Oracle Essbase 11 Development Cookbook

Over 90 advanced development recipes to build and take your Oracle Essbase Applications further

Jose R. Ruiz

[PACKT] enterprise 🎔
PUBLISHING   professional expertise distilled

BIRMINGHAM - MUMBAI

Oracle Essbase 11 Development Cookbook

First published: January 2012

Production Reference: 1170112

Published by Packt Publishing Ltd.
Livery Place
35 Livery Street
Birmingham B3 2PB, UK.

ISBN 978-1-84968-326-5

www.packtpub.com

Cover Image by Sandeep Babu (sandyjb@gmail.com)

Credits

Author
Jose R. Ruiz

Reviewers
Alexia Rodriguez Alwine
Satyanarayana Bodhanapu

Acquisition Editor
Kerry George

Lead Technical Editor
Susmita Panda

Technical Editor
Llewellyn F. Rozario

Copy Editor
Neha Shetty

Project Coordinator
Vishal Bodwani

Proofreaders
Aaron Nash
Chris Smith

Indexer
Rekha Nair

Production Coordinator
Arvindkumar Gupta

Cover Work
Arvindkumar Gupta

About the Author

Jose R. Ruiz is an Oracle Essbase 11 Certified Implementation Specialist with over nine years experience in developing enterprise-level Essbase applications. He has maintained and conducted post-production development on 18 Essbase databases. In addition, Jose Ruiz has been charged with developing E-commerce, Fixed Assets, Balance Sheets, Point of Sales, and Inventory databases.

Jose Ruiz is currently working with Oracle consultants on designing, developing, and implementing an Inventory, Purchase Order, and Sales Data Mart and an Essbase database at his current employer.

I would like to thank my colleagues and friends Peter Beddoe and Alexia Alwine for their review and advice. In addition, I would like to thank my wife, Yaneth C. Ruiz, for her support and patience throughout this endeavor.

About the Reviewer

Alexia Rodriguez Alwine is a Project Manager with extensive experience in the pharmaceutical and consumer products industries. She has worked with Unilever, Inc. and several of its subsidiaries; Steifel Laboratories, a GlaxoSmithKline company; and BE Aerospace. In addition to serving as a Project Manager, she has served as Hyperion Administrator, Systems Analyst, and Finance Manager. Her experience with Oracle includes Web Analysis, Financial Reporting, FDM, HFM, Hyperion Planning, Oracle Upgrades, and Essbase Migration Projects. She also has experience with SAP and Data Mart implementation.

Alexia graduated with a bachelor's degree in economics, communications, and international relations from the University of Pennsylvania. She received her MBA from the University of Florida. In her spare time, she researches and conducts workshops concerning the impact of technology on the family.

www.PacktPub.com

Support files, eBooks, discount offers, and more

You might want to visit www.PacktPub.com for support files and downloads related to your book.

Did you know that Packt offers eBook versions of every book published, with PDF and ePub files available? You can upgrade to the eBook version at www.PacktPub.com and, as a print book customer, you are entitled to a discount on the eBook copy. Get in touch with us at service@packtpub.com for more details.

At www.PacktPub.com, you can also read a collection of free technical articles, sign up for a range of free newsletters and receive exclusive discounts and offers on Packt books and eBooks.

PACKTLiB®

http://PacktLib.PacktPub.com

Do you need instant solutions to your IT questions? PacktLib is Packt's online digital book library. Here, you can access, read, and search across Packt's entire library of books.

Why Subscribe?

- ▶ Fully searchable across every book published by Packt
- ▶ Copy and paste, print, and bookmark content
- ▶ On demand and accessible via web browser

Free Access for Packt account holders

If you have an account with Packt at www.PacktPub.com, you can use this to access PacktLib today and view nine entirely free books. Simply use your login credentials for immediate access.

Instant Updates on New Packt Books

Get notified! Find out when new books are published by following @PacktEnterprise on Twitter, or the *Packt Enterprise* Facebook page.

Table of Contents

Preface

Oracle Essbase 11 Development Cookbook will help you learn the tools necessary for the development of Essbase databases in Oracle Essbase version 11.1.2.1. Here you will find over 90 recipes that explain everything from how to use a relational data model to building and loading an Essbase database in Essbase Studio. The book also goes over how to build the Block Storage (BSO) databases and explains some of the options are exclusive to building an Aggregate Storage (ASO) database. In this book, we will be using Essbase Studio, Essbase Integration Services (EIS), and Essbase Administration Service (EAS) to build databases, and we will discuss the strengths of each tool. Moreover, we discuss how to create Calculation Scripts, use MaxL to automate your processes, and integrate data. Finally, we step through how to effectively implement security, and how to build dynamic reports. The reader is encouraged to use these recipes as the foundation for their own customized databases and scripts.

What this book covers

Chapter 1, Understanding and Modifying Data Sources. This chapter explains how to prepare your data source to build hierarchies and load data in Essbase databases. Because you should not have to rebuild the wheel, we cover some tools that will assist us in extracting hierarchies from existing Essbase databases for the purpose of setting up your star schema in a relational environment. The goal of this chapter is to show the reader the components needed to maintain metadata in a relational environment and set up that environment to support drill-through reporting. This being said, most of the techniques used in this chapter can be implemented using flat files as well.

Chapter 2, Using Essbase Studio. We will begin this chapter by discussing advantages of and disadvantages of Essbase Studio when compared to development tools like Essbase Integration Services (EIS) and Essbase Administration Services (EAS). This chapter also has some of the more basic yet necessary steps needed to build your database using Essbase Studio. We will review how to create a data source, minischema, and manipulate data elements with Common Platform Language (CPL).

Chapter 3, Building the BSO Cube. In this chapter, we build and deploy the TBC Block Storage (BSO) database using Essbase Studio. We also explore the building of TBC databases using Essbase Integration Services (EIS).

Chapter 4, Building the ASO Cube. This chapter explains some of the options exclusive to building the Aggregate Storage (ASO) model. In addition, we learn how to build a Measure dimension from the fact table, and how to build a drill-through report in Essbase Studio.

Chapter 5, Using EAS for Development. This chapter explains how to build the Sample Basic database using the Essbase Administration Services (EAS) outline editor, build rules, load rules, and flat files. We also explore the use of Text and Date measures, outline formulas in the BSO model, and MDX in an aggregate storage database.

Chapter 6, Creating Calculation Scripts. In this chapter, we learn how to use calculation scripts to run complex formulas that require multiple passes through the Essbase database, data allocations, copying data, clearing data, aggregating data, and some best practices for optimizing your calculations' performance.

Chapter 7, Using MaxL to Automate Process. This chapter teaches you how to automate the updating, building, and loading of an Essbase database. This chapter more specifically shows MaxL script techniques designed to make scripts reusable and portable. These techniques will allow us to move our automation from development to staging or production without having to re-write our MaxL script before migration.

Chapter 8, Data Integration. This chapter explains how to integrate data in between Essbase and relational databases. In addition, we discuss how to move data between Essbase databases.

Chapter 9, Provisioning Security using MaxL Editor or Shared Services. This chapter shows how to use Shared Services and MaxL to set up security. Essbase has very flexible and powerful security features. This functionality, if planned carefully, can make your database more intuitive and customized to the needs of each end user.

Chapter 10, Developing Dynamic Reports. In this chapter, you will learn how to build a more dynamic Financial Report. Moreover, we discuss how to build a simple Web Analysis Report for an even more dynamic user experience.

What you need for this book

You will need the following software to complete the recipes in this book:

1. Oracle EPM Essbase 11.1.2.1
2. Essbase Studio 11.1.2.1
3. Essbase Integration Services (EIS)
4. Financial Report & Web Analysis

5. SQL Server 2008/ Oracle 11g

6. Essbase Outline Extractor

7. Star Integration Server – Express Edition

Who this book is for

If you are an experienced Essbase developer, Essbase Database Designer or Database Administrator, then this book is for you. This book assumes that you have good knowledge of Oracle Essbase.

Conventions

In this book, you will find a number of styles of text that distinguish between different kinds of information. Here are some examples of these styles, and an explanation of their meaning.

Code words in text are shown as follows: "enter connection: \'TBC'::'TBC. dbo.MEASURES'.'CHILD'||" - "||connection : \'TBC'::'TBC.dbo. MEASURES'.'MEASURES_ALIAS' in the textbox."

A block of code is set as follows:

```
Create Table PRODUCTS(
    PRODUCTID    int         NOT NULL,
    SKU          varchar(15) NULL,
    SKU_ALIAS    varchar(25) NULL,
    Constraint PK_PRODUCTS_PRODUCTID Primary Key (PRODUCTID)
);
```

New terms and important words are shown in bold. Words that you see on the screen, in menus or dialog boxes for example, appear in the text like this: "Click on cell **F2,** then click on the box to the right and bottom of the cell, and drag it down to cell **F12**."

Warnings or important notes appear in a box like this.

Tips and tricks appear like this.

Reader feedback

Feedback from our readers is always welcome. Let us know what you think about this book—what you liked or may have disliked. Reader feedback is important for us to develop titles that you really get the most out of.

To send us general feedback, simply send an e-mail to feedback@packtpub.com, and mention the book title via the subject of your message.

If there is a topic that you have expertise in and you are interested in either writing or contributing to a book, see our author guide on www.packtpub.com/authors.

Customer support

Now that you are the proud owner of a Packt book, we have a number of things to help you to get the most from your purchase.

Downloading the example code

You can download the example code files for all Packt books you have purchased from your account at http://www.PacktPub.com. If you purchased this book elsewhere, you can visit http://www.PacktPub.com/support and register to have the files e-mailed directly to you.

Errata

Although we have taken every care to ensure the accuracy of our content, mistakes do happen. If you find a mistake in one of our books—maybe a mistake in the text or the code—we would be grateful if you would report this to us. By doing so, you can save other readers from frustration and help us improve subsequent versions of this book. If you find any errata, please report them by visiting http://www.packtpub.com/support, selecting your book, clicking on the **errata submission form** link, and entering the details of your errata. Once your errata are verified, your submission will be accepted and the errata will be uploaded on our website, or added to any list of existing errata, under the Errata section of that title. Any existing errata can be viewed by selecting your title from http://www.packtpub.com/support.

Piracy

Piracy of copyright material on the Internet is an ongoing problem across all media. At Packt, we take the protection of our copyright and licenses very seriously. If you come across any illegal copies of our works, in any form, on the Internet, please provide us with the location address or website name immediately so that we can pursue a remedy.

Please contact us at copyright@packtpub.com with a link to the suspected pirated material.

We appreciate your help in protecting our authors, and our ability to bring you valuable content.

Questions

You can contact us at questions@packtpub.com if you are having a problem with any aspect of the book, and we will do our best to address it.

1
Understanding and Modifying Data Sources

In this chapter, we will cover the following topics:

- ▶ Setting up an Account or Measures dimension with a parent-child reference
- ▶ Setting up dimensions with a generation reference
- ▶ Adding columns for outline formulas
- ▶ Adding the Solve Order column to tables that have ASO formulas
- ▶ Adding and populating the Sort Order Column
- ▶ Adding tables for varying attributes
- ▶ Determining hierarchies in relational tables
- ▶ Using the Essbase Outline Extractor to extract dimensions
- ▶ Using Star Analytics to build your star schema from existing Essbase cubes

Introduction

In this chapter, we will build components into our relational environment that will allow us to successfully build an **Essbase** database and facilitate drill-through reporting. Although we are discussing relational data sources, the properties, attributes, and concepts discussed in this chapter can be used to build hierarchies off data sources such as flat files for example. The techniques used here can be used in tools like Essbase Administrative Services, Essbase Integration Services, and Essbase Studio. This chapter also has recipes on the Essbase Outline Extractor and Star Analytics. These two tools allow us to extract hierarchies from existing Essbase cubes. We would use these tools to extract existing hierarchies or modify existing hierarchies to build all or parts of our star schema.

Setting up an Account or Measures dimension with a parent-child reference

In this recipe, we will set up a relational table in a parent-child reference format. We will also review the type of properties that can go in each column and their definitions. The **Account** or **Measure** dimension is normally the most dynamic dimension in a financial database and it is recommended that you use the parent-child structure to build the dimension in a relational environment. The parent-child reference also allows ragged hierarchies without having to add columns to your tables when an additional level or generation is needed. We will also review an alternative method, which requires us to use the measures field in our fact table to build our Measure dimension.

Getting ready

To get started, open your SQL Server Management Studio, and add a database called TBC. For this recipe, we are using T-SQL, but the PL\SQL equivalent will be provided where applicable. You should add a **SCHEMA** called TBC using tools such as **TOAD, SQL Developer**, or **Golden**, if you are using Oracle.

How to do it...

1. Run the following scripts to create the Measures table. We can change the script below to PL/SQL by replacing int with INTEGER and varchar() with VARCHAR2(). A screenshot of the table follows the script:

```
  --This is the syntax in T-SQL
create table MEASURES
(
    SORTKEY            int              not null,
    MEASURESID         int              not null,
    PARENT             varchar(85)      null      ,
```

```
CHILD                 varchar(85)              not null,
MEASURES_ALIAS        varchar(85)              null     ,
CONSOLIDATION         varchar(85)              null     ,
TWOPASSCALC           varchar(85)              null     ,
STORAGE               varchar(85)              null     ,
VARIANCEREPORTING     varchar(85)              null     ,
TIMEBALANCE           varchar(85)              null     ,
SKIP                  varchar(85)              null     ,
UDA                   varchar(85)              null     ,
FORMULA               varchar(255)             null     ,
COMMENT_ESSBASE       varchar(85)              null     ,
constraint PK_MEASURES primary key (MEASURESID)
)
Go
```

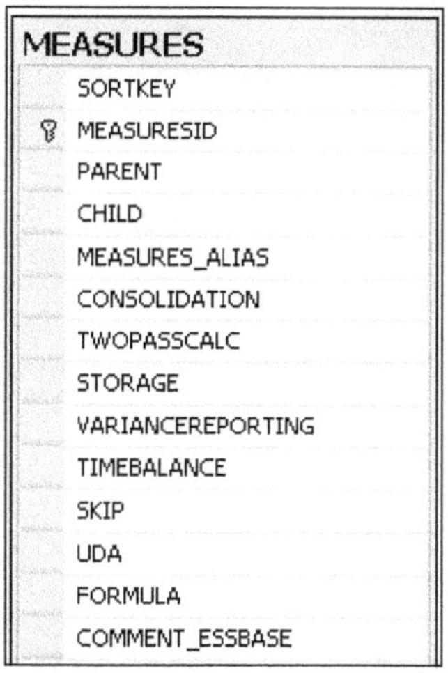

MEASURES

- SORTKEY
- 🔑 MEASURESID
- PARENT
- CHILD
- MEASURES_ALIAS
- CONSOLIDATION
- TWOPASSCALC
- STORAGE
- VARIANCEREPORTING
- TIMEBALANCE
- SKIP
- UDA
- FORMULA
- COMMENT_ESSBASE

2. Execute the following scripts to add the data to your table:

```
INSERT INTO MEASURES (SORTKEY,MEASURESID,PARENT,CHILD,MEASURES_
ALIAS,
  CONSOLIDATION,TWOPASSCALC,STORAGE,VARIANCEREPORTING,
  TIMEBALANCE,SKIP,UDA,FORMULA,COMMENT_ESSBASE)
  VALUES (100,1,'Measures','Profit','','+','',
'X','','','','','','');
```

```
INSERT INTO MEASURES (SORTKEY,MEASURESID,PARENT,CHILD,MEASURES_
ALIAS,
   CONSOLIDATION,TWOPASSCALC,STORAGE,VARIANCEREPORTING,
   TIMEBALANCE,SKIP,UDA,FORMULA,COMMENT_ESSBASE) VALUES
   (200,2,'Profit','Margin','','+','','X','','','','','','');

INSERT INTO MEASURES (SORTKEY,MEASURESID,PARENT,CHILD,MEASURES_
ALIAS,
   CONSOLIDATION,TWOPASSCALC,STORAGE,VARIANCEREPORTING,TIMEBALANCE,
   SKIP,UDA,FORMULA,COMMENT_ESSBASE) VALUES
   (300,3,'Margin','Sales','','+','',
   '','','','','','','');

INSERT INTO MEASURES (SORTKEY,MEASURESID,PARENT,CHILD,ME
ASURES_ALIAS,CONSOLIDATION,TWOPASSCALC,STORAGE,VARIANCE
REPORTING,TIMEBALANCE,SKIP,UDA,FORMULA,COMMENT_ESSBASE)
VALUES (400,4,'Margin','COGS','Cost of Goods Sold','-
','','','E','','','','','');

INSERT INTO MEASURES (SORTKEY,MEASURESID,PARENT,CHILD,MEASURES_
ALIAS,
   CONSOLIDATION,TWOPASSCALC,STORAGE,VARIANCEREPORTING,TIMEBALANCE,
   SKIP,UDA,FORMULA,COMMENT_ESSBASE) VALUES
   (500,5,'Profit','Total Expenses','','-
','','X','E','','','','','');

INSERT INTO MEASURES (SORTKEY,MEASURESID,PARENT,CHILD,MEASURES_
ALIAS,
   CONSOLIDATION,TWOPASSCALC,STORAGE,VARIANCEREPORTING,TIMEBALANCE,
   SKIP,UDA,FORMULA,COMMENT_ESSBASE) VALUES
   (600,6,'Total Expenses','Marketing','','+',
   '','','E','','','','','');

INSERT INTO MEASURES (SORTKEY,MEASURESID,PARENT,CHILD,MEASURES_
ALIAS,
   CONSOLIDATION,TWOPASSCALC,STORAGE,VARIANCEREPORTING,TIMEBALANCE,
   SKIP,UDA,FORMULA,COMMENT_ESSBASE) VALUES
   (700,7,'Total Expenses','Payroll','','+','','',
   'E','','','','','');

INSERT INTO MEASURES (SORTKEY,MEASURESID,PARENT,CHILD,MEASURES_
ALIAS,
   CONSOLIDATION,TWOPASSCALC,STORAGE,VARIANCEREPORTING,
   TIMEBALANCE,SKIP,UDA,FORMULA,COMMENT_ESSBASE) VALUES
   (800,8,'Total Expenses','Misc','Miscellaneous','+',
```

```
'','','E','','','','','');

INSERT INTO MEASURES (SORTKEY,MEASURESID,PARENT,CHILD,MEASURES_
ALIAS,
    CONSOLIDATION,TWOPASSCALC,STORAGE,VARIANCEREPORTING,TIMEBALANCE,
    SKIP,UDA,FORMULA,COMMENT_ESSBASE) VALUES
    (900,9,'Measures','Inventory','','~','','O','','','','','');

INSERT INTO MEASURES (SORTKEY,MEASURESID,PARENT,CHILD,MEASURES_
ALIAS,
    CONSOLIDATION,TWOPASSCALC,STORAGE,VARIANCEREPORTING,
    TIMEBALANCE,SKIP,UDA,FORMULA,COMMENT_ESSBASE) VALUES
    (1000,10,'Inventory','Opening
      Inventory','','+','','','E','F','','',
    'IF(NOT @ISMBR(Jan)) "Opening Inventory"=@PRIOR("Ending
      Inventory");ENDIF;"Ending Inventory"="Opening
      Inventory"+Additions-Sales;','');

INSERT INTO MEASURES (SORTKEY,MEASURESID,PARENT,CHILD,MEASURES_ALI
AS,CONSOLIDATION,TWOPASSCALC,STORAGE,VARIANCEREPORTING,TIMEBALANCE
,SKIP,UDA,FORMULA,
COMMENT_ESSBASE) VALUES (1100,11,'Inventory','Additions','','~',''
,'','E','','','','','');

INSERT INTO MEASURES (SORTKEY,MEASURESID,PARENT,CHILD,MEASURES_
ALIAS,
    CONSOLIDATION,TWOPASSCALC,STORAGE,VARIANCEREPORTING,
    TIMEBALANCE,SKIP,UDA,FORMULA, COMMENT_ESSBASE) VALUES
    (1200,12,'Inventory','Ending
      Inventory','','~','','','E','L','','','','');

INSERT INTO MEASURES (SORTKEY,MEASURESID,PARENT,CHILD,MEASURES_ALI
AS,CONSOLIDATION,TWOPASSCALC,STORAGE,VARIANCEREPORTING,TIMEBALANCE
,SKIP,UDA,FORMULA,
COMMENT_ESSBASE) VALUES (1300,13,'Measures','Ratios','','~','',
'O','','','','','','');

INSERT INTO MEASURES (SORTKEY,MEASURESID,PARENT,CHILD,MEASURES_
ALIAS,
    CONSOLIDATION,TWOPASSCALC,STORAGE,VARIANCEREPORTING,TIMEBALANCE,
    SKIP,UDA,FORMULA, COMMENT_ESSBASE) VALUES
    (1400,14,'Ratios','Margin %','','+','T','X','','','','',
      'Margin % Sales;','');

INSERT INTO MEASURES (SORTKEY,MEASURESID,PARENT,CHILD,MEASURES_
ALIAS,
```

```
CONSOLIDATION,TWOPASSCALC,STORAGE,VARIANCEREPORTING,TIMEBALANCE,
SKIP,UDA,FORMULA, COMMENT_ESSBASE) VALUES
(1500,15,'Ratios','Profit %','','~','T','X','','','','',
  'Profit % Sales;','');

INSERT INTO MEASURES (SORTKEY,MEASURESID,PARENT,CHILD,MEASURES_
ALIAS,
  CONSOLIDATION,TWOPASSCALC,STORAGE,VARIANCEREPORTING,TIMEBALANCE,
  SKIP,UDA,FORMULA, COMMENT_ESSBASE) VALUES
  (1600,16,'Ratios','Profit per Ounce','','~','T','X','','','','',
    'Profit/@ATTRIBUTEVAL(Ounces);','');
```

How it works...

The MEASURES table has the following columns:

COLUMN	DESCRIPTION
SORTKEY	This column is the integer that helps you sort the MEASURES in the order that you want them to appear in the hierarchy
MEASURESID	This ID is used as the PRIMARY KEY in the MEASURES table and as a FOREIGN KEY in the fact table
PARENT	This column is the Parent in the hierarchy
CHILD	This column is the Child of the Parent column
MEASURES_ALIAS	This is a more intuitive description of Measures normally defined by the business
CONSOLIDATION	This field has the aggregation type for the Child column
TWOPASSCALC	This field has the value "T" if the aggregation requires a second pass through the outline for the results to be right
STORAGE	Storage can have many values and will determine how or if the data in the outline is stored or dynamically calculated
VARIANCEREPORTING	The Variance Reporting column is used to mark Expense accounts for reporting variances
TIMEBALANCE	The Time Balance column is used with your time dimension to determine whether to use LIFO, FIFO, or the Average method for a specific measure
SKIP	The Skip column works with Time Balance to determine how to treat #MISSING or Zero values
UDA	The User Defined Attribute is useful for many purposes including outline formulas, calculation formulas, and the retrieval of data by the criteria defined by the business
FORMULA	These are the outline formulas used in the BSO model
COMMENT_ESSBASE	These are simply comments on the meta-data stored in this table

In step 2, we load the data. The following are descriptions of what goes into some of these columns as per Oracle's documentation.

These are the valid **Consolidations** values:

TYPE	TYPE DESCRIPTION	TYPE LONG DESCRIPTION
%	Percent	Expresses as a percentage of the current total in a consolidation
*	Multiplication	Multiplies by the current total in a consolidation
+	Addition	Adds to the current total in a consolidation
-	Subtraction	Subtracts from the current total in a consolidation
/	Division	Divides by the current total in a consolidation
^	Never	Excludes from all consolidations in all dimensions
~	Ignore	Excludes from the consolidation

This is the valid **Two Pass** value:

TYPE	TYPE DESC	TYPE LONG DESCRIPTION
T	Two Pass Calculation	Requires a two-pass calculation (applies to accounts dimensions only)

These are the valid **Storage** values:

TYPE	TYPE DESC	TYPE LONG DESCRIPTION
N	Never Share	Never allows data sharing
O	Label Only	Tags as label only (store no data)
S	Store Data	Sets member as stored member (non-Dynamic Calc and not label only)
V	Dynamic Calc and Store	Creates as Dynamic Calc and Store
X	Dynamic Calc	Creates as Dynamic Calc

This is the valid **Variance Reporting** value:

TYPE	TYPE DESC	TYPE LONG DESCRIPTION
E	Expense	Treats as an expense item (applies to accounts dimensions only)

These are the valid **Time Balance** values:

TYPE	TYPE DESC	TYPE LONG DESCRIPTION
A	Average	Treats as an average time balance item (applies to accounts dimensions only)
F	First	Treats as a first time balance item (applies to accounts dimensions only)
L	Last	Treats as a last time balance item (applies to accounts dimensions only)

These are the valid **Skip** options per Oracle's Documentation:

TYPE	TYPE DESC	TYPE LONG DESCRIPTION
B	Missing and Zeros	Skips #MISSING data and data that equals zero when calculating the parent value
M	Missing	Skips #MISSING data when calculating the parent value
Z	Zeros	Skips data that equals zero when calculating the parent value

There's more...

Using the parent-child reference table structure will depend on whether we know that our Measures and Accounts are going to change often. The structure of your fact table will have to change if you decide to use Measure tables. A fact table that has the Measures going down a table vertically, as rows, will allow us to use the Measures column in the fact table to join to the MEASURES table. The following screenshot illustrates how this design will look:

```
┌──────────────────────────────┐
│ MEASURES                     │
│     SORTKEY                  │
│  ⚷  MEASURESID               │
│     PARENT                   │       ┌──────────────────────────┐
│     CHILD                    │       │ SALES                    │
│     MEASURES_ALIAS           │       │     STATEID              │
│     CONSOLIDATION            │       │     PRODUCTID            │
│     TWOPASSCALC              │       │     SCENARIOID           │
│     STORAGE          ⊶───────────────○< MEASURESID             │
│     VARIANCEREPORTING        │       │     SUPPLIERID           │
│     TIMEBALANCE              │       │     TRANSDATE            │
│     SKIP                     │       │     AMOUNT               │
│     UDA                      │       └──────────────────────────┘
│     FORMULA                  │
│     COMMENT_ESSBASE          │
│                              │
└──────────────────────────────┘
```

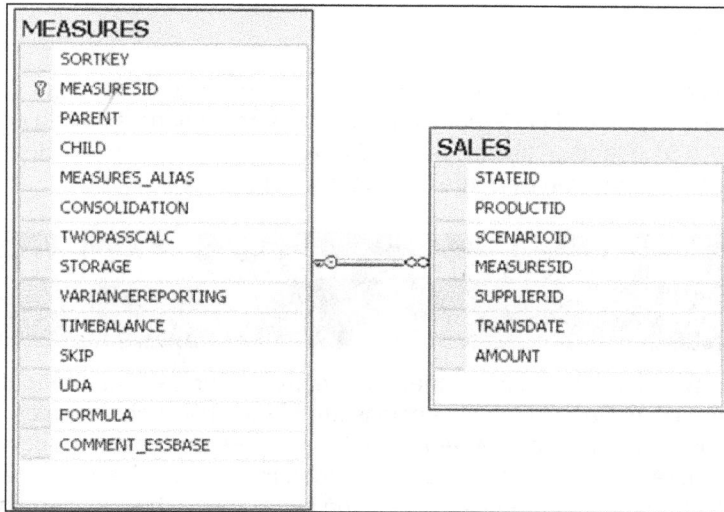

We can easily add accounts or change parent-child associations using this format without having to modify the fact table. On the other hand, if our fact table has Measures horizontally, in columns, then the Measures dimension will have to be built in Essbase Studio or Essbase Integration Services instead. The following screenshot is an example of what a fact table, with Measures as columns, would look like:

```
┌──────────────────────────────┐
│ SALESFACT                    │
│     STATEID                  │
│     PRODUCTID                │
│     SCENARIOID               │
│     SUPPLIERID               │
│     TRANSDATE                │
│     SALES                    │
│     COGS                     │
│     MARKETING                │
│     PAYROLL                  │
│     MISC                     │
│     OPENINGINVENTORY         │
│     ADDITIONS                │
└──────────────────────────────┘
```

The Beverage Company (**TBC**) sample database's SALES and SALESFACT tables are examples of the two different formats.

See also

You can find an example of the MEASURES dimension being built in the recipe *Creating hierarchies using a Parent-child reference table* in *Chapter 3*. For an example on how to build the MEASURES dimension using Essbase Studio from the fact table, refer to the recipe *Building a Measures dimension from the fact table* in *Chapter 4*.

Setting up dimensions with a generation reference

In this recipe, we will build a table in a generation reference format. The SUPPLIER is a geographical dimension. Geographic dimensions are natural hierarchies, which means that the generations are related to each other naturally and there is normally a one-to-many relationship. A generation reference format is common in a relational environment as it can be used to conduct relational reporting as well. The same cannot be said about the parent-child structure.

Getting ready

To get started, open your SQL Server Management Studio, and add a **TBC** database. Add a **SCHEMA** using a tool such as TOAD, SQL Developer, or Golden, if you are using Oracle.

How to do it...

1. Run the following scripts to create the SUPPLIER table. We can change the script below to PL/SQL by replacing int with INTEGER and varchar() with VARCHAR2(). Following the scripts is a screenshot of the table:

    ```
    --This is the syntax in T-SQL
    create table SUPPLIER
    (
      SUPPLIERID          int                   not null,
      SUPPLIER_ALIAS      varchar(50)           null    ,
      ADDRESS             varchar(25)           null    ,
      CITY                varchar(25)           null    ,
      STATE               varchar(25)           null    ,
      ZIP                 varchar(20)           null    ,
      COUNTRY             varchar(25)           null    ,
      constraint PK_SUPPLIER primary key (SUPPLIERID)
    )
    go
    ```

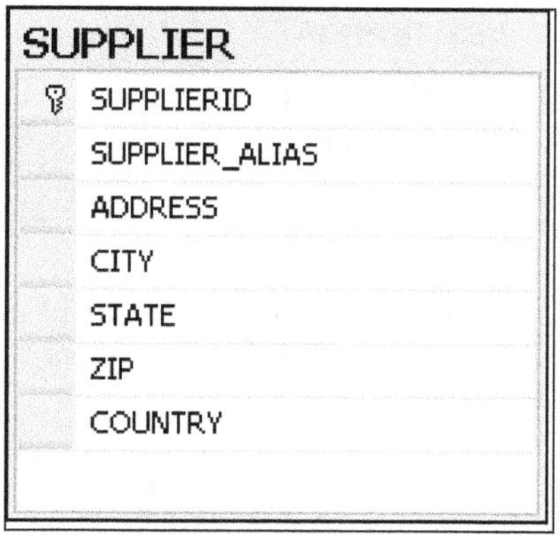

SUPPLIER

- 🔑 SUPPLIERID
- SUPPLIER_ALIAS
- ADDRESS
- CITY
- STATE
- ZIP
- COUNTRY

2. Execute the following scripts to add data to the SUPPLIER table:

```
INSERT INTO SUPPLIER
  (SUPPLIERID,SUPPLIER_ALIAS,ADDRESS,CITY,STATE,ZIP,COUNTRY)
  VALUES (1,'High Tech Drinks','1344 Crossman
    Ave','Sunnyvale','California','94675','USA');

INSERT INTO SUPPLIER
  (SUPPLIERID,SUPPLIER_ALIAS,ADDRESS,CITY,STATE,ZIP,COUNTRY)
  VALUES (2,'East Coast Beverage','900 Long Ridge
    Rd','Stamford','Connecticut','92001','USA');

INSERT INTO SUPPLIER
  (SUPPLIERID,SUPPLIER_ALIAS,ADDRESS,CITY,STATE,ZIP,COUNTRY)
  VALUES (3,'Cool Canadian','1250 Boul Rene
    Levesque','Montreal','New York','H3B-W4B','Canada');
```

3. Select from the SUPPLIER table to see the results:

```
Select * From SUPPLIER;
```

How it works...

In step 1, the SUPPLIER table was created and in step 2 the data was populated. A generation in Essbase begins with generation 1 at dimension because the name of the cube in the outline is generation 0. We can tell from the structure of the table that it is clearly set up in **generation reference** as depicted in the following grid:

COLUMN	DESCRIPTION
SUPPLIERID	The PRIMARY KEY and a FOREIGN KEY
COUNTRY	Generation 2
STATE	Generation 3

COLUMN	DESCRIPTION
CITY	Generation 4
ZIPCODE	Generation 5
ADDRESS	Generation 6

> The generation reference will allow us to create ragged hierarchies, but requires the handling of null values by your development tool.

See also

For more information on how to build the SUPPLIER dimension using Essbase Studio, refer to the recipe *Creating hierarchies using a Generation reference table* in *Chapter 3*.

Adding columns for outline formulas

In this recipe, we will add columns to our MEASURES table, so that we can later add a formula to the dimension's members. The importance of this is apparent when you consider that the **Aggregate Storage (ASO)** model does not use the same syntax as the **Block Storage (BSO)** model for their outline formulas. The ASO outline uses **Multidimensional Expressions (MDX)**, which is the standard syntax convention for OLAP applications. We can use our table for both BSO and ASO applications by adding an additional column for the ASO model's formulas.

Getting ready

To get started, open SQL Server Management Studio, and add a database called TBC. In this recipe, we are using T-SQL, but the PL-SQL equivalent for the examples has been included in the following code snippet. The MEASURES dimension was created in the recipe *Setting up an Account or Measure dimension with parent-child reference* in *Chapter 1*. We need to complete step 1 of the aforementioned recipe before we continue.

How to do it...

1. Execute the following script to add a column to the MEASURES table. Following the script is the screenshot of the table after the modification:

    ```
    --This is the syntax in T-SQL
    Alter Table MEASURES Add FORMULA_MDX VARCHAR(4000) NULL;
    --This is the syntax in PL\SQL
    Alter Table MEASURES ADD FORMULA_MDX VARCHAR2(4000) NULL;
    ```

```
--Delete content of the table to avoid issues with executing this
  execise
Delete From MEASURES;
```

2. Execute the following script to add a row with the new formula:

```
--This is the syntax for both T-SQL and PL\SQL
INSERT INTO MEASURES (SORTKEY,MEASURESID,PARENT,CHILD,MEASURES_
ALIAS,CONSOLIDATION,TWOP
  ASSCALC,STORAGE,VARIANCEREPORTING,TIMEBALANCE,SKIP,UDA,FORMULA,
  COMMENT_ESSBASE, FORMULA_MDX) Values(0, 14, 'Ratios', 'Margin
  %', '', '+', 'T', 'X', '', '', '', '', 'Margin % Sales;', '',
  '[Measures].[Sales] / [Measures].[Margin];');


INSERT INTO MEASURES (SORTKEY,MEASURESID,PARENT,CHILD,MEASURES_
ALIAS,CONSOLIDATION,TWOP
  ASSCALC,STORAGE,VARIANCEREPORTING,TIMEBALANCE,SKIP,UDA,FORMULA,
  COMMENT_ESSBASE, FORMULA_MDX) Values(0, 15, 'Ratios', 'Profit
  %', '', '~', 'T', 'X', '', '', '', '', 'Profit % Sales;', '',
  '[Measures].[Sales] / [Measures].[Profit];');
```

How it works...

In step 1, the column FORMULA_MDX is added to the MEASURES table. The script in step 2 adds the new rows with the FORMULA_MDX column included. The objective of this recipe is to show you that the syntax is different every time you use a table for both an ASO and BSO set of applications, so you need to have two formula columns. You can see how different the syntax is in the following code snippet, but if you need a more detailed explanation on this, please visit: http://www.oracle.com/technetwork/middleware/bi-foundation/4395-calc-to-mdx-wp-133362.pdf. This is Oracle's white paper on *Converting Calc Formulas to MDX in an Essbase Outline*.

FORMULA	FORMULA_MDX
Margin % Sales;	Measures.Sales / Measures.Margin;
Profit % Sales;	Measures.Sales / Measures.Profit;

Adding the solve order column to tables that have ASO formulas

In this recipe, we will include an additional column to our MEASURES table to specify the solve order for the hierarchy. The ASO outline does not have the Two Pass Calc option in its Account dimension; as a result, you will have to specify the solve order by adding an additional column.

Getting ready

To get started, open SQL Server Management Studio, and add a database called TBC. In this recipe, we are using T-SQL, but the PL\SQL equivalent is provided in the examples. The MEASURES dimension was created in the recipe *Setting up an Account or Measure dimension with parent-child reference* in *Chapter 1*. We need to complete step 1 of the aforementioned recipe before we continue.

How to do it...

1. Execute the following script to add the FORMULA_MDX and SOLVE_ORDER columns to the MEASURES table, if it does not exist:

```
--This is the script in T-SQL
Alter Table MEASURES Add FORMULA_MDX VARCHAR(4000) NULL;
Alter Table MEASURES Add SOLVE_ORDER INT NULL;
--This is the script in PL-SQL
Alter Table MEASURES ADD FORMULA_MDX VARCHAR2(4000) NULL;
Alter Table MEASURES Add SOLVE_ORDER INTEGER NULL;
```

```
MEASURES
    SORTKEY
🔑  MEASURESID
    PARENT
    CHILD
    MEASURES_ALIAS
    CONSOLIDATION
    TWOPASSCALC
    STORAGE
    VARIANCEREPORTING
    TIMEBALANCE
    SKIP
    UDA
    FORMULA
    COMMENT_ESSBASE
    FORMULA_MDX
    SOLVE_ORDER
```

2. Execute the following scripts to add the formula and the solve order values to the MEASURES table:

```
INSERT INTO MEASURES
    (SORTKEY,MEASURESID,PARENT,CHILD,MEASURES_ALIAS,
    CONSOLIDATION,TWOP ASSCALC,STORAGE,VARIANCEREPORTING,
    TIMEBALANCE,SKIP,UDA,FORMULA,COMMENT_ESSBASE,FORMULA_MDX,
    SOLVE_ORDER) Values(0, 14, 'Ratios', 'Margin %', '', '+', 'T',
    'X', '', '', '', '', 'Margin % Sales;', '', '
    [Measures].[Sales] / [Measures].[Margin];', 20);


INSERT INTO MEASURES
    (SORTKEY,MEASURESID,PARENT,CHILD,MEASURES_
ALIAS,CONSOLIDATION,TWOP
    ASSCALC,STORAGE,VARIANCEREPORTING,TIMEBALANCE,SKIP,UDA,FORMULA,
COMMENT_ESSBASE, FORMULA_MDX, SOLVE_ORDER) Values(0, 15, 'Ratios',
    'Profit %', '', '~', 'T', 'X', '', '', '', '', 'Profit % Sales;',
    '', '[Measures].[Sales] / [Measures].[Profit];', 20);
```

3. Select from the table to see the values that you added:

```
Select * From MEASURES;
```

How it works...

We started this recipe by adding the SOLVE_ORDER column to the MEASURES table. We also added two new rows with the SOLVE_ORDER populated. The objective of this recipe is to show you that the SOLVE_ORDER value has to be higher than its respective components in order for the formula to return the correct values. We should consider the following steps when assigning SOLVE_ORDER:

1. Set up in SOLVE_ORDER in increments of tens or twenties for clarity and consistency.

2. When the default is not specified, SOLVE_ORDER is zero, but it is good practice to always specify the SOLVE_ORDER to remove ambiguity and define the calculation's priority.

Adding and populating the Sort Order Column

In previous releases of Essbase, a developer had the option of building a hierachy in ascending or descending alphabetical order via a build rule. If you wanted to sort the hierarchies in a different order, then you would go into **Essbase Administrative Services** (**EAS**). Then, open the outline, and drag and drop the members in the order that the business wanted or extract the dimension using an Outline Extract utility, sort the hierarchy, and use a build rule to rebuild the dimension. In contrast, when we are using Essbase Studio, in version 11.1.2.1, we are going to have to define the Sort Order in the relational environment. If you have the Oracle's data-governance software **Data Relationship Management** (**DRM**), this task will be handled there, but this recipe shows you how to load the Sort Order field with some SQL knowledge and Excel.

Getting ready

To get started, open SQL Server Management Studio, and add a database called TBC, if you have not already done it. In this recipe, we are using T-SQL and providing the PL\SQL equivalent where the syntax is different. You need to add a SCHEMA instead and use a tool like TOAD or Golden, if you are using Oracle. You should also open an Excel workbook.

How to do it...

1. Execute the following query to create the YEARS table. We can change the script below to PL/SQL by replacing int with INTEGER and varchar() with VARCHAR2():

```
--For T-SQL user
Create Table YEARS(
    YEARID      int       NOT NULL,
    YEAR        int       NULL,
```

```
QUARTER      varchar(80)     NULL,
MONTH        varchar(80)     NULL,
MONTH_ALIAS  varchar(80)     NULL,
Constraint PK_YEAR_YEARID Primary Key(YEARID Asc)
);
```

2. Execute the following script to add the **SORT_ORDER** column:

```
--This is the syntax in T-SQL
Alter Table YEARS Add SORT_ORDER INT NULL;
--This is the syntax in PL/SQL
Alter Table YEARS Add SORT_ORDER INTEGER NULL;
```

3. Open Excel and enter the YEARS dimension's data starting with field **A1**, as follows:

	A	B	C	D	E
1	1	2011	QTR1 11	Jan 2011	January 2011
2	2	2011	QTR1 11	Feb 2011	February 2011
3	3	2011	QTR1 11	Mar 2011	March 2011
4	4	2011	QTR2 11	Apr 2011	April 2011
5	5	2011	QTR2 11	May 2011	May 2011
6	6	2011	QTR2 11	Jun 2011	June 2011
7	7	2011	QTR3 11	Jul 2011	July 2011
8	8	2011	QTR3 11	Aug 2011	August 2011
9	9	2011	QTR3 11	Sep 2011	September 2011
10	10	2011	QTR4 11	Oct 2011	October 2011
11	11	2011	QTR4 11	Nov 2011	November 2011
12	12	2011	QTR4 11	Dec 2011	December 2011

4. Sort the hierarchy manually, if it does not look right in the order specified in the preceding screenshot. Enter the number 1 in cell **F1** and formula =F1+1 in cell **F2.**

	A	B	C	D	E	F
1	1	2011	QTR1 11	Jan 2011	January 2011	1
2	2	2011	QTR1 11	Feb 2011	February 2011	2

5. Click on cell **F2,** then click on the box to the right and bottom of the cell, and drag it down to cell **F12**.

	A	B	C	D	E	F
1	1	2011	QTR1 11	Jan 2011	January 2011	1
2	2	2011	QTR1 11	Feb 2011	February 2011	2
3	3	2011	QTR1 11	Mar 2011	March 2011	3
4	4	2011	QTR2 11	Apr 2011	April 2011	4
5	5	2011	QTR2 11	May 2011	May 2011	5
6	6	2011	QTR2 11	Jun 2011	June 2011	6
7	7	2011	QTR3 11	Jul 2011	July 2011	7
8	8	2011	QTR3 11	Aug 2011	August 2011	8
9	9	2011	QTR3 11	Sep 2011	September 2011	9
10	10	2011	QTR4 11	Oct 2011	October 2011	10
11	11	2011	QTR4 11	Nov 2011	November 2011	11
12	12	2011	QTR4 11	Dec 2011	December 2011	12

6. Enter the following concatenation string in cell **G1**, select **G1**, and press *CTRL+C*. Select range **G2:G12**, and press *CTRL+V* to paste the concatenation string:

```
="Insert Into TIME Values (" & A1 & ", " & B1 & ", '"& C1 & "', '"
    & D1 & "', '" & E1 & "', '" & F1 & "');"
```

7. Copy range **G1:G12**, open up SQL Management Studio, connect to the TBC database, paste the range in the query window, and execute the following queries:

```
Insert Into YEARS Values(1, 2011, 'QTR1 11', 'Jan 2011',
    'January 2011', '1');
Insert Into YEARS Values(2, 2011, 'QTR1 11', 'Feb 2011',
    'February 2011', '2');
Insert Into YEARS Values(3, 2011, 'QTR1 11', 'Mar 2011',
    'March 2011', '3');
Insert Into YEARS Values(4, 2011, 'QTR2 11', 'Apr 2011',
    'April 2011', '4');
Insert Into YEARS Values(5, 2011, 'QTR2 11', 'May 2011',
    'May 2011', '5');
Insert Into YEARS Values(6, 2011, 'QTR2 11', 'Jun 2011',
    'June 2011', '6');Insert Into YEARS Values(7, 2011,
    'QTR3 11', 'Jul 2011', 'July 2011', '7');
Insert Into YEARS Values(8, 2011, 'QTR3 11', 'Aug 2011',
    'August 2011', '8');
Insert Into YEARS Values(9, 2011, 'QTR3 11', 'Sep 2011',
    'September 2011', '9');
Insert Into YEARS Values(10, 2011, 'QTR4 11', 'Oct 2011',
    'October 2011', '10');
```

```
Insert Into YEARS Values(11, 2011, 'QTR4 11', 'Nov 2011',
   'November 2011', '11');
Insert Into YEARS Values(12, 2011, 'QTR4 11', 'Dec 2011',
   'December 2011', '12');
```

How it works...

The following are the steps in this recipe:

1. We added the YEARS table to the TBC database.
2. We added the SORT_ORDER column to the YEARS table.
3. We added an integer used to sort the members.
4. We also entered the YEARS dimension into an Excel sheet and sorted our YEARS hierarchy.
5. After placing the SORT_ORDER into column **F1**, we pasted the correct SORT_ORDER and concatenate Insert statements together with the values in Excel.
6. Finally, we used the Insert statements in the Excel workbook to update the YEARS table using the SQL Management Studio.

The following is what your YEARS hierarchy should look like without the SORT_ORDER column:

2011		
	QTR1 11	
		Feb 2011
		Jan 2011
		Mar 2011
	QTR2 11	
		Apr 2011
		Jun 2011
		May 2011
	QTR3 11	
		Aug 2011
		Jul 2011
		Sep 2011
	QTR4 11	
		Dec 2011
		Nov 2011
		Oct 2011

Essbase Studio will enter February into the outline before January, May will be after June, August will be before July, and the fourth quarter will be completely out of order. For this reason, it is suggested that you add a SORT_ORDER column to all of your dimension tables.

See also

Refer to the *Using Sort Order on data elements* recipe in *Chapter 2* to learn how to set the sort order for your metadata elements.

Adding tables for varying attributes

The varying attributes is an attribute dimension that maps to multiple dimensions. The concept of varying attributes in a relational environment is depicted by creating a mapping table. In this recipe, we will build a mapping table that joins the SALESMAN table to the Product and Market tables. We will also see how this format works for a varying attribute.

Getting ready

To get started, open SQL Server Management Studio, and add a database called TBC. In this recipe, we are using T-SQL, but the PL\SQL equivalent is provided in the examples.

How to do it...

1. Create and populate a SALESMAN table with following script. We can change the script below to PL/SQL by replacing int with INTEGER and varchar() with VARCHAR2():

```
--This is the syntax in T-SQL
Create Table SALESMAN(
   SALESMANID        int            NOT NULL,
   SALESMANNAME      varchar (80)   NULL,
   Constraint PK_SALESMAN_SALESMANID Primary Key (SALESMANID)
);
go
--This scripts enter the data into the SALEMAN table
   Insert Into SALESMAN Values(1, 'John Smith');
   Insert Into SALESMAN Values(2, 'Jose Garcia');
   Insert Into SALESMAN Values(3, 'Johnny Blaze');
```

2. Create and populate a PRODUCTS table:

```
--This is the syntax in T-SQL
Create Table PRODUCTS(
   PRODUCTID    int          NOT NULL,
   SKU          varchar(15)  NULL,
```

```
   SKU_ALIAS    varchar(25) NULL,
   Constraint PK_PRODUCTS_PRODUCTID Primary Key (PRODUCTID)
);
--Insert data into PRODUCTS table
Insert Into PRODUCTS Values(1, '100-10', 'Cola');
Insert Into PRODUCTS Values(2, '100-20', 'Diet Cola');
Insert Into PRODUCTS Values(3, '100-30', 'Caffeine Free Cola');
```

3. Create and populate a MARKETS table:

```
--This is the syntax in T-SQL
Create Table MARKETS(
   STATEID       int          NOT NULL,
   STATE         varchar(25)  NULL,
   Constraint PK_MARKETS_STATEID Primary Key (STATEID)
);
--Insert data into MARKETS table
Insert Into MARKETS Values(1, 'New York');
Insert Into MARKETS Values(2, 'Massachusetts');
Insert Into MARKETS Values(3, 'Florida');
```

4. Create and populate a SALESMANMAP table:

```
--This is the syntax in T-SQL
Create Table SALESMANMAP(
   SALESMANID   int NOT NULL,
   STATEID      int NOT NULL,
   PRODUCTID    int NOT NULL,
   Constraint PK_SALESMANMAP Primary Key (STATEID, PRODUCTID)
);

--Insert data into the SALESMANMAP table
Insert Into SALESMANMAP Values(1,1,2);
Insert Into SALESMANMAP Values(1,2,3);
Insert Into SALESMANMAP Values(2,1,1);
Insert Into SALESMANMAP Values(2,2,2);
Insert Into SALESMANMAP Values(3,3,1);
Insert Into SALESMANMAP Values(3,3,3);
```

5. Execute the following scripts to join the tables:

```
Alter Table SALESMANMAP Add  Constraint FK_SALESMANMAP_PRODUCTID
Foreign Key(PRODUCTID)
References PRODUCTS (PRODUCTID);

Alter Table SALESMANMAP Add  Constraint FK_SALESMANMAP_SALESMANID
Foreign Key(SALESMANID)
References SALESMAN (SALESMANID);
```

```
Alter Table SALESMANMAP Add  Constraint FK_SALESMANMAP_STATEID
Foreign Key(STATEID)
References MARKETS  (STATEID);
```

6. Execute the following query to see the relationship between the `Market`, `Product`, and `Salesman`:

```
Select
    T4.SALESMANID, T2.SALESMANNAME, T4.STATEID,
    T3.STATE, T4.PRODUCTID, T1.SKU_ALIAS
    From PRODUCTS T1, SALESMAN T2, MARKETS T3, SALESMANMAP T4
    Where T1.PRODUCTID = T4.PRODUCTID and
    T2.SALESMANID = T4.SALESMANID and
    T3.STATEID = T4.STATEID and
    T2.SALESMANNAME = 'John Smith'
```

How it works...

The relationships between the tables created and populated in steps 1 through 4 are shown in the following diagram:

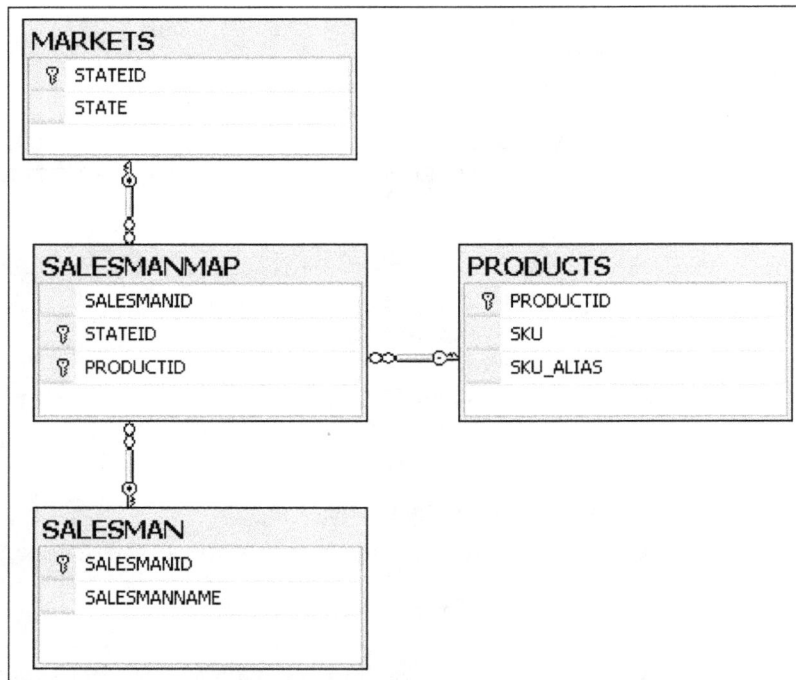

The **SALESMANMAP** table joins the other three tables of which **SALESMAN** is the varying attribute. Salesman varies depending on the state and product you want to report on. We can retrieve the relationship between tables using the query shown in step 5. The results for this query are displayed in the following screenshot:

	SALESMANID	SALESMANNAME	STATE...	STATE	PRODUCTID	SKU_ALIAS
1	1	John Smith	1	New York	2	Diet Cola
2	1	John Smith	2	Massachusetts	3	Caffeine Free Cola

The important thing to note about this varying attribute example is that it is possible for two Salesmen to conduct business in the same Market, but it is not possible for the same two Salesmen to sell the same Product in the same Market. This logic is maintained by the constraints placed on the **SALESMANMAP** mapping table.

See also

Refer to the *Adding tables to a Minischema* recipe in *Chapter 2* to add the varying attribute example to the TBC database. Refer to the *Setting Essbase Properties* recipe in *Chapter 3* to learn how to set the varying attributes' properties.

Determining hierarchies in relational tables

In this recipe, we will determine hierarchies in relational models. This recipe will also go over some of the main attribute dimension types. Attribute dimensions are dynamic dimensions that allow users to report on their data without increasing the foot print of the database. Attributes work in a similar way to an alternate hierarchy, but unlike an alternate hierarchy you can use an attribute dimension to conduct cross tab reporting on a different axis than your base dimension.

Getting ready

To get started, open SQL Server Management Studio, and add a database TBC, or if you are using Oracle you can add schema TBC and use TOAD or Golden to complete the recipe.

How to do it...

1. Execute the following script to add the Product Table. We can change the script below to PL/SQL by replacing int with INTEGER and varchar() with VARCHAR2():

```
--Create Product Table T-SQL
create table PRODUCT
(
```

```
        PRODUCTID          int                    not null,
        FAMILYID           int                    null     ,
        SKU                varchar(15)            null     ,
        SKU_ALIAS          varchar(25)            null     ,
        CAFFEINATED        varchar(5)             null     ,
        OUNCES             int                    null     ,
        PKGTYPE            varchar(15)            null     ,
        INTRODATE          datetime               null     ,
        constraint PK_PRODUCT primary key (PRODUCTID)
)
Go
```

2. Execute the following queries to load data into the table you have just created. The SKUs do not repeat in this table, but as part of your discovery phase you should make sure that this is the case as duplicates will throw off your findings. The scripts that follow this step will help you do just that.

```
--Insert values into product table. This syntax should work with
    either Pl/SQL or T-SQL
Insert into PRODUCT Values(1 , 1 , '100-10', 'Cola', 'TRUE', 12,
    'Can', 'Mar 25 1996 12:00AM');
Insert into PRODUCT Values(2 , 1 , '100-20', 'Diet Cola',
    'TRUE', 12, 'Can', 'Apr  1 1996 12:00AM');
Insert into PRODUCT Values(3 , 1 , '100-30', 'Caffeine Free Cola',
    'FALSE', 16, 'Bottle', 'Apr  1 1996 12:00AM');
Insert into PRODUCT Values(4 , 2 , '200-10', 'Old Fashioned',
    'TRUE', 12, 'Bottle', 'Sep 27 1995 12:00AM');
Insert into PRODUCT Values(5 , 2 , '200-20', 'Diet Root Beer',
    'TRUE', 16, 'Bottle', 'Jul 26 1996 12:00AM');
Insert into PRODUCT Values(6 , 2 , '200-30', 'Sasparilla',
    'FALSE', 12, 'Bottle', 'Dec 10 1996 12:00AM');
Insert into PRODUCT Values(7 , 2 , '200-40', 'Birch Beer',
    'FALSE', 16, 'Bottle', 'Dec 10 1996 12:00AM');
Insert into PRODUCT Values(8 , 3 , '300-10', 'Dark Cream', 'TRUE',
    20, 'Bottle', 'Jun 26 1996 12:00AM');
Insert into PRODUCT Values(9 , 3 , '300-20', 'Vanilla Cream',
    'TRUE', 20, 'Bottle', 'Jun 26 1996 12:00AM');
Insert into PRODUCT Values(10, 3 , '300-30', 'Diet Cream', 'TRUE',
    12, 'Can', 'Jun 26 1996 12:00AM');
Insert into PRODUCT Values(11, 4 , '400-10', 'Grape', 'FALSE', 32,
    'Bottle', 'Oct  1 1996 12:00AM');
Insert into PRODUCT Values(12, 4 , '400-20', 'Orange', 'FALSE',
    32, 'Bottle', 'Oct  1 1996 12:00AM');
Insert into PRODUCT Values(13, 4 , '400-30', 'Strawberry',
    'FALSE', 32, 'Bottle', 'Oct  1 1996 12:00AM');
```

3. Execute the following script to determine the SKU count in the PRODUCT table:

```
--Retrieve SKU count for both PL\SQL and T-SQL
Select Count(SKU) From PRODUCT;
```

4. Execute the following scripts to determine the cardinality between the SKU and the CAFFEINATED columns:

```
--Determine if there is one-to-many relationship between SKU and
  Caffeinated for both PL\SQL and T-SQL
Select SKU, Count(CAFFEINATED) As Cnt
  From PRODUCT
  Group By SKU
  Having Count(CAFFEINATED) = 1;

Select CAFFEINATED, Count(SKU) As Cnt
  From PRODUCT T1
  Group By CAFFEINATED;
```

5. Execute the following scripts to determine the cardinality between the SKU and the OUNCES columns:

```
--Determine if there is one-to-many relationship between SKU and
  Ounces for both PL\SQL and T-SQL
Select SKU, Count(OUNCES) As Cnt
  From PRODUCT
  Group By SKU
  Having Count(OUNCES) = 1;

Select OUNCES, Count(SKU) As Cnt
  From PRODUCT
  Group By OUNCES;
```

6. Execute the following scripts to determine the cardinality between the SKU and PKGTYPE columns:

```
--Determine if there is one-to-many relationship between SKU and
  PKGTYPE for both PL\SQL and T-SQL
Select SKU, Count(PKGTYPE) As Cnt
  From PRODUCT
  Group By SKU
  Having Count(PKGTYPE) = 1;

Select PKGTYPE, Count(SKU) As Cnt
  From PRODUCT
  Group By PKGTYPE;
```

7. Execute the following script to determine the cardinality between the SKU and INTRODATE columns:

```
--Determine if there is one-to-many relationship between SKU and
   IntroDate for both PL\SQL and T-SQL
Select SKU, Count(INTRODATE) As Cnt
   From PRODUCT
   Group By SKU
   Having Count(INTRODATE) = 1;


Select INTRODATE, Count(SKU) As Cnt
   From PRODUCT
   Group By INTRODATE;
```

8. Execute the following scripts to determine the cardinality between the SKU and PRODUCTID columns:

```
--Determine if there is a relationship between SKU and PRODUCTID
for both PL\SQL and T-SQL
Select SKU, Count(PRODUCTID) As Cnt
   From PRODUCT
   Group By SKU
   Having Count(PRODUCTID) = 1;


Select PRODUCTID, Count(SKU) As Cnt
   From PRODUCT
   Group By PRODUCTID;
```

9. Execute the following scripts to determine the cardinality between the PRODUCTID and FAMILYID columns:

```
--Determine if there is one-to-many relationship between PRODUCTID
   and FAMILYID for both PL\SQL and T-SQL
Select PRODUCTID, Count(FAMILYID) As Cnt
   From PRODUCT
   Group By PRODUCTID
   Having Count(PRODUCTID) = 1;


Select FAMILYID, Count(PRODUCTID) As Cnt
   From PRODUCT
   Group By FAMILYID;
```

How it works...

The first and second steps setup a `Product Table` and populate it with data. The third step retrieves a count of the SKUs in your Product table. You will need this count to determine if the attribute column has a one-to-many relationship with the SKU. This query returned exactly 13 valid SKUs.

The first script in step 4 returns a row for every time the SKU rolls up to one parent. You can see in the following screenshot, that there are exactly 13 rows signifying that each SKU rolls up to one CAFFEINATED value.

This query returns the value, as shown in the following screenshot:

```
Select SKU, Count(CAFFEINATED) As Cnt
   From PRODUCT
   Group By SKU
   Having Count(CAFFEINATED) = 1;1;
```

	SKU	Cnt
1	100-10	1
2	100-20	1
3	100-30	1
4	200-10	1
5	200-20	1
6	200-30	1
7	200-40	1
8	300-10	1
9	300-20	1
10	300-30	1
11	400-10	1
12	400-20	1
13	400-30	1

The second script in step 4 shows you that the CAFFEINATED column has a true and false value, which makes this column a good candidate for a Boolean attribute dimension. The reason this is a Boolean attribute is because it has exactly either of the two values TRUE or FALSE. The counts from this query and the previous one shows you that there are one-to-many relationships as SKUs rollup to only one CAFFEINATED value, but a single CAFFEINATED value can have many SKU children.

This script returns **TRUE** and **FALSE** values as depicted in the following screenshot:

```
Select CAFFEINATED, Count(SKU) As Cnt
  From PRODUCT T1
  Group By CAFFEINATED;
```

	CAFFEINATED	Cnt
1	FALSE	6
2	TRUE	7

The scripts in step 5 show a one-to-many relationship between SKU and OUNCES. Script 2 of step 5 shows that OUNCES will make a good candidate for a NUMERIC attribute dimension. A NUMERIC attribute type is as the word implies a number. We can use a NUMERIC attribute's value in calculating scripts or outline formulas to create formulas based on the attribute assigned.

This query returns a list of numeric values as depicted in the following screenshot:

```
Select OUNCES, Count(SKU) As Cnt
  From PRODUCT
  Group By OUNCES;
```

	OUNCES	Cnt
1	12	5
2	16	3
3	20	2
4	32	3

The scripts in step 6 show a one-to-many relationship between SKU and PKGTYPE as it returns exactly 13 unique records. Script 2 of step 6 shows the PKGTYPE that would make a good TEXT attribute or an alternate dimension. A TEXT attribute allows for a comparison in calculations and a selection of a member based on the attribute assigned. Text attributes are the default attribute in Essbase.

This query returns a list of text values as depicted in the following screenshot:

```
Select PKGTYPE, Count(SKU) As Cnt
  From PRODUCT
  Group By PKGTYPE;
```

	PKGTYPE	Cnt
1	Bottle	10
2	Can	3

The scripts in step 7 also show a one-to-many relationship between SKU and INTRODATE. Script 2 of step 7 shows that INTRODATE is, as the name implies, a date and as such will make a good DATE attribute dimension. You can use DATE attributes in calculation as well. We can compare different Products, for example, based on the DATE attribute for specific Market. Date attributes from January 1, 1970 through January 1, 2038 are supported.

This query returns a list of date values as depicted in the following screenshot:

```
Select INTRODATE, Count(SKU) As Cnt
  From PRODUCT
  Group By INTRODATE;
```

	INTRODATE	Cnt
1	1995-09-27 00:00:00.000	1
2	1996-03-25 00:00:00.000	1
3	1996-04-01 00:00:00.000	2
4	1996-06-26 00:00:00.000	3
5	1996-07-26 00:00:00.000	1
6	1996-10-01 00:00:00.000	3
7	1996-12-10 00:00:00.000	2

Moreover, in step 8 you will see a one-to-one relationship between SKU and PRODUCTID, which means there is exactly one PRODUCTID for each SKU, and one SKU will rollup to exactly one parent. Script 2 of step 8 shows that this will more than likely be the main rollup in your PRODUCT dimension. This is also intuitive as the SKU in this case is the column representing the PRODUCT:

	PRODUCTID	Cnt
1	1	1
2	2	1
3	3	1
4	4	1
5	5	1
6	6	1
7	7	1
8	8	1
9	9	1
10	10	1
11	11	1
12	12	1
13	13	1

Finally, the relationship between FAMILYID and PRODUCTID is a one-to-many relationship, shown in step 9. A possible outcome of these findings is to create a dimension and hiearchy with three generations as depicted in the following table:

DIMENSION	GENERATION	LEVEL
PRODUCT	1	2
FAMILYID	2	1
SKU	3	0

There's more...

In real world situations, you may come across scenarios where your relationships are not always one-to-one or one-to-many. Keep a note of these exceptions as you may need to concatenate columns, create alternate rollups with shared members, add a prefix or suffix, create a new dimension, or turn on duplicate members in your outline in order to deal with these issues. We will go over some of these in other chapters. That said, the preceding scripts will help you see these discrepancies before you begin building your cube, which will save you time later in your development. In addition, note that when building a BSO cube you can only assign attributes to a sparse dimension.

See also

Refer to the recipes *Adding attribute dimensions to hierarchies* and *Setting Essbase Properties* in *Chapter 3* to learn how to set up attribute dimensions and their properties in Essbase Studio.

Using the Essbase Outline Extractor to extract dimensions

In this recipe, we are going to use the **Essbase Outline Extractor** to extract the meta-data from the Sample Basic database in parent-child format. The Essbase Outline Extractor is a free product and can be downloaded from **AppliedOLAP**'s website: http://www.appliedolap.com/free-tools/outline-extractor. The version you should consider for Essbase 11.1.2.1 for now is essbase_outline_extractor_11.1.2. This tool can assist you in extracting your metadata from an existing Essbase cube. We can then use its output to load **Data Relationship Management** (**DRM**) or a relational environment.

Getting ready

To get started, click on the **Start** menu to open the Essbase Outline Extractor.

How to do it...

1. Click on **Programs** and select **olapunderground | Essbase Outline Extractor | Essbase Outline Extractor**.

2. Click on the **Do not show this message again** checkbox and click on **Proceed** if you get the following prompt:

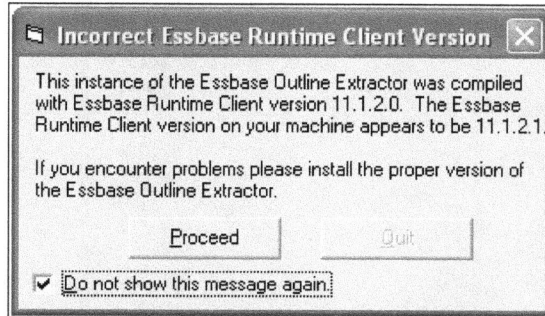

3. You should now see the extract utility, as follows:

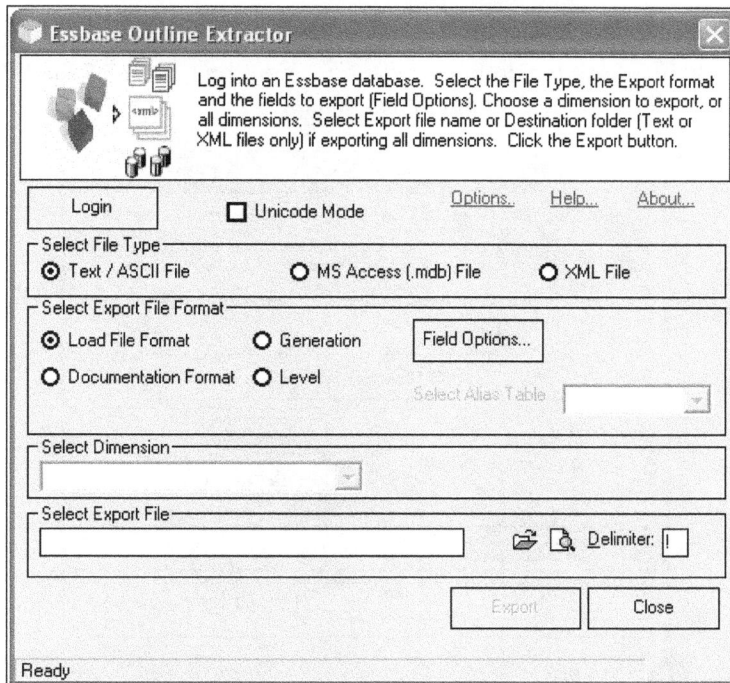

4. Click on the **Login** button on the top left and enter the server you want to log in to. Enter your username and password.

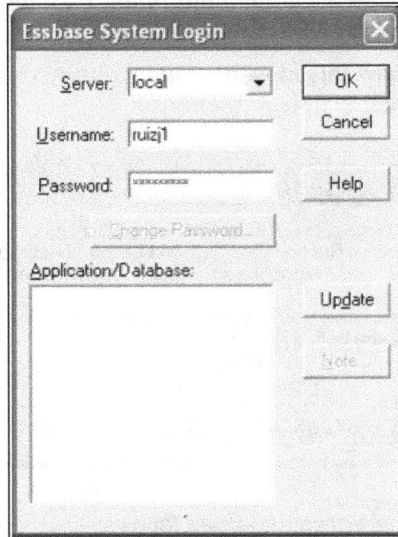

5. Click on the **Sample.Basic** application and database, and click on the **OK** button.

6. You should now have the option to select a dimension from the **Select Dimension** combo box. Click on the **Product** dimension.

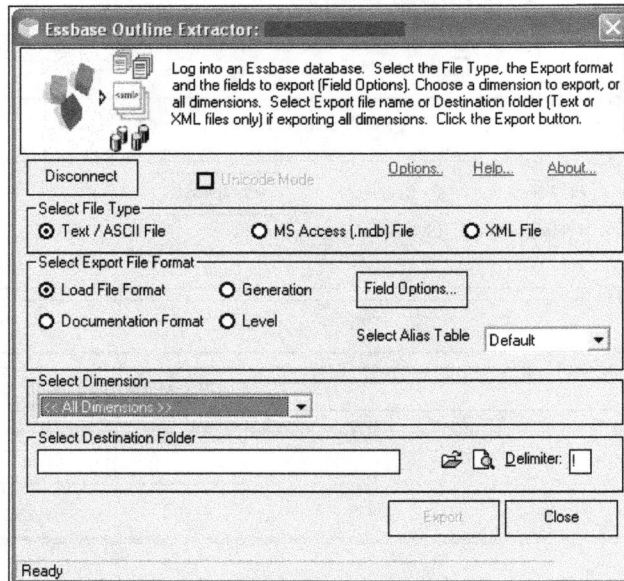

7. Click on the **Load File Format** radio button and the **Field Options** command button. Select all the checkboxes except **Currency Name/Category** in this menu as it is not applicable in this case.

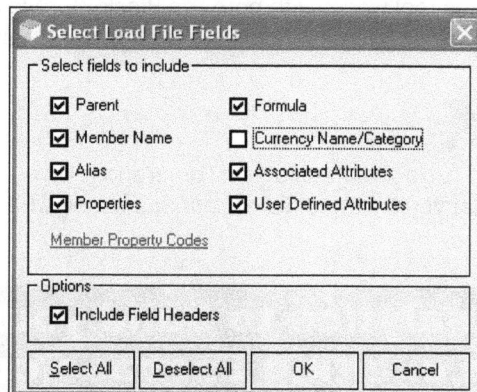

8. Click on the **Browser** button circled in the following screenshot and select a file location and filename.

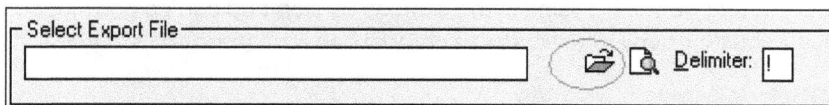

9. You have the option to change the file's delimiter as well, but the exclamation mark (**!**) character should work fine.

10. Click on the **Export** button.

11. A file should be produced in the location you specified, delimited by the bang or exclamation character, and in a parent-child format. The column headers in this file should be as follows:

COLUMN HEADERS
PARENT0,Product
CHILD0,Product
ALIAS0,Product
PROPERTY0,Product
FORMULA0,Product
OUNCES0,Product
CAFFEINATED0,Product
PKGTYPE0,Product

How it works...

In this recipe, we used the Essbase Outline Extractor to extract the metadata for the `Product` dimension into a text file. This tool works with both the Block Storage and Aggregate storage model, but may have issues when the dimension member count is very large.

There's more...

You can also use the tool to extract dimensions in Generation, Level, and Documentation Format. It is encouraged that you try the different options to see what format best fits your needs.

Using Star Analytics to build your star schema from existing Essbase cubes

In this recipe, we will be using a third party tool called Star Integration Server Manager to build a star schema from an existing cube. The purpose of using this tool in this recipe is to quickly move the meta-data of your Essbase, Planning, or HFM applications to a relational environment. The tool we will be using is the express version and can be downloaded from the Star Analytics website: `http://www.staranalytics.com/products/index.htm`.

Getting ready

To get started, open Microsoft SQL Server and add a database called `BASIC`. Microsoft SQL Server is being used for this example, but you can use Oracle, Sybase, Teradata, DB2, MySQL, or a text file to extract your outline.

How to do it...

1. Click on **Programs** and select **Star Analytics | Star Integration Server Manager**.
2. Double-click on **Connection Manager** on the left-hand side, and click on the **New Connection** button. The **New HyperionEssbase Connection** menu will appear on the screen, as follows:

3. Enter a **Sample** for your **Connection Name** and enter your **Essbase Server**.

4. Enter a **Sample** for the **Application** parameter value, **Basic** for the **Database** parameter value, **Basic** for your **Outline** parameter value, and your **User Name** and **Password**. Click on the **Test** button to test your connection, click the **OK** button on the pop up menu, and click on the **Save and Close** button.

5. Double-click on **Connection Manager**, select **SQL Server using SQL Server login** in the **Connection Type**, and enter **Basic** for the **Name**.

6. Enter your **SQL Server** name into the parameter value, **Basic** for the **Database** parameter, and enter your **Login Name** and **Password**.

7. Click on the **Test** button to test your connection, click the **OK** button on the popup menu, and click the **Save and Close** button.

8. Click on the **New Essbase Selection** button and select the **Selection Information** tab. In the **Source Connection** drop-down select **Sample: Hyperion Essbase**, and in the **Target Connection** drop-down select **Basic: SQLServer-SQLLogin**.

9. Check all the **Export** checkboxes in the **Column Selections** grid, and check on the **Spin** checkbox for **Measures**. Your screen will look like the following screenshot:

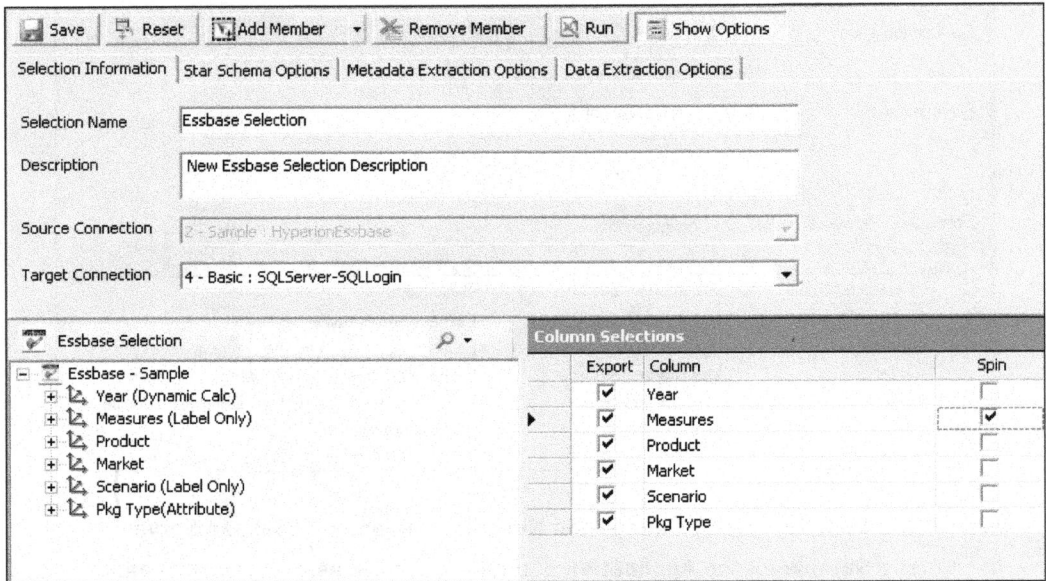

10. Click on the **Run** button in the **Run Selection** prompt and select **Yes** to run the **Current Selection**. Click on the **OK** button in the **Run Completion** on the pop up.

11. Verify that all your tables were created in the **Running Essbase Selection** in the local dialog box, and click on the **Close** button. Your screen should look as follows:

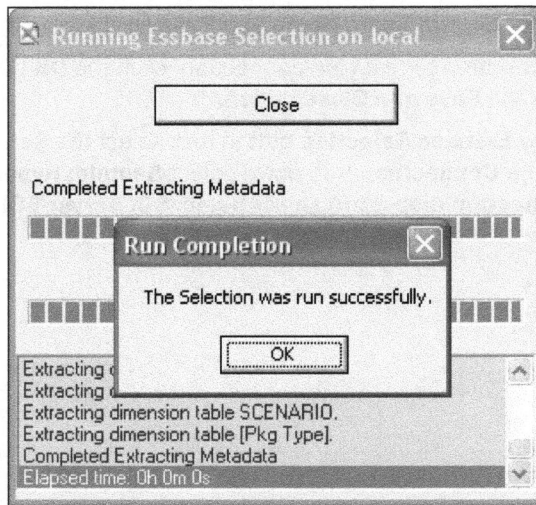

How it works...

In this recipe, we created a connection to our relational database and a connection to Essbase. We then used the tool to define the dimensions we wanted to include in our star schema. Finally, we created a star schema using the Sample Basic database with our selections. You should see six tables in your Basic relational database. The results of this exercise are available in script `3265_01_08_tsql.sql`.

See also

The Sample Basic database comes with the Essbase installation, but if you would like to build it, refer to the *Adding an Application and Database on an Essbase server* recipe in *Chapter 5*.

2

Using Essbase Studio

In this chapter, we will cover the following topics:

- ► Creating a TBC database and connecting to the data source
- ► Adding user-defined tables
- ► Building your minischema
- ► Setting up joins in a minischema
- ► Adding tables to a minischema
- ► Using a text file as the data source
- ► Working with Common Platform Language (CPL)
- ► Using Sort Order on data elements

Introduction

In this chapter, we will go over some basic, yet necessary Essbase Studio recipes. The first question that we should discuss, is why begin developing with Essbase Studio as opposed to **Essbase Administration Services** (**EAS**) or **Essbase Integration Services** (**EIS**)? The most obvious answer is that Oracle has announced that their long-term vision is to replace EAS and EIS with Essbase Studio. Please visit the following URL for more information on the Oracle Essbase Road Map: `http://communities.ioug.org/Portals/2/Oracle_Essbase_Roadmap_Sep_09.pdf`.

That said, version 11.1.2.1, the version this book is written for, requires that you use Essbase Studio in conjunction with EAS for a set of tasks. Please see the following advantages and disadvantages of Essbase Studio for more details.

Advantages of Essbase Studio

▶ Essbase Studio is integrated with all new features of 11.x

▶ Ease of migrating Integration Service catalog to Essbase Studio catalog via migration utility

▶ As opposed to EIS, Essbase Studio gives developers the option of deploying all dimensions, one or a set of dimensions, or performing a data load via MaxL

▶ Provides an intuitive user interface with wizards that simplifies data model design, cube design, and application building and deployment

▶ Provides one environment for the designing of all data models

▶ Provides the ability to create drill-through reporting as opposed to EAS

▶ Provides the ability to build a dimension library that can be used to build other applications

▶ Powerful CPL for the modification of data elements

▶ Provides for the creation of calendar hierarchies with built-in wizards

Disadvantage of Essbase Studio

▶ The EAS and EIS development tools are both more mature than Essbase Studio

▶ Essbase Studio will need to be used in conjunction with EAS for the following development tasks in version 11.1.2.1 or later

▶ Configurations of certain Essbase Application settings need to be done in EAS

▶ Creation of substitution variables is available only with EAS

▶ Creation of security filters is available only with EAS

▶ Dragging and dropping of members which are not in Measures dimension is only supported in EAS

▶ Calculation, rules, report scripts, MaxL, and MDX editors are not available in Essbase Studio

▶ Creation of partitions is not available in Essbase Studio

Creating TBC sample database and connecting to the data source

The first step in using Essbase Studio is to connect to the data source. In this recipe, we will be creating The Beverage Company (TBC) sample database and we will also be creating a SQL Server data source connection.

Getting ready

To get started, open SQL Server Management Studio, and add a database called `TBC`. We are using the SQL Server scripts in this example, but Oracle has provided the Oracle, DB2, Teradata, and MySQL scripts.

How to do it...

1. Open SQL Server Management Studio, select the **TBC** database, click on the **File** menu, select **Open**, and click on **File...**. Open the following script: ...\Oracle\ Middleware\EPMSystem11R1\products\Essbase\EssbaseStudio\Server\ sqlscripts\tbc_create_sqlsrv.sql.

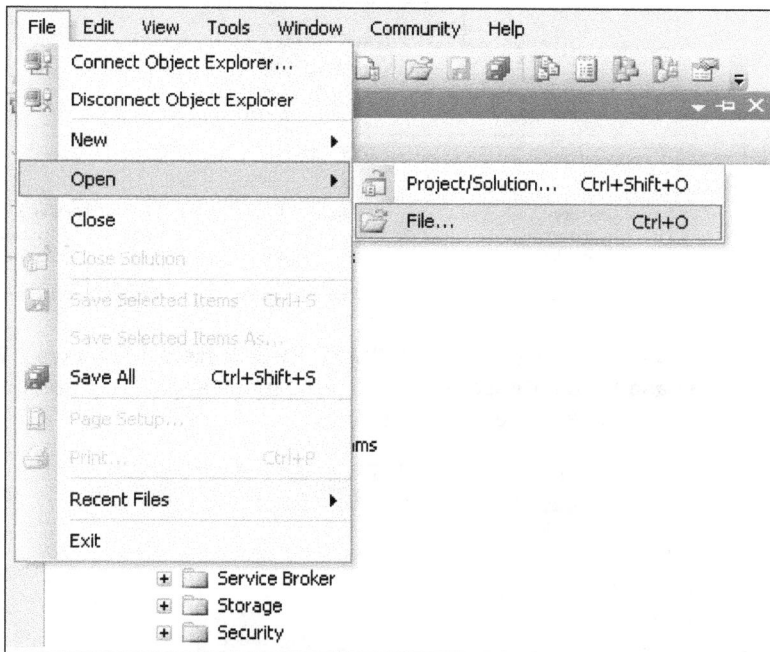

2. Make sure **TBC** is selected in your **Available Database** window and click on **Execute**.

3. Click on the **File** menu, select **Open**, and click on **File...**. Open the following script:...\ Oracle\Middleware\EPMSystem11R1\products\Essbase\EssbaseStudio\ Server\sqlscripts\tbc_sampledata.sql

4. Make sure the **TBC** database is selected in your **Available Database** window and click on **Execute**.

5. The TBC database should look like the following screenshot. Take a minute to examine the Star Schema.

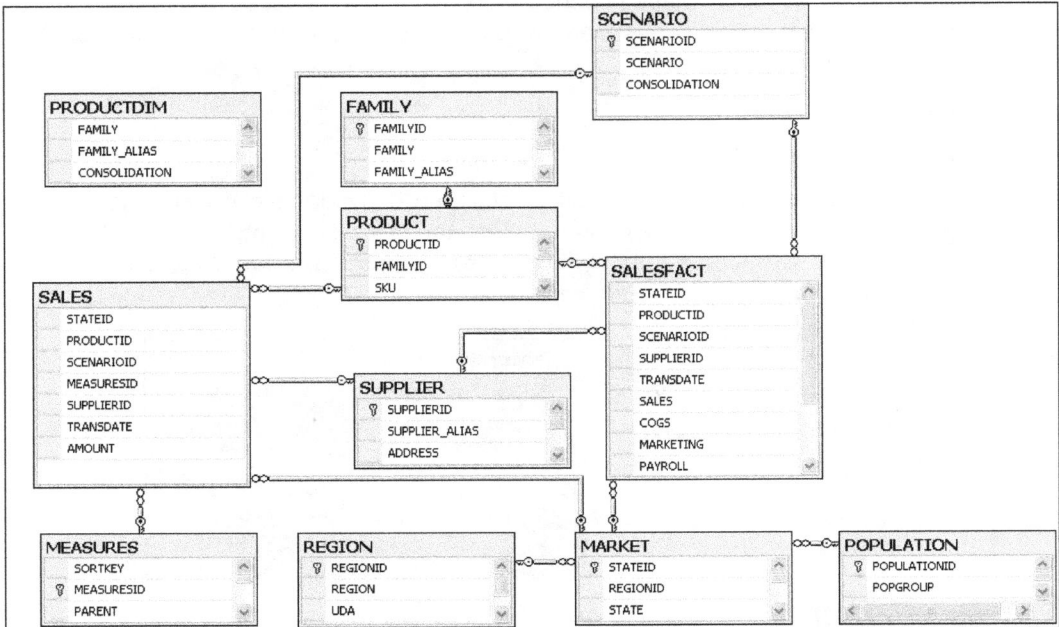

SCENARIO
- SCENARIOID
- SCENARIO
- CONSOLIDATION

PRODUCTDIM
- FAMILY
- FAMILY_ALIAS
- CONSOLIDATION

FAMILY
- FAMILYID
- FAMILY
- FAMILY_ALIAS

PRODUCT
- PRODUCTID
- FAMILYID
- SKU

SALESFACT
- STATEID
- PRODUCTID
- SCENARIOID
- SUPPLIERID
- TRANSDATE
- SALES
- COGS
- MARKETING
- PAYROLL

SALES
- STATEID
- PRODUCTID
- SCENARIOID
- MEASURESID
- SUPPLIERID
- TRANSDATE
- AMOUNT

SUPPLIER
- SUPPLIERID
- SUPPLIER_ALIAS
- ADDRESS

MEASURES
- SORTKEY
- MEASURESID
- PARENT

REGION
- REGIONID
- REGION
- UDA

MARKET
- STATEID
- REGIONID
- STATE

POPULATION
- POPULATIONID
- POPGROUP

6. Click on the **Start** menu and then click **Oracle EPM System | Essbase | Essbase Studio | Essbase Studio Console**. The following menu should pop up and allow you to enter the server, username, and password:

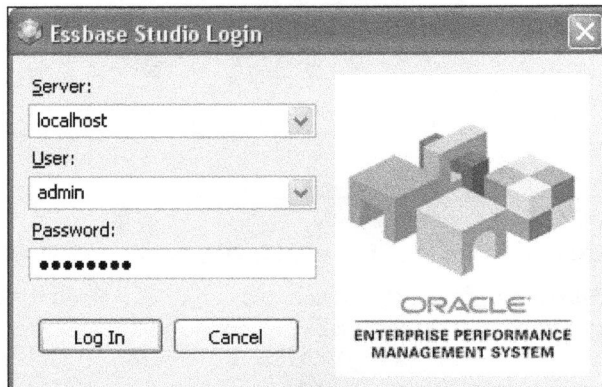

Essbase Studio Login

Server:
localhost

User:
admin

Password:
••••••••

Log In   Cancel

ORACLE
ENTERPRISE PERFORMANCE
MANAGEMENT SYSTEM

7. Enter your information and click on the **Log In** button. **Oracle Essbase Studio** should open. On the right-hand side you should see two tabs. Right-click on the **Data Sources** tab node, and click on **New** and **Data Sources...**

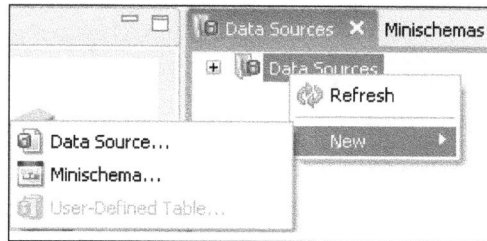

8. In the **Connection Wizard** enter the **Connection Name** and the **Connection Description**. Select the **Data Source Type** from the drop-down. Enter the **Server Name**, your **User Name** and **Password**, and select your **Database Name**.

9. Click on the **Test Connection** button to verify that the parameters you entered are correct. If the connection is successful a prompt should pop up. Click on the **Next** button to select tables.

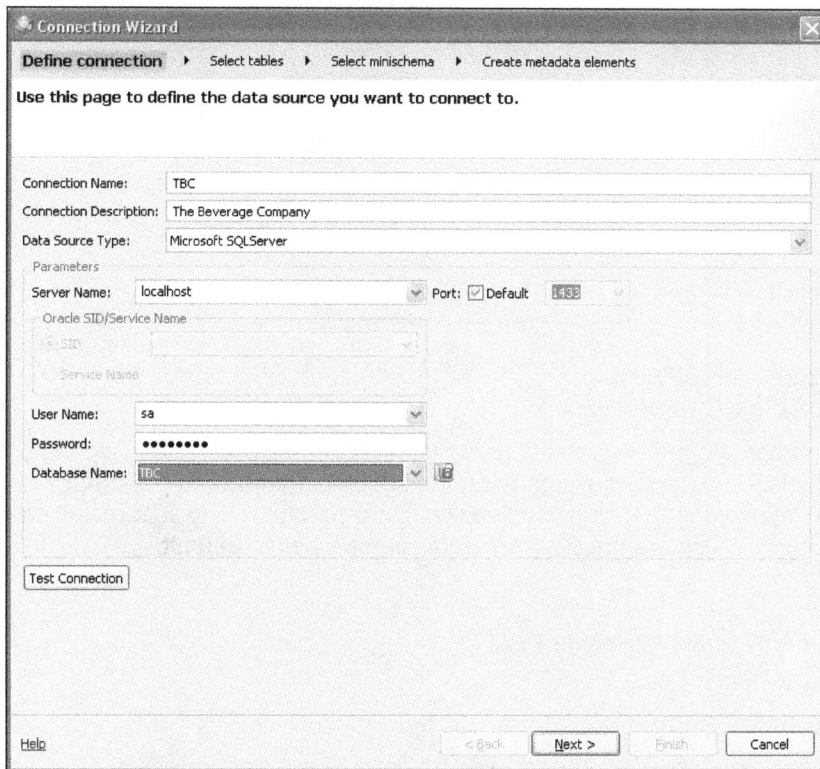

10. In the **Select tables** tab, press *Shift* and select all the tables from `TBC.dbo.FAMILY` to `TBC.dbo.SUPPLIER`. Click on the right arrow button to move the tables to the **Tables in Data Source** list box. Then, click on the **Finish** button. You should get a **Data Source Created successfully** prompt.

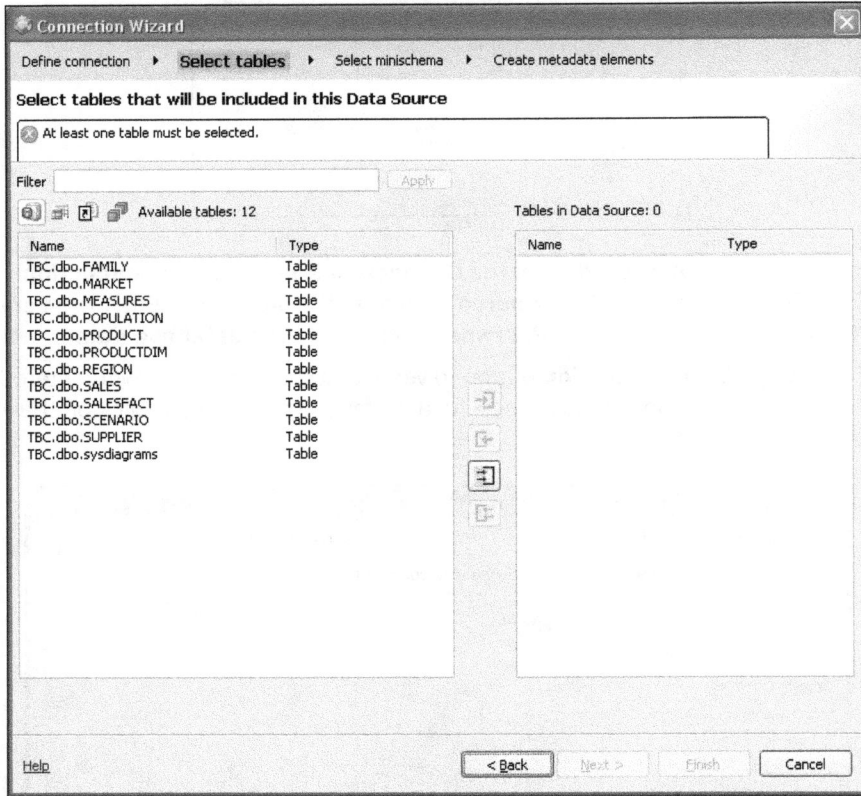

How it works...

In steps 1 through 5, you set up the `TBC` database that comes with Essbase Studio. We logged in and opened the Connection Wizard to set up our data source. In addition, we entered the data source's information and necessary parameters to successfully connect to your data source. These are the available data source types by default:

- Oracle
- Oracle Business Intelligence
- Microsoft SQLServer
- IBM DB2
- Essbase server

▶ Dimension server

▶ Text file

Finally, we select the tables, views, alias, or synonyms that we need from the data source. The **Select tables** tab allows you to filter your selections. The buttons under the **Filter** textbox will show tables, views, aliases, and synonyms. We can continue to add the minischema and data elements using the **Connection Wizard**. If you would like more details on the different data source connections, then use the following website to open the Oracle Essbase Studio document: `http://download.oracle.com/docs/cd/E17236_01/epm.1112/est_user.pdf`

Adding user-defined tables

The user-defined table is used to create a view within Essbase Studio. User-defined tables should give you some flexibility without having to change the data source. This functionality is going to be important when defining your metadata. Furthermore, this flexibility is valuable in environments where the Essbase developers cannot modify the data source at the risk of impacting other Essbase applications or relational reporting. In this recipe, we will add a user-defined table to our data source and then add that table to the TBC minischema.

Getting ready

To get started, click on the **Start** menu and navigate to **Oracle EPM System | Essbase | Essbase Studio | Essbase Studio Console**. On the login menu, enter the server, username, and password.

How to do it...

1. Right-click on TBC Data Source under the **Data Sources** node. Then click on **New** and select **User-Defined Table...**:

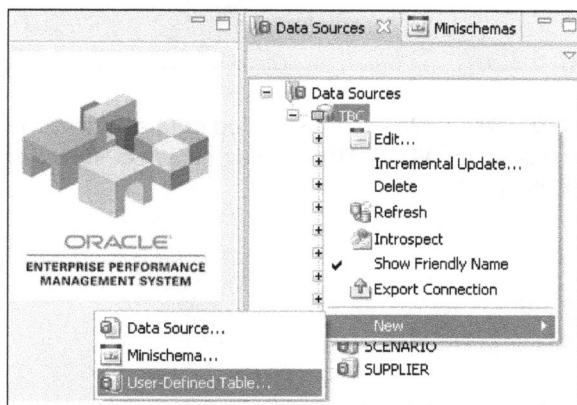

2. Enter a **Table name** in the available textbox and the following script to create the user-defined table in the **Table Definition** textbox:

```
--This is T-SQL Calendar Script
Select Distinct YEAR(T1.TRANSDATE) as YEAR,
                        MONTH(T1.TRANSDATE) as MONTH,
                        DATENAME(month, T1.TRANSDATE) as
MONTHNAME,
                        T1.TRANSDATE
From SALES T1


--This is PL-SQL Calendar Script
Select Unique TO_CHAR(T1.TRANSDATE, 'YYYY') as YEAR,
                 TO_CHAR(T1.TRANSDATE, 'MM') as MONTH,
                 TO_CHAR(T1.TRANSDATE, 'MONTH') as MONTHNAME,
                 T1.TRANSDATE
From SALES T1
```

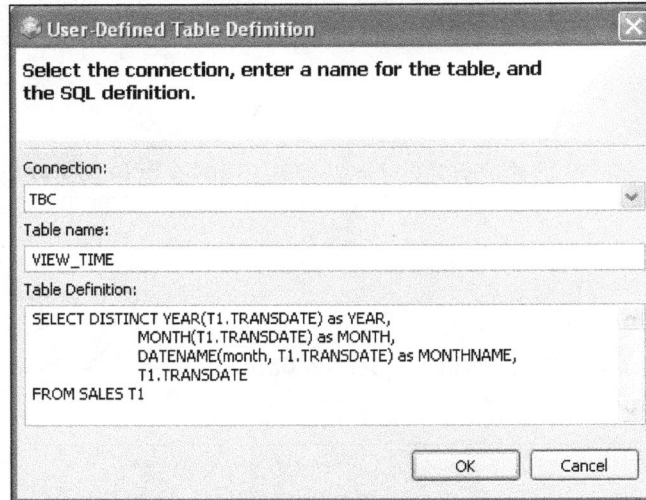

3. Click on the **VIEW_TIME** table in your selected data source to view field names. You can then right-click on the **VIEW_TIME** node and select **View Sample Data** to see some of the view's data.

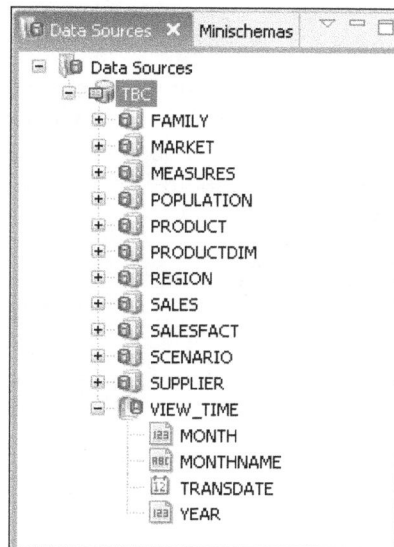

How it works...

The user-defined table is added to the data source in the preceding steps with a SQL select query. The user-defined table is a view or virtual view into the data source schema. This functionality is powerful in facilitating the creation of hierarchies. We will be able to use this table in the minischema just like a regular table from the data source. If performance becomes an issue with a user-defined table, you should consider creating a table or materialized view in the data source instead.

Building your minischema

The minischema is a structure that defines the relationships between your tables, or in the case of parent-child recursive relationships, within the same table. In the preceding recipe, *Creating TBC database and connecting to the data source*, we had an opportunity to continue with the process and build the minischema and data elements. We separated the steps to focus on each component individually, but the **Connection Wizard** would have been a seamless approach to building your data source connection, minischema, and data elements. In this recipe, we will create a minischema using the **Minischema Wizard** in Essbase Studio.

Getting ready

To get started, click on the **Start** menu and navigate to **Programs | Oracle EPM System | Essbase | Essbase Studio**. The login menu will pop up. Enter your server, username, password, and click the **Login** button.

How to do it...

1. On the right-hand side of your Essbase Studio screen, you are going to see two tabs. Click on the **Minischemas** tab, right-click on the **Minischema** node, click on **New** in the menu, and select **Minischema...**. The following menu will pop up. Enter TBC in the **Minischema Name**, optionally enter the **Minischema Description**, and click on the **Next** button:

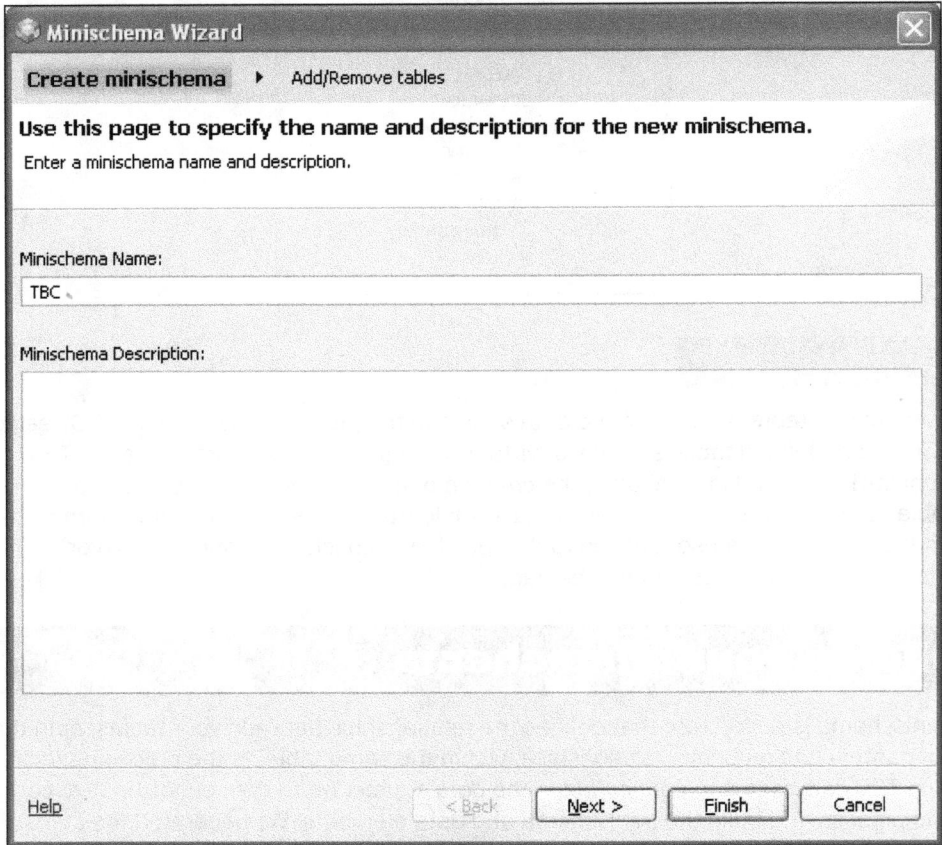

```
┌─────────────────────────────────────────────────────────────────────────┐
│  ● Minischema Wizard                                              [ X ]    │
├─────────────────────────────────────────────────────────────────────────┤
│  Create minischema      ▶   Add/Remove tables                             │
├─────────────────────────────────────────────────────────────────────────┤
│  Use this page to specify the name and description for the new minischema.│
│  Enter a minischema name and description.                                 │
│                                                                           │
│  Minischema Name:                                                         │
│  ┌─────────────────────────────────────────────────────────────────────┐ │
│  │ TBC                                                                   │ │
│  └─────────────────────────────────────────────────────────────────────┘ │
│  Minischema Description:                                                   │
│  ┌─────────────────────────────────────────────────────────────────────┐ │
│  │                                                                       │ │
│  │                                                                       │ │
│  │                                                                       │ │
│  │                                                                       │ │
│  │                                                                       │ │
│  │                                                                       │ │
│  │                                                                       │ │
│  └─────────────────────────────────────────────────────────────────────┘ │
│                                                                           │
│  Help              [ < Back ]  [ Next > ]  [ Finish ]  [ Cancel ]         │
└─────────────────────────────────────────────────────────────────────────┘
```

2. Make sure your connection is correct in the **Add/Remove tables** tab. Enter **PRODUCT** into the **Filter** textbox and click on the **Apply** button to filter. The **PRODUCT** table should be the only one appearing in the **Available Tables** list box, if you are using the TBC data source.

3. Remove **PRODUCT** from the **Filter** textbox and click on **Apply**. Click on the **PRODUCT** table, and click on the add button. If you hover over this button, then it should give you a tool tip that says **Add selected tables to the schema**. Click on the **Add related tables** button to get all the tables related to PRODUCT. Your screen **Minischema Wizard** should appear as follows:

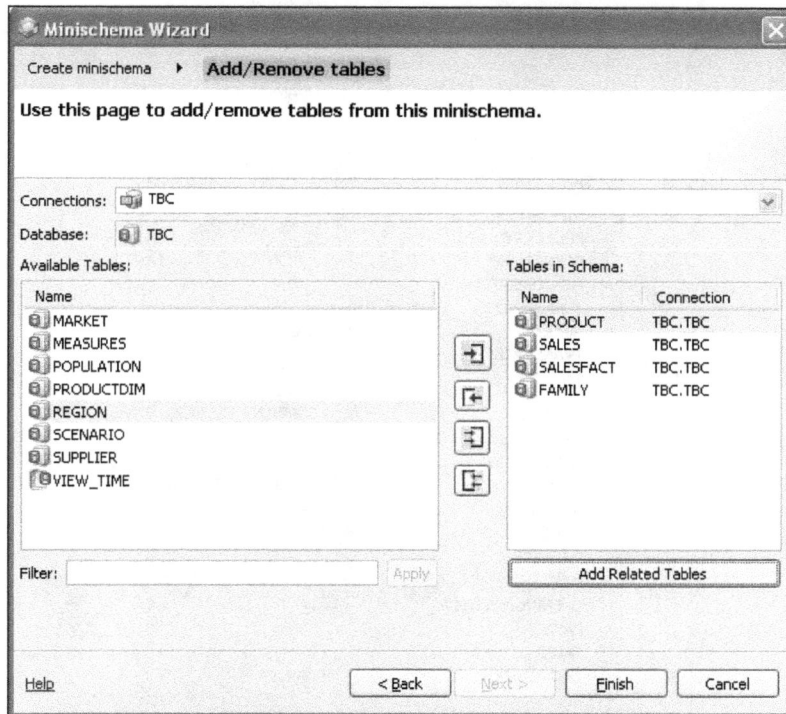

4. Click on the **Add all** button to add all tables to the **Tables in Schema** list box. If you hover over the button, then you should get a tool tip that says **Add all tables to the schema**. Click on the **Finish** button. Your minischema for the TBC database should look as follows:

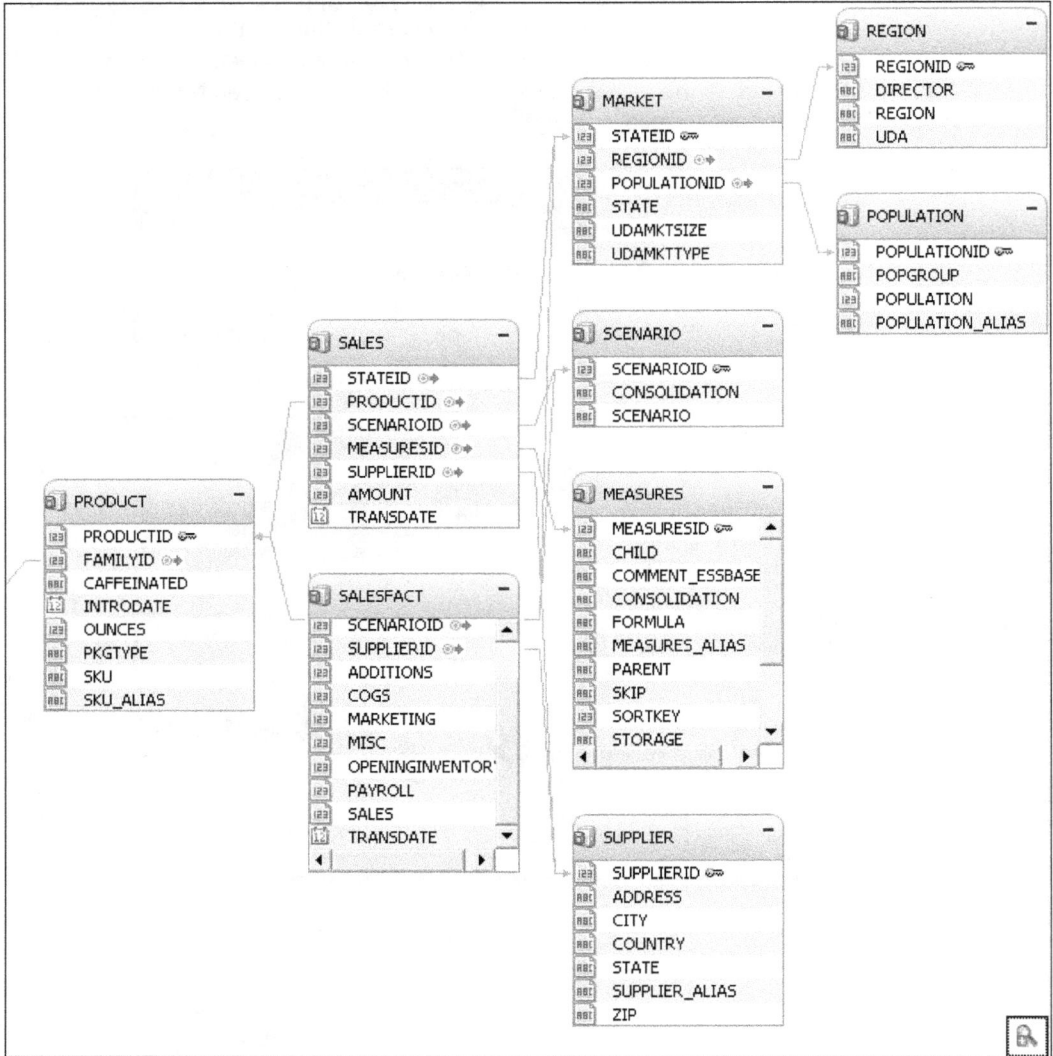

How it works...

In this recipe, we worked with the **Minischema Wizard** to place the TBC data source into a minischema. We were able to filter tables, select related tables, and choose all the tables included in the TBC data source. The minischema reflects the relationships between the tables at the physical data source. We are now ready to define additional relationships and create data elements.

See also

The relationships in the minischema will be used by Essbase Studio in data loads, creating hierarchies, measures dimensions, and in building drill-through reports. Refer to the recipe *Setting up joins in a minischema* in this chapter to learn how to set up a relationship between tables.

Setting up joins in a minischema

When you create a minischema, if there are any joins in the data source they will be visible in the minischema diagram. In the TBC minischema, in the recipe *Building your minischema*, there are no visible recursive (parent-child) relationships. Any user-defined tables that you define in the data source will also not have any relationships assigned to them. These relationships will impact the queries that Essbase Studio generates. If you do not understand the relationships in your data source, then you will most likely not build a cube that truly defines how the business functions. Defining relationships between tables can be done manually by adding joins or by using inspection. In this recipe, we will practice both methods.

Getting ready

To get started with Essbase Studio, click on the **Start** menu and navigate to **Programs | Oracle EPM System | Essbase | Essbase Studio**. The login menu will pop up. Enter your server, username, and password, and click on the **Login** button.

How to do it...

1. On the right-hand side of your screen you will see two tabs. Click on the **Minischemas** tab, click on the **+** sign next to the **Minischema** node to expand, and double-click on the TBC minischema to open.

2. Right-click on the **MEASURES** table in the minischemas and select **Add join...** in the menu:

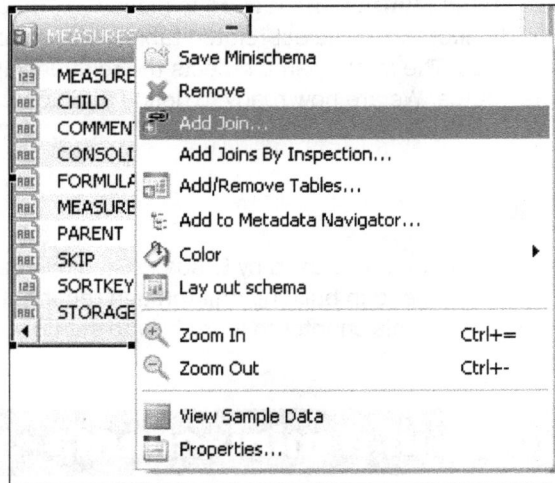

3. In the menu that pops up, select **MEASURES** in the combo box on the right. Then click on the first column's cell and select **CHILD**. After this click on the first cell and select **PARENT**, and then click the **OK** button:

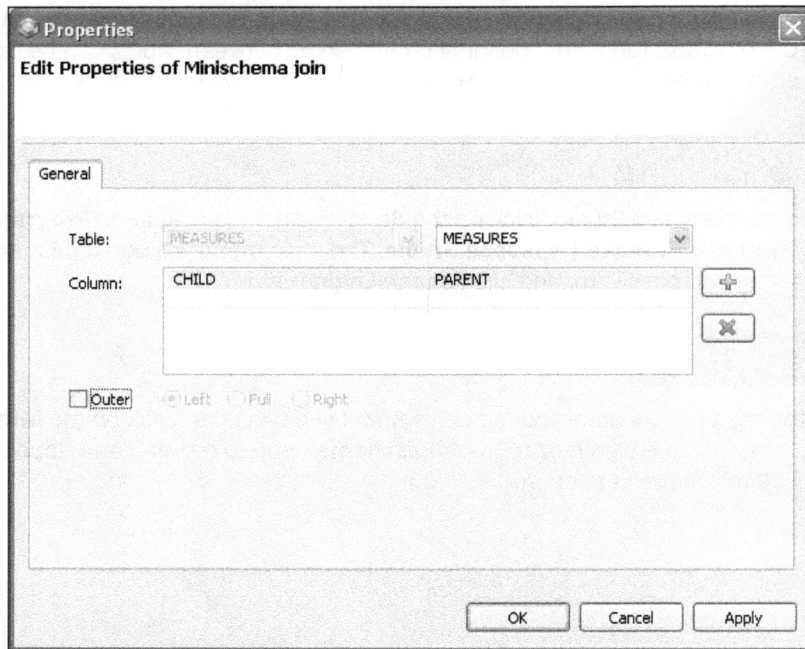

4. Click on the **SALES** table, select the **TRANSDATE** column, and drag the column to the **VIEW_TIME** user-defined table created in a preceding recipe, *Adding user defined tables*, to create a join.

5. You can double-click on the line representing the join between **SALES** and **VIEW_TIME** to see the columns that join the tables. You can also see the relationship if you hover over the line.

How it works...

This recipe shows you how to create a recursive relationship between the CHILD and PARENT columns in the **MEASURES** table and how to create join between the **SALES** and user-defined table **VIEW_TIME** by dragging and dropping the **TRANDATE** from the **SALES** to the **VIEW_TIME** table. Note that in the Properties menu you have the option of selecting your join type. The default join is an INNER join, which signifies that the records returned will be inclusive. The option to have a left, right, or full outer join is also available.

There's more...

1. If you right-click anywhere on the minischema screen, then you will get a menu that allows you to select **Add Joins By Inspection...**:

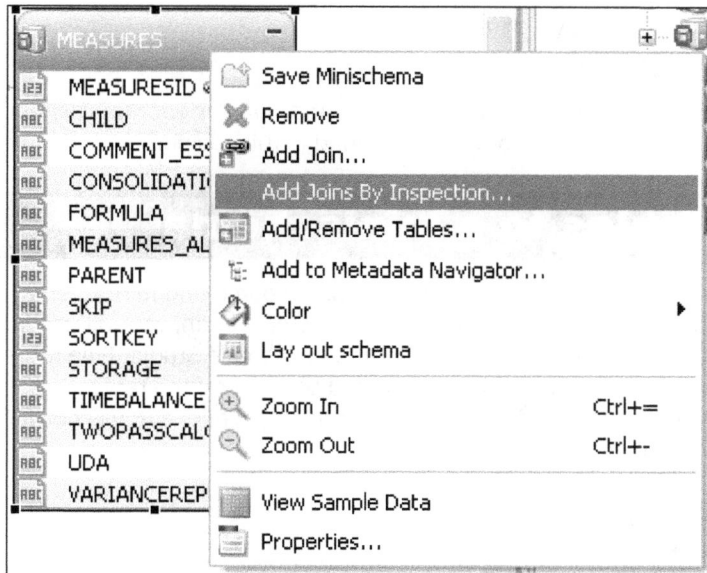

2. A menu, like the one shown in the following screenshot, will allow you to select the relationships that you feel are valid, and then select **OK** to apply them to your minischema:

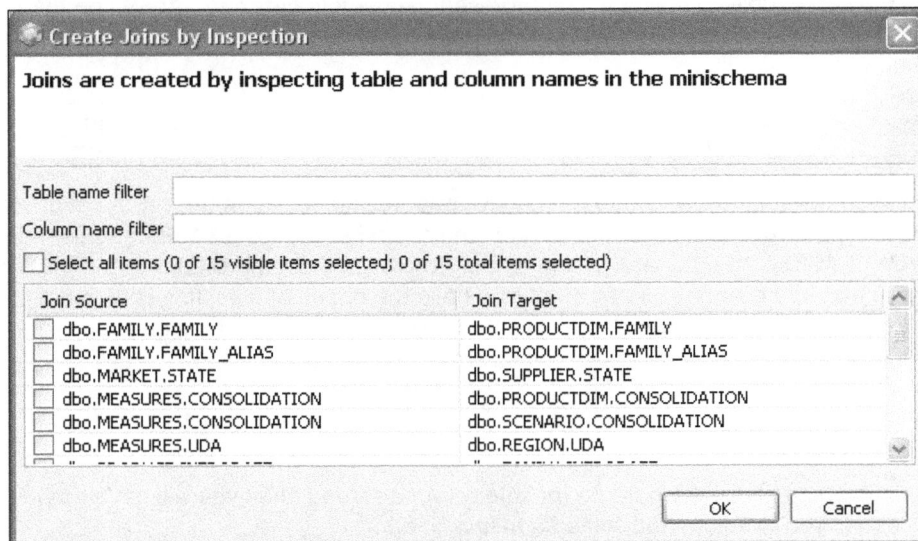

See also

Reviewing the recipes *Adding User-defined tables* and *Building your minischema* in this chapter will help you explore the components found in this recipe.

Adding tables to a minischema

In this recipe, we will add two new tables to your data source and minischema. We will begin this recipe by adding tables to your relational data source. Then, you will use incremental updates to add the two tables to your data source in Essbase Studio. Finally, we are going to add the tables to the minischema. This task would be easier if the tables already existed in your data source in Essbase Studio, but in real-world applications this is normally the order in which these changes take place.

Getting ready

Open your SQL Server Management Studio and open the TBC database. If you have not created the database, then see the recipe *Creating TBC database and connecting to the data source* in this chapter. The example is done using T-SQL, but the PL-SQL equivalent for the examples is as follows.

How to do it...

1. In SQL Server Management Studio, click on **File | Open File...** to open the `tsql_script_3265_02_01.sql` file included within this chapter for T-SQL, and click on **Execute**. If you are using Oracle, then use the `plsql_script_3265_02_01.sql` file instead in your favorite data management tool.

2. Click on the **Start** menu and **Programs | Oracle EPM System | Essbase | Essbase Studio**. The login menu will pop up. Enter your server, username, and password, and click on the **Login** button.

3. In Essbase Studio, on the right-hand side of your screen, you are going to see two tabs. Click on the **Data Source** tab, right-click on the **TBC** data source, and click on **Incremental Update**.

4. Click on the *Shift* key, select `TBC.dbo.SALESMAN` and `TBC.dbo.SALESMANMAP`, and click on the single right arrow button to add the tables to the **Tables in Data Source** list box. Click on **OK**.

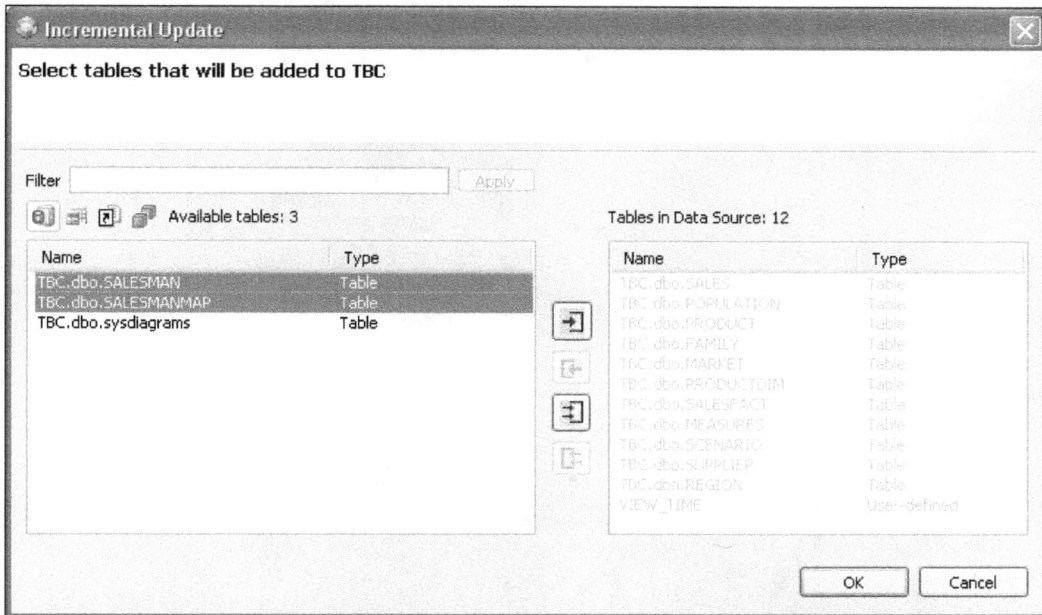

Incremental Update	☒

Select tables that will be added to TBC

Filter [_____] Apply

Available tables: 3   Tables in Data Source: 12

Name	Type		Name	Type
TBC.dbo.SALESMAN	Table		TBC.dbo.SALES	Table
TBC.dbo.SALESMANMAP	Table		TBC.dbo.POPULATION	Table
TBC.dbo.sysdiagrams	Table		TBC.dbo.PRODUCT	Table
			TBC.dbo.FAMILY	Table
			TBC.dbo.MARKET	Table
			TBC.dbo.PRODUCTDIM	Table
			TBC.dbo.SALESFACT	Table
			TBC.dbo.MEASURES	Table
			TBC.dbo.SCENARIO	Table
			TBC.dbo.SUPPLIER	Table
			TBC.dbo.REGION	Table
			VIEW_TIME	User-defined

OK   Cancel

5. Click on the **Minischema** tab, right-click on the **TBC** minischema, and select **Edit...**.

6. Right-click anywhere in the minischema diagram and select **Add/Remove Tables...**.

7. In the **Properties** menu, click on the double right arrow to add the **SALESMAN** and **SALESMANMAP** table to the minischema:

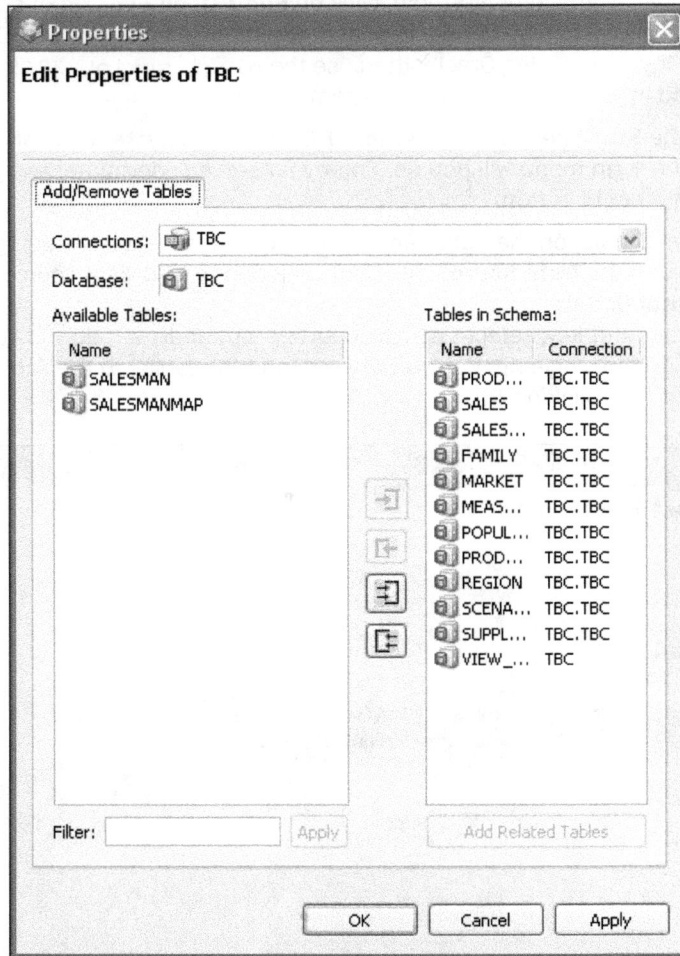

How it works...

In this recipe, we first added the SALESMAN and SALESMANMAP tables to the TBC relational database by running the scripts included in this chapter. We then executed an Incremental update of the TBC data source in Essbase Studio. Finally, we used the Properties menu to add the tables to the minischema.

See also

For additional information on the TBC data source and how to create it, see recipe *Creating TBC database and connecting to the data source* in this chapter.

Using a text file data source

The ability to load data from many different data sources is one of the reasons why Essbase is such a flexible tool. In this recipe, we will see how to use text files as the data source and how to add a text file to a new minischema using the Connection Wizard.

Getting ready

To get started with Essbase Studio, click on the **Start** menu and navigate to **Programs | Oracle EPM System | Essbase | Essbase Studio**. The login menu will pop up. Enter your server, username, and password, and click on the **Log In** button.

How to do it...

1. On the right-hand side of your Essbase Studio screen, you are going to see two tabs. Click on the **Data Sources** tab and right-click on the **Data Source** node. Then click on **New** and **Data Source...**.

2. When the data source menu pops up, enter the connection name `tbc_sample_text` and select **Text** as the **Data Source Type**. Click the **Browse** button to the right of the **Location** textbox. The following **Text File Location** dialog should be displayed:

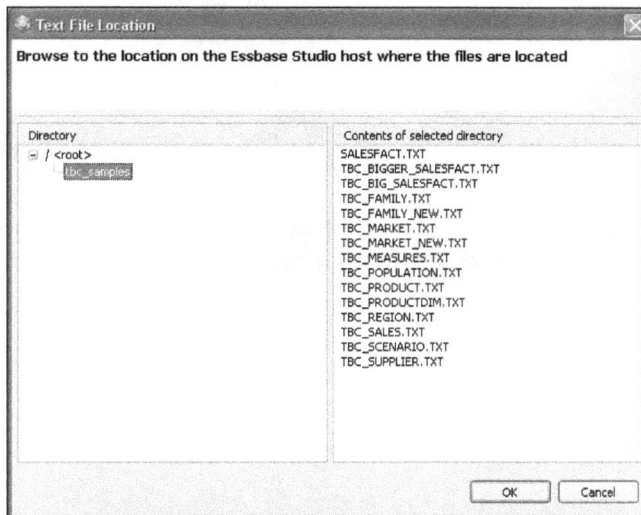

3. Double-click on **tbc_samples** and then click on **OK**. In the **Connection Wizard** make sure the **Column names in the first row** checkbox is enabled, click on the **Comma** delimiter radio button, and click on the **NEXT** button.

4. Select the **TBC_BIGGER_SALESFACT.txt** file. Your **Connection Wizard** should look like the following image:

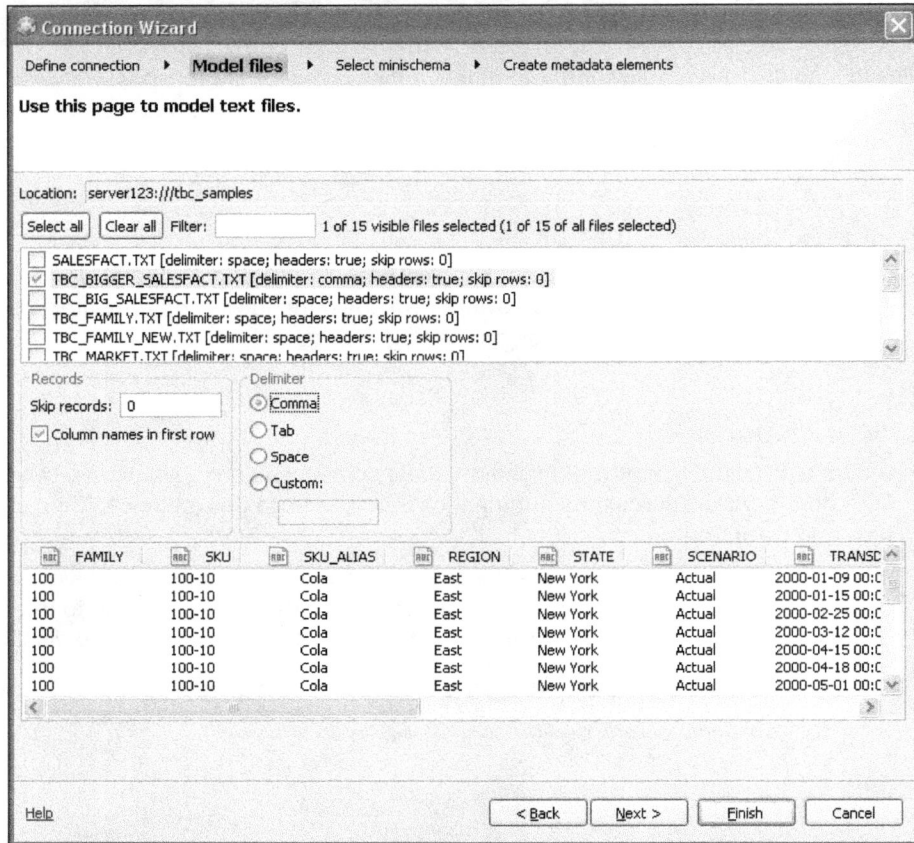

5. You should now see the **Select minischema** tab. Select the **Create a new schema diagram** radio button, leave the `tbc_samples_text Schema`, and click on the **Next** button:

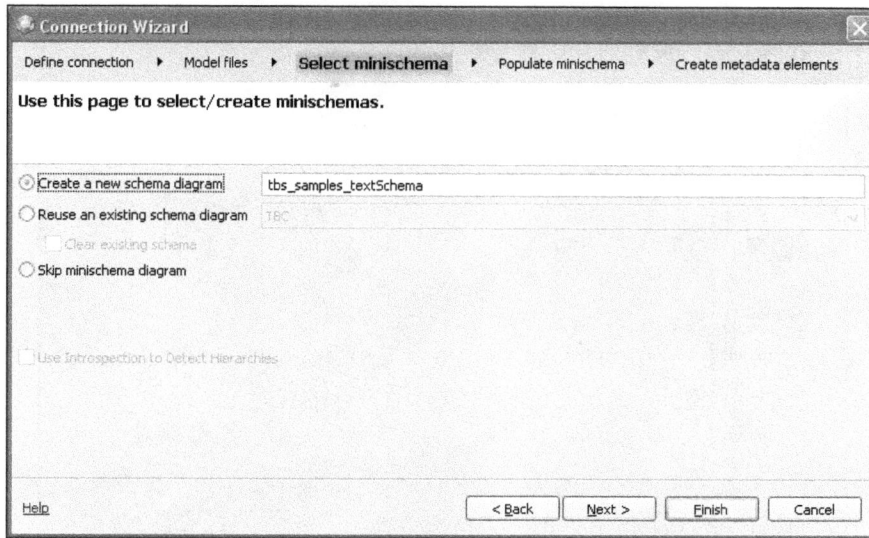

6. In the **Populate minischema** tab, click on the double right arrow to move all available files to the **Tables in Schema** list box and click on the **Next** button:

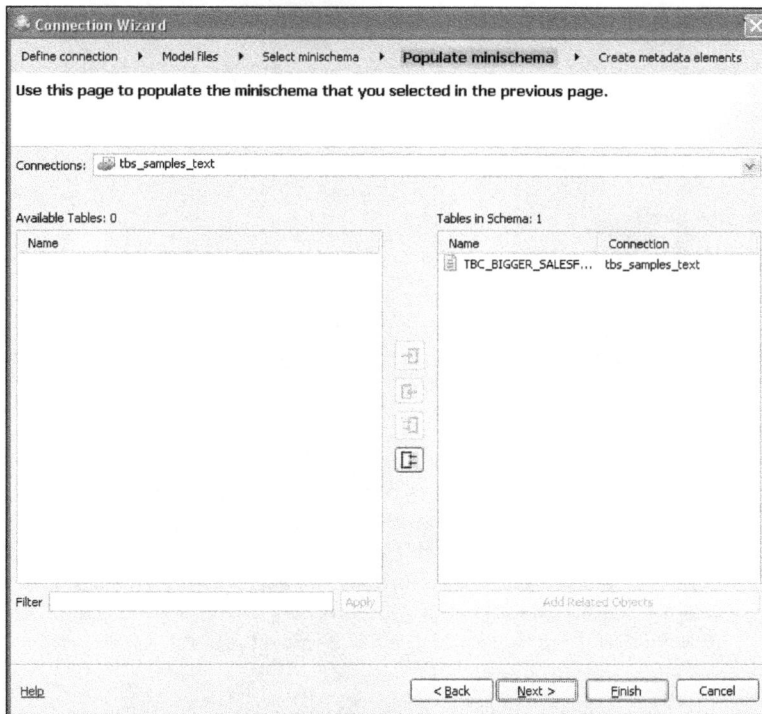

7. In the **Create metadata elements** tab, check **tbc_sample_text** and **TBC_BIGGER_ SALESFACT.txt** and click on the **Finish** button:

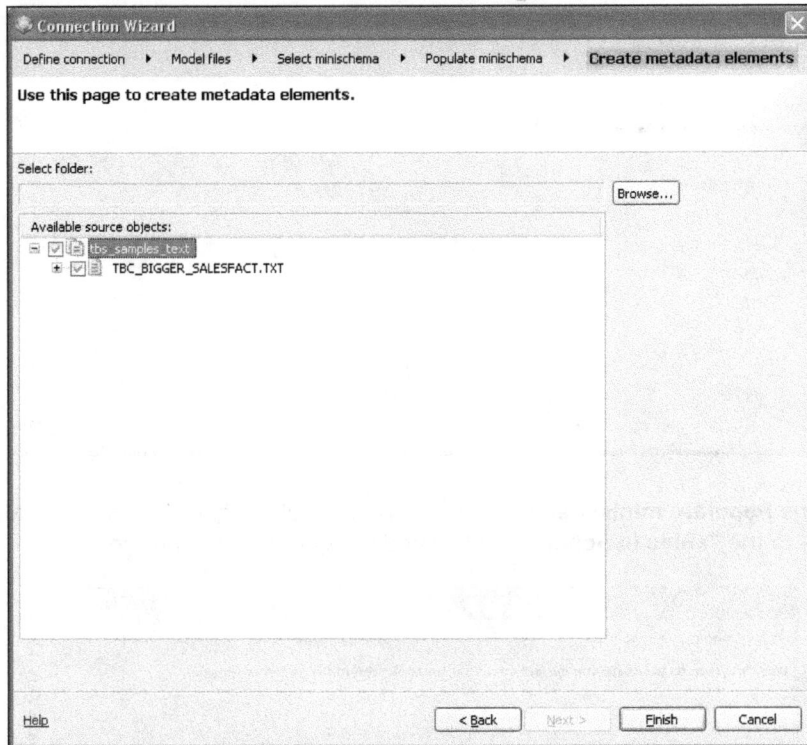

How it works...

In this recipe, we created a text data source using the `tbc_sample` text files. If you want to add your own text files, add a folder and drop your text files under the root directory: `..\Oracle\Middleware\EPMSystem11R1\products\Essbase\EssbaseStudio\ Server\`

> These files are set up in the directory `MIDDLEWARE_HOME/user_ projects/epmsystem1/BPMS/bpms/bin` by the administrator to protect the content from unauthorized use. The Essbase administrator can change the location of this path by modifying the `server. datafile.dir` property in the `server.properties` file. The text file LOCATION dialog box root directory will change to the directory specified in the `server.datafile.dir` property.

We also specified the delimiter for the text file, and set up a minischema and metadata elements for the text file by using the **Connection Wizard**.

Working with Common Platform Language (CPL)

CPL is the syntax that you will need to use on your data elements or dimension elements to apply functions, filters, and operators. In this recipe, we will use the `MonthShortName` function and concatenate data elements using CPL.

Getting ready

To get started with Essbase Studio, click on the **Start** menu and **Programs | Oracle EPM System | Essbase | Essbase Studio**. The login menu will pop up. Enter your server, username, password, and click on the **Log in** button.

How to do it...

1. In Essbase Studio, on the right side of your screen, you will see two tabs. Click on the **Minischema** tab, click and hold the **MEASURES** folder, and drag it under the **MetaData Navigator** root directory. Repeat the same step for the **SALES** folder.

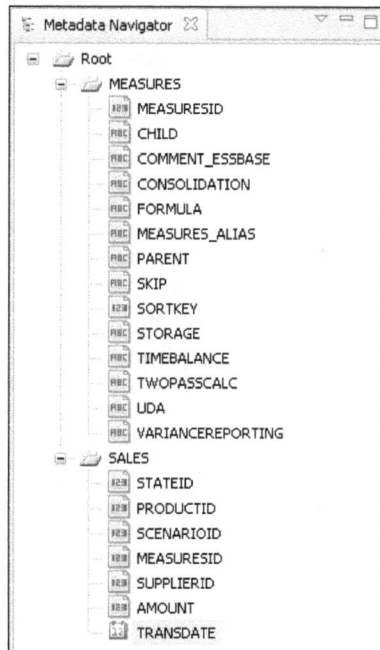

```
Metadata Navigator
Root
  MEASURES
    MEASURESID
    CHILD
    COMMENT_ESSBASE
    CONSOLIDATION
    FORMULA
    MEASURES_ALIAS
    PARENT
    SKIP
    SORTKEY
    STORAGE
    TIMEBALANCE
    TWOPASSCALC
    UDA
    VARIANCEREPORTING
  SALES
    STATEID
    PRODUCTID
    SCENARIOID
    MEASURESID
    SUPPLIERID
    AMOUNT
    TRANSDATE
```

2. Right-click on the **SALES** folder, click on **New**, and then **Dimension Element**:

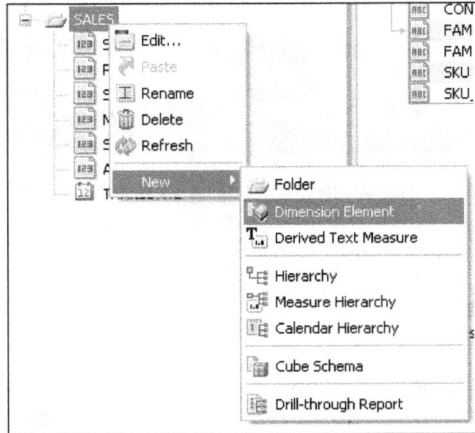

3. Change the name to MonthShortName, select the **Function** tab, drill down on **All functions**, and click on the **monthShortName** function. Click on the **Source** tab and highlight **$$DateOperand$$** in between the parentheses. Next, drill down on the **SALES** table, double-click on **TRANSDATE** to select it, click on the **Apply** button, and then on **OK**. The value in the Caption Binding textbox will be **'monthShortName'(connection : \'TBC'::'TBC.dbo.SALES'.'TRANSDATE')**, as shown in the following screenshot:

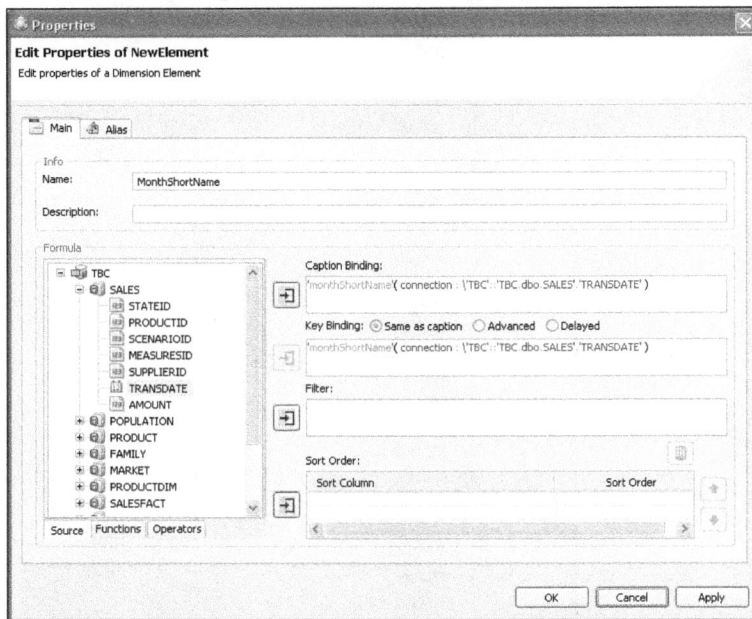

4. Right-click on the **MonthShortName** dimension element and select **View Sample Data**.

	MonthShortName
1	Jan
2	Feb
3	Mar
4	Apr
5	May
6	Jun
7	Jul
8	Aug
9	Sep
10	Oct
11	Nov
12	Dec

5. Click on the **Tool** menu, select **Alias Set Manager**, click on the plus **+** sign, and enter TBC for the name of your **Alias set**:

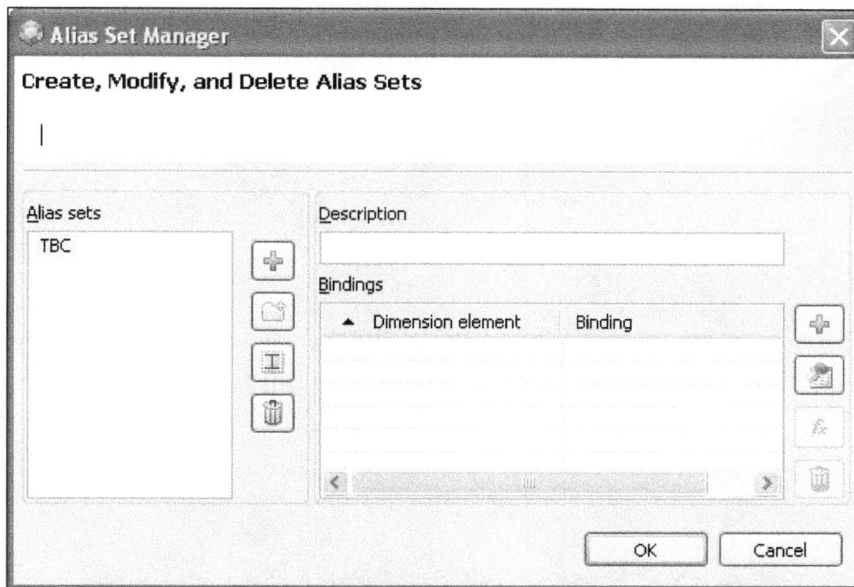

6. Drill down on the **MEASURES** folder under the **Metadata Navigator** frame, double-click on **CHILD**, select the **Alias** tab, select the first row with TBC in the name, click on the **FX** button, and enter connection: \`'TBC'::'TBC.dbo. MEASURES'.'CHILD'||" - "||connection : \`'TBC'::'TBC.dbo. MEASURES'.'MEASURES_ALIAS'` in the textbox. You could also use the window below to select the values in the **Edit Alias Binding** menu, and click on **OK**. Click on **Apply**, and then on **OK** in the **Properties** window. The following is what your menu should look like:

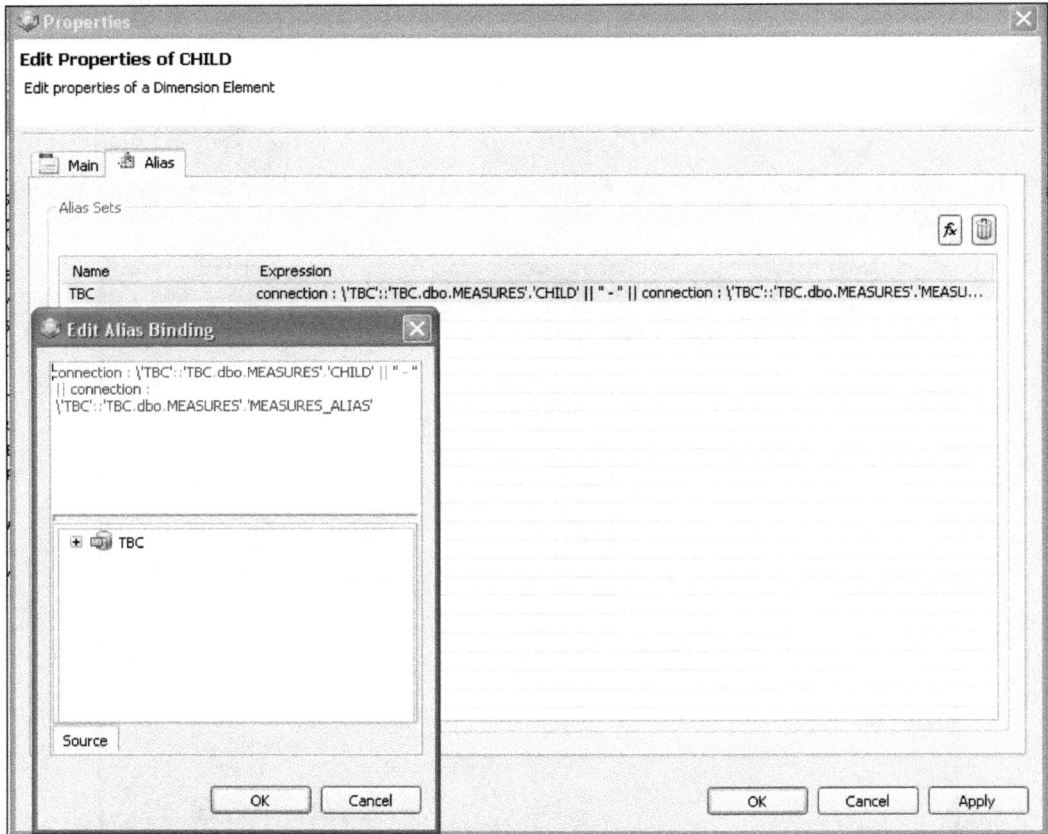

How it works...

The CPL function `MontShortName` is used in this recipe to parse `TRANSDATE` into an abbreviation of the month. We also created an Alias set and concatenated the `CHILD` to the `MEASURES_ALIAS` data element to create a unique Alias binding. CPL is a powerful syntax that would merit several recipes. The CPL Reference (*Appendix D*) of the *Oracle Essbase Studio User's Guide* covers all the CPL functionality. You can find this document at `http://download.oracle.com/docs/cd/E17236_01/epm.1112/est_user.pdf`. Reading *Appendix D* will help you understand the rules of the syntax and experiment with the functions.

Using Sort Order on data elements

Businesses will often ask for certain members to be in a specific order in the outline, and for this reason, it is important to have the Sort Order columns in each of your tables. In this recipe, we will use the Sort Order or Sort Key column of a table to specify the order of the members in a hierarchy.

Getting ready

To get started with Essbase Studio, click on the **Start** menu and navigate to **Programs | Oracle EPM System | Essbase | Essbase Studio**. The login menu will pop up. Enter your server, username, password, and click on the **Log In** button.

How to do it...

1. On the right side of your Essbase Studio screen, you are going to see two tabs. Click on the **Minischema** tab and drag the **MEASURES** folder under the **MetaData Navigator** root directory.

2. Drill down on the **MEASURES** folder and double-click on the **CHILD** member.

3. Select the **SORTKEY** data element and use the single right arrow to add to the **Sort Order** selection. Make sure the order attribute is **Ascending**, by clicking on the **Apply** button, and then on **OK**, as shown in the following screenshot:

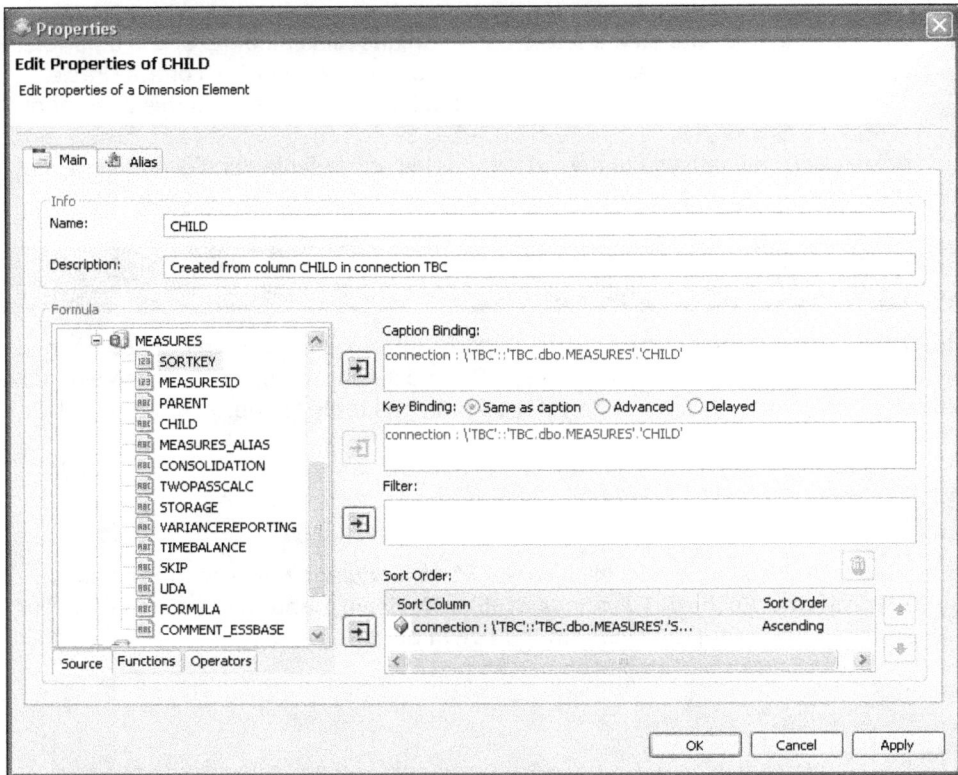

4. Right-click on the **CHILD** data element and select **View Sample Data**.

How it works...

This recipe covered how to set up the order of the members in the outline. Although there are cases where ascending alphanumeric order is fine, the order of the members in the outline often changes to make the outline more visually intuitive for the users and to help in reporting.

3
Building the BSO Cube

In this chapter, we will cover the following topics:

- ▶ Creating hierarchies using a parent-child reference table
- ▶ Creating hierarchies using a Generation reference table
- ▶ Adding attribute dimensions to hierarchies
- ▶ Building a Calendar dimension
- ▶ Creating date elements
- ▶ Creating Alias tables
- ▶ Developing Cube Schema and an Essbase model
- ▶ Setting Essbase properties
- ▶ Deploying a cube
- ▶ Creating an OLAP Model in EIS
- ▶ Creating an OLAP Metaoutline in EIS

Introduction

In this chapter, we will continue with the **The Beverage Company** (**TBC**) sample database which we started in *Chapter 2, Using Essbase Studio*, with Essbase Studio, and we will conduct some of these same tasks using **Essbase Integration Service** (**EIS**). On the other hand, we will not be discussing the building of a Block Storage database in **Essbase Administration Services** (**EAS**) as these tasks are covered in *Chapters 5, 6, 7,* and *8*.

The following is a summary of the application development steps in Essbase Studio:

1. Prep Data Source
2. Create Data Source Connection
3. Create minischema, user-defined tables, and add joins
4. Select data elements
5. Create or modify metadata elements, date elements, and hierarchies
6. Create alias tables
7. Create Essbase schema and Essbase Models
8. Set Essbase properties
9. Build drill-through reports
10. Deploy Essbase cubes

Building an Essbase application in EIS will require some of the same steps but these tasks can be accomplished within the OLAP Model and OLAP Metaoutline in contrast.

Creating hierarchies using a parent-child reference table

In this recipe, we will build a hierarchy using a parent-child reference. The parent-child reference is the most flexible format for building hierarchies. In this recipe, we will work with the **MEASURES** dimension as this table in the TBC database is set up in a parent-child format.

Getting ready

To get started, click on the **Start** menu and navigate to **Programs | Oracle EPM System | Essbase | Essbase Studio**. The login menu will pop up. Enter your server, username, and password, and click on the **Log in** button.

How to do it...

1. On the right side of your Essbase Studio screen you are going to see two tabs. Click on the **Minischemas** tab, drill down on **Minischema** node, and double-click on **TBC Minischema**.
2. In the **Minischema** window, right-click on the **MEASURES** table. Then click on **Add Joins...**. Select **MEASURES** in the combobox on the right and click on the **PARENT** metadata element from the following drop-down list.
3. On the left column, select **CHILD from the drop down list**, click on **Apply**, and then **OK**.

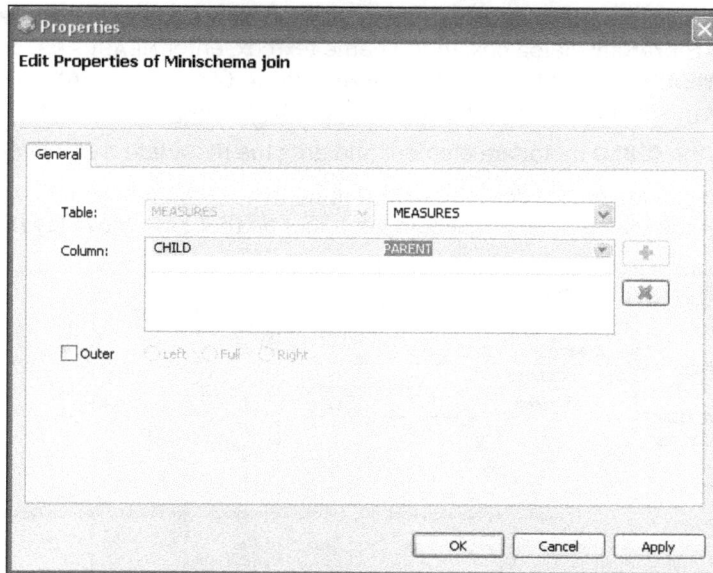

4. Drill down on the TBC Minischema in the **Minischemas** tab. Click on the **MEASURES** folder, and drag to the **Metadata Navigator** on the left side of the Essbase Studio screen.

5. Right-click on the **Root** directory under **Metadata Navigator**. Click on **New** and then on **Folder**. Enter HIERARCHIES in the name textbox for the folder in the **Properties** menu. Click on **Apply**, and then on **OK**.

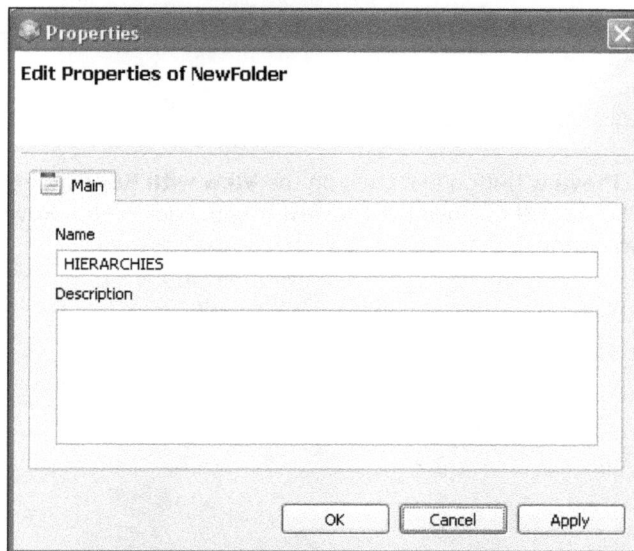

6. Right-click on the **HIERARCHIES** folder. Click on **New** and then on **Hierarchy** to open the **Edit Hierarchy** dialog box. In the name textbox, enter MEASURES, drill down on the **MEASURES** folder in **Metadata Navigator**. Click on the **PARENT** metadata element (just copied over in the root directory), and drag under the **Hierarchy** column.

7. Click on the **CHILD** metadata element and drag the metadata element under **PARENT**.

8. Use the right arrow to indent the **CHILD** metadata element. If you hover over the right arrow (in the dialog box), you should get a tool tip that says **Move level right**.

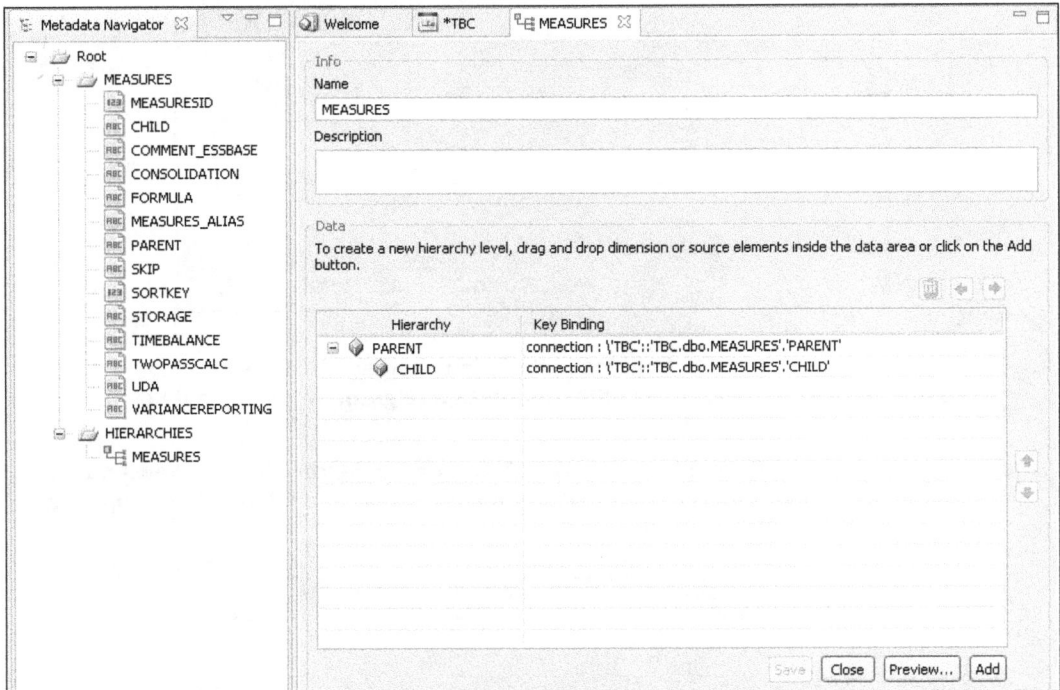

9. Click on the **Preview** button and then on the **View with Key Binding** button to see the hierarchy. Click on **OK** to close the **Preview** menu. Click on the **Save** button, and then on the **Close** button.

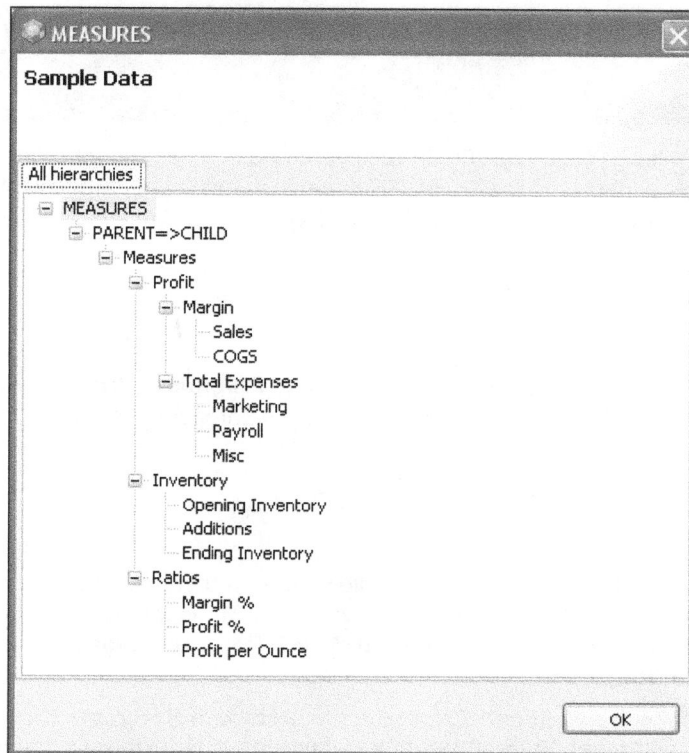

```
MEASURES                                    [X]

Sample Data


┌─────────────┐
│All hierarchies│
├─────────────┴──────────────────────────────┐
│  ⊟ MEASURES                                 │
│     ⊟ PARENT=>CHILD                         │
│        ⊟ Measures                           │
│           ⊟ Profit                          │
│              ⊟ Margin                       │
│                 ─ Sales                     │
│                 ─ COGS                      │
│              ⊟ Total Expenses               │
│                 ─ Marketing                 │
│                 ─ Payroll                   │
│                 ─ Misc                      │
│           ⊟ Inventory                       │
│              ─ Opening Inventory            │
│              ─ Additions                    │
│              ─ Ending Inventory             │
│           ⊟ Ratios                          │
│              ─ Margin %                     │
│              ─ Profit %                     │
│              ─ Profit per Ounce             │
│                                             │
│                              ┌──────────┐   │
│                              │    OK    │   │
│                              └──────────┘   │
└─────────────────────────────────────────────┘
```

How it works...

We began this recipe by making sure that the **MEASURES** table had a self join between the **PARENT** and **CHILD** columns. This join represents a recursive relationship in the Minischema. The **MEASURES** folder is dragged from the TBC Minischema to your **Metadata Navigator** to create a metadata element folder. You then create a folder where you will create the **MEASURES** hierarchy, by opening the **Edit Hierarchy Dialog box**, and dragging the elements from the **Metadata Navigator** to the Hierarchy column to create the hierarchy. Finally, we use the **Preview** button to view what your **MEASURES** hierarchy will look like.

See also

For information on how to create the TBC Minischema, review the recipes *Creating TBC database and connecting to the data source* and *Building your Minischema* in *Chapter 2*.

Creating hierarchies using a generation reference table

In this recipe, we will be using a SUPPLIER table, created in a generation reference, to build the SUPPLIER dimension. The SUPPLIER dimension has a geographical hierarchy. A geographical hierarchy is a natural hierarchy, which makes it an excellent candidate for a generation reference table.

Getting ready

To get started, click on the **Start** menu and navigate to **Programs | Oracle EPM System | Essbase | Essbase Studio**. The login menu will pop-up. Enter your server, username, and password, and click on the **Log in** button.

How to do it...

1. On the right side of your Essbase Studio screen, you are going to see two tabs. Click on the **Minischemas** tab, drill down on the **Minischema** node, drill down on the TBC minischema, select the **SUPPLIER** folder, and drag the folder to the **Metadata Navigator**.

2. Right-click on the **Root** directory under the **Metadata Navigator**, click on **New**, and then on **Folder**. Enter HIERARCHIES in the name textbox for the folder in the **Properties** menu. Click on **Apply**, and then on **OK**.

3. Right-click on the **HIERARCHIES** folder. Click on **New**, and then on **Hierarchy**.

4. Enter SUPPLIER in the **Name** textbox in the **Edit Hierarchy** dialog box; drill down on the **SUPPLIER** folder in **Metadata Navigator**. Click on the **COUNTRY** metadata element member and drag to the hierarchy window.

5. Click on **COUNTRY** under the **Hierarchy** column. Click on the **Add** button, select **Add Child**, drill down on **SUPPLIER** in the **Select Entity** dialog box, select **STATE**, and click on **OK**. The following is an image of the **Select Entity** menu, which shows you how to add a physical element from the Source Navigator:

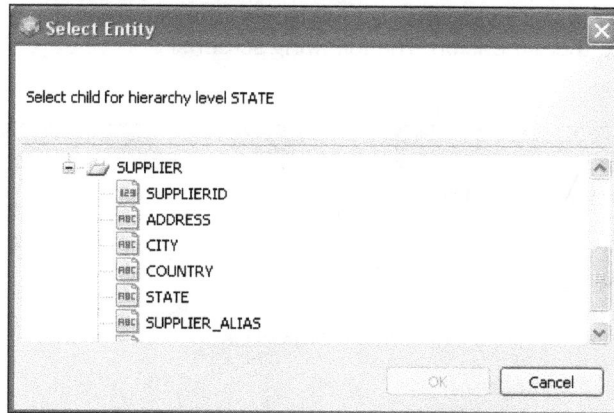

6. Click on **CITY** in **MetaData Navigator** and drag on top of **STATE**. The **CITY** metadata element should be added as a child of **STATE**.

7. Click on **ZIP** in the **Metadata Navigator** and drag on top of **CITY**. The **ZIP** should display as a child of **CITY**.

8. Click on **ADDRESS** in the **Metadata Navigator** and drag on top of **ZIP**. The **ADDRESS** should display as a child of **ZIP**.

9. Click on **SUPPLIER_ALIAS** in the **Metadata Navigator** and drag on top of the ZIP metadata element. Your screen should look like the following screenshot:

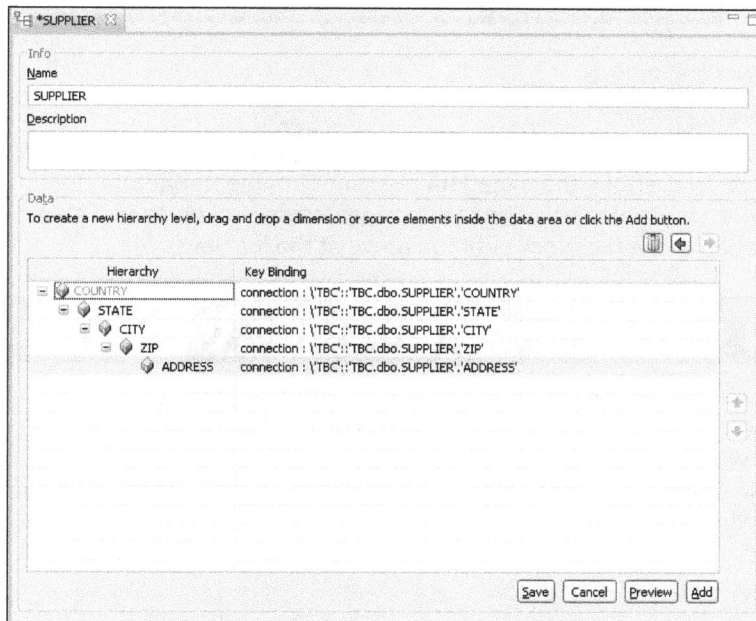

10. You should click on the **Preview** button to view the hierarchy. Then, click on the **Save** button to add the dimension. The following screenshot is what your hierarchy should look like:

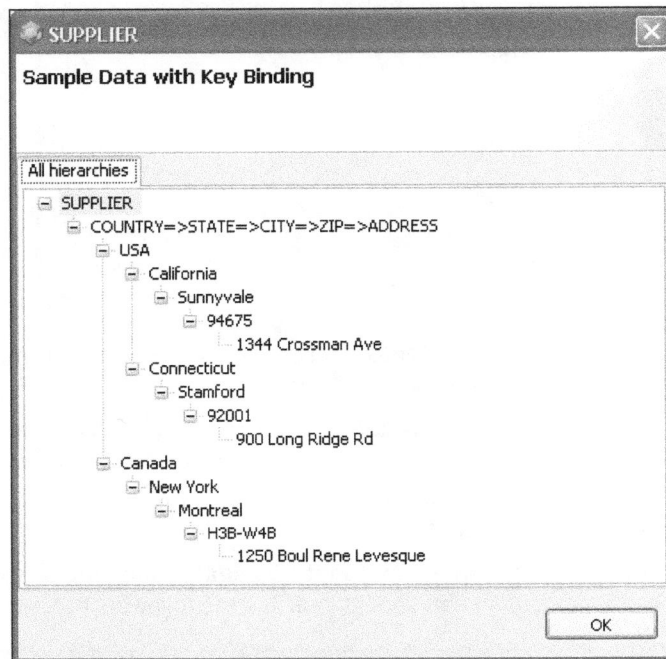

How it works...

This recipe shows you how to set up the geographical or generation reference dimension called SUPPLIER by dragging the metadata element from the Metadata Navigator to the Edit Hierarchy dialog box. The task is repeated several times and each time it adds another generation to the hierarchy until you arrive at the leaf level.

Adding attribute dimensions to hierarchies

In this recipe, we are going to set up the PRODUCT dimension that we discussed in the recipe *Determining hierarchies in relational tables* in *Chapter 1, Understanding and Modifying Data Sources*. We discussed the theory behind the one-to-one or one-to-many relationship of a hierarchy in *Chapter 1*. In contrast, we will create the base dimension PRODUCT and its attribute dimensions in this recipe.

Getting ready

To get started, click on the **Start** menu and navigate to **Programs | Oracle EPM System | Essbase | Essbase Studio**. The login menu will pop up. Enter your server, username, and password, and click on the **Log in** button.

How to do it...

1. On the right side of your Essbase Studio screen, you are going to see two tabs. Click on the **Minischemas** tab, drill down on **Minischema** node, drill down on the **TBC Minischema**, select the **PRODUCT(s)** folder, and drag the folder to the **Metadata Navigator**. Repeat the same exercise for the **FAMILY** and **SALESMAN** folder created in the recipe *Adding tables to a Minischema* in *Chapter 2*.

2. Right-click on the **Root** directory under the **Metadata Navigator**. Click on **New**, and then on **Folder**. Enter HIERARCHIES in the name textbox for the folder in the properties menu. Click on **Apply**, and then on **OK**.

3. Right-click on the **HIERARCHIES** folder, click on **New**, and then on **Hierarchy**.

4. Click and drag the **FAMILY** metadata element from the **FAMILY** folder in the **Metadata Navigator** to the hierarchy window. Click on the **SKU** metadata element and drag it to the Hierarchy window under the **FAMILY** metadata element. Use the right arrow to indent the **SKU** metadata element right.

5. Click and drag the **CAFFEINATED** metadata element from the **PRODUCT** folder in the **Metadata Navigator** to the hierarchy window. Click on the **SKU** metadata element and drag it on top of **CAFFEINATED**. The **SKU** metadata element should appear as a child of **CAFFEINATED** in your dialog box.

6. Click and drag the **INTRODATE** dimension element from the **PRODUCT** folder in the **Metadata Navigator** to the **Edit Hierarchy** dialog box. Click on the **SKU** metadata element and drag it on top of **INTRODATE**. **SKU** should appear as a child of **INTRODATE** in your dialog.

7. Click and drag the **OUNCES** dimension element from the **PRODUCT** folder in the **Metadata Navigator** to the **Edit Hierarchy** window. Click on the **SKU** metadata element and drag it to the hierarchy window under the **OUNCES**. You can use the right arrow to indent the **SKU** metadata element.

8. Click and drag the **PKGTYPE** metadata element from the **PRODUCT** folder in the **Metadata Navigator** to the hierarchy window. Click on **SKU** and drag on top of **PKGTYPE**. **SKU** will show as a child of **PKGTYPE**.

9. Drill down on the **SALESMAN** folder and drag the **SALESMANNAME** metadata element to the hierarchy column. Click on **SKU** in the **PRODUCT** folder and drag on top of **SALESMANNAME**.

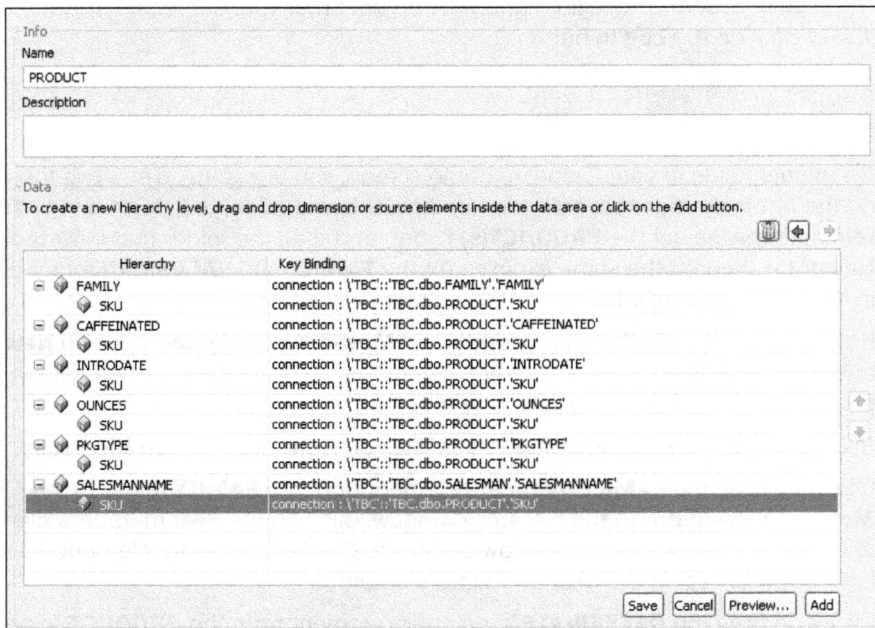

10. Click on the **Preview...** button to view the dimensions. It will look like the following screenshot:

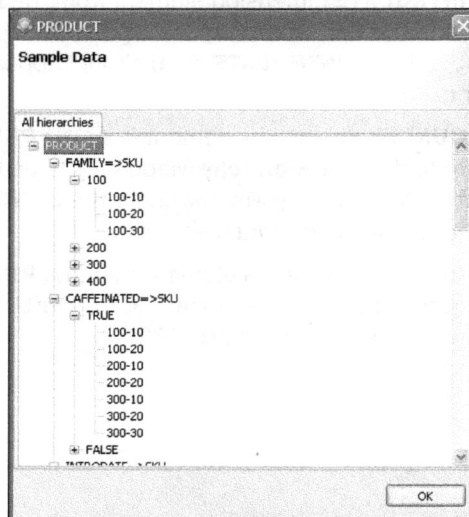

How it works...

We began this recipe by moving the **PRODUCT** and **FAMILY** folders from the TBC Minischema to the **Metadata Navigator**. We then set up the **HIEARCHIES** folder and built the **PRODUCT** hierarchy by dragging and dropping the **FAMILY** and **SKU** for the base dimension's hierarchy. We also set up the **CAFFEINATED, INTRODATE, OUNCES, PKGTYPE,** and **SALESMANNAME** attribute dimensions. Finally, we used the **Preview...** button to view a sample of the base dimension and attribute dimensions. When building attribute dimensions, note that all members from the base dimension we associate to the attribute must be at the same level, and we can only associate attributes to sparse dimensions.

See also...

After you complete the building of the Essbase Model, you will need to use the Essbase Properties menu to specify the attribute type. Refer to the recipe *Determining hierarchies in relational tables* in *Chapter 1* to determine what types of attribute dimensions you have. To find out how to change the properties using the Essbase Properties menu, review the *Setting Essbase Properties* recipe later in this chapter.

Building a Calendar dimension

In this recipe, we will create a Fiscal calendar using the CALENDAR dimension functionality in Essbase Studio. The Calendar dimension was a long awaited function in Essbase. Prior to the Calendar dimension, you had to create your own template in an Essbase cube. When you were designing another cube, you would simply copy that dimension from one outline to the next. This worked fine if you only had to worry about a simple Gregorian calendar, but it was slightly more challenging for retail, broadcast calendars, or fiscal calendars. In this recipe, we will be building the 4-5-4 fiscal calendar for a retail company. The retail calendar comes from the National Federation Retailer and is designed to track year over year data across multiple years. The 4-5-4 is the pattern that is used in the quarters. Using this pattern, the first month of the quarter will have four weeks, the second month five weeks, and the last month has four weeks. This calendar also takes into account the extra week in leap years.

Getting ready

To get started, click on the **Start** menu and navigate to **Programs | Oracle EPM System | Essbase | Essbase Studio**. Log in to Essbase Studio using your server, username, and password.

How to do it...

1. Right-click on the **Root** directory under the **Metadata Navigator**; click on **New**, and then on **Folder**. Enter **HIERARCHIES** in the name textbox for the folder in the **Properties** menu, click on **Apply**, and then on **OK**.

2. Right-click on the **HIEARCHIES** folder; click on **New**, and then on **Calendar Hierarchy**. The **Edit Calendar Hierarchy** dialog box will pop up.

3. Type in **TIME** into the **Hierarchy Name** textbox.

4. In the **Edit Calendar Hierarchy** dialog box under **Modeling Parameters** click on the **Start Date** combobox. Select **01/30/2000**, and click on the **OK** button.

5. In the **End Date** combobox select **02/03/2001**, click on the **OK** button, and leave Sunday selected for **First day of the Week**.

6. In the **Time Depth area**, click on the **Year**, click on the **Edit** button, select **Year 2006** for the format, and click on the **OK** button.

7. Click down on **Quarter** and then click on the **Edit** button, select **Quarter 1 2006**, and click on the **OK** button.

8. Click down on **Month** and then click on the **Edit** button, select **January 2006**, and click on the **OK** button.

9. Click down on **Week**. Click on the **Edit** button, select **Week 1 2006**, and then click on the **OK** button.

10. Click down on **Day**. Click on the **Edit** button, select **January 02 2006**, and then click on the **OK** button.

11. Select the **Fiscal** radio button. Click on **Semantic Rules**, and in the **Fiscal Calendar** dialog box and the **Year semantic rules** session, select the **Starting week – number in month** radio button.

12. Select **February** in the **Month** combobox and **Week 1** in the **Week** combobox.

13. In the **Month Semantic Rules** section, select the **By Qtr-Month Pattern**, select **4-5-4** from the **Week Pattern** combobox, and **December** in the **Month having extra week** combobox. Your screen should look like the following screenshot:

14. In the **Fiscal Calendar** dialog box and **Year semantic rules** session select the **Ending week – number in Month** radio button.

15. Select **January** in the **Month** combobox and **Week 4** in the **Week** combobox.

16. In the **Month Semantic Rules** section, select the **By Qtr-Month Pattern**, select **4-5-4** from the **Week Pattern** combobox, and **December** in the **Month having extra week** combobox. Your screen should look like the following screenshot; click on the **OK** button:

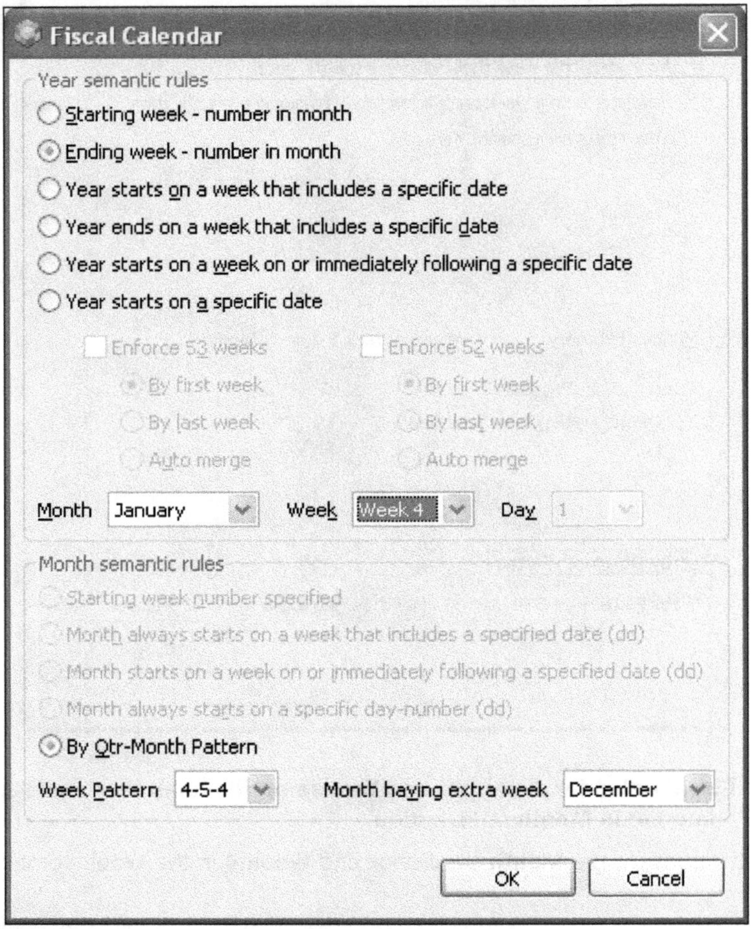

17. Right-click on the **TIME** hierarchy in the **Metadata Navigator** and select **Preview Hierarchy**. Your hierarchy should look like the following screenshot:

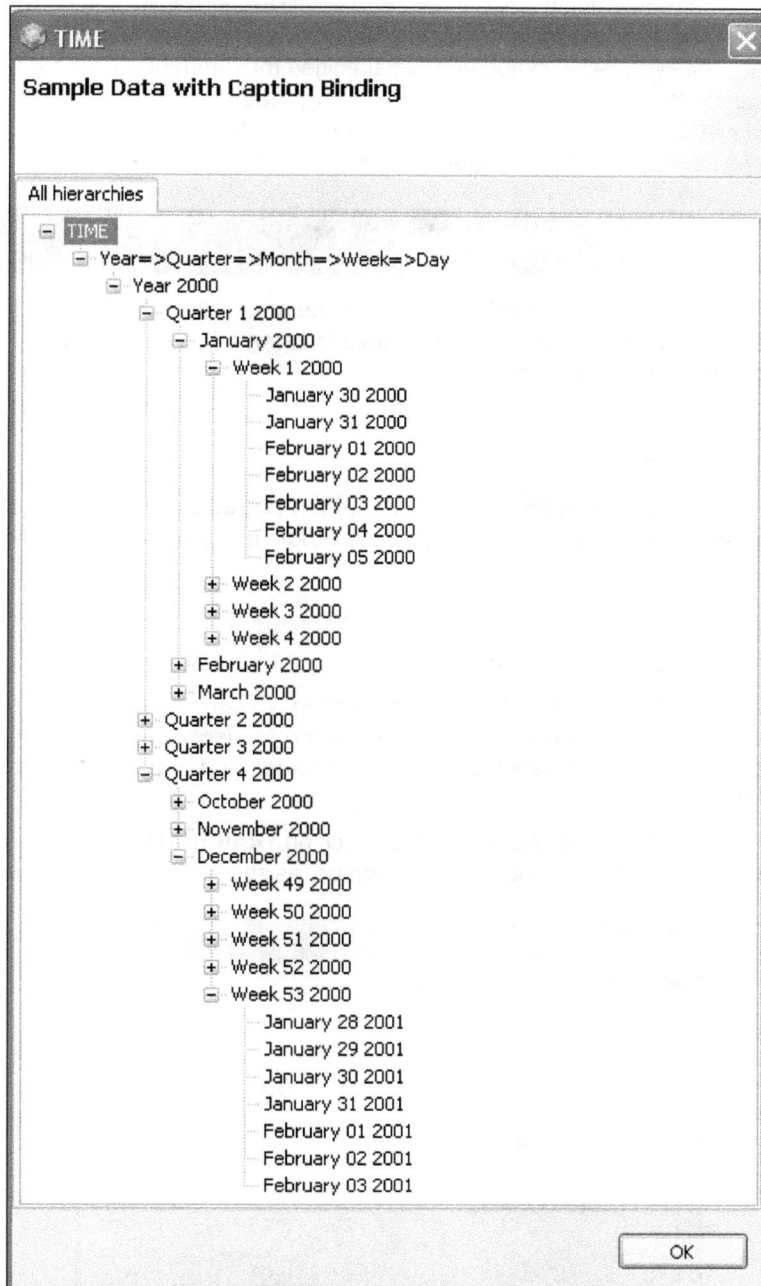

How it works...

We began this recipe by opening the `Edit Calendar Hierarchy`. We selected the range that we were going to use to model our calendar hierarchy and the beginning day of the weeks under `Modeling Parameters`. In addition, we specified the depth of our time dimension and formatted our dates. Moreover, we set up the `Starting week`, `Ending Week`, and the `Qtr by Month Pattern`. Finally, we previewed our hierarchy in the `Metadata Navigator`. The example that was used is based on the National Federation Retailer retail calendar.

Creating date elements

In this recipe, we are going to use the **TRANSDATE** date metadata element in the **SALESFACT** table to create date elements. This is an alternative to using a Calendar dimension or building a Calendar table in the relational environment.

Getting ready

To get started, click on the **Start** menu and navigate to **Programs | Oracle EPM System | Essbase | Essbase Studio** . Then log in to Essbase Studio using your server, username, and password.

How to do it...

1. On the right side of your Essbase Studio screen, you are going to see two tabs. Click on the **Minischemas** tab, drill down on the **Minischema** node, drill down on the TBC minischema, select the **SALESFACT** folder, and drag the folder to the **Metadata Navigator**.

2. Drill down on the **SALESFACT** table, right-click on **TRANSDATE**, and select **Create Date Element...**. The selection menu should pop up, as shown in the following screenshot:

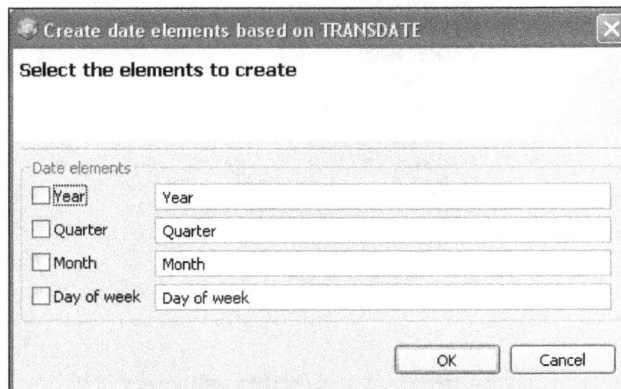

3. Select **Year, Quarter, Month**, and **Day of week** by selecting the check boxes and clicking on the **OK** button. In this step, you are specifying what date elements you need.

4. You should now see the date element in the **SALESFACT** folder.

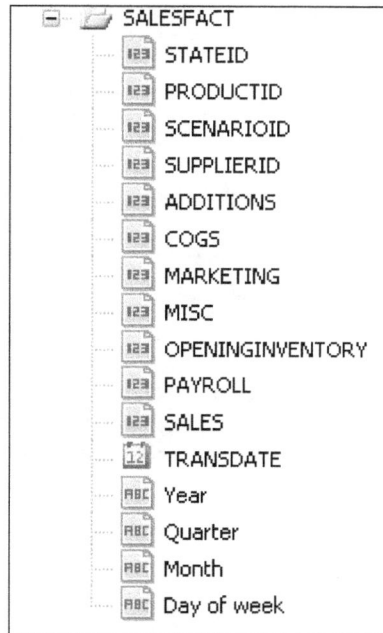

5. If you have not already done it, right-click on the **Root** directory under the **Metadata Navigator**. Click on **New**, and then on **Folder**. Enter HIERARCHIES in the **Name** textbox. Then click on **Apply** and then on **OK**.

6. Right-click on the **HIERARCHIES** folder, and click on **New**. Select Hierarchy; enter Year in the **Name** textbox.

7. Drill down on the **SALESFACT** table and drag-and-drop the date element Year to the hierarchy column.

8. Drag and drop the **Quarter** date element on top of the **Year** in the hierarchy column. Repeat the same step for the **Month** date element. Your screen will look like the following screenshot:

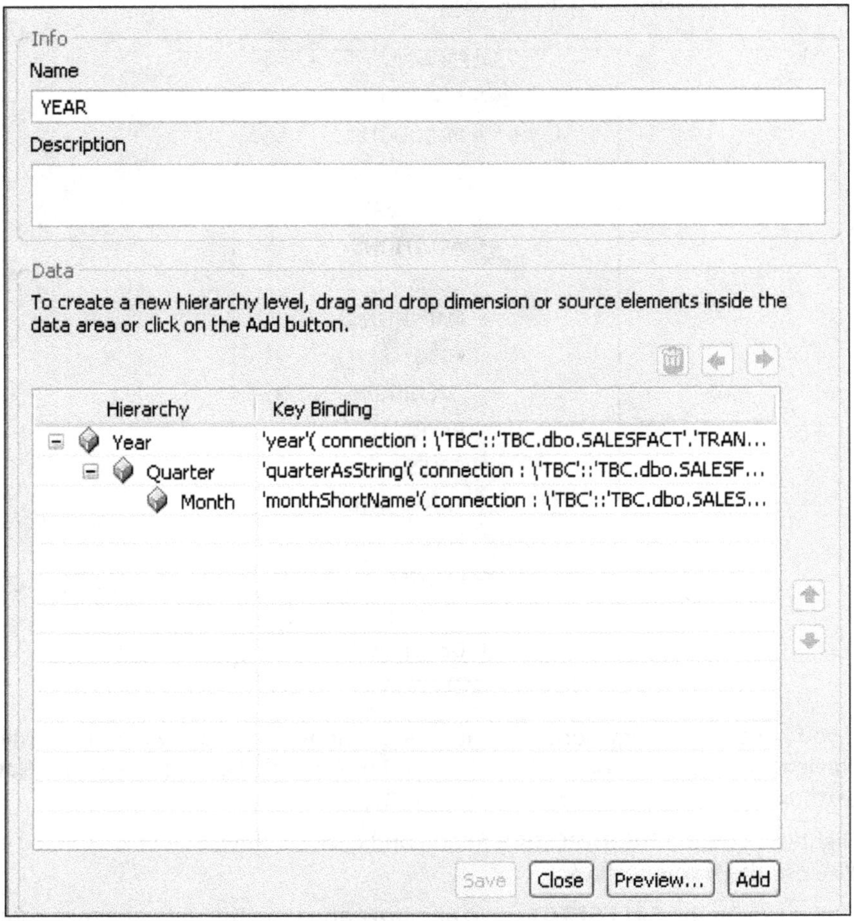

9. You can use the **Preview...** button to view what the hierarchy will look like then click on the **Save** button to save the YEAR hierarchy.

How it works...

In this recipe, we used the **TRANSDATE** dimension element to create a set of date elements. If you double-click on the **Year** date element, you will notice that it has **Common Platform Language** (**CPL**) in its Caption Binding that allows you to format **TRANSDATE**. This is the CPL that the Year date element contains `'year' ( connection : \'TBC'::'TBC.dbo.SALESFACT'.'TRANSDATE')`. The date element simply allows you to create these without having to type the CPL.

Creating Alias tables

In this recipe, we will create an Alias set or table to give more descriptive names to the members in the outline. In a business environment, it is common for the same functions to have different names depending on the recipient of the information. Version 11.1.2.1 now supports 32 alias tables, or 32 different ways of naming the same member. This is, of course, far more than the average application needs, but it gives you a lot of flexibility for reporting purposes.

Getting ready

To get started, click on the **Start** menu and navigate to **Programs | Oracle EPM System | Essbase | Essbase Studio**. Log in to Essbase Studio using your server, username, and password.

How to do it...

1. In Essbase Studio, click on the **Tools** Menu and **Alias Set Manager** to display the **Alias Set Manager** dialog box. Click on the **+** sign in the middle of the dialog box, and enter `Default` for the name of your Alias set. Then click on the **OK** button.

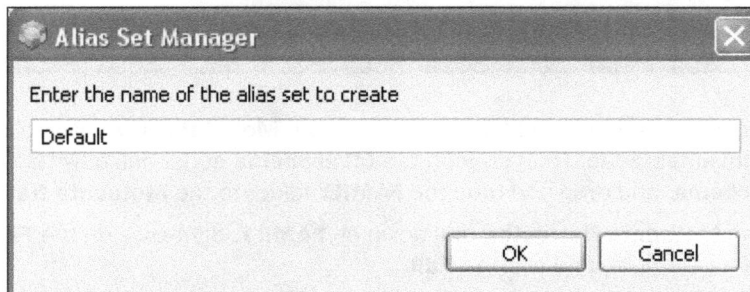

2. On the right-hand side of your **Alias Set Manager** dialog, click on the **+** sign to establish an alias binding.

3. In the **Create a New Binding** dialog box, drill down on **MEASURES** on the left side and select **CHILD**. Drill down on the **MEASURES** folder on the right side, double-click the **MEASURES_ALIAS**, and click on the **OK** button. Your dialog box should look like the following screenshot:

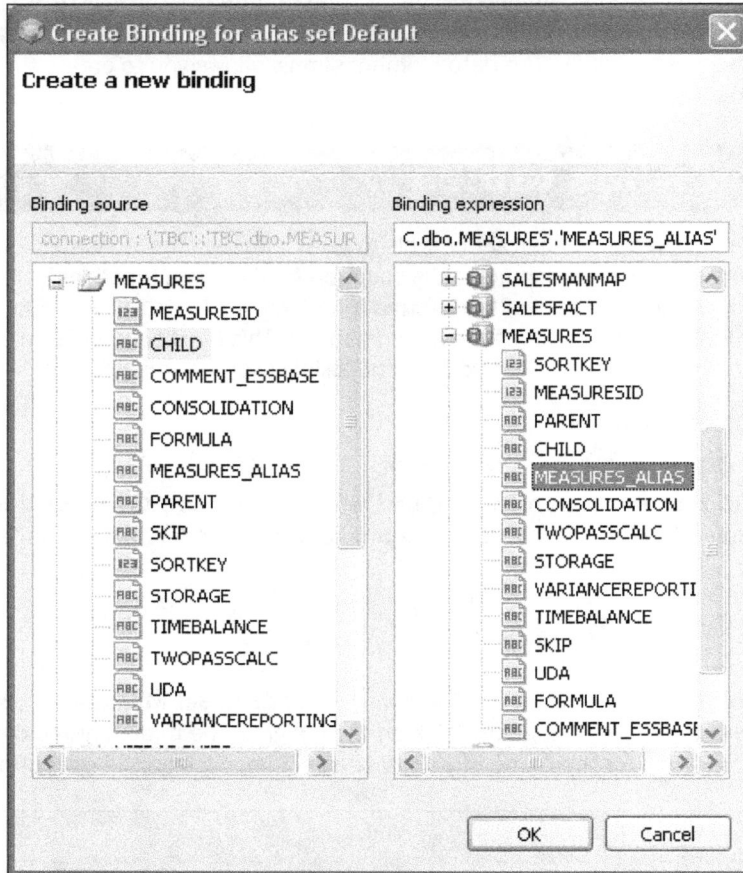

4. If you have not added the **FAMILY** folder to your **Metadata Navigator**, click on the **Minischema** tab. Then click on the **Minischema** node, drill down on the **TBC Minischema**, and drag-and-drop the **FAMILY** folder to the **Metadata Navigator**.

5. Click on **Metadata Navigator**, drill down on **FAMILY**, right-click on the **FAMILY** metadata element, and click on **Edit...**.

6. In the **Properties** dialog box, select the **Alias** tab, select the **Default row**, click on the **FX** button, drill down on **FAMILY** in the **Edit Alias Binding** menu, double-click on **FAMILY_ALIAS**, and click on the **OK** button.

7. Click on the **Apply** button, and click on **OK**. Your menu should look like the following screenshot:

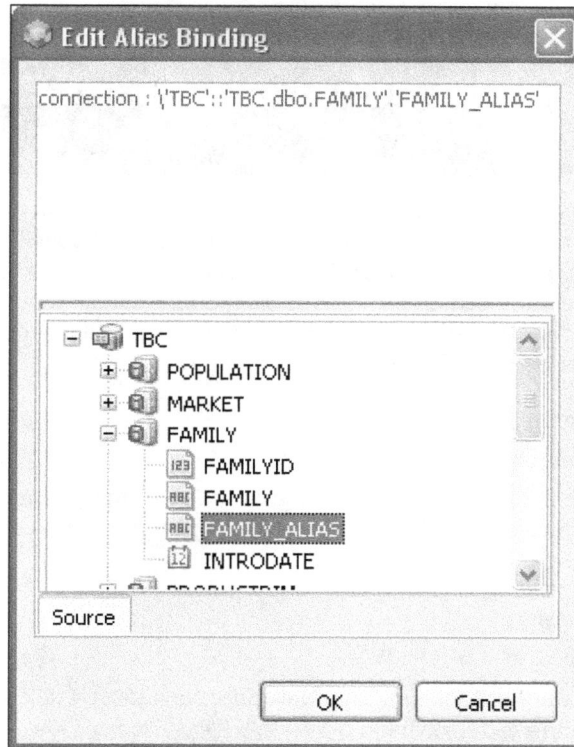

How it works...

In this recipe, we built an Alias set using the **Alias Set Manager**. Then, we used the **Create a New Binding** dialog box to bind the **MEASURE** metadata element to the **MEASURES_ALIAS** alias. We were also able to bind the metadata element **FAMILY** to **FAMILY_ALIAS** using the **Properties** dialog by right-clicking and editing the **FAMILY** metadata element in the **Metadata Navigator**.

There's more...

If you would like an opportunity to practice adding an Alias to the default alias table, then the SKU metadata element has a SKU_ALIAS in the PRODUCT table and the POPULATION metadata element has a POPULATION_ALIAS in the POPULATION attribute dimension table. In addition, the SUPPLIER dimension has a SUPPLIER_ALIAS metadata element that you can use to assign an Alias to the ADDRESS metadata element.

Developing cube schema and an Essbase model

In this recipe, we will use the TBC hierarchies to set up a **cube schema** and Essbase model. The cube schema is an object or foundation structure that specifies the hierarchies, measures, and defines data bindings of an Essbase cube. You can also build an Essbase model when you build a cube schema. The Essbase model is a star schema developed from the relational model. The Essbase models will be used to specify the Essbase cubes' properties, attributes, alias, transformations, and drill-through reports.

Getting ready

To get started, click on the **Start** menu and navigate to **Programs | Oracle EPM System | Essbase | Essbase Studio** and log in to Essbase Studio using your server, username, and password.

How to do it...

1. Right-click on the **Root** folder of the **Metadata Navigator**. Click on **New** and select **Folder**, and in the textbox type in CUBE_SCHEMAS. Click on **OK**.

2. Right-click on the **CUBE_SCHEMAS** folder, click on **New**, then click on **Cube Schema**, and enter in TBC_Schema in the **Cube Schema Name** textbox.

3. Click and drag the following hierarchies to the **Hierarchies** list box: **MEASURES, TIME, PRODUCT, MARKET, SUPPLIER,** and **SCENARIO**. Note that the order in which you drag these to the list box is the order in which they will appear in the Essbase cube. We will be able to modify the order of hierarchies again while setting up the Essbase properties.

4. Click on the **SALE** folder, select **AMOUNT**, and drag it to the **Measures/Measure Hierarchy** list box. Click on the **Next** button.

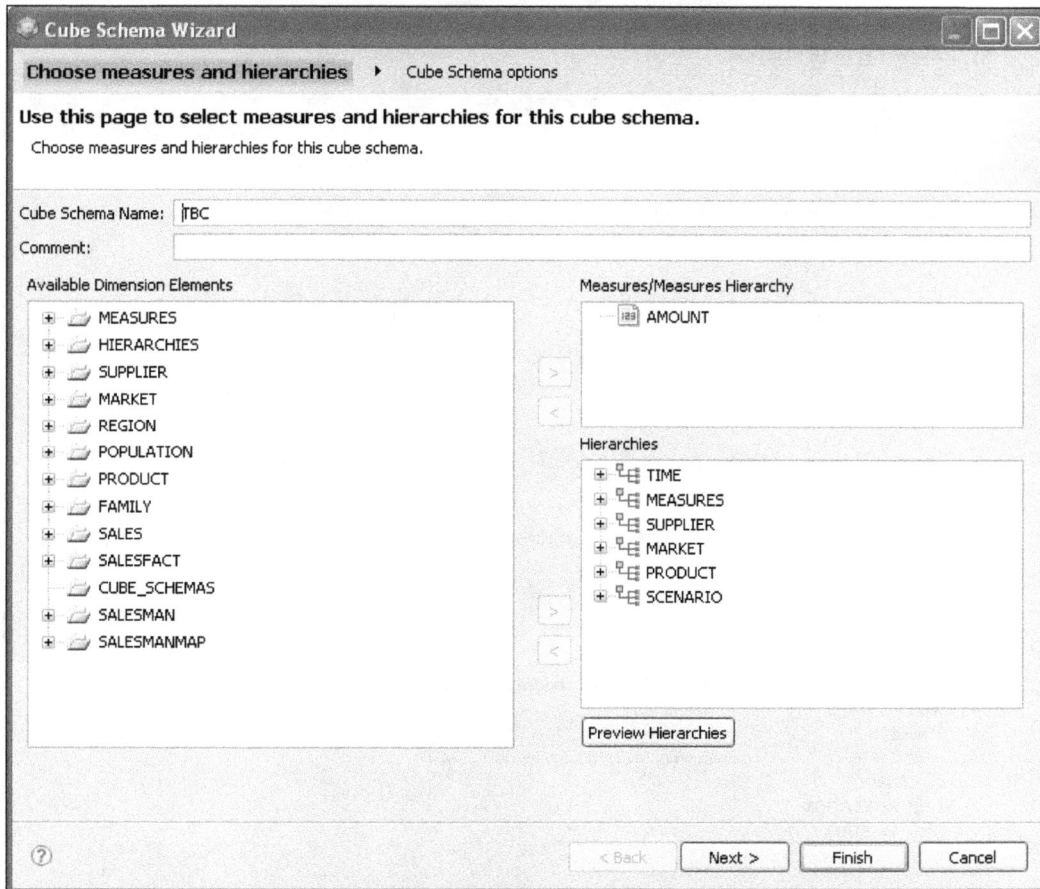

5. In the **Cube Schema** tab, check **Create Essbase Model** and **Override default data load binding**. Select the **Accounts Dimension** combobox and select **MEASURES**. This is important as you don't want Essbase Studio to make the **AMOUNT** measure the Account dimension. Click on the **Next** button.

6. Click on **AMOUNT**, and double-click on **Data Load Binding**.

7. In the **Default load Binding** dialog box, drill down on the **TBC** and **SALES** folders, and double-click on **AMOUNT**. The following is what your screen should look like at the **Define data load mappings** tab. We have not created the SCENARIO or MARKET dimension in prior recipes, but you can see what their structure is in the following screenshot:

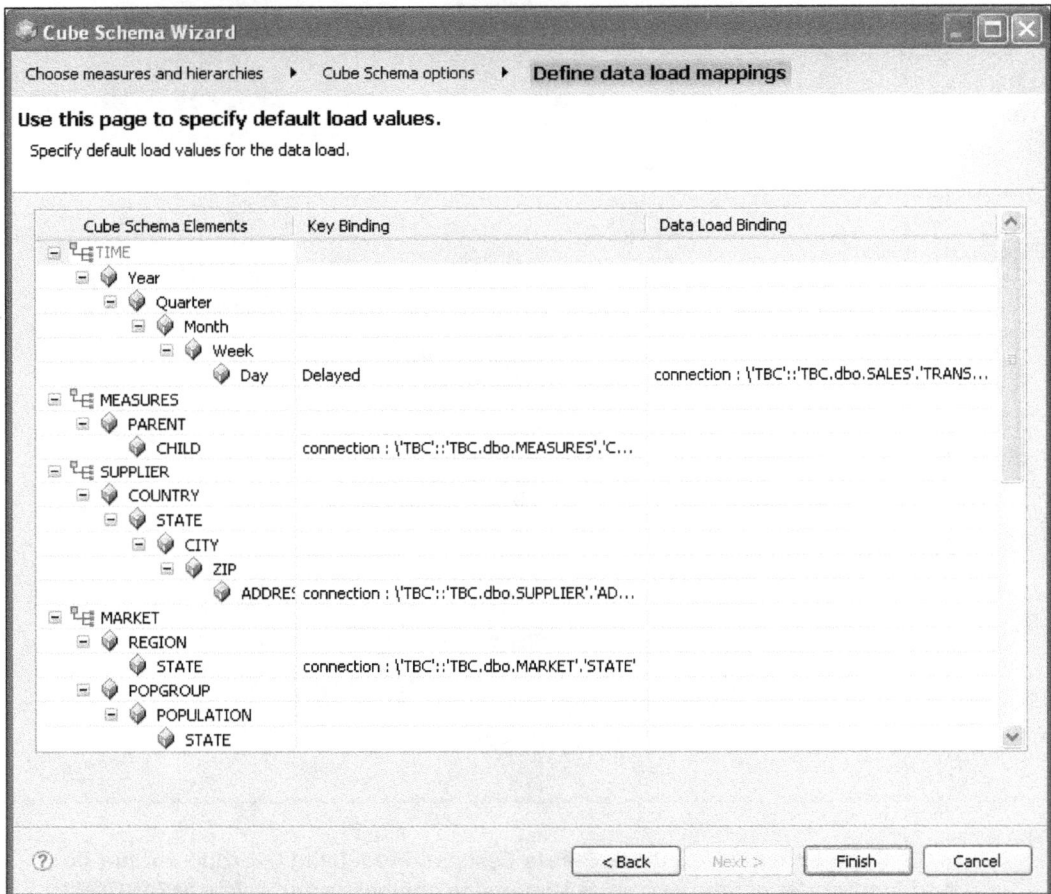

8. Click on the **OK** button and then on **Finish** to generate the Essbase model. The following screenshot is the Essbase Model:

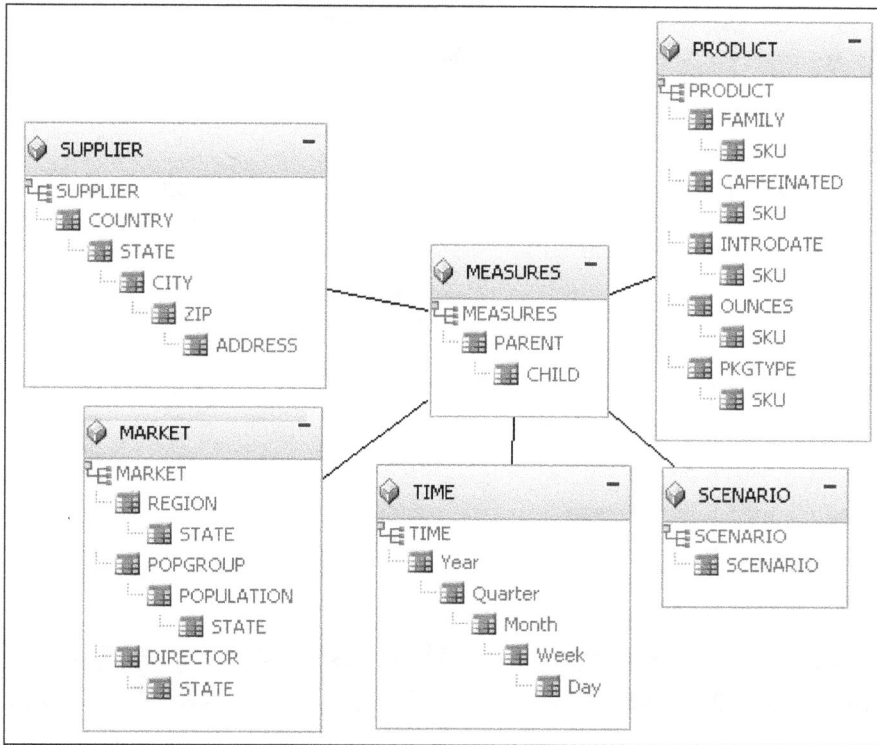

How it works...

In this recipe, we used the **Cube Schema Wizard** to select our cube's hierarchies and measures. The order that you select the hierarchies in the **Cube Schema Wizard** is the order in which they will be set in, in the database outline. This is important for the BSO model as the order of the dense and sparse dimensions will impact performance.

> Essbase Studio will not give you the Essbase properties you need to determine your dense or sparse dimension. We have to go to Essbase Administrative Services and load data before you can establish what the settings should be for the dense. That said, this database was set up in an hour glass shape with the largest dense dimension on top and the largest sparse dimension second to last. The SCENARIO dimension, a flat dense dimension, was set up as an anchor dimension at the bottom. This structure will, in most cases, improve calculation performance.

In the **Cube Schema** options tab, you selected **Override the default data load bindings** because we are using a Calendar dimension and have to specify the binding for this dimension to continue. We selected to create the Essbase Model, and we made the **MEASURES** dimension the account dimension. Finally, we defined the data load mapping by binding the element using the **Data Load Binding** dialog.

There's more...

This recipe uses all the dimensions we built in this chapter and two additional ones that were not covered, SCENARIO and MARKET. The structures of the SCENARIO and MARKET dimensions are specified in this recipe.

See also

You can review the following recipes in this chapter to see how to create the PRODUCT, MEASURE, TIME, and SUPPLIER dimensions:

- ▶ Creating hierarchies using a parent-child reference table
- ▶ Creating hierarchies using a generation reference table
- ▶ Adding attribute dimensions to hierarchies
- ▶ Building a Calendar dimension

Setting Essbase properties

In this recipe, we will use the Essbase Properties dialog to set up the default Alias table, set the dense and sparse setting for our dimensions, select all external source properties for the MEASURES dimension, and specify the attribute types for the MARKET and PRODUCT dimensions. We will also use the Transformation tab to add a suffix to the STATE metadata member in the SUPPLIER, so that it does not overlap with the MARKET dimension's STATE metadata member.

Getting ready

To get started, click on the **Start** menu and navigate to **Programs | Oracle EPM System | Essbase | Essbase Studio** and log in to Essbase Studio using your server, username, and password.

How to do it...

1. Right-click on the **TBCModel** created in recipe *Developing Cube Schema and an Essbase model* in this chapter, and select **Essbase Properties...**.

2. Click on the **Default** button to set all properties to default.

3. Click on the **TBCModel** root, click on the **Alias** tab, select **Default**, and use the right arrow to move to the **Selected Tables** list box. Your cube will now have a **Default** alias table.

4. Select the **MEASURES** dimension, click on the **Info** tab, and select **Dense** in the **Dimension Storage** session. Repeat the same step for the TIME and SCENARIO dimensions.

5. Select the **PRODUCT** dimension, click on the **Info** tab, and select **Sparse** in the **Dimension Storage** session. Repeat the same steps for the MARKET and SUPPLIER dimensions. Your BSO cube will now have dense and sparse settings for its outline.

6. Drill down on the **MEASURES** dimension and select **CHILD**. Click on the **Info** tab, in the **Consolidation** session. Select the **External Source** radio button, and select **CONSOLIDATION** from the combobox.

7. In the **Data Storage** session, select **STORAGE** in the combobox under **External Source**.

8. In the **Two Pass Calculation** session, select the **External Source** radio button, and select **TWOPASSCALC** in the combobox.

9. Select the **Account Info** tab. In the **Time Balance** session, select the **External Source** radio button, and select **TIMEBALANCE**.

10. In the **Skip** session, select the **External Source** radio button, and select **SKIP** from the combobox.

11. In the **Variance Reporting** session, select the **External Source** radio button, and select **VARIANCEREPORTING** from the combobox.

12. Select the **Formula** tab. In the **Formula** session, select the **From External Source** radio button and select **FORMULA** from the combobox.

13. Select the **UDAs** tab. In the **Add a new UDA** session, select **External Source**, and select **UDA** from the combobox.

14. Drill down on **MARKET** dimension, click on the **POPGROUP** attribute dimension, and select the **General** tab. In the **Attribute Setting** session, check Essbase Attribute for STATE, in **Attribute Dimension Name** change the value to **POPULATION**, and in the **Attribute Type**, select **Numeric**.

15. Click on the **DIRECTOR** attribute under the **MARKET** dimension. In the **General** tab in the **Attribute Settings** session, check Essbase Attribute for STATE, and in the **Attribute Type**, select **String**.

16. Drill down on the **PRODUCT** dimension and click on the **CAFFEINATED** attribute dimension. In the **General** tab in the **Attribute Setting** session, check **Essbase Attribute** for **SKU**, and in the **Attribute Type**, select **Boolean**.

17. Repeat the same steps for attribute dimensions INTRODATE, PKGTYPE, and OUNCES, but make sure to remember that the Attribute Type for INTRODATE is Date/Time, the Attribute Type for PKGTYPE is String, and the Attribute Type for OUNCES is Numeric.

18. Select the **SALEMANNAME** varying attribute dimension. In the **Attribute Setting** session of the **General** tab, check **Essbase Attribute** for **SKU**. In **Attribute Dimension Name** change the value to **SALESMAN**, and in the **Attribute Type** select **String**.

19. Click on **Edit...**, click on **Create as Varying Attribute**, and use the arrows to move the **MARKET** dimension to the top. Select **STATE** for the leaf level column. Under **Type**, select **Individual**. Click on the **From** column and enter connection : \'TBC'::'TBC.dbo.MARKET'.'STATE' in the **Expression** textbox, or select **STATE** from the left-hand side.

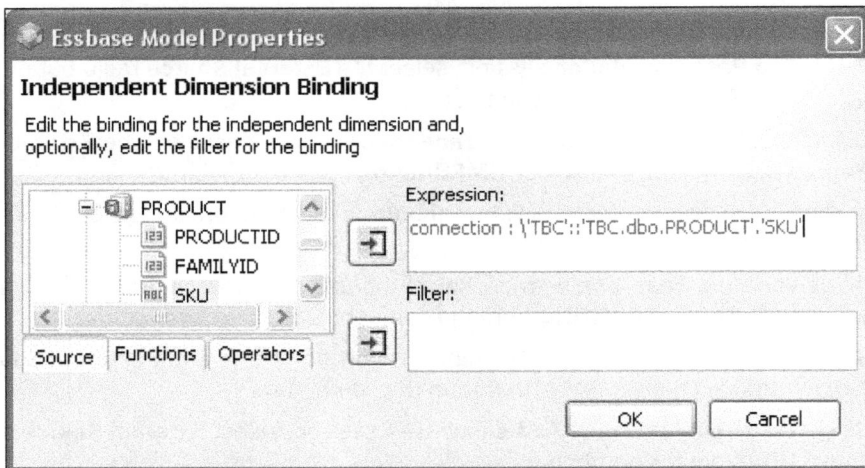

20 Drill down on the **SUPPLIER** dimension and select **STATE**. In the **Rules for Prefix / Suffix construction** session of the **Transformation** tab, enter ellipses ... into the custom **Suffix** textbox. Under this session, you should see a preview session with **STATE...**.

21. Drill down on the **TIME** dimension and in the **Info** tab make the storage of Year, Quarter, Month, and Week **Dynamic Calc**.

How it works...

In this recipe, we set dense and sparse settings for our dimension and used the External Sources provided in the MEASURES table to set up properties. We also set up six attribute dimensions and the one varying attribute. The difference between the attributes dimension and the varying attribute dimension is that attribute dimensions are only associated to one dimension, the base dimension, while a varying attributes associations can, as the name implies, vary across multiple dimensions.

Deploying a cube

In this recipe, we will deploy the TBC cube that we set up in the recipes *Developing Cube Schema and Essbase model* and *Setting Essbase properties* in *Chapter 3*. We will be adding an Application and Database using Essbase Administration Service, incrementally building the outline, and loading the TBC data.

Getting ready

To get started, click on the **Start** menu and navigate to **Programs | Oracle EPM System | Essbase | Essbase Studio**. Log in to Essbase Studio using your server, username, and password.

How to do it...

1. Click on the **Start** menu and navigate to **Programs | Oracle EPM System | Essbase | Administration Services | Start Administration Services Consol**. The login menu will pop up. Enter your administration server, username, password, and click on the **Log in** button.

2. Drill down on Essbase Server. Drill down on localhost of your Essbase Server, right-click on **Applications**, click on **Create Applications**, click on **Using Block Storage** in the menu and enter in TBC in the **Application name** textbox, and click on **OK**.

3. Right-click on the **TBC** application and select **Create Database....** In the **Create Database** dialog box, enter TBC for your database name, and click on the **OK** button.

4. Right-click on **TBCModel** created in the *Developing Cube Schema and Essbase model* recipe in this chapter, and select **Cube Deploymernt Wizard**.

5. In the following menu, enter your connection, Essbase server, username, and password, and click on the **Login** button:

6. In the **Essbase Server connection options**, enter your Essbase Server Connection, select **TBC** for the Application, and select **TBC** for the Database. Then, click on **Next**.

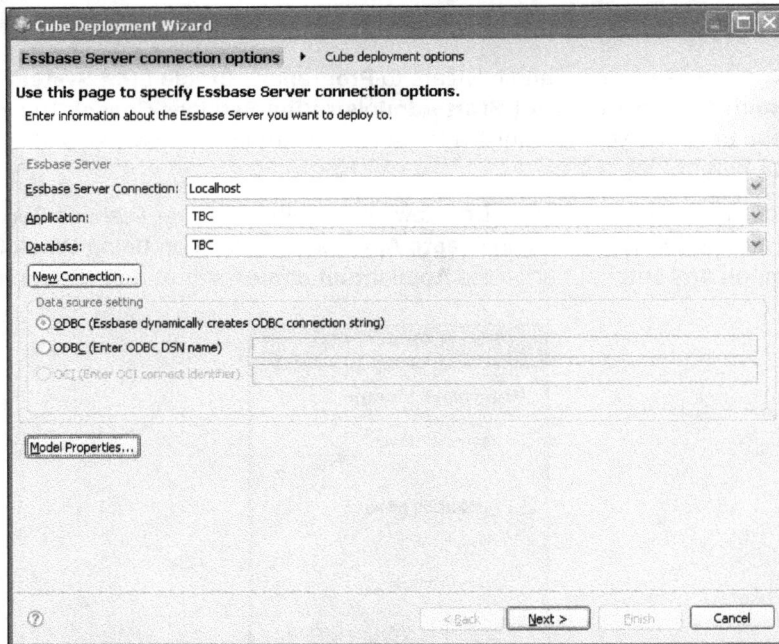

7. In the **Cube Deployment** options tab, select the **Build Outline** radio button, then select the **Incremental Load** checkbox, and click on the **Next** button.

8. In the Incremental load tab of the **Cube Deployment Wizard**, click on **Update** or **Rebuild selected hierarchies** radio button. Select the **TIME** dimension, click on the **Update** button, and then on the **Finish** button.

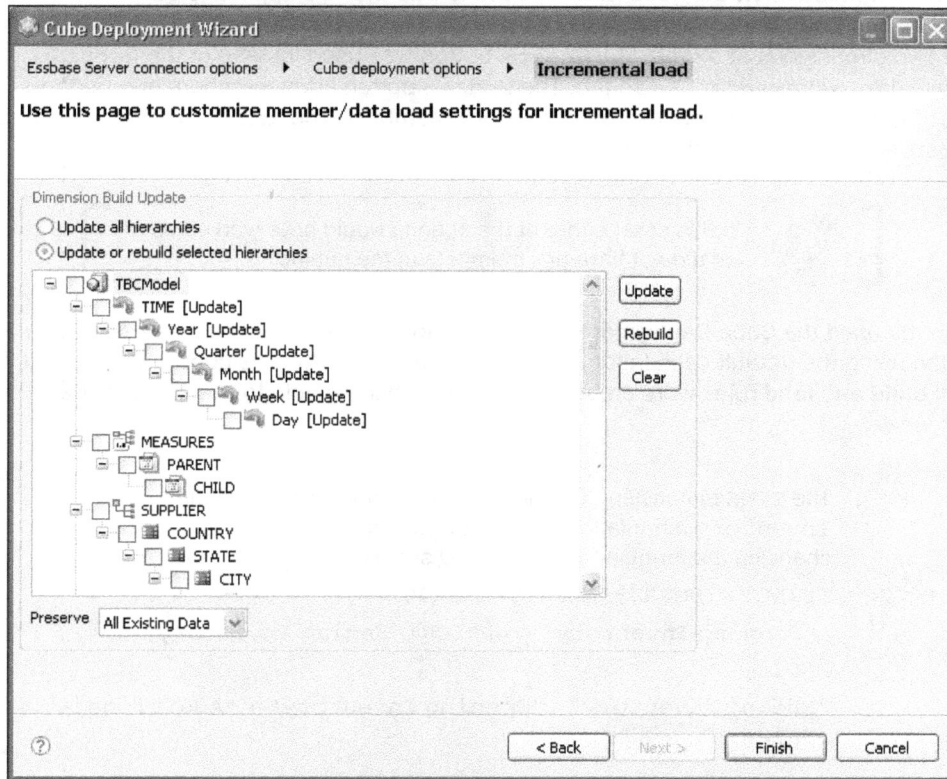

9. If you received no errors, repeat steps 5 through 7 for the remainder of the dimensions except for the PRODUCT dimension. The reason for this method is that building one dimension at a time will help you better understand which dimensions have errors.

10. Repeat steps 5 through 7 for the PRODUCT dimension, but exclude the **SALESMAN** varying attribute. The varying attribute dimension will sometimes return an error if the base dimension and associated dimensions are not complete.

11. Repeat steps 5 through 7, this time only selecting the **SALESMAN** attribute.

12. Right-click on the **TBCModel**, and select **Cube Deployment Wizard**. In the **Cube Deployment Wizard**, enter your Essbsase Server for the Essbase Server Connection. Select **TBC** for the Application and select **TBC** for the Database. In the **Load task type** session, click on the **Load Data** radio button, and click on the **Finish** button.

13. In **Essbase Administrative Service**, right-click on the **TBC** database, click on **Execute Calculation...**, select **Default**, and click on **OK**.

How it works...

Essbase Administration Services (**EAS**) is used to add the TBC application and TBC database. The Cube Deployment Wizard is then used to incrementally build the TBC outline one or two dimensions at a time. The `Update` button was used instead of the `Rebuild` button in the `Incremental Load` tab. The `Update` button adds members and updates the properties of a member, but does not remove any members. The `Rebuild` button removes all members and rebuilds the hierarchy.

> In this case, either of the options would have worked as we did not have any members in the outline.

Finally, you used the Cube Deployment Wizard to load data into your database and calculate the cube using the default calculation. In EAS, you will notice that the cube was modified and all **build** and **load** rules were created. You should also be able to retrieve data using Smart View.

> The `TIME` dimension that we built in *Chapter 3* will cause the `Opening Inventory` formula to not validate. You can resolve this issue by changing the formula to the following syntax:
>
> ```
> IF(NOT @ISMBR("January 30 2000"))
>  "Opening Inventory" = @PRIOR("Ending Inventory");
> ENDIF;
> "Ending Inventory"= "Opening Inventory" + "Additions"->Sales;
> ```

Creating an OLAP Model in EIS

In this recipe, we will build an **OLAP Model** using **Essbase Integration Services** (**EIS**). The EIS environment has some similarities and many differences when compared to Essbase Studio. To begin, we will have to set up an ODBC for the connection to the TBC database created in the first recipe of *Chapter 2*. The metadata catalog needs to be created before using EIS. The metadata catalog is created when you first install EIS or can be create by following the instructions in the Oracle Essbase Integration Service Adminstrator's Guide at the following link: http://download.oracle.com/docs/cd/E17236_01/epm.1112/eis_sysadmin.pdf. That said, the Essbase Studio minischema and the OLAP Model in EIS are very similar in practice. Both development tools have logical representations of the data source, which are used to create the relationship between the dimension tables in your star schema to your fact table.

Getting ready

To get started, click on the **Start** menu and navigate to **Programs | Oracle EPM System | Integration Services-Console**. If you have not created your Metadata Catalog review, then visit: `http://download.oracle.com/docs/cd/E17236_01/epm.1112/eis_sysadmin.pdf`.

How to do it...

1. If the **OLAP Metadata Catalog Setup** dialog box shows and the metadata catalog has already been set up, then uncheck the **Show this dialog at Startup** checkbox, as shown in the following screenshot, and click on **Close**:

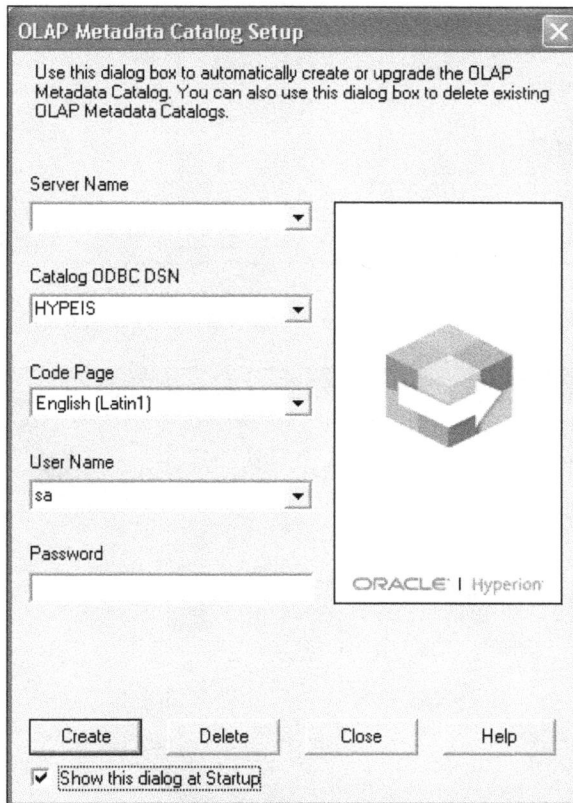

2. In the **Login** screen, enter your Essbase Integration Services Server, OLAP Metadata Catalog, User name, and password.

3. Enter your Essbase server, User Name, password, and click on the **OK** button. Your login screen should have looked like the following screenshot:

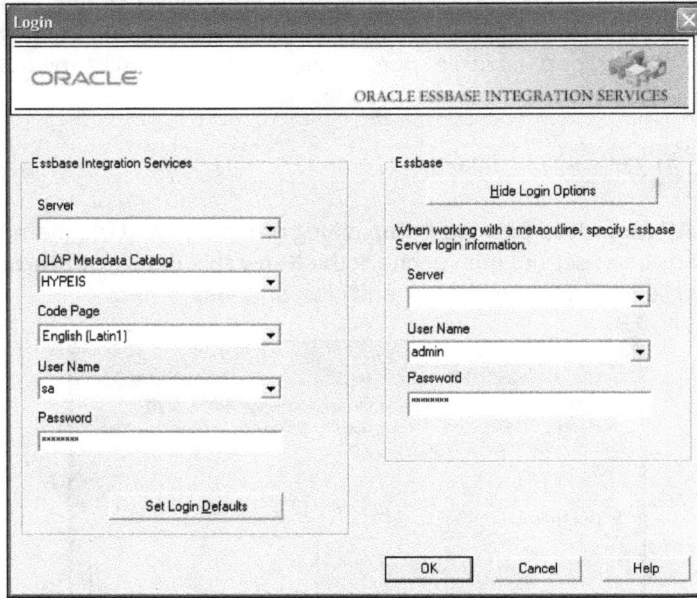

4. Click on the **OLAP Model** icon in the **Welcome** dialog and click on the **Open** button.

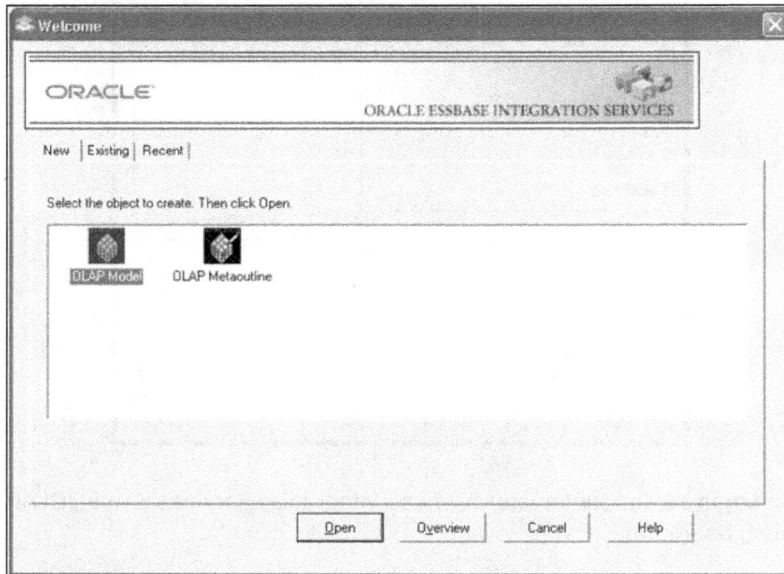

5. Select the **Data Source**. Enter your data source **User Name** and **Password**, and then click on the **OK** button. The **Data Source** is populated in this dialog box when you set up a **System ODBC**. In our case, the TBC database is created in *Chapter 2*.

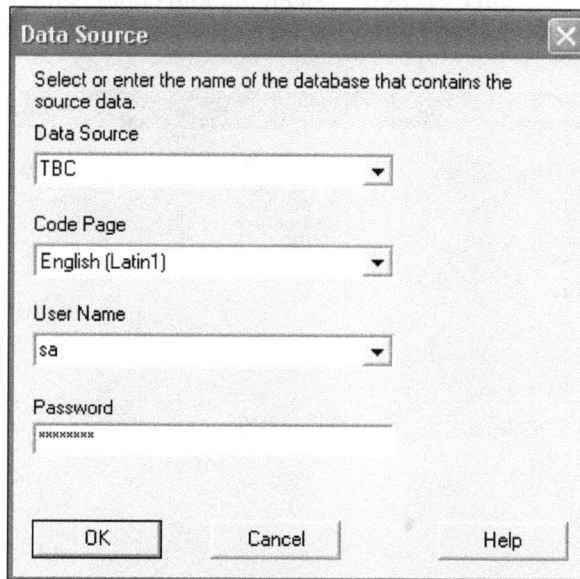

6. On the left side of your screen, drill down on database owner (**dbo**) and **Tables**. Click on the **SALES** table and drag-and-drop on the work area. Click the **Yes** button on the **Would you like to create a Time dimension?** prompt.

7. Click the **No** button on the **Would you like to add an Accounts dimension?** prompt. Your screen should like the following image:

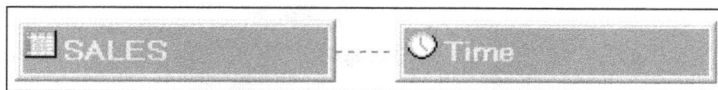

8. Click the **MARKET** table and drag to the work area; click the **Yes** button on the **Do you want to add the table (MARKET) to current model?** prompt. Repeat the same steps for the MEASURES, PRODUCT, SCENARIO, MARKET, and SUPPLIER tables. Right-click on each table and click **View Columns** to expand the table and view columns.

9. Click on the **Add Joins Mode** button 🖉, select the **PRODUCT** table, and drag to the **SALES** table. Make sure **PRODUCT** is the name and **Default** is the **Dimension** type. Click on the **OK** button, and then on **PRODUCTID** in the **Product** listbox. Select **PRODUCTID** in the **SALES** listbox, click on the **Add** button, and then on **Close**. Repeat the same steps for the SCENARIO, MARKET, and SUPPLIER tables.

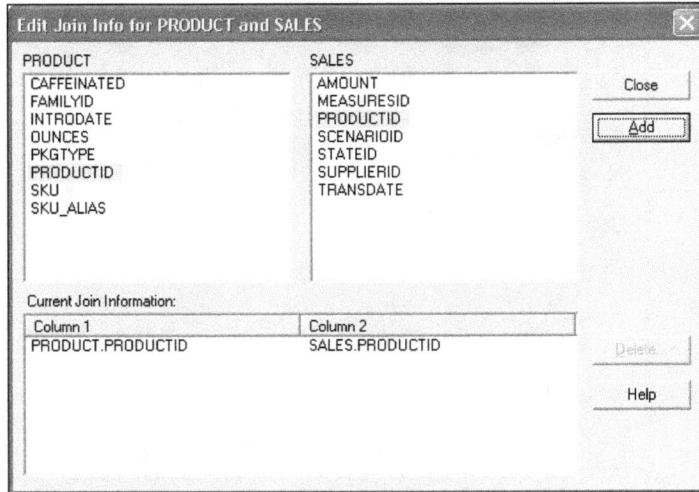

10. Right-click on the **MEASURES** table. Click on **Properties...** and select the **Physical Joins** tab. Select **CHILD** in the **CHILD** listbox, select **PARENT** in the **PARENT** listbox, click on the **Add** button, and then on the **Close** button.

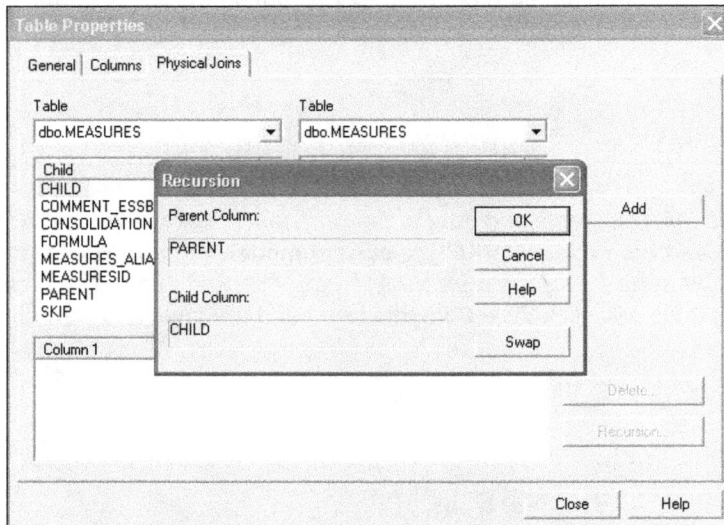

11. Click on the **MEASURES** table and drag to the **SALES** table. Make sure **MEASURES** is the name. Click the **OK** button and then **MEASURESID** in the **MEASURES** listbox. Click on **MEASURESID** in the **SALES** listbox, and click on the **Add** button, and then on **Close**.

12. Double-click on the join between the **SALES** and **Time** tables. Make sure **Time** is the name and **Time** is the **Dimension Type**. Click on the **OK** button, and then on **TRANSDATE** in the **Product** listbox. Select **TRANSDATE** in the **Sales** listbox, click the **Add** button, and then on **Close**.

13. Right-click on the **Time** table, select **Rename**, type YEAR, and click on **Enter**. Your **OLAP Model** should look like the following screenshot:

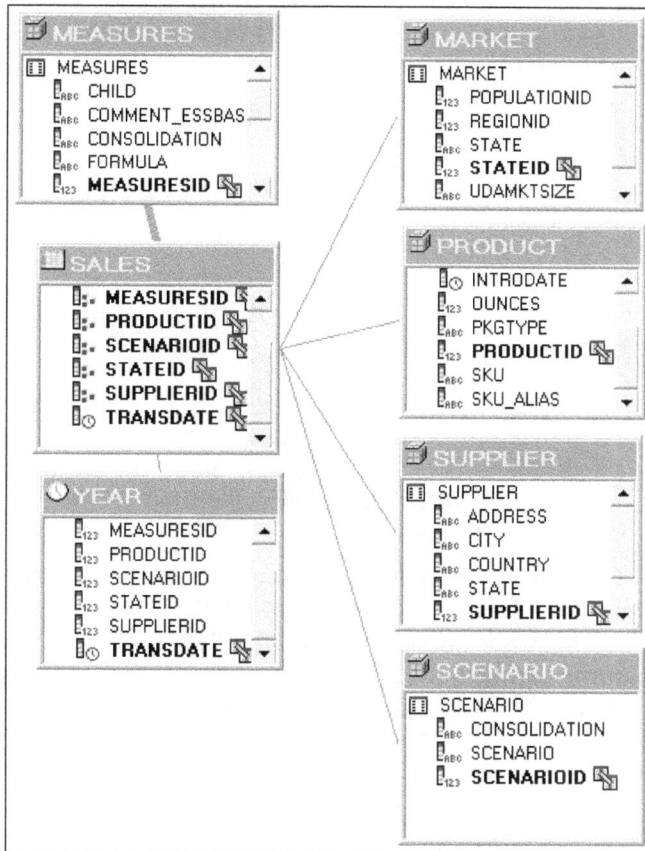

14. Right-click on the **YEAR** table, select **Properties...**, click on the **Columns** tab, and select **TRANSDATE**. Click on the **Date-Hierarchy** button, select **Quarter**, **Month**, click on **OK**, and then on **Close**.

15. Select the **FAMILY** table and drag to the work area; click on the **Yes** button on the **Do you want to add the table (FAMILY) to current model?** prompt.

16. Click on the **FAMILY** table and drag your mouse to the **PRODUCT** table. In the **Edit Join Info for FAMILY and PRODUCT** dialog box, select **FAMILYID** in the **FAMILY** listbox, select **FAMILYID** in the **PRODUCT** list box, click on the **Add** button, and then on **Close**.

17. Right-click on **PRODUCT** in the **PRODUCT** table and select the **Columns** tab. Hold *Shift* and select **CAFFEINATED, INTRODATE, OUNCES,** and **PKGTYPE**. Click on the **Attribute** button, and then on **Close**. The **PRODUCT** and **FAMILY** table should look like the following screenshot:

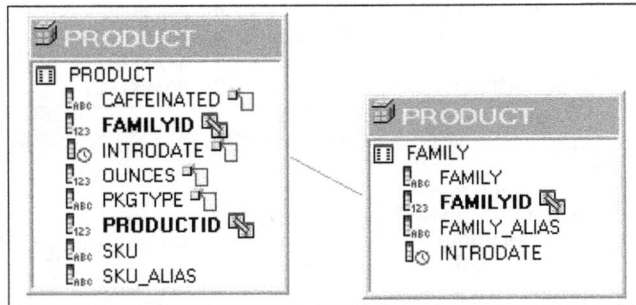

18. Click on the **REGION** table and drag to the work area; click the **Yes** button for the **Do you want to add the table (REGION) to current model?** prompt. Repeat the same steps for the POPULATION table.

19. Click on the **REGION** table and drag your mouse to the **MARKET** table in the **Edit Join Info for REGION and MARKET** dialog box. Select **REGIONID** in the **REGION** listbox, select **REGIONID** in the **MARKET** list box, click on the **Add** button, and then on **Close**.

20. Click on the **POPULATION** table and drag your mouse to the **MARKET** table; in the **Edit Join Info for POPULATION and MARKET** dialog box select **POPULATIONID** in the **REGION** listbox, select **POPULATIONID** in the **MARKET** listbox, click on the **Add** button, and then on **Close**. The MARKET and its relations should look like the following screenshot:

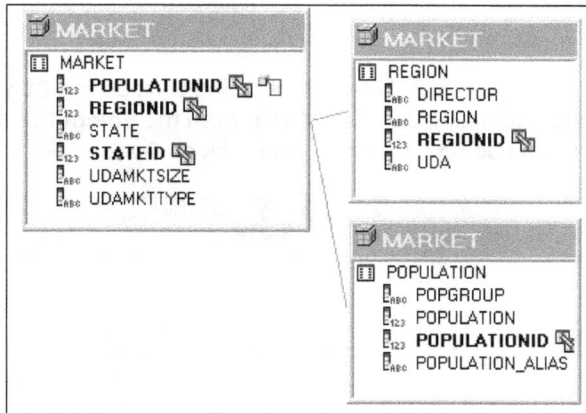

21. Click the **File** menu, and then the **Save** menu; in the **Save New OLAP Model** dialog box, type in **TBC** in the **OLAP Model Name**, and click **OK**.

How it works...

In this recipe, we added the dimension and fact tables to the OLAP Model. We set up joins between dimension and fact tables and recursive joins for the parent-child relationship in the MEASURE dimension. We also assigned attribute dimensions in the PRODUCT dimension. In addition, the OLAP Model can also be used to create reusable hierarchies and specify data transformations.

Creating an OLAP metaoutline in EIS

In this recipe, we will build an **OLAP metaoutline** in the EIS. The OLAP metaoutline is used to determine the structure and content of your Essbase outline. In contrast to Essbase Studio, we will be using the OLAP metaoutline to accomplish tasks like building hierarchies, creating a cube schema, creating an Essbase model, and setting Essbase properties. Building an OLAP metaoutline will require us to define our measures, create the hierarchies within our dimension, define the organizational structure of groups of members, and define members among other tasks.

Getting ready

To get started, click on the **Start** menu and **Programs | Oracle EPM System | Integration Services-Console**. We should complete the recipe *Creating an OLAP Model in EIS* in this chapter as we will build on the OLAP Model completed there.

How to do it...

1. Click on the **File** menu in EIS. Select **New...**, and click on the **OLAP Metaoutline** icon in the **Welcome** dialog box. Select **TBC** from the **Select the model that the metaoutline should be on** combobox, and click on **Open**.

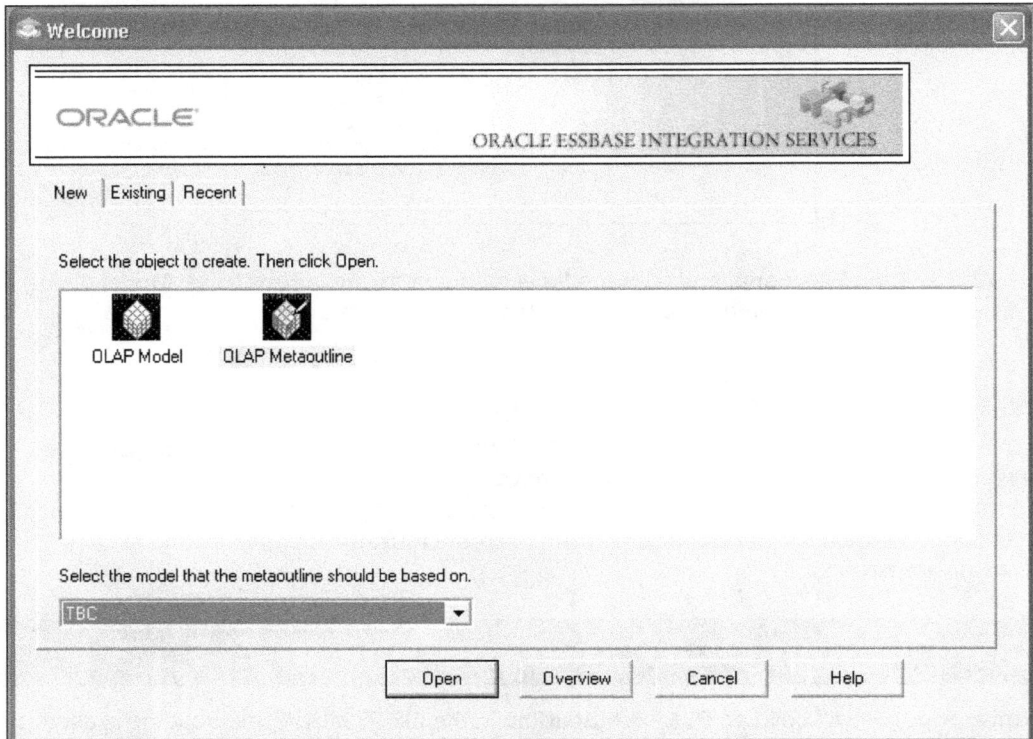

2. In the **Data Source** dialog box, select your relational database, the **Data Source** should be **TBC**. Enter your Data Source User Name, Password, and click on **OK**.

3. Expand each dimension on the left window pane by clicking on the **+** sign next to each. Click on the **Quarter_Month** hierarchy and drag to the window on the right. Your screen should look like the following screenshot:

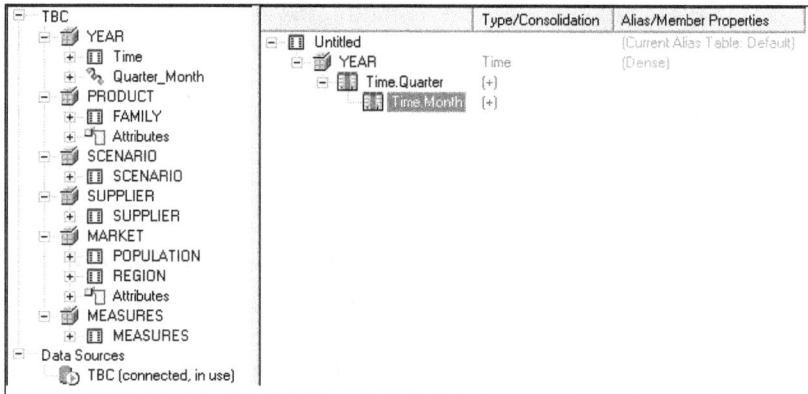

4. Drill down on **MEASURES** by clicking the **+** sign, click **CHILD**, and drag to the right window pane. Right-click on the **MEASURES.CHILD** column, click on **Properties**, select the **MemberInfo** tab, click on the **From Database Column** radio button, and select **CONSOLIDATION** in the combobox in the **Consolidation** session.

5. Click on the **From Database Column** radio button and select the **TWOPASSCALC** column from combobox in the **Two Pass Calculation** session.

6. Click on the **From Database Column** radio button and select the **STORAGE** column in the combobox from the **Data Storage** session. Your screen should look like the following screenshot:

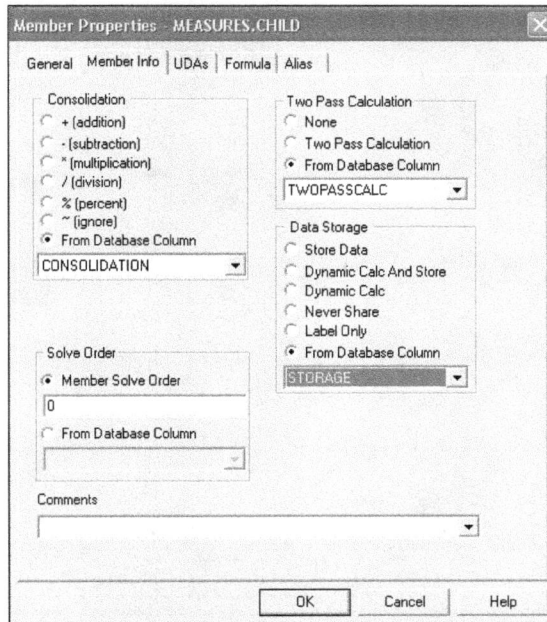

7. Click on the **UDAs** tab, then click the **From Database Column** radio button, select the **UDA** column in the combobox in the **New UDA** session, and click on the **Add to List** button.

8. Click the **Formula** tab, select the **From Database Column** radio button, and click the **FORMULA** column.

9. Click on the **Alias** tab, and then select the **MEASURES_ALIAS** column in the **Alias** combobox.

10. Click on the **Add** button and then on the **OK** button in the **Members Properties - MEASURES.CHILD** dialog box.

11. Select the **MEASURES**. Click on the **Edit** menu, select **Properties | Member Info**, and select the **Account** radio button under **Dimension Type**. Select **Dense** under the dimension **Storage** and **Label Only** under **Data Storage**. Click on **OK**. These steps make the **MEASURES** dimension into your **Account** dimension and the **Data Storage** for the **MEASURES** member.

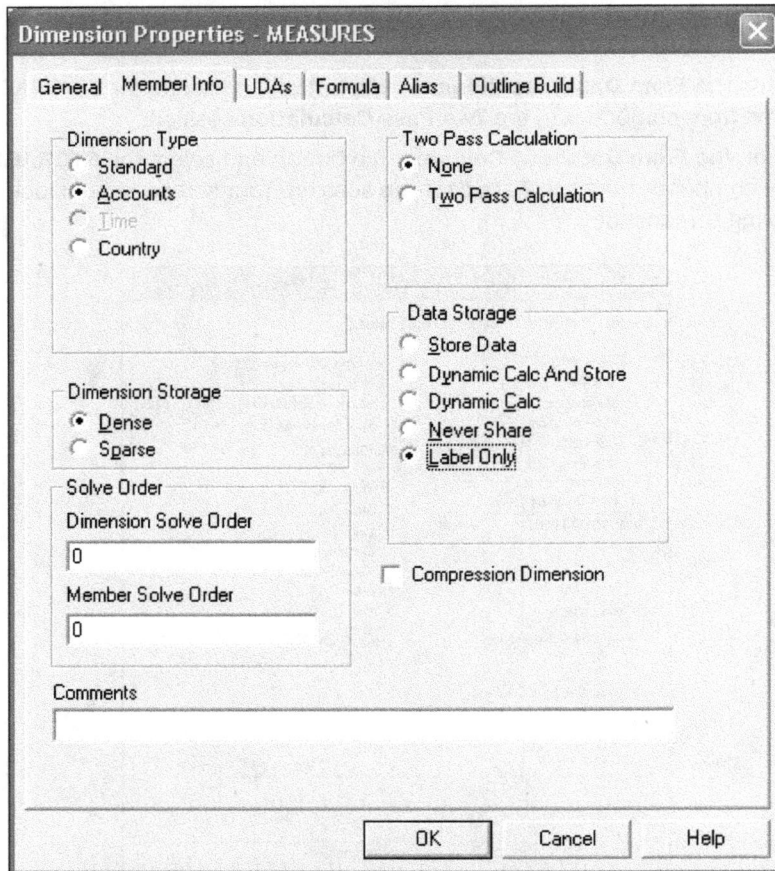

12. Under the **MARKET** dimension, expand **REGION** and **MARKET** in the left window pane, and click on **REGION** and drag to the right pane under **MEASURES**.

13. Click on **STATE** under **MARKET** and drag to the right pane on top of **REGION.REGION**. Your screen should look like the following screenshot:

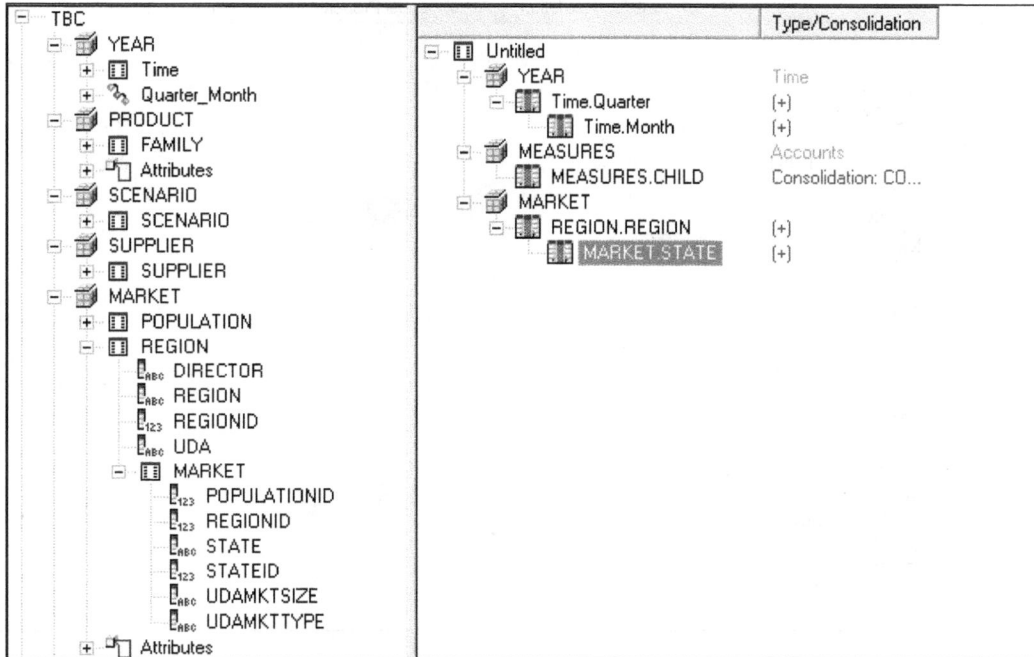

14. Under the **PRODUCT** dimension, expand **FAMILY** and **PRODUCT** in the left window pane. Click on **FAMILY** and drag to the right pane under **MARKET**.

15. Click on **SKU** under **PRODUCT** and drag to the right pane on top of **FAMILY.FAMILY**.

16. Under the **SCENARIO** dimension, expand **SCENARIO** in the left window pane, click on **SCENARIO**, and drag to the right pane under **PRODUCT**.

17. Under the **PRODUCT** dimension, expand **Attributes** in the left window pane, click on **PRODUCT.CAFFEINATED**, and drag to the right pane under **SCENARIO**. Repeat the same step for PRODUCT.INTRODATE, PRODUCT.OUNCES, and PRODUCT.PKGTYPE.

18. Click on the **TBC** root on the left pane. Click on the **Edit** menu, and select **Properties**; in the **OLAP Metaoutline Properties** dialog box, click on the **Database Measures** tab, then on the **Add** button. Select **MEASURESID**, and click on **OK** twice. Your screen should look like the following image:

	Type/Consolidation	Alias/Member Properties	Formula
TBC		(Current Alias Table: Default)	
YEAR	Time	(Dense)	
Time.Quarter	[+]		
Time.Month	[+]		
MEASURES	Accounts	(Dense)	
MEASURES.CHILD	Consolidation: CO...	(Alias: MEASURES_ALIAS)...	Formula: FORMULA
MARKET		(Sparse)	
REGION.REGION	[+]		
MARKET.STATE	[+]		
PRODUCT { CAFFEINATED, I...		(Sparse)	
FAMILY.FAMILY	[+]		
PRODUCT.SKU	[+]		
SCENARIO		(Dense)	
SCENARIO.SCENARIO	[+]		
CAFFEINATED	(Text)		
PRODUCT.CAFFEINATED			
INTRODATE	(Date)		
PRODUCT.INTRODATE			
OUNCES	(Numeric)		
PRODUCT.OUNCES			
PKGTYPE	(Text)		
PRODUCT.PKGTYPE			

19. Click on the **File** menu. Select **Save**, type TBC in the **Meta Outline Name** textbox, and click on **OK**.

20. Click on the **Start** menu and navigate to **Programs | Oracle EPM System | Essbase | Administration Services | Start Administration Services Consol**. The login menu will pop up. Enter your Administration Server, username, password, and click on the **Log in** button.

21. Drill down on Essbase Server, and drill down on **EssbaseCluster-1** of your Essbase Server. Right-click on **Applications**, click on **Create Applications**, and then on **Using Block Storage** in the menu. Enter in **TBC_EIS** in the Application name textbox and click on **OK**.

22. Right-click on the **TBC_EIS** application and select **Create Database....** In the **Create Database** dialog box, enter **TBC** for your database name, and click on **OK**. The reason why we added the application and database this way is that the default for outline deployment is the aggregate storage database, and we want a BSO application.

23. Return to the **EIS** application, click on the **Outline** menu, and then on **Member** and **Data Load...**. Type **TBC_EIS** in the **Application Name** textbox, type **TBC** in the **Database Name** textbox, select the **Use default calc script** radio button, click on **Next**, and then on **Finish**. A prompt will pop up when finished, letting you know that it has successfully loaded **Essbase Server:TBC_EIS:TBC**. Click on **OK** and then on **Close** to exit.

How it works...

In this recipe, we started by creating the TBC OLAP meta outline by selecting our YEAR or Time dimension hierarchy. We then selected the MEASURES.CHILD to define our MEASURES dimension, set all the MEASURES dimension's properties, and specified the MEASURES dimension as our Accounts dimension. We also selected the MARKET, PRODUCT, and SCENARIO dimensions for our TBC database Essbase outline and defined all dense and sparse settings for the dimensions. Moreover, we selected attribute dimension for the PRODUCT dimension. Finally, we created a BSO application and database in Essabase Administrative Services and deployed our TBC_EIS application.

4

Building the ASO Cube

In this chapter, we will cover the following topics:

- ► Using the Connection Wizard to set up an ASO cube
- ► Building a Measures dimension from the fact table
- ► Creating an ASO Cube Schema and an Essbase Model
- ► Understanding Essbase model properties for the ASO cube
- ► Designing a drill-through report
- ► Using the View dimension for Dynamic Time Series reporting

Introduction

This chapter is designed to show some of the differences we will need to consider when developing an **Aggregate Storage Option** (**ASO**) database in contrast to the classic **Block Storage Option** (**BSO**) database. In addition, we will also create a drill-through report in Essbase Studio to complete the tasks discussed in *Chapter 3*'s list of development tasks.

> There is one database type that we will not be discussing but is worth mentioning here for your information. The **XOLAP** (**eXtended On-Line Analytic Processing**) database has hierarchies and an outline, just like the ASO and BSO database types, but when a user requests data, a SQL Script is generated and the relational data source is queried. The process of designing the XOLAP database is similar to the database modeling we completed in the previous chapters, but it does have some differences in its work flow and user guidelines. Review the **Oracle Essbase Studio User's Guide** for more information on XOLAP.

Using the Connection Wizard to set up an ASO cube

In this recipe, we will create a Data Source and minischema for the ASOsamp application. We will also set up joins for tables that have a recursive relationship, and identify the dimensions, attributes, and fact tables in our model. Finally, we will review why the ASO model is a good choice for the ASOsamp application.

Getting ready

To get started, open **SQL Server Management Studio**, and add a database called ASOsamp. We are using the SQL Server scripts in this example, but Oracle PL SQL scripts are available as well.

How to do it...

1. Open up SQL Server Management Studio, click on the **ASOsamp** database, click on the **File** menu, select **Open**, and click on **File....**

2. Open the script, 3265_04_01tsql.sql.

3. Make sure that **ASOsamp** is selected in your **Available Database** window.

4. Click on **Execute**.

5. Click on the **File** menu, and then on **Open**, and click on **File....** Open the script 3265_04_01_sampledata.sql.

6. Make sure that **ASOsamp** is selected in your **Available Database** window and click on **Execute**.

7. Click on the **Start** menu and navigate to **Oracle EPM System | Essbase Studio | Essbase Studio Console**.

8. Enter the **Server, username**, and **password** at the log in menu , and click on **OK**.

9. On the right-hand side of Essbase Studio, you should see two tabs, right-click on the **Data Sources** tab node, click on **New**, and then on **Data Sources....**

10. In the **Connection Wizard**, enter the **Connection Name**, and enter the **Connection Description**.

11. Select the **Data Source Type** from the drop down, enter **Server Name, User Name, Password**, and select your **Database Name**. Click on the **Test Connection** button to verify that the parameters you entered are correct. A **Connection is Successful** prompt should pop up. Click on the **Next** button to select tables.

12. In the **Select Table** tab, click on *Shift* and select all the tables from the left-hand side listbox. Click on the right arrow button to move the tables to the **Tables in Data Source** listbox. Click on the **Next** button.

13. Click on the **Create a new schema diagram** radio button, in the **Minischema** tab. Leave the **ASOsampSchema** in the textbox, and click on the **Next** button.

14. All the tables that you chose in step 12 should be in the **Table in Schema** listbox. Click on the **Next** button.

15. In the **Create Metadata Element** tab, click on **ASOsamp** to select all the tables you want in your **Metadata Navigator**, and click on the **Finish** button.

16. We should see the following minischema diagram. The fact table is in the center of the diagram and all other tables join directly or indirectly to it. All the tables that directly join to the fact table are Dimension tables and all tables that join to the dimension tables are attribute dimensions. Notice that there isn't a Measures dimension. We are going to have to build the Measures dimension using the fact table.

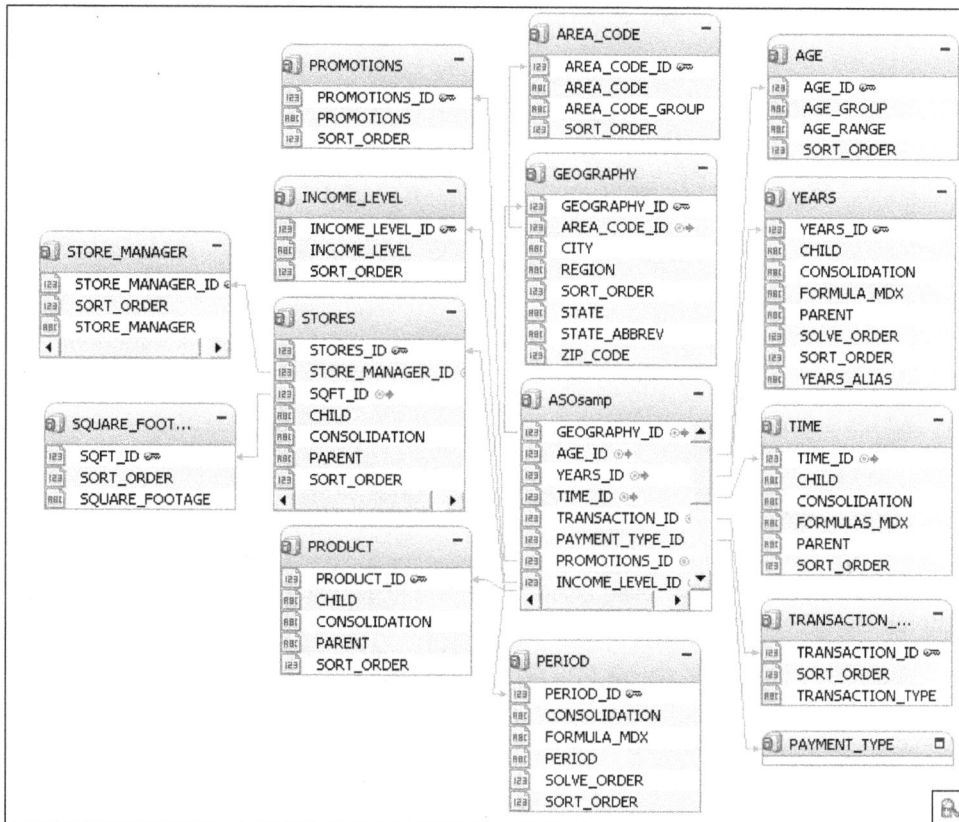

17. Right-click on the **STORES** table and click on **Add Join...**; select **STORES** in the **Properties of Minischema Join** menu, select **PARENT** in the column area, and then click on **OK**. We will need to repeat these same steps for the **TIME** and **YEARS** tables as both table are in parent-child format.

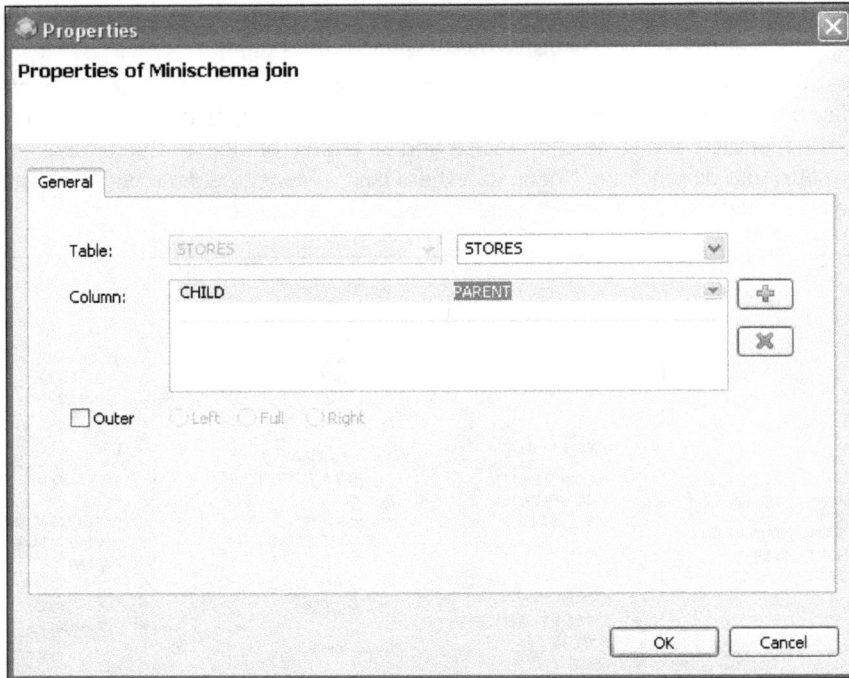

How it works...

In this recipe, we created the ASOsamp Data Source, minischema, and Data Element using the Connection Wizard. We then discussed some simple guidelines to determine the fact table, dimension tables, and attribute dimensions in the ASOsamp Star Schema. The fact table is clearly the ASOsamp table as it is at the centre of the star schema, and all other tables either directly or indirectly join to it. The tables that join to the fact table directly are your dimensions. The following is the list of dimensions in the ASOsamp:

 ▸ STORES
 ▸ PRODUCTS
 ▸ TRANSACTION TYPE
 ▸ AGE
 ▸ INCOME LEVEL
 ▸ PAYMENT TYPE

- ▶ PERIOD
- ▶ PROMOTIONS
- ▶ YEARS
- ▶ TIME
- ▶ GEOGRAPHY

Also, the GEOGRAPHY and STORES have attribute dimensions associated with them. The reason why this is an ASO cube is that it has 12 stored dimensions, counting Measures. Although in theory it is possible to have a BSO database with 12 dimensions, when a BSO database exceeds 10 dimensions, calculation and retrieval performance will begin to degrade. The ASOsamp application will clearly exceed the number of dimensions optimal for a BSO cube. The ASO databases are very good for storing large amounts of data. They have a small foot print and can accommodate a large hierarchy with millions of members. If you need a more detailed explanation on the differences in syntax between the BSO and ASO model, then refer to Oracle's White Paper on **Converting Calc Formulas to MDX in an Essbase Outline** here: `http://www.oracle.com/technetwork/middleware/bi-foundation/4395-calc-to-mdx-wp-133362.pdf`.

Building a Measures dimension from the fact table

In this recipe, we will build a Measures dimension from a column in the ASOsamp fact table. The ASOsamp fact table has measures as columns instead of rows. For this reason, the Measures dimension in the ASOsamp star schema is not in its own table, and we have to build its structure in Essbase Studio. We will have to define formulas and other Essbase Properties, but this is done after we build the Cube Schema and Essbase Model.

Getting ready

To get started with Essbase Studio, click on the **Start** menu and navigate to **Programs | Oracle EPM System | Essbase | Essbase Studio**, then click on **Start Server** to make sure your Essbase Studio Server is running. When the Start Server command prompt gives you the console command, log in to Essbase Studio using your server, username, and password.

How to do it...

1. Right-click on the **ASOsamp** folder in your **Metadata Navigator**. Select **New** and then **Folder**, and type in HIERARCHIES in the properties menu.

2. Right-click on the **HIERARCHIES** folder, select **New** and then **Measure Hierarchy**, and type in Measures in the **Name** textbox of the **Edit Hierarchy** dialog box.

3. In the **Metadata Navigator**, drill down on the **ASOsamp** fact table and drag-and-drop the following elements: **Original Price**, **Price Paid**, **Returns**, **Units**, and **Transactions** one at a time to the **Edit Hierarchy** dialog box, under **Hierarchy**. They should all fall underneath each other, as siblings, in the preceding order listed.

4. Select **Transactions** in the **Edit Hierarchy** dialog box, click on the **Add** button on the lower-right hand side, select **Add user-defined sibling**, and replace **NewMember** in the cell with **Ratios**. You are going to see **Unspecified** in the **Key Binding** column. You do not need to specify a Key Binding for this or the other **Ratios**.

5. Select **Ratios** in the **Edit Hierarchy** dialog box, click on the **Add** button, select **Add user-defined child**, and replace the **Member1** in the cell with **Avg Units/Transaction**.

6. Select **Avg Units/Transaction** in the **Edit Hierarchy** dialog box, click on the **Add** button, select **Add user-defined sibling**, and replace the **Member2** in the cell with **% of Total**. Click on the **Save** button. The **Edit Hierarchy** dialog box will look as follows:

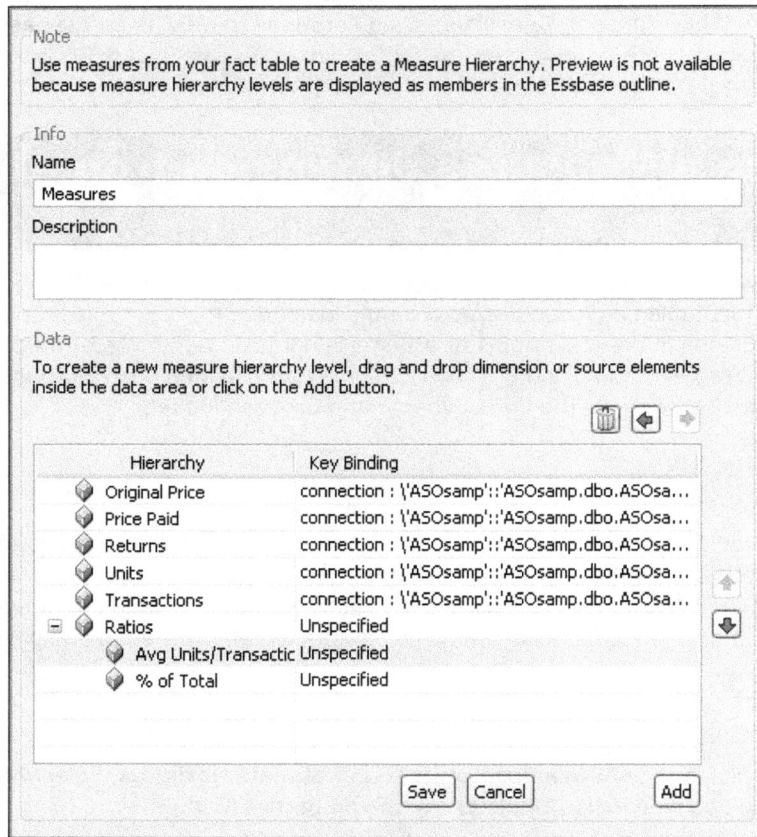

Note

Use measures from your fact table to create a Measure Hierarchy. Preview is not available because measure hierarchy levels are displayed as members in the Essbase outline.

Info

Name

Measures

Description

Data

To create a new measure hierarchy level, drag and drop dimension or source elements inside the data area or click on the Add button.

Hierarchy	Key Binding
Original Price	connection : \'ASOsamp'::'ASOsamp.dbo.ASOsa...
Price Paid	connection : \'ASOsamp'::'ASOsamp.dbo.ASOsa...
Returns	connection : \'ASOsamp'::'ASOsamp.dbo.ASOsa...
Units	connection : \'ASOsamp'::'ASOsamp.dbo.ASOsa...
Transactions	connection : \'ASOsamp'::'ASOsamp.dbo.ASOsa...
⊟ Ratios	Unspecified
Avg Units/Transactic	Unspecified
% of Total	Unspecified

Save | Cancel | Add

How it works...

In this recipe we built the Measures dimension off the fact table. This was a very manual process as you can see. In real world situations, you may need to use this method, as your fact table may not always have all the data in one single column and measures as rows. This task may be difficult for financial account dimensions that have accounts added often from the companies' chart of accounts. In this case, a parent-child format would be easier to maintain.

There's more...

This is not the last time we are going to have to modify this Measures dimension. After we build the Cube Schema and Essbase Model, we are going to edit the Essbase properties and enter the Consolidations, Solve Order, Storage, and formulas. These are the properties of the Measures dimension, as follows:

MEMBER	ALIAS	CONSOLIDATION	SOLVE ORDER	STORAGE	FORMULA
Original Price		+			
Price Paid		~			
Returns		~			
Units	Items per Package	~			
Transactions	No. of Packages	~			
Ratios		~		O	
Avg Units/ Transaction		+	20		[Units]/[Transactions]
% of Total		~	20		Transactions/ (Transactions, Time, [Transaction Type], [Payment Type], Promotions,Age, [Income Level], Products, Stores, Geography)

To complete the ASOsamp cube, we are also going to have to set up the Time, Years, Product, and Stores dimensions as parent-child hierarchies. Moreover, the Payment Type, Promotions, Transaction Type, Period, Age, Geography, and Income Level dimensions need to be set up as generation hierarchies. Remember that Geography has an attribute dimension called Area Code.In addition, the Store dimension has Store Manager and Square Footage as the attribute dimensions.

See also

To complete the rest of the hierarchies in this ASOsamp cube, the following recipes in *Chapters 2* and *3* will help us get started:

- ▶ Using Sort Order on data elements
- ▶ Creating hierarchies using a parent-child reference table
- ▶ Creating hierarchies using a `Generation` reference table
- ▶ Adding attribute dimensions to hierarchies

Creating an ASO Cube Schema and an Essbase Model

In this recipe, we will create a Cube Schema and an Essbase Model for the ASOsamp application. This process is similar to the one we discussed in the recipe *Developing Cube Schema and Essbase Model* in *Chapter 3*; but it is not the same. Our Time and Year dimensions are not being generated via a Calendar Hierarchy and as such we don't have to worry about Key Bindings. In addition, when you are building an ASO model's Cube Schema, the order that you choose the hierarchies is only important for display purposes and should not impact performance, as the concepts of dense and sparse are not relevant to the ASO model. You will recall that in a Block Storage application, we need to build the cube in an hour glass shape with a larger dense dimension on top and the largest sparse dimension on the button. This best practice does not apply to ASO.

Getting ready

To get started with Essbase Studio, click on the **Start** menu and navigate to **Programs | Oracle EPM System | Essbase | Essbase Studio | Essbase Studio Console**. Use the login menu to enter your server, username, and password, and click on the **Log In** button.

How to do it...

1. Right-click on the **ASOsamp** folder in your **Metadata Navigator**. Select **New** and then **Folder**, and type in CUBE_SCHEMA in the properties menu.

2. Right-click on the **CUBE_SCHEMA** folder, click on **New**, select **Cube Schema**, and type in ASOsamp in the **Cube Schema Name** textbox. Optionally, enter a description in the following textbox, drill down on the **ASOsamp** folder on the left side, drill down on the **HIERARCHIES** dimension, select **Measures**, and use the arrows on the right to move to the **Measures/Measures Hierarchy** listbox.

3.   Select the Years hierarchy from the **Cube Schema Wizard** dialog box and use the arrow to move to the **Hierarchies** listbox. Repeat the same steps for the Time, Transaction Type, Payment Type, Promotions, Age, Income Level, Products, Stores, Geography, and Period hierarchies. Your screen will look like the following screenshot:

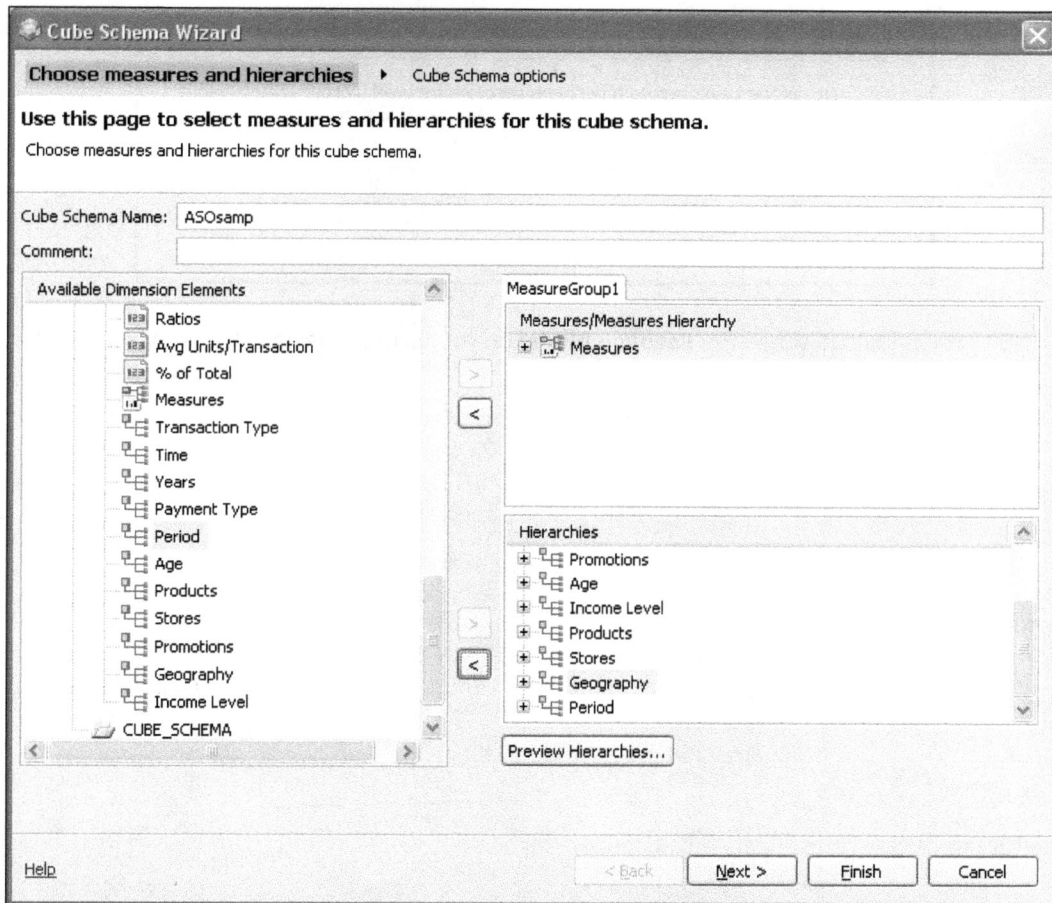

4. Click on the **Next** button, click on the **Create Essbase Model** checkbox, leave the name of the model as **ASOsampModel**, and click on the **Finish** button. If you receive the following menu, click the **Yes** button as we will define the measures with Delay binding in the properties menu.

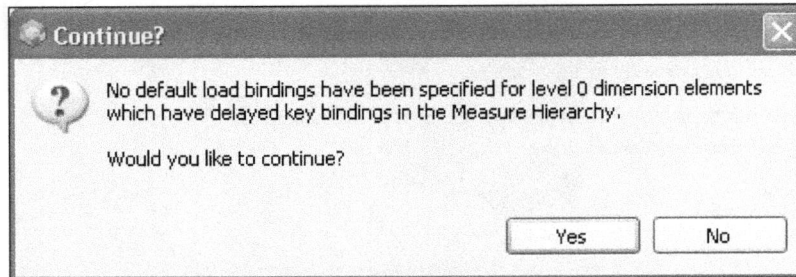

> **Continue?**
>
> ? No default load bindings have been specified for level 0 dimension elements which have delayed key bindings in the Measure Hierarchy.
>
> Would you like to continue?
>
> [Yes]   [No]

5. You should now see the **Essbase Model** on your screen. Review the Essbase Model for the complete set of dimensions.

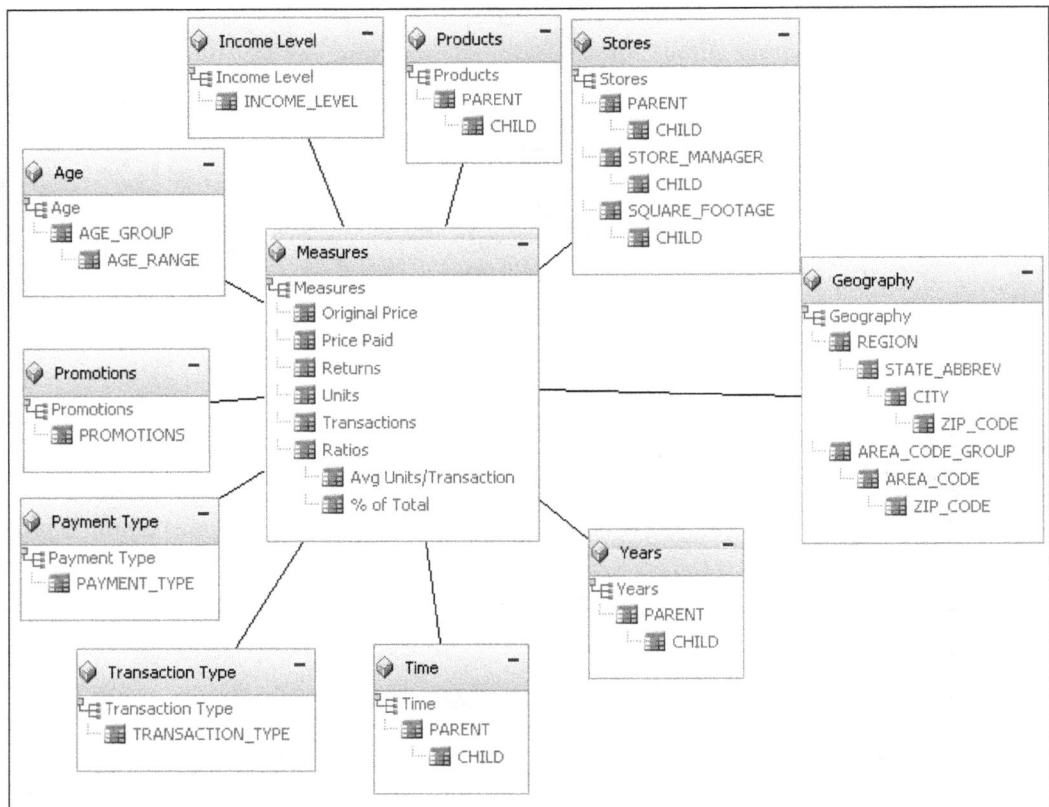

How it works...

In this recipe, we built a Cube Schema and Essbase Model for the ASOsamp data source. As you can see, we don't always have to specify Key Bindings when building a Cube Schema. The reason for having to specify Key Bindings, in the *Developing Cube Schema and Essbase model* recipe in *Chapter 3*, was that we were using a Calendar hierarchy and had to bind this hierarchy to our fact table. We also discussed how the order of the hierarchies in the ASO model is not as relevant as in the BSO model, because the dense and sparse dimension settings do not apply.

Understanding Essbase Model properties for the ASO cube

In this recipe, we will set up the Essbase properties for the ASOsamp Essbase Model. In the *Building a Measures dimension from the fact table* recipe in this chapter, we saw that Measure dimensions had several properties that we needed to set as this hierarchy was created using the fact table in Essbase Studio. In addition, we need to set dimensions properties for each hierarchy using properties that are exclusive to the ASO model.

Getting ready

To get started with Essbase Studio, click on the **Start** menu and **Programs | Oracle EPM System | Essbase | Essbase Studio | Essbase Studio Console**. Use the login menu to enter your server, username, and password, and click on the **Log In** button.

How to do it...

1. Right-click on the **ASOsamp** folder in your **Metadata Navigator**. Drill down on the **CUBE_SCHEMA** folder, right-click on **ASOsampModel Essbase Model**, and select **Essbase Properties**.

2. Click on the **ASOsampModel** root in the **General** tab and select the **ASO storage model** checkbox.

3. The **Adjustments to ASO Model** dialog box will let you know that the Measures dimension has been set as the compression dimension. The dialog also shows that there is no dimension set as accounts. Click on **Close**.

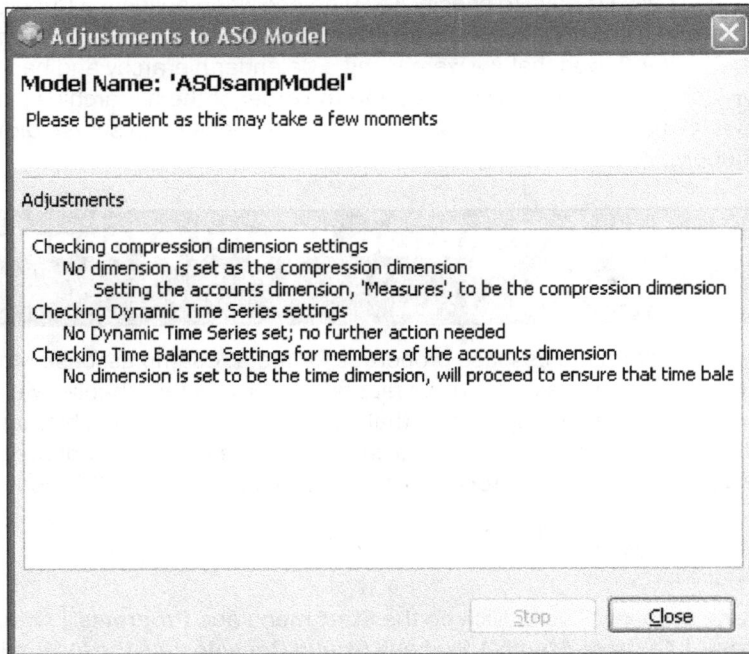

4. Click on the **Years** hierarchy, select the **Outline Build** tab, and select the **Dynamic at dimension level** radio button. Repeat the same step for the `Time` and `Period` hierarchies.

5. Click on the **Product** hierarchy, select the **Outline Build** tab, and select the **Multiple-hierarchy enabled** level radio button.

6. Drill down on the **Time** dimension, select the **PARENT** metadata element, click on the **Info** tab, and select **External Source**; choose **ASO_STORAGE** from the drop-down list under the **ASO Storage Option** section.

7. Select the **Original Price** element under the **Measures** dimension, and then click on **+** in the **Info** tab. Repeat the same step for **Price Paid**, **Returns**, **Unit**, **Transaction**, **Avg Units/Transaction**, and **% of Total**.

8. Click on **Ratio** and select the **~** Ignoret consolidation to not consolidate the member. Click on the **Ratios** member and select the **Dynamic** radio button under the **Aggregate Storage Options** section.

9. Click on the **Avg Units/Transaction** measure, select the **Formula** tab, and enter `[Units]/[Transactions]`. Click on **% of Total** measure, select the **Formula** tab, and enter the following formula. This formula references multiple dimensions and may cause problems at deployment time if the dimensions it references are not complete: `Transactions/(Transactions,Time,[Transaction Type],[Payment Type],Promotions,Age,[Income Level],Products, Stores,Geography)`.

How it works...

In this recipe, we specified that we were working with an ASO storage model in the `General` tab. Essbase Model Properties then validated the property choices to make sure that they did not violate rules of the ASO model. We then used the `Outline Build` tab to specify what hierarchy type we wanted to use for each of the dimensions. Your choices in the `Outline Build` tab are stored at dimension level, Dynamic at dimension level, and Multiple Hierarchy Enabled at dimension level. The following table defines these hierarchy storage settings:

HIERARCHY	DESCRIPTION
Stored Hierarchy	Members of stored hierarchies are obviously stored when aggregated according to the outline structure.
Dynamic Hierarchy	Essbase calculates members at the retrieval time. The order that a formula is evaluated is defined by the member's solve order.
Multiple Hierarchy Enabled	The Dimension with Multiple Hierarchy Enabled can have alternate hierarchies with both stored and dynamic rollups.

You may have also noticed that the Measures dimension is automatically set as the Account dimension and Dynamic at dimension level. The Account dimension is by default the compression dimension and the compression dimension is always set to Dynamic at the dimension level. You will see this in the `Outline Build` tab. You will need to choose a compression dimension that increases compression while decreasing retrieval time. The `Account` dimension is normally the best choice, but this may not always be the case. Finally, we set up the consolidations for the Measures dimension and define the MDX formulas for the Avg Units/Transaction and % of Total ratios.

There's more...

▸ There are external Formulas, Consolidation, Solve Order, and Alias Sets that need to be set or assigned to the ASOsamp cube if you want to complete all the Essbase properties.

[
When deploying the ASOsamp application, you should consider deploying the outline metadata first without specifying the External Source formulas or Measures formulas covered in this recipe first. The formulas may cause errors due to the fact that the dimensions being referenced may not be completed.
]

See also

▶ Review the recipes *Setting Essbase properties* and *Creating Alias tables* in *Chapter 3* if you want to learn how to set the additional properties and create an alias set for the ASOsamp cube.

Designing a drill-through report

In this recipe, we will build a drill-through report using Essbase Studio. There are times when a user may require more information on what makes up a number while conducting analysis in Essbase. Drill-through reporting allows the user to select the intersection that contains the data in question and drill into the relational data. This functionality has historically been handled via **Essbase Integration Services** (**EIS**) and this development tool is still used for this purpose in the field. That said, Essbase Studio will have parity with EIS, as per Oracle's road map in the near future. Please visit the following URL for more information on the Oracle Essbase Road Map: http://communities.ioug.org/Portals/2/Oracle_Essbase_ Roadmap_Sep_09.pdf

Getting ready

To get started with Essbase Studio, click on the **Start** menu and **Programs | Oracle EPM System | Essbase | Essbase Studio | Essbase Studio Console**. Use the login menu to enter your server, username, and password, and click on the **Log In** button.

How to do it...

1. Right-click on the **ASOsamp** folder in your **Metadata Navigator**, select **New** and then **Folder**, and type DRILL_THROUGH_REPORTS.

2. Right-click on the **DRILL_THROUGH_REPORTS** folder, click on **New**, then **Drill-through report**. Type in **ASO_Report** in the **Name** textbox, click on the **Add** button, and select **Measures** hierarchy. Repeat the same steps of "adding" for the Years and Transaction type hierarchies.

3. Unselect the **PARENT** metadata element in the **Years** hierarchy. Your screen should look like the following screenshot:

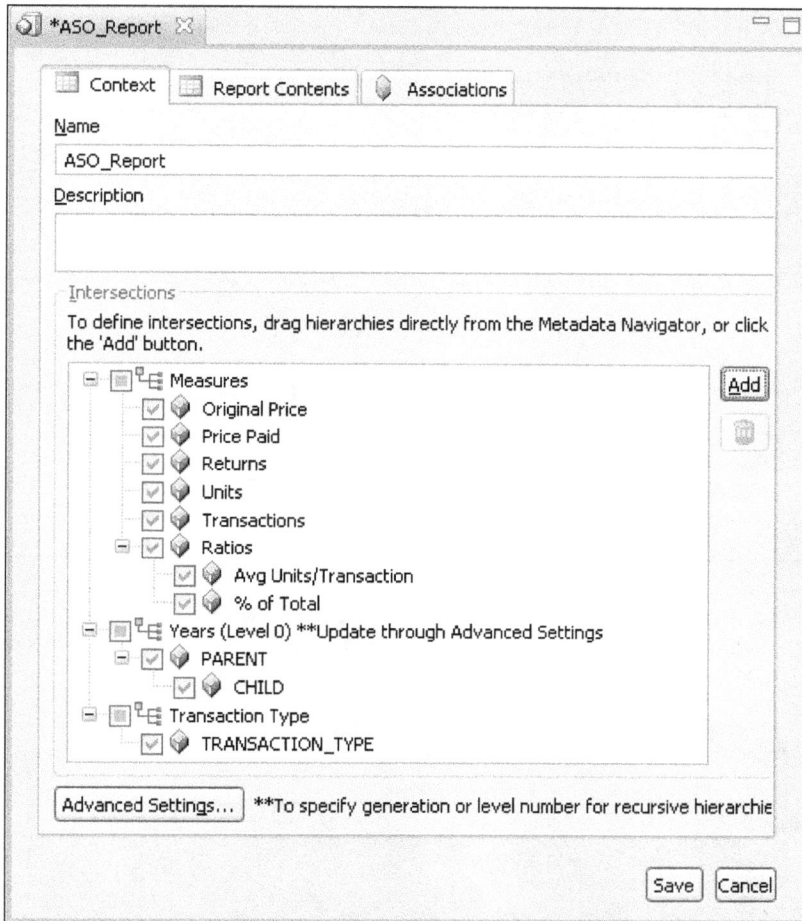

4. Click on the **Report Contents** tab. Click on **Add**, select the **CHILD** metadata element from the **YEARS** folder under **ASOsamp**, click on the **Display Name** cell, and change the value to **YEAR**.

5. Click on the **Add** button and select **Transaction Type** from the **Transaction Type** folder.

6. Click on the **Add** button, open **ASOsamp**, select **Original Price**, press the *Shift* key, select **Transactions**, and click on the **OK** button.

7. Click on the **Sort Order** cell next to YEAR and select **ASC**. Repeat the last step for the **TRANSACTION_TYPE**'s **Sort Order**. Your screen will look like the following screenshot:

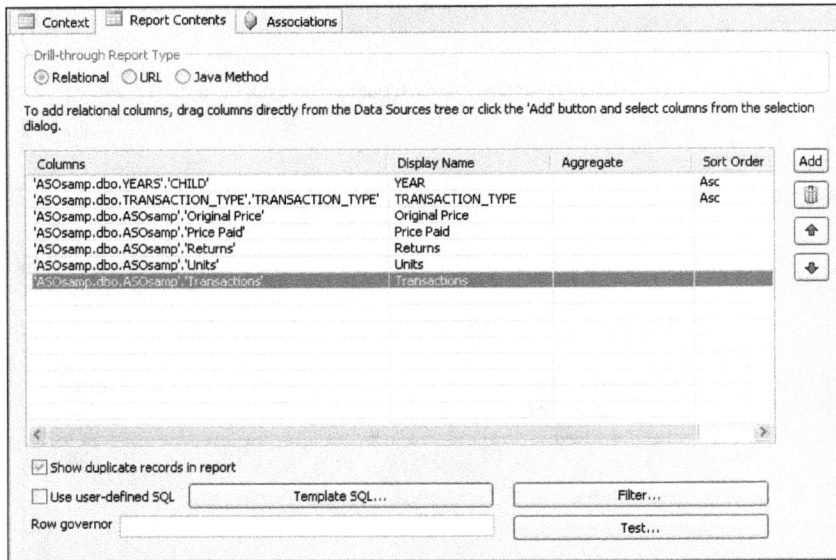

8. Click on the **Test...** button and type `Sale` in **Transaction Type Column Value**. Click on the **Column Value** next to **CHILD**. Enter **Curr Year**, and click on the **Show Results** button. Your screen will look like the following screenshot:

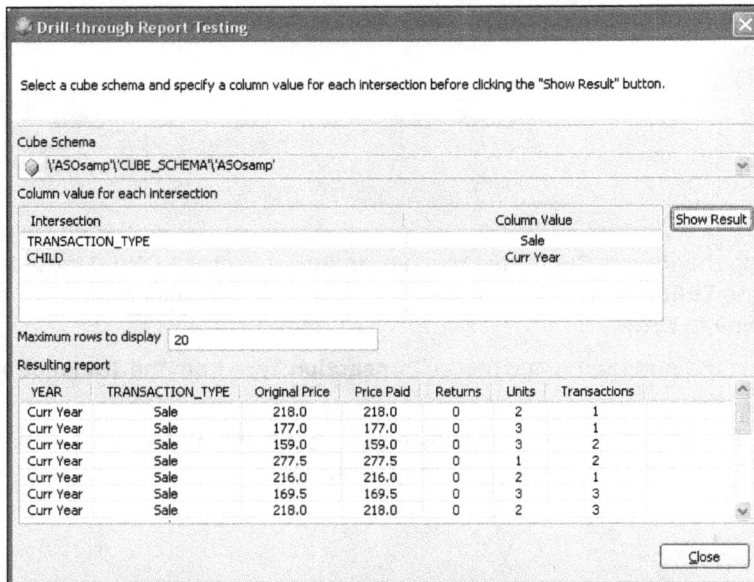

9. Click on the **Close** button and select the **Use user-defined SQL** checkbox.

10. Select the **Template SQL...** button in the **Template SQL** dialog box and click on the **Get Standard SQL** button to see the SQL statement. You can use this screen to modify system-generated SQL statements. Click on the **Cancel** button, and uncheck the **Use user-defined SQL** checkbox. Your screen should look as follows in the Template SQL dialog box:

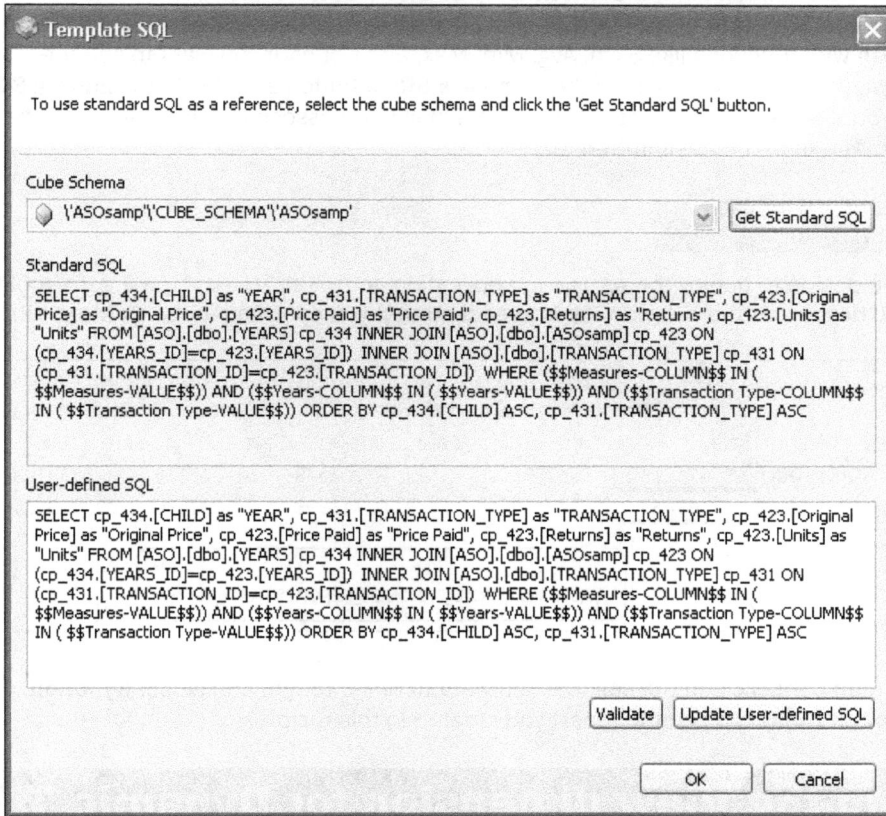

Template SQL

To use standard SQL as a reference, select the cube schema and click the 'Get Standard SQL' button.

Cube Schema

\'ASOsamp'\'CUBE_SCHEMA'\'ASOsamp'   [Get Standard SQL]

Standard SQL

```
SELECT cp_434.[CHILD] as "YEAR", cp_431.[TRANSACTION_TYPE] as "TRANSACTION_TYPE", cp_423.[Original
Price] as "Original Price", cp_423.[Price Paid] as "Price Paid", cp_423.[Returns] as "Returns", cp_423.[Units] as
"Units" FROM [ASO].[dbo].[YEARS] cp_434 INNER JOIN [ASO].[dbo].[ASOsamp] cp_423 ON
(cp_434.[YEARS_ID]=cp_423.[YEARS_ID]) INNER JOIN [ASO].[dbo].[TRANSACTION_TYPE] cp_431 ON
(cp_431.[TRANSACTION_ID]=cp_423.[TRANSACTION_ID]) WHERE ($$Measures-COLUMN$$ IN (
$$Measures-VALUE$$)) AND ($$Years-COLUMN$$ IN ( $$Years-VALUE$$)) AND ($$Transaction Type-COLUMN$$
IN ( $$Transaction Type-VALUE$$)) ORDER BY cp_434.[CHILD] ASC, cp_431.[TRANSACTION_TYPE] ASC
```

User-defined SQL

```
SELECT cp_434.[CHILD] as "YEAR", cp_431.[TRANSACTION_TYPE] as "TRANSACTION_TYPE", cp_423.[Original
Price] as "Original Price", cp_423.[Price Paid] as "Price Paid", cp_423.[Returns] as "Returns", cp_423.[Units] as
"Units" FROM [ASO].[dbo].[YEARS] cp_434 INNER JOIN [ASO].[dbo].[ASOsamp] cp_423 ON
(cp_434.[YEARS_ID]=cp_423.[YEARS_ID]) INNER JOIN [ASO].[dbo].[TRANSACTION_TYPE] cp_431 ON
(cp_431.[TRANSACTION_ID]=cp_423.[TRANSACTION_ID]) WHERE ($$Measures-COLUMN$$ IN (
$$Measures-VALUE$$)) AND ($$Years-COLUMN$$ IN ( $$Years-VALUE$$)) AND ($$Transaction Type-COLUMN$$
IN ( $$Transaction Type-VALUE$$)) ORDER BY cp_434.[CHILD] ASC, cp_431.[TRANSACTION_TYPE] ASC
```

[Validate] [Update User-defined SQL]

[OK] [Cancel]

11. Click on the **Association** tab, select the **ASOsampModel**, and click on the **Save** button.

How it works

If you are familiar with how SQL works, then the steps that are about to be described should be easier to understand. In the **Context** tab of the Drill-Through Report dialog, we specified the intersection where you can drill-through using the report. This is almost like specifying the Where clause in a SQL statement. We specified the columns that users will see when they conduct the drill through in the **Content** tab. You also created the Order by and Select clauses of the SQL statement. The Group by clause can be determined by using the column **Aggregate** with functions like Sum, Avg, Min, Max, and Count. If you want to see the SQL statement, then you could click on the **Template SQL...** button and the **Get Standard SQL** button. You were also able to test your report. Finally, you associated the query with the **ASOsampModel** in the **Association** tab.

There's more

When you decide to deploy the ASOsamp application, in Smart View you will get a tool tip when you hover over the cell with the intersection that you specified in the **Context** tab.

	A	B	C	D	E	F	G
1		Original Price	Price Paid	Returns	Units	Transactions	Ratios
2		Sale	Sale	Sale	Sale	Sale	Sale
3	Curr Year	35821213.25	35579920.48	0	204678	216376	0.945936703
4	Prev Year	69083459.25	68473545.67	0	413993	401230	1.031809685
5							
6			Drill Through:				
7			\'ASOsamp'\'DRILL_THROUGH_REPORTS'\'ASO_Report'				

You can then right-click on the cell that you want to drill-through, and select **Hyperion**, and **Drill-Through Report** to see the report you created in this recipe.

Using the View dimension for Dynamic Time Series reporting

In this recipe, we will be using a View dimension called Period to conduct effective **Dynamic Time Series reporting** in the ASO cube. Dynamic Time Series is a functionality that is out-of-the-box with the BSO model and is used to retrieve, for example, your period-to-date, quarter-to-date, and year-to-date values.

Getting ready

To get started with **Smart View**, open a new Excel workbook, click on the **Smart View** tab, click on the **Open** button, log in to your Essbase Server, right-click on the ASOsamp cube, and select **Ad hoc analysis**.

How to do it...

1. Drag-and-drop the **Measures** to the rows in your Excel spreadsheet from your **POV** menu.

2. Drag-and-drop the **Years**, **Time**, **Period**, and **Transaction Type** dimensions from your **POV** to the columns in your Excel sheet. Layout your cross tab report as shown in the following screenshot:

	A	B	C	D	E	F	G	H	I
1		Curr Year	Curr Year	Curr Year	Curr Year	Curr Year	Curr Year	Curr Year	Curr Year
2		Per	Per	Per	Per	Per	Per	Q-T-D	Y-T-D
3		Jan	Feb	Mar	Qtr1	Apr	May	May	May
4		Sale	Sale	Sale	Sale	Sale	Sale	Sale	Sale
5	Original Price	7080780.75	3347300.25	5296496.5	15724577.5	3438830.5	6985555.25	10424385.75	26148963.25
6	Price Paid	7061055.74	3292406.39	5279595.96	15633058.09	3428968.54	6877279.53	10306248.07	25939306.16
7	Returns	0	0	0	0	0	0	0	0
8	Units	39718	19670	29530	88918	20010	39461	59471	148389
9	Transactions	41932	20766	31578	94276	21154	41796	62950	157226
10	Ratios	0.947200229	0.94722142	0.935144721	0.943166872	0.945920393	0.94413341	1.890053803	4.719620173

3. Click on the **Refresh** button on your **POV** to retrieve your data.

How it works

The grid you created in the preceding section has **Per** in range **B2:G2**. Per is the only stored member of the View dimension and shows the data as stored or aggregated by other dimensions. In column H, we are using the Q-T-D time series member to retrieve the quarter-to-date for May, in this case. In column **H**, you can see the sum of **Apr** and **May** or column **F** and **G** as this is the quarter-to-date calculation. In column I, we are using Y-T-D time series member to retrieve the year-to-date for May, the Time dimension member you selected. This formula returns the sum of **Jan** through **May**.

These are the MDX formulae for Q-T-D and Y-T-D, respectively. We will go over MDX in more detail when we discuss ASO outline formula, but this is what MDX is doing in general. The PeriodsToDate function is used to sum the current member of the Time dimension with respect to generation 4, the quarters, for the Q-T-D time series member.

In the Y-T-D time series member's case we will sum the current member of the Time dimension with respect to generation 1, the top member of the Time dimension.

The following is the MDX formula for the Q-T-D (quarter-to-date) member in the **Period** dimension:

```
Q-T-D = SUM( PeriodsToDate( [Time].Generations(4),
[Time].CurrentMember ), [Period].[Per] )
```

The following is the MDX formula for the Y-T-D (year-to-date) member in the **Period** dimension:

```
Y-T-D = SUM( PeriodsToDate( [Time].Generations(1),
[Time].CurrentMember ), [Period].[Per] )
```

> The View or Time Series dimension is a technique published by a gentleman called Gary Crisci. His work was published in a document titled *Leveraging Analytic Dimension in an Essbase Aggregate Storage Model with MDX*. This document is included with this chapter in the `caat_presenters_upd.pdf`. In this document he discusses how to use MDX to overcome the Dynamic Time Series limitations of the ASO model and, among other things, how to conduct time balance reporting using the View dimension. Mr. Crisci also has a blog where he discusses similar topics: `http://garycris.blogspot.com/`

5
Using EAS for Development

In this chapter, we will cover the following topics:

- ▸ Adding an application and database on an Essbase server
- ▸ Using the outline editor to add dimensions
- ▸ Using dimension build rules to add parent-child dimensions
- ▸ Creating dimension build rules to add a base and attribute dimensions
- ▸ Using dimension build rules to add parents to attribute dimensions
- ▸ Creating load rules for flat file data loads
- ▸ Creating substitution variables
- ▸ Using If/Else logic and substitution variables in outline formulas
- ▸ Using Text measures on a BSO cube
- ▸ Using Date measures on a BSO cube
- ▸ Using different outline formula logic at the parent level
- ▸ Creating a load rule for SQL data load using substitution variables
- ▸ Using MDX in aggregate storage applications

Introduction

In this chapter, the first recipe *Adding an application and database on an Essbase server* is used to build the outline from a `Basic.otl` outline file, which is included in this book. This recipe is important as the `Sample Basic` database is used in the next five chapters. In the following five recipes, we will build and load the `Sample Basic` database using the **Outline Editor** and **dimension build rules**. Moreover, we will also discuss more intermediate topics such as creating and using substitution variables, applying If/Else logic, and creating Text and Date measures to name a few. In addition, we will touch on the more advanced topics of creating **SQL load rules**. Finally, we will build an `Aggregate Storage` database from a `Sample.otl` file and apply some MDX outline formula. You might be asking yourself, based on the first four chapters, why use **Essbase Administrative Service** (**EAS**) to develop Essbase databases? The most important reason is that it is the most matured development tool for developing Essbase databases. You will find in the next four chapters that there are functions and editors in EAS that have yet to be integrated into **Essbase Studio** or **Essbase Integration Sevice** (**EIS**) as of version 11.1.2.x.

Adding an application and database on an Essbase Server

In this recipe, we will be adding an application and database using EAS. We will also replace the outline file with a completed outline, populate the database with data, and run the default calculation. In addition, we will discuss some of the objects created when you add a BSO application and database.

Getting ready

To get started, click on the **Start** menu and navigate to **Programs | Oracle EPM System | Essbase | Essbase Administration Services | Start Administration Services Console**. In the Log in menu, enter your Administration Server, Username, Password, and click on the **Log in** button.

How to do it...

1. In EAS, drill down on the **Essbase Servers** node, and expand on your **EssbaseCluster-1 or your Essbase Server**.

2. Right-click on **Applications**, select **Create application**, click on **Using block storage**, enter `Sample` in the **Application name** textbox, and then click on the **OK** button, as shown in the following screenshot:

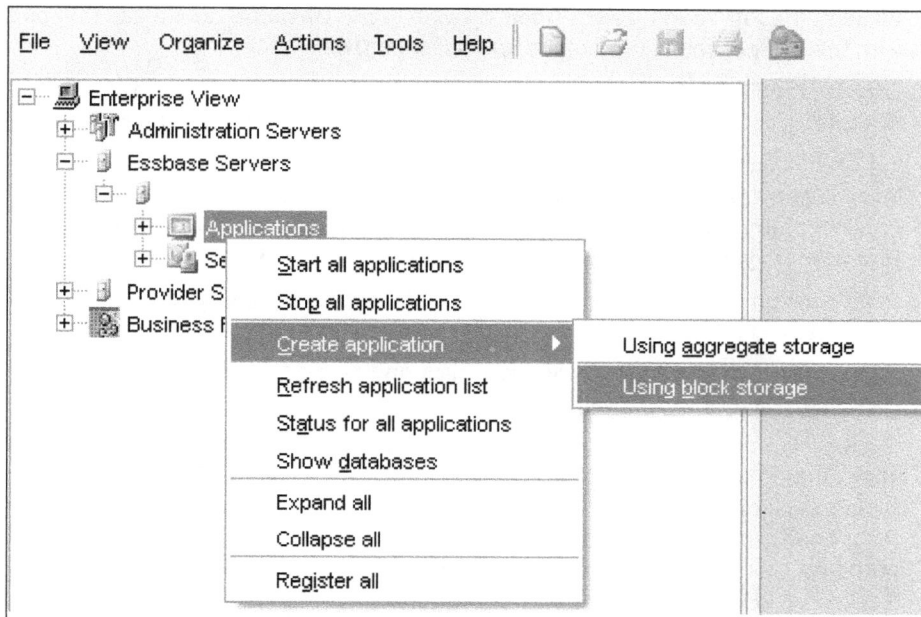

3. Right-click on the **Sample** application, select **Create Database**, enter `Basic` in the **Database name** textbox, and then click on the **OK** button. In this window, you can also choose to **Allow duplicate member names** and set the **Database type** to **Normal** or **Currency**. Leave the **Database Type** as **Normal** and do not select **Allow Duplicate Member Names**, as shown in the following screenshot:

4. Click on the **File** menu, select **Open**, browse to the **Basic.otl** outline file that comes with this recipe, select the outline, and click on **OK**.

5. Click on the **File** menu, select **Save As**, click on the **Essbase Server tab**, click on the **Sample** application, and click on the **Basic** database. Select the **Basic.otl** file and then click on **OK**.

6. You will see a pop-up asking if you want to replace the existing file. Click on **Yes**. Another prompt will open asking you, **The outline has been saved to the new location. Do you want to open it?** Click on **Yes**.

7. Right-click on the **Sample** application, click on **Stop**, select **Application**, and click **Yes**.

8. Right-click on the **Sample** application, click on **Start**, select **Application**, and click **Yes**.

9. Right-click on the **Basic** database and select **Load data**. In the **Data Load** menu, click on the **Find Data File** button; select the **BasicExport.txt** file included in this recipe, click on the **OK** button in the menu, and then click on the **OK** button in the **Data Load** menu. If you have problems loading this file, then place it in the following path and try again: `..\Oracle\Middleware\user_projects\epmsystem1\ EssbaseServer\essbaseserver1\app\Sample\Basic`

10. Right-click on the **Basic** application, click on **Execute calculation**, select **(Default)**, and then click on **OK**.

How it works...

In this recipe, we created a BSO application and database. We replaced the existing outline with the `Basic.otl` file that is already populated with dimensions. In addition, we stopped and started the application as a best practice as there are times that the outline does not override the existing one immediately if you are using the file system to make changes. Moreover, we loaded the data for the `Basic` database using an export file called `BasicExtract.txt` without a load rule. Finally, we ran the default calculation to aggregate the data in the cube. The following are a few things to keep in mind when creating an application or database in Essbase:

- Essbase application and database names must be less than eight characters

- Do not use spaces, tabs, or the following characters in the application or database names: {* [] : ; , = > < . + ? ' / \ |}

- In a `Block Storage` database, you can only have one application, but each application can have multiple databases

- In an `Aggregate Storage` database, you can only have one application and database

- Multiple databases in one application may cause problems when applying a security filter

If you open the `. .\Oracle\Middleware\user_projects\epmsystem1\`
`EssbaseServer\essbaseserver1\app\Sample\Basic` path in version 11.1.2.1, you will
see that objects were created, as shown in the following screenshot:

Name ▲	Size	Type	Date Modified
trig		File Folder	5/18/2011 11:02 AM
Basic	1 KB	Data Base File	5/18/2011 11:16 AM
Basic.dbb	1 KB	DBB File	5/18/2011 11:15 AM
Basic.esm	2 KB	ESM File	5/18/2011 11:19 AM
Basic.ind	1 KB	IND File	5/18/2011 11:05 AM
Basic.otl	10 KB	OTL File	5/18/2011 11:03 AM
Basic.tct	1 KB	TCT File	5/18/2011 11:19 AM
ess00001.ind	8,024 KB	IND File	5/18/2011 11:19 AM
ess00001.pag	825 KB	PAG File	5/18/2011 11:19 AM

The following graph shows the description of the files created as per the *Oracle Essbase
Database Administrator's Guide*:

File Extension	Description
db	Database file, defining the name, location, and other database settings
dbb	Backup of database file
esm	Essbase kernel file that manages pointers to data blocks and contains control information used for database recovery
ind	Essbase index file
otl	Essbase outline file
pag	Essbase database data (page) file
tct	Essbase database transaction control file that manages all commits of data, and follows and maintains all transactions

Using the outline editor to add dimensions

In this recipe, we will be adding a new application and database to our Essbase Server. We
will use the Outline Editor to add the `Year` and `Scenario` dimensions to our outline. In
addition, we will set up our `Year` dimension as our `Time` dimension and add time-series
functionality to our database. We will also add two calculated members in the `Scenario`
dimension to take advantage of Essbase's variance reporting functionality. This recipe is the
first of five recipes used to build and load the `Sample Basic` database.

Getting ready

To get started, click on your **Start** menu and navigate to **Programs | Oracle EPM System | Essbase | Essbase Administration Services | Start Administration Services Console**. In the Log in menu, enter your Administration Server, Username, Password, and click on the **Log in** button.

How to do it...

1. In EAS, drill down on the **Essbase Servers** node, expand on your **Essbase Server**, right-click on **Applications**, select **Create application**, click on **Using block storage**, enter **Sample** in the **Application name** textbox, and click on the **OK** button.

2. Right-click on the **Sample** application, select **Create Database**, enter **Basic** in the **Database name** textbox, and click on the **OK** button.

3. Drill down on the **Sample** application and Basic database, right-click on the **Outline**, and click on **Edit**.

4. Right-click on the **Outline: Basic** node in the **Outline Editor**, select the **Add a child to the selected member button**, enter **Year**, press the *Enter* key, and then press *Esc*.

5. Click on the **Year** dimension, then on the **Time Dimension Type** button ; click the **Add a child to the selected member** button, enter Qtr1, press the *Enter* key, and then press *Esc*. This step sets up the Year dimension as the Time dimension.

6. Select the **Qtr1** member and click on the **Dynamic Calc Member** button. Repeat the same step for the **Year** member.

7. Click on the **Qtr1** member, select the **Add a child to the selected member** button, enter **Jan**, press the *Enter* key, and then press *Esc*.

8. Select member **Jan**, click on the **Add a sibling to the selected member** button, enter **Feb**, press the *Enter* key, and then press *Esc*. Repeat steps 5 through 8 for the remaining Year dimension members as shown in the following table:

PARENT	CHILD	STORAGE
Qtr1	Mar	Stored
Year	Qtr2	Dynamic Calc
Qtr2	Apr	Stored
Qtr2	May	Stored
Qtr2	Jun	Stored
Year	Qtr3	Dynamic Calc
Qtr3	Jul	Stored
Qtr3	Aug	Stored
Qtr3	Sep	Stored

PARENT	CHILD	STORAGE
Year	Qtr4	Dynamic Calc
Qtr4	Oct	Stored
Qtr4	Nov	Stored
Qtr4	Dec	Stored

9. Right-click on the **Year** dimension, select **Dynamic Time Series** in the **Define Dynamic Time Series Member** menu, enable **H-T-D**, and select **Gen 1**.

10. Enable **Q-T-D**, select **Gen 2**, and click on **OK**. Your **Define Dynamic Time Series Member** menu should look like the following screenshot:

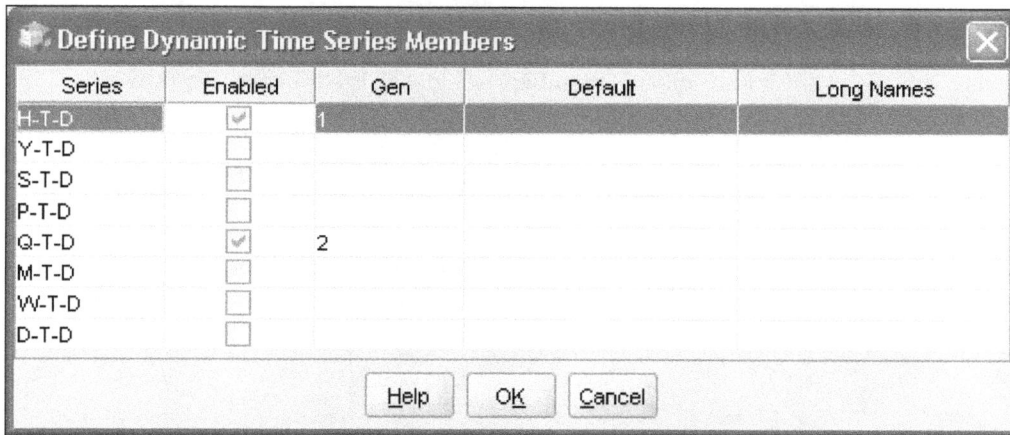

11. Click on the **Year** dimension, select the **Add a sibling to the selected member** button, enter Scenario, press the *Enter* key, and then *Esc*.

12. Click on the **Scenario** dimension and click on the **Label Only** button.

13. Click on the **Add a child to the selected member** button, enter Actual, and press the *Enter* key.

14. Enter Budget and press the *Enter* key.

15. Enter Variance and press the *Enter* key.

16. Enter Variance %, press the *Enter* key, and then press *Esc*.

17. Click on the **Budget** scenario and click on the **Exclude from Consolidation** or the tilde button.

18. Right-click on the **Variance** scenario, click on **Edit Member Properties** in the **Information** tab, and change the **Two Pass Calculation** setting to **True**.

19. Change the **Consolidation** setting to (**~**) **Ignore**.

20. Change the **DataStorage** setting to **Dynamic Calc**.

21. Select the **Formula** tab and enter formula @VAR (Actual, Budget) ;. Repeat steps 18 through 21 for the **Variance %** scenario, but change the formula to @ VARPER (Actual, Budget) ;.

22. Click on the **Verify** button and then on the **Save** button.

How it works...

In this recipe, we started by creating the Sample Basic database and adding a Year dimension to its outline. We made the Year dimension our Time dimension, which means that this will be the dimension used for Time Balance and Dynamic Time Series reporting. We modified the Dynamic Time Series options in the **Define Dynamic Time Series Member** menu by enabling H-T-D (history-to-date) and Q-T-D (Quarter-to-Date) and associated the H-T-D to generation 1 and Q-T-D to generation 2. These options allow us to see period-to-date calculation dynamically by using H-T-D (Apr) and Q-T-D (Feb), in Smart View for example. The results of these dynamically calculated members would look like the following table:

Member	Payroll
Jan	4056
Feb	4056
Mar	4056
Apr	4081
Q-T-D(Feb)	8112
H-T-D(Apr)	16249

The Q-T-D (Feb) dynamically calculated function returns the sum of Jan and Feb. The H-T-D (Apr) dynamically calculated function returns the sum of Jan, Feb, Mar, and Apr.

In addition, we added a Scenario dimension with two stored scenarios and two dynamically calculated members. The @VAR and @VARPER functions in the Scenario dimension are used in conjunction with the variance reporting function in our Measures dimension to make sure that when an Account is marked as Expense, the value that is returned is negative if the Actual amount is greater than the Budget amount. A negative number would bring attention to the fact that Expense was higher than the Budget amount. Here are a few pointers that you should consider when building a Block Storage outline manually:

1. Do not have any Dynamic Calc values rolled up to stored value. This will slow down calculations as Essbase has to calculate the Dynamic Calc member every time for the Stored member parent.

2. When you have an implied share (a situation where only one member rolls up to one parent) make sure to tag the parent as Never Share.

3. The `Time` and `Account` dimensions are by default set as `Dense` dimension because these are normally the most likely to have data for each combination of dimensions. You will need to verify that this is the case after you load data.

4. Use the consolidation properties and outline to conduct calculation when possible, in contrast to using calculation scripts or the member formula.

5. Make sure you lay out your dimensions in an hourglass shape to ensure good calculation performance. This is a good practice but you still need to analyze your database performance when you load data and make adjustments for calculation and data retrieval performance.

6. Avoid placing dimensions in your database that do not apply to the subject area as a whole. A distributed approach, with a separate database per subject area, makes for a more intuitive user experience. It will increase the speed of your reporting, decrease security overhead, and will provide a marginal increase in maintenance.

7. Setting all the parent's storage as `Dynamic Calc` or `Label only` in your `Dense` dimension and storing it in your `Sparse` dimension gives us the flexibility of only having to aggregate the `Sparse` dimension, which normally takes less time to complete.

Using dimension build rules to add the parent-child dimension

In this recipe, we will set up a dimension build rule to modify the outline of the `Sample Basic` database. This recipe will be using the parent-child reference to build our `Measures` dimension.

Getting ready

To get started, click on your **Start** menu and navigate to **Programs | Oracle EPM System | Essbase | Essbase Administration Services | Start Administration Services Console**. In the Log in menu, enter your Administration Server, Username, Password, and click on the **Log in** button.

How to do it...

1. Open a new Excel workbook.

2. Enter the values as shown in the following table, and save them as tab delimited on your `Sample Basic` database directory for ease of use with the name `Measures.txt`. The URL for the `Sample Basic` database is as follows for version 11.1.2.x:

   ```
   ..\ Oracle\Middleware\user_projects\epmsystem1\
       EssbaseServer\essbaseserver1\app\Sample\Basic.
   ```

3. This table has all the members and properties you need for the `Measures` dimension in a parent child format:

Parent	Child	Measures_Alias	Properties	Formula
Measures	Profit		+X	
Profit	Margin		+X	
Margin	Sales		+	
Margin	COGS	Cost of Goods Sold	-E	
Profit	Total Expenses		-XE	
Total Expenses	Marketing		+E	
Total Expenses	Payroll		+E	
Total Expenses	Misc	Miscellaneous	+E	
Measures	Inventory		~O	
Inventory	Opening Inventory		+EF	
Inventory	Additions		~E	
Inventory	Ending Inventory		~EL	
Measures	Ratios		~O	
Ratios	Margin %		+TX	Margin % Sales;
Ratios	Profit %		~TX	Profit % Sales;
Ratios	Profit per Ounce		~TX	

4. In EAS, drill down on **EssbaseCluster-1 | Applications | Sample | Basic**, right-click on **Outline,** and click on **Edit**.

5. Right-click on the **Outline: Basic** node. In the **Outline Editor**, select the **Add a child to the selected member** button, enter **Year**, and press the *Enter* key. Choose the **Year** dimension instead of the **Outline: Basic** node. If you have already built it in the preceding recipe, in the **Outline Editor**, select the **Add a child to the selected member** button, enter `Measures`, press the *Enter* key, and then press *Esc*.

6. Click on the **Measures** dimension, click on the **Account Dimension Type** button, and click on **Save**.

7. Under the **Basic** database, right-click on **Rules Files**, and click on **Create Rules Files**.

8. Click on **File**, select **Open data files**, click on the **Essbase Server** tab, select **Measures.txt**, and click on **OK**.

9. Click on **Field1**, select the **Field** menu, and click on **Properties**.

10. Click on the **Dimension Build Properties** tab and double-click on **Measures** under dimension.

11. Double-click on **Parent** under **Field | Type**, and click on the **Next** (**>>**) button.

12. Double-click on **Measures** under **Dimension**.

13. Double-click on **Child** under **Field | Type**, and click on the **Next** (**>>**) button. The last five steps set up the recursive or parent relationship between **Field1** and **Field2**.

14. Double-click on **Measures** under **Dimension**.

15. Double-click on **Alias** under **Field | Type**, and click on the **Next** (**>>**) button to select the alias field for your measure.

16. Double-click on **Measures** under **Dimension**.

17. Double-click on **Property** under **File | Type** to set the properties, and click on the **Next** (**>>**) button. If you lose your place while conducting these steps, then you can drag the **Field Properties** menu to the side to see the value in the grid behind it.

18. Double-click the **Measures** under **Dimension**.

19. Double-click on **Formula** under **File | Type** to set the **Formula** property. Click on the **Next** (**>>**) button, and click on **OK**.

20. Click on the **Dimension Build** button in the **Data Prep Editor** to set the rule as a dimension build.

21. Click on the **Data Source Properties** button, select the **Header** tab, and enter the value **1** for **Number of lines to skip**. Click on **OK**. You can hover over the buttons to view the **Data Source Properties** tooltip, as shown in the following screenshot:

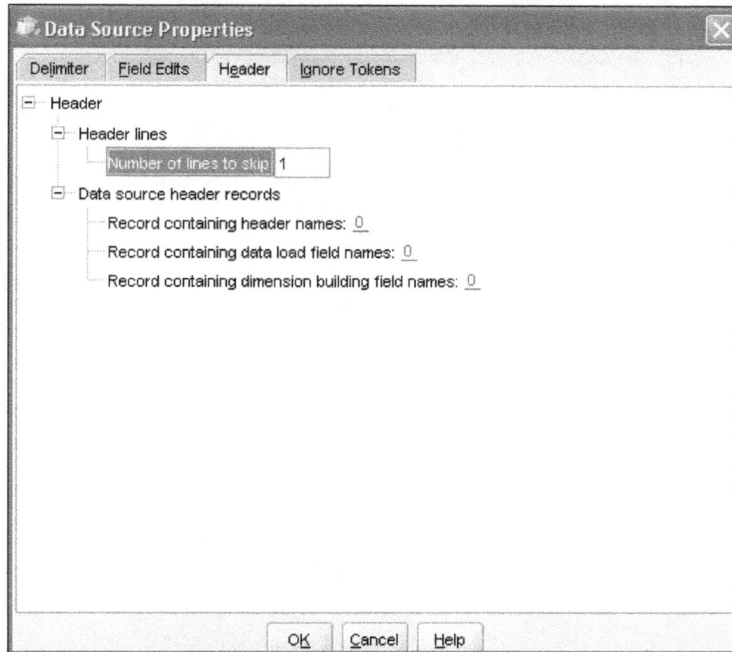

22. Click on the **Dimension Build Setting** button [icon] and select the **Dimension Build Settings** tab.

23. Double-click on **Measures**, select **Allow Properties Changes**, select **Allow Properties Formula Changes** under **Existing members**, click on **Use parent/child reference** under **Build method**, and click on **OK**.

24. Click on the **Validate** button, click on **File**, select **Save**, type **Measures** for the dimension build rule name, and click on **OK**.

25. Right-click on the **Basic** database, and click on **Load data**; under **Mode** select **Build only**, click on the **Find Data File** button, select the **Essbase Server** tab, click on **Measures**, and then click on **OK**.

26. Click on the **Find Rules File** button, click on **Measures.rul**, and then click on **OK** on the menu and the **Data Load** menu to execute the load rule. You will get a dialog letting you know the status of the load rule after it runs.

How it works...

In this recipe, we created a dimension build rule to add the hierarchy of the Measures dimension in parent-child reference, the alias, all properties, and a set of formulas. Your Measures dimension should look like the following image:

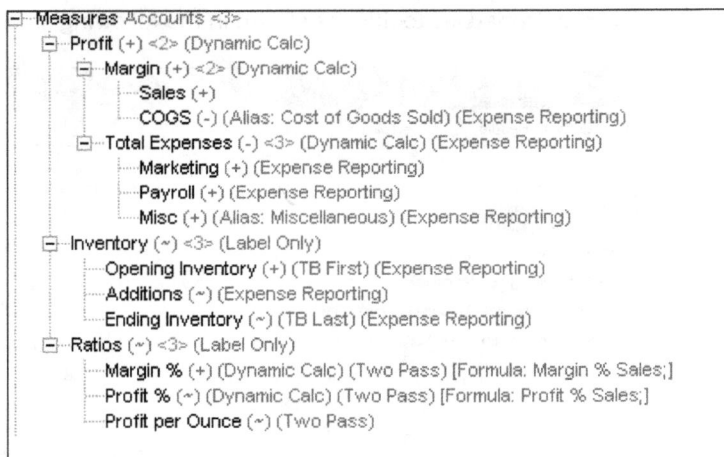

```
Measures Accounts <3>
    Profit (+) <2> (Dynamic Calc)
        Margin (+) <2> (Dynamic Calc)
            Sales (+)
            COGS (-) (Alias: Cost of Goods Sold) (Expense Reporting)
        Total Expenses (-) <3> (Dynamic Calc) (Expense Reporting)
            Marketing (+) (Expense Reporting)
            Payroll (+) (Expense Reporting)
            Misc (+) (Alias: Miscellaneous) (Expense Reporting)
    Inventory (~) <3> (Label Only)
        Opening Inventory (+) (TB First) (Expense Reporting)
        Additions (~) (Expense Reporting)
        Ending Inventory (~) (TB Last) (Expense Reporting)
    Ratios (~) <3> (Label Only)
        Margin % (+) (Dynamic Calc) (Two Pass) [Formula: Margin % Sales;]
        Profit % (~) (Dynamic Calc) (Two Pass) [Formula: Profit % Sales;]
        Profit per Ounce (~) (Two Pass)
```

See also

Review the recipe *Setting up an Account or Measure dimensions with a parent child reference* in *Chapter 1* for an explanation of all the properties that can be added using the parent-child reference.

Creating dimension build rules to add a base and attribute dimensions

In this recipe, we will set up a build rule to modify the outline of the `Sample Basic` database. This recipe will be using the `Generation` reference, but we will discuss several other build methods that we can use with the dimension build rule.

Getting ready

To get started, click on your **Start** menu and navigate to **Programs | Oracle EPM System | Essbase | Essbase Administration Services | Start Administration Services Console**. In the Log in menu, enter your Administration Server, Username, Password, and click on the **Log In** button.

How to do it...

1. In EAS, drill down on **EssbaseCluster-1 | Applications | Sample | Basic**, right-click on **Outline**, and click on **Edit**.

2. Right-click on the **Outline: Basic** node. In the **Outline Editor**, select the **Add a child to the selected member** button, enter **Product**, and press the *Enter* key. If you already built the **Measures** dimension in the preceding recipe select the **Measures** dimension instead of the **Outline: Basic** node and click the **Add a sibling to the selected member** button instead.

3. Enter **Ounces** for the dimension name, press the *Enter* key, and then press *Esc*. Click on the **Ounces** dimension, then on the **Add a child to selected member** button, and enter **32**. Hovering over the buttons in the Outline Editor will give you a tooltip with the name or function of the button.

4. Click on the **Ounces** dimension, click on **Attribute Dimension Type**, click **Yes** at the prompt, click on the **Edit properties for the selected member(s)** button, change the **Attribute Type** to **Numeric**, click on **OK**, and then click on **Yes** when prompted.

5. Right-click on the **Ounce** dimension, click on the **Add a sibling to selected member** button, enter the **Intro Date**, press the *Enter* key, and then press *Esc*.

6. Click on the **Intro Date** dimension, click on the **Add a child to selected member** button, and enter **03-25-1996**.

7. Click on the **Intro Date** dimension, click on the **Attribute Dimension Type** button, click on **Yes** when prompted, click on the **Edit properties for the selected member(s)** button, change the **Attribute Type** to **Date**, click on **OK**, and then click on **Yes** when prompted.

8. Click on the **Intro Date** dimension, click on the **Add a sibling to selected member** button, enter **Pkg Type**, press the *Enter* key, and then press *Esc*. Click on the **Pkg Type** dimension, click on the **Add a child to selected member** button, and enter **Can**.

9. Click on the **Pkg Type** dimension, click on the **Add a sibling to selected member** button, then enter **Caffeinated**, press the *Enter* key, and then press *Esc*.

10. Click on **Caffeinated**, click on the **Attribute Dimension Type** button, and click on **Yes**. Click on the **Edit properties for the selected member(s)** button, change the **Attribute Type** to **Boolean**, click on **OK**, and then click on **Yes**.

11. Right-click on the **Product** dimension, click on **Edit member properties**, click on the **Attribute** tab, select **Caffeinated**, **Intro Date**, **Ounces**, and **Pkg Type**, click on the **Assign** button, and then click on **OK**.

12. Click on **Verify** and **Save** in the **Outline Editor** window.

13. Open up an Excel workbook; enter the values as in the following grid, and save the tab as delimited on your `Sample Basic` database directory for ease of use with the name `Product.txt`. The URL for the `Sample Basic` database is as follows:

    ```
    ..\ Oracle\Middleware\user_projects\epmsystem1\EssbaseServer\
        essbaseserver1\app\Sample\Basic
    ```

    The following table has all the member properties and attribute dimensions for the Product dimension.

FamilyID	Family_Alias	SKU	SKU_Alias	Caffeinated	Ounces	PkgType	IntroDate
100	Colas	100-10	Cola	TRUE	12	Can	03-25-1996
100	Colas	100-20	Diet Cola	TRUE	12	Can	04-01-1996
100	Colas	100-30	Caffeine Free Cola	FALSE	16	Bottle	04-01-1996
200	Root Beer	200-10	Old Fashioned	TRUE	12	Bottle	09-27-1996
200	Root Beer	200-20	Diet Root Beer	TRUE	16	Bottle	07-26-1996
200	Root Beer	200-30	Sasparilla	FALSE	12	Bottle	12-10-1996
200	Root Beer	200-40	Birch Beer	FALSE	16	Bottle	12-10-1996
300	Cream Soda	300-10	Dark Cream	TRUE	20	Bottle	06-26-1996
300	Cream Soda	300-20	Vanilla Cream	TRUE	20	Bottle	06-26-1996
300	Cream Soda	300-30	Diet Cream	TRUE	12	Can	06-26-1996
400	Fruit Soda	400-10	Grape	FALSE	32	Bottle	10-01-1996
400	Fruit Soda	400-20	Orange	FALSE	32	Bottle	10-01-1996
400	Fruit Soda	400-30	Strawberry	FALSE	32	Bottle	10-01-1996

14. Drill down on the your Essbase Server in EAS and the **Applications** node, select the **Sample Basic** database, right-click on the **Basic** database, click on **Create**, and select **Rules File**.

15. Click on the **File** menu, click on **Open data file**, select the **Product.txt** file from the menu, and click on **OK**.

16. Click on the **Dimension build field** button [icon] in **Data Prep Editor** to specify that you plan to use this rule to conduct a dimension build.

17. Click on the **Data Source Properties** button, select the **Header** tab, enter a value of **1** for **Number of lines to skip**, and click on **OK**. You can hover over the buttons to view the **Data Source Properties** tooltip.

18. Click on the **Field1** column and click on the **Field Properties** button [icon].

19. In the **Field Properties** menu, select the **Dimension Build Properties** tab, and in the **Field definition** session, under **Dimension**, double-click on **Product**.

20. Under **Field | Type**, double-click **Generation**, enter **2** in the **Number** field, and click on the **Next** button. Your screen should look like the following screenshot assuming that you completed the **Year**, **Measure**, and **Scenario** dimensions:

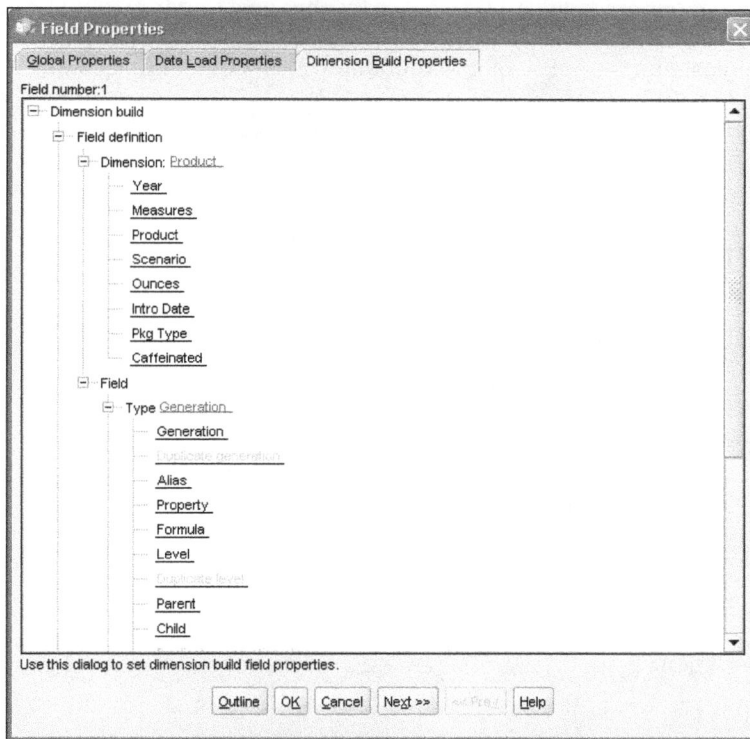

21. Under **Field definition | Dimension**, double-click on **Product**, under **Field | Type**, double-click on **Alias**, and then click on the **Next** button.

22. Under **Field | Type**, double-click on **Generation**, enter **3** for **Number**, and click on the **Next** button.

23. Under **Field definition | Dimension**, double-click on **Product**, under **Field | Type**, double-click on **Alias**, and then click on the **Next** button.

24. Under **Field definition | Dimension**, double-click on **Product**, under **Field | Type | Attribute Dimension**, double-click on **Caffeinated**, and then click on the **Next** button.

25. Under **Field definition | Dimension**, double-click on **Product**. Under **Field | Type | Attribute Dimension**, double-click on **Ounces**, and then click on the **Next** button.

26. Under **Field definition | Dimension**, double-click on **Product**, under **Field | Type | Attribute Dimension**, double-click on **Pkg Type**, and then click on the **Next** button.

27. Under **Field definition | Dimension**, double-click on **Product**, under **Field | Type | Attribute Dimension**, double-click on **Intro Date**, and then click on the **OK** button.

28. Click on the **Dimension Build settings** button [icon] and select the **Dimension Build Setting** tab.

29. In the **Dimension Build Settings | Dimension**, double-click on **Product**, and under **Existing members**, enable **Allow property changes**. Under **Attribute Members**, enable **Allow association changes**. Under **Build method**, select **Use generation references**, and then click on the **OK** button, as shown in the following screenshot:

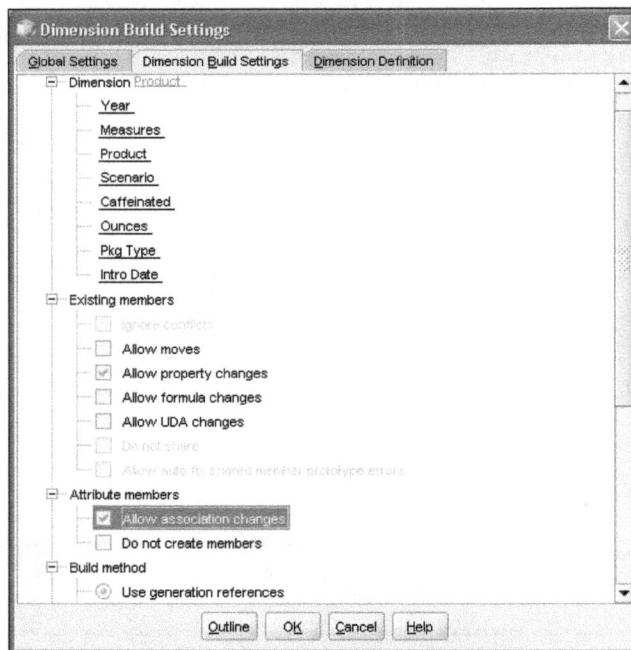

30. Click on the **Validation** button and click on **Yes**.

31. Click on the **File** menu, click on the **Save** button, and type **Product** for the name of your build rule.

32. Right-click on the **Sample Basic** database, select **Load Date** in the Data Load menu, click on the **Find Data File** button, select the **Product.txt** file, and click on **OK**.

33. Click on the **Find Rule File** button, select the **Product.rul** file, click on **OK**, select **Mode** and **Build Only** in the **Data Load** menu, and click on the **OK** button.

34 The **Data Load Results** dialog box should show **Success** for the **Status**.

How it works...

In this recipe, we created a dimension build rule to add the `Product` base dimension, the attribute dimensions, and associate the attributes to the `Product` base dimensions in the `Sample Basic` outline. The following are a few facts that you should consider when using attribute dimensions:

1. Attribute dimensions can only be associated to sparse dimensions.
2. Attribute dimension types are Numeric, Text, Date, and Boolean.
3. Attribute dimensions can be used for cross-tab reporting.
4. You can use attribute dimensions in outline formulas and calc scripts.
5. Attribute dimensions can be used to specify numeric ranges.
6. Attribute dimensions can only be associated to one level in a hierarchy.

There's more...

The build rules give us several build options as depicted in the following **Dimension Build Settings** menu:

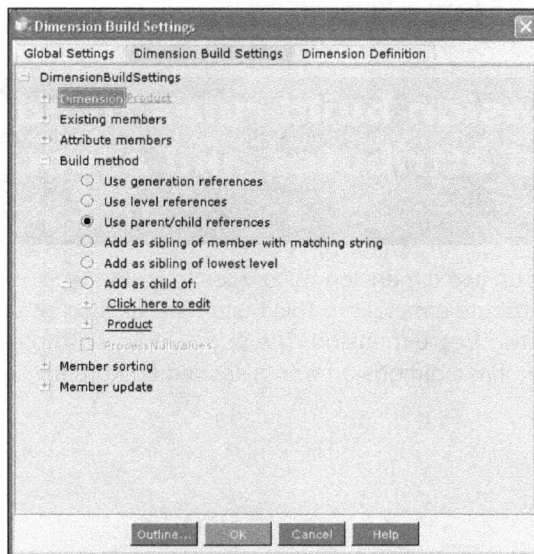

The following table describes these options in more detail:

Build method	Description
Use generation reference	All records set up in the top-down data source organized from left to right and from the highest level to the lowest level
Use level references	All records set up in the bottom-up data source organized from left to right and from the lowest level to the highest level
Use parent-child references	All records specify a new child member that is to roll up to the specified parent
Add as sibling of member with matching string	Add new members by matching strings to existing members
Add as sibling of lowest level	Add new members as siblings of members at level 0
Add as child of	Add all new members as children of a specified parent, in most cases a dummy parent

> The Sample Basic database that comes with Essbase will include dimension build rules that you can use to practice building the outline manually.

See also

Review the recipe *Adding an Application and Database on an Essbase server* to understand how to create the Sample Basic database.

Using dimension build rules to add user-defined attributes and associate dimensions

In this recipe, we will set up two dimension build rules to build the Market base dimension and the Population attribute dimension. This build rule will also be used to add user-defined attributes to the Market dimension. The Population attribute will then be associated to the Market base dimension with a second build rule.

Chapter 5

Getting ready

To get started, click on your **Start** menu and navigate to **Programs | Oracle EPM System | Essbase | Essbase Administration Services | Start Administration Services Console**. In the Log in menu, enter your Administration Server, Username, Password, and click on the **Log In** button.

How to do it...

1. In EAS, drill down on **EssbaseCluster-1 | Applications | Sample | Basic**, right-click on the **Outline**, and click on **Edit**.

2. Right-click on the **Outline: Basic** node. In the **Outline Editor**, select the **Add a child to the selected member** button, enter **Market**, and press the *Enter* key. Choose the **Product** dimension instead of the **Outline: Basic** node if you have already built the **Product** dimension in the preceding recipe and click the **Add a sibling to the selected member** button.

3. Enter **Population** for the dimension name, press the *Enter* key, and then press *Esc*. Click on the **Population** dimension, and select the **Add a child to selected member** button.

4. Enter **Small**, press the *Enter* key, and then press *Esc*.

5. Click on **Small**, select the **Add a child to selected member** button, enter **3000000**, press the *Enter* key, and then press *Esc*.

6. Click on the **Population** dimension, click on **Attribute Dimension Type**, click on **Yes** at being prompted. Click on the **Edit properties for the selected member(s)** button; change the **Attribute Type** to **Numeric**, click on **OK**, and then click on **Yes** at being prompted.

7. Right-click on the **Market** dimension, click on **Edit member properties**, click on the **Attribute** tab, select **Population**, click on the **Assign** button, and then click on **OK**.

8. Click on **Verify** and **Save** in the **Outline Editor** window.

9. Open up an Excel workbook; enter the values as shown in the following table, and save as tab delimited in your `Sample Basic` database directory for ease of use with the name `Market.txt`. The URL for the `Sample Basic` database is as follows:

```
..\Oracle\Middleware\user_projects\epmsystem1\EssbaseServer\
  essbaseserver1\app\Sample\Basic
```

157

The following table provides the members, user defined attributes, attributes of the Market dimension, and the hierarchy for the Population dimension:

Region	State	udamktsize	udamkttype	Popgroup	Population	POPULATION_ALIAS
East	New York	Major Market		Large	21000000	18,000,001–21,000,000
East	Massachusetts	Major Market		Medium	9000000	6,000,001–9,000,000
East	Florida	Major Market		Medium	15000000	12,000,001–15,000,000
East	Connecticut	Small Market		Small	6000000	3,000,001–6,000,000
East	New Hampshire	Small Market		Small	3000000	LT/= 3,000,000
West	California	Major Market		Large	33000000	30,000,001–33,000,000
West	Oregon	Small Market		Small	6000000	3,000,001–6,000,000
West	Washington	Small Market		Small	6000000	3,000,001–6,000,000
West	Utah	Small Market		Small	3000000	LT/= 3,000,000
West	Nevada	Small Market	New Market	Small	3000000	LT/= 3,000,000
South	Texas	Major Market		Large	21000000	18,000,001–21,000,000
South	Oklahoma	Small Market		Small	6000000	3,000,001–6,000,000
South	Louisiana	Small Market	New Market	Small	3000000	LT/= 3,000,000
South	New Mexico	Small Market		Small	3000000	LT/= 3,000,000
Central	Illinois	Major Market		Medium	12000000	9,000,001–12,000,000
Central	Ohio	Major Market		Medium	12000000	9,000,001–12,000,000
Central	Wisconsin	Small Market		Small	6000000	3,000,001–6,000,000
Central	Missouri	Small Market		Small	6000000	3,000,001–6,000,000
Central	Iowa	Small Market		Small	3000000	LT/= 3,000,000
Central	Colorado	Major Market	New Market	Small	6000000	3,000,001–6,000,000

10. Drill down on the your Essbase Server in EAS and in the **Applications** node, select the **Sample Basic** database, right-click on the **Basic** database, click on **Create**, and select **Rules File**.

11. Click on the **File** menu, click on **Open data file**, select the **Market.txt** file from the menu, and click on **OK**.

12. Click on the **Data Source Properties** button, select the **Header** tab, enter the value **1** for **Number of lines to skip**, and click on **OK**. You can hover over the buttons to view the **Data Source Properties** tooltip.

13. Click on the **Dimension build field** button [image] in **Data Prep Editor** to specify that you plan to use this rule to conduct a dimension build.

14. Click on the **Field1** column and click on the **Field Properties** button [image].

15. Under the **Field Properties** menu, select the **Dimension Build Properties** tab, and in the **Field definition** session under **Dimension**, double-click on **Market**.

16. Under **Field | Type**, double-click on **Generation**, enter **2** for **Number**, and click on the **Next** button.

17. Under the **Field Properties** menu, select the **Dimension Build Properties** tab, and in the **Field definition** session under **Dimension**, double-click on **Market**.

18. Under **Field | Type**, double-click on **Generation**, enter **3** for **Number**, and click on the **Next** button.

19. Under the **Field Properties** menu, select the **Dimension Build Properties** tab, and in the **Field definition** session under **Dimension**, double-click on **Market**.

20. Under **Field | Type**, double-click on **UDA**, and click on the **Next** button.

21. Under the **Field Properties** menu, select the **Dimension Build Properties** tab, and in the **Field definition** session under **Dimension**, double-click on **Market**.

22. Under **Field | Type**, double-click on **UDA**, enter **2** for **Number**, and click on the **Next** button.

23. Under the **Field Properties** menu, select the **Dimension Build Properties** tab, and in the **Field definition** session under **Dimension**, double-click on **Population**.

24. Under **Field | Type**, double-click on **Generation**, enter **2** for **Number**, and click on the **Next** button.

25. Under the **Field Properties** menu, select the **Dimension Build Properties** tab, and in the **Field definition** session under **Dimension**, double-click on **Population**.

26. Under **Field | Type**, double-click on **Generation**, enter **3** for **Number**, and click on the **Next** button.

27. In the **Field Properties** menu, select the **Dimension Build Properties** tab, and in the **Field definition** session under **Dimension**, double-click on **Population**.

28. Under **Field | Type**, double-click on **Alias**. Your screen should look like the following image:

29. Click on the **Dimension Build settings** button and select the **Dimension Build Setting** tab.

30. In the **Dimension Build Settings | Dimension**, double-click on **Market**. Under **Existing members**, enable **Allow property changes** and under **Build method** select **Use generation references**

31. Double-click on **Population**. Under **Existing members**, enable **Allow property changes** and under **Build method** select **Use generation references**, and then click on the **OK** button.

32. Click on the **Validation** button and then on **OK**.

33. Click on the **File** menu, click on the **Save** button, and type **Market** for the name of your build rule.

34. We will now start our second dimension build rule using the work you completed for the Market rule file. Select the **GEN3, Population** field and click on the **Move Field** button.

35. Select the **GEN3, Population** field in **Move Field**, move in between **GEN3, Market** and **UDA3, Market** by using the **Up** button, and then click on **OK**, as shown in the following screenshot:

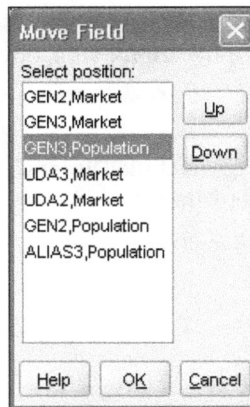

36. Click on the **GEN3, Population** column and click on the **Field Properties** button.

37. Select the **Dimension Build Properties** tab, double-click on **Market Dimension**, and double-click **Population** under **Field | Type | Attribute Dimensions**.

38. Click on the **Next (>>)** button and select the **Ignore field during dimension build** checkbox. Repeat this step for the remaining three fields. We ignore these fields because we do not need them to associate our attributes to the `Market` dimension.

39. Click on the **Dimension Build Settings** button, select the **Dimension Build Setting** tab, and under **Dimension Build Settings | Dimension** double-click on **Market**.

40. Under **Existing Member**, enable **Allow property changes**.

41. Under **Attribute members**, enable **Allow Association changes** and **Do not create members**, and click on the **OK** button.

42. Click on the **Validation** button and then click on **OK**.

43. Click on the **File** menu, click the **Save as** button, and type **AttrMkt** for the name of your build rule.

44. Right-click on the **Basic** database and select **Load Date**. In the **Data Load** menu click on the **Find Data File** button, select the **Market.txt** file, and click on **OK**.

45. Click on the **Find Rule File** button, select the **Market.rul** file, and then click on **OK**. Select **Mode** and **Build Only** in the **Data Load** menu, and click on the **OK** button. Repeat the last three steps for the **AttrMkt** build rule to associate the population attributes.

46. The **Data Load Results** dialog box should show **Success** for **Status**.

How it works...

In this recipe, we created a dimension build rule to build the Market, Population, and assign the UDAs to the lowest and upper levels of the Market dimension. We were able, in this recipe, to reuse the first build rule and text files for two purposes. In the second dimension build rule, we used the Market dimension rule as our starting point. We also associated the Population attribute to the lowest level of the Market. The following image is what your hierarchies should look like:

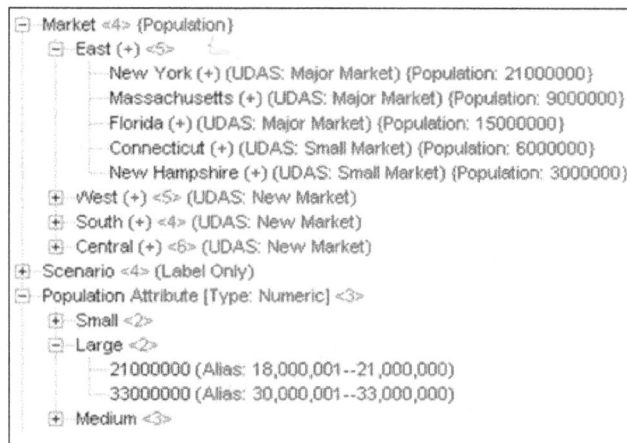

```
□ Market «4» {Population}
    □ East (+) <5»
            New York (+) (UDAS: Major Market) {Population: 21000000}
            Massachusetts (+) (UDAS: Major Market) {Population: 9000000}
            Florida (+) (UDAS: Major Market) {Population: 15000000}
            Connecticut (+) (UDAS: Small Market) {Population: 6000000}
            New Hampshire (+) (UDAS: Small Market) {Population: 3000000}
    ⊞ West (+) <5» (UDAS: New Market)
    ⊞ South (+) <4» (UDAS: New Market)
    ⊞ Central (+) <6» (UDAS: New Market)
⊞ Scenario <4» (Label Only)
□ Population Attribute [Type: Numeric] <3»
    ⊞ Small <2»
    □ Large <2»
            21000000 (Alias: 18,000,001--21,000,000)
            33000000 (Alias: 30,000,001--33,000,000)
    ⊞ Medium <3»
```

Creating load rules for flat file data loads

In this recipe, we will set up a load rule to quickly load from a flat file into our Sample Basic database.

Getting ready

To get started, click on your **Start** menu and navigate to **Programs | Oracle EPM System | Essbase | Essbase Administration Services | Start Administration Services Console**. In the Log in menu, enter your Administration Server, Username, Password, and click on the **Log in** button.

How to do it...

1. Open up an Excel workbook; enter the values in the following image, and save the tab as delimited on your `Sample Basic` database directory with the name `LoadRuleExample.txt` for ease of use. The URL for the `Sample Basic` database is as follows in version 11.1.2.x:

   ```
   ..\ Oracle\Middleware\user_projects\epmsystem1\
   EssbaseServer\essbaseserver1\app\Sample\Basic
   ```

	A	B	C	D	E
1	Scenario	Product	Market	Year	Payroll
2	Actual	100-10	Florida	Jan	1000
3	Actual	100-10	Florida	Feb	1000
4	Actual	100-10	Florida	Mar	1000
5	Actual	100-10	Florida	Apr	1000
6	Actual	100-10	Florida	May	1000
7	Actual	100-10	Florida	Jun	1000
8	Actual	100-10	Florida	Jul	1000
9	Actual	100-10	Florida	Aug	1000
10	Actual	100-10	Florida	Sep	1000
11	Actual	100-10	Florida	Oct	1000
12	Actual	100-10	Florida	Nov	1000
13	Actual	100-10	Florida	Dec	1000

2. Drill down on the Essbase Server in EAS and the **Applications** node. Select the **Sample Basic** database, right-click on the **Basic** database, select **Create**, and then **Rules File**. The **Data Prep Editor** should now be visible, as shown in the following screenshot:

	Scenario	Product	Market	Year	Payroll
2	Actual	100-10	Florida	Jan	1000
3	Actual	100-10	Florida	Feb	1000
4	Actual	100-10	Florida	Mar	1000
5	Actual	100-10	Florida	Apr	1000
6	Actual	100-10	Florida	May	1000

3. Click on the **File** menu, click on the **Open** data file, select the **LoadRuleExample.txt** file from the menu, and click on **OK**, as shown in the following screenshot:

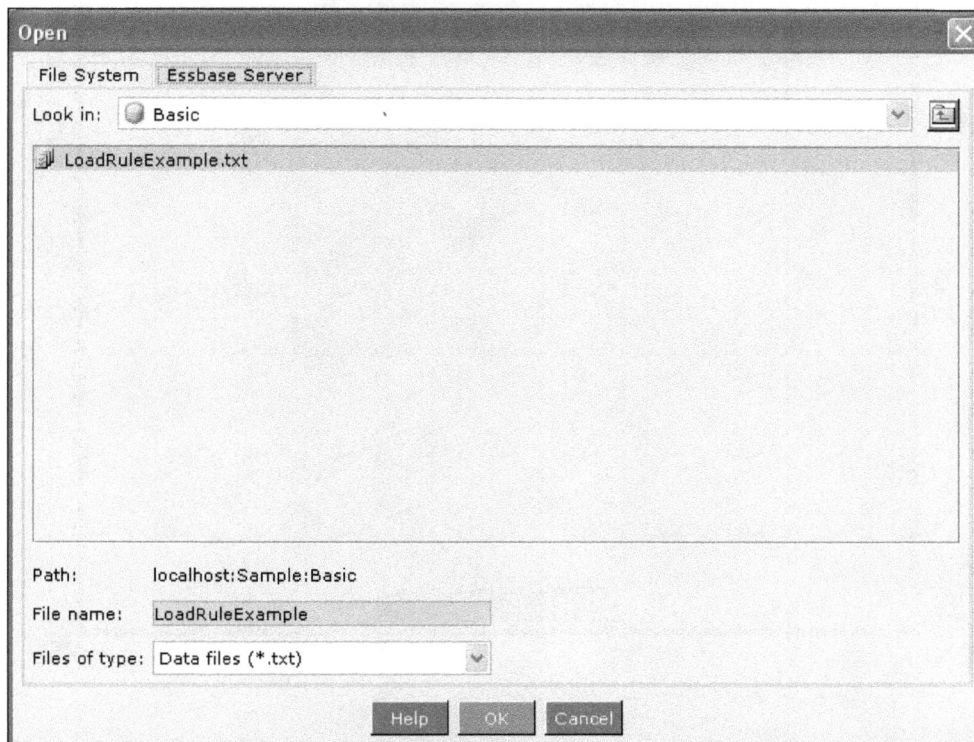

4. Click on the **Data Source Properties** dialog box 🔲, click on the **Header** tab, select the **Record containing data load field names** radio button, enter **1** in the textbox, and click on **OK**. If you see more fields to the right of the **Payroll** measure, then remove them from the text file and repeat the steps.

5. Click on the **Validate rule file** button 🔲 and click on **OK** on being prompted.

6. Click on the **File** menu, click on **Save**, call the load rule **LDSamp**, and click on **OK**.

7. Right-click on the **Basic** database, select **Load data...**, in the **Data Load** menu click on the **Find Data File** button, select the **LoadRuleExample.txt** file, and click on **OK**.

8. Click on the **Find Rule File** button, select the **LDSamp.rul** file, click on **OK**, and click on **OK** on the **Data Load** menu.

9. The **Data Load Results** dialog box will pop up letting you know if your load was successful, if it has failed, or is partially loaded. If it is partially loaded, then you will find the error file at the following URL: `..\Oracle\Middleware\EPMSystem11R1\products\Essbase\eas\client\dataload.err`

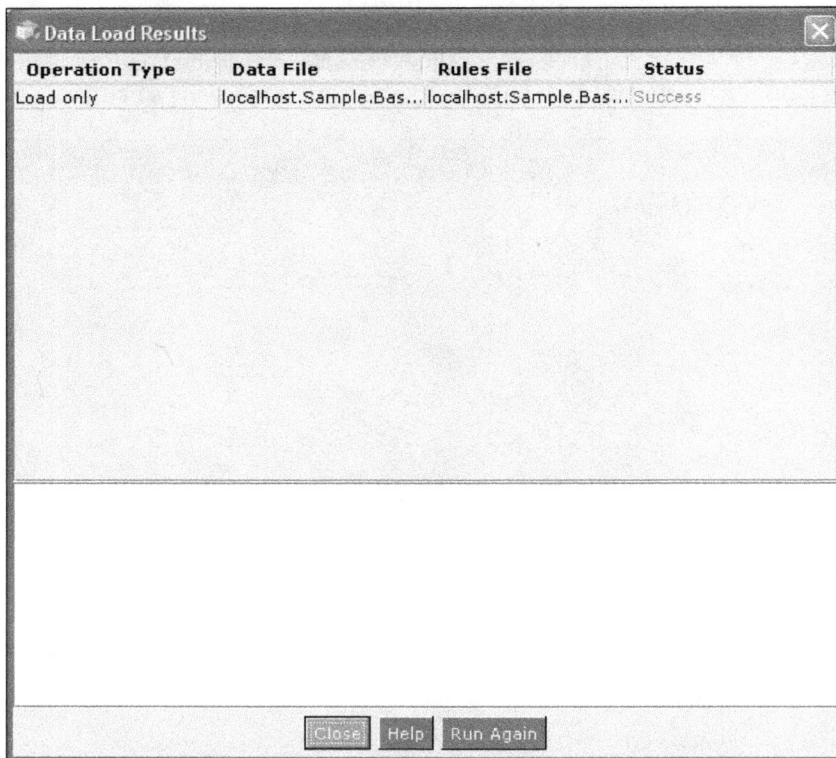

Operation Type	Data File	Rules File	Status
Load only	localhost.Sample.Bas...	localhost.Sample.Bas...	Success

Close   Help   Run Again

How it works...

In this recipe, we created a load rule to load data from a simple flat file. We started by building the flat file and dropping it in the **Basic** database directory. Then, we created the load rule and named it LDSamp.rul. What made creating the load rule simple was the fact that all the dimensions were clearly defined in the first row of the flat file. We were able to use **Record containing data load field names** in the **Data Source Properties** dialog box instead of defining each of the fields one at a time. Finally, we loaded the data from our simple flat file into the **Basic** database using our LDSamp load rule.

Creating substitution variables

In this recipe, we will go over how to set up substitution variables for different types of applications. The substitution variable is a global place holder for information that changes often. We will be setting up substitution variables at the Essbase Server level, at the application level, and at the database level. Moreover, we will discuss what the order of precedence is for substitution variables that have the same names at different levels. Finally, we will create substitution variables for use in date ranges and SQL queries in data load rules.

Getting ready

To get started, click on your **Start** menu and navigate to **Programs | Oracle EPM System | Essbase | Essbase Administration Services | Start Administration Services Console**. In the Log in menu, enter your Administration Server, Username, Password, and click on the **Log in** button.

1. Right-click on your Essbase Server in EAS, select **Edit**, and click on **Variables**.

2. In the **Substitution Variables** menu, click down on the cell under **Application**, select **(all apps)**, click down on the cell under the **Database** column, and select **(all dbs)**.

3. Click on the cell under **Variable**, type **CurMth**, select the cell under **Value**, type in **Apr**, and click on the **Set** button.

4. Repeat steps 1 through 3 for the variables:

Application	Database	Variable	Value
(all apps)	(all dbs)	PrevMth	Mar
Sample	(all dbs)	CurMth	Apr
Sample	Basic	CurMth	Mar
Sample	Basic	SQLCurMth	"Mar"
Sample	Basic	CurMthTD	Jan:Apr

How it works...

In this recipe we set up the `CurMth` and `PrevMth` substitution variables at the server level by selecting the (all apps) application and the (all dbs) database. In addition, we set up the `CurMth` variable as an application level and database level variable to be able to understand precedence. The variable at the database level takes precedence over the variable at the application level. The variable at the application level, if there is a conflict, will take precedence over the variable at the server level. Moreover, we set up the `SQLCurMth` variable to be used on SQL queries enclosed in double single quotes. Finally, we set up `CurMthTD` to keep track of date ranges.

There's more...

Although we will not be able to view existing substitution variables in the New Variable menu, we can create a substitution variable by completing the following steps in EAS as well:

1. Right-click on your Essbase Server in EAS, select **Create**, and click on **Variables**.

2. In the **New Variable** menu, click on the **Application** combo box, select **(all apps)**, click down on the **Database** combo box, and select **(all dbs)**.

3. Enter **NextMth** in the **Name** textbox. In **Value** textbox enter **May**, and click on **OK**.

There's more...

We can also keep track of duplicate members in outlines and the MDX syntax by using substitution variables. You will need to specify duplicate member names, in substitution variables, by using the qualifier name and enclosing them in double quotes as follows:

```
"[2000].[Qtr1]"
```

If you are using the substitution variable in an MDX statement, then it must be enclosed in ([]) brackets. However, if you're not using it in an MDX statement, then enclose them in double quotes (" ").

> Substitution variables can be used in report scripts, calculation scripts, partitions, outline formulas, load rules, MaxL scripts, web analysis, financial reports, and security filters to develop, decrease maintenance, and make these objects more dynamic based on information that changes frequently.

See also

Review *Adding an Application and Database on an Essbase server* to understand how to create the `Sample Basic` database. Review *Adding or changing substitution variables with MaxL* in *Chapter 7* to find out how to use MaxL to create or edit substitution variables.

Using If/Else logic and substitution variables in outline formulas

In this recipe, we are going to be setting up substitution variables for the outline formulas. We will then set up an outline to not only use If/Else logic, but also allow the user to conduct the "what if" analysis on a forecast scenario. We will use the `Adjust Data` menu in `Smart View` to increase the selected cell values by three percent and submit this data into Essbase. In addition, we will run a calculation from `Smart View` and validate the results of the If/Else logic.

Getting ready

To get started, click on your **Start** menu and navigate to **Programs | Oracle EPM System | Essbase | Essbase Administration Services | Start Administration Services Console**. In the Log in menu, enter your Administration Server, Username, Password, and click on the **Log in** button.

How to do it...

1. In EAS, drill down on the **Essbase Servers** node, right-click on your **Essbase Server**, select **Edit**, click on **Variables**, and enter the **CurMthTD** and **FcstMthTD** substitution variables as follows. Refer to the recipe *Creating substitution variables* in this chapter for more details.

Application	Database	Variable	Value
Sample	Basic	CurMthTD	Jan:Apr
Sample	Basic	FcstMthTD	May:Dec

2. Select the **Basic** database in the **Sample** application. Double-click on the **Basic** outline to open.

3. Drill down on the **Measures** dimension and the **Ratios** hierarchy. Right-click on the member **Profit per Ounce**, click on **Add Sibling** from the drop-down menu, enter **Adjustment Rate** as the member name, press the *Enter* key, and then press *Esc*.

4. Click on the **Adjustment Rate** member and select the ^ (karat) or **Never Consolidate Member** button.

5. Drill down on your `Scenario` dimension and right-click on the **Budget** member, enter **Forecast** for the new member name, press the *Enter* key, and then press *Esc*.

6. Right-click on the **Forecast** member, click on **Edit member properties**; in the **Information** tab, change the consolidation to (**~**) **ignore**, click on the **Formula** tab, enter the following formula, use the **Verify** button to validate the formula syntax, and click on the **OK** button:

```
IF (NOT @ISMBR("Adjustment Rate"))
   IF(@ISMBR(&CurMthTD))
               "Actual";
     ELSEIF( @ISMBR(&FcstMthTD))
               "Budget" * "Adjustment Rate"->"Forecast";
     ELSEIF(NOT @ISLEV("Year", 0))
        @SUMRANGE(@CURRMBR("Measures"),
          @CURRMBRRANGE(Year, LEV, 0, , 0));
     ELSE
         #MISSING;
   ENDIF;
ENDIF;
```

7. Click on the **Save** button to save the outline. Make sure the **All data** radio button is selected, and click on **OK**.

8. Open an Excel session. Open a connection to your **Smart View** by pressing the **Open** button in the `Smart View` ribbon. Select **Private Connections** in your **Smart View** panel, enter your username and password in the **Connect to Data Source** menu, and click on **Connect**.

9. Drill down on **Sample** application, right-click on the **Basic** database, and **Ad hoc analysis**, and set up your spreadsheet as follows:

	A	B
1		Florida
2		100-10
3		Forecast
4		Adjustment Rate
5	Jan	0
6	Feb	0
7	Mar	0
8	Apr	0
9	May	0
10	Jun	0
11	Jul	0
12	Aug	0
13	Sep	0
14	Oct	0
15	Nov	0
16	Dec	0

10. Select **B9**, enter **1** as the value, and copy and paste the value from cell **B10** to **B16**. The cell should turn yellow. Select range **B9:B16**, and click on the **Adjust** button in your Essbase ribbon. Next, in the **Adjust Data** menu, click on the **Increase selected cell(s) by fixed percentage** radio button, type **3** into the textbox, and click on the **Adjust Data** button. This feature is available in version **11.1.x**.

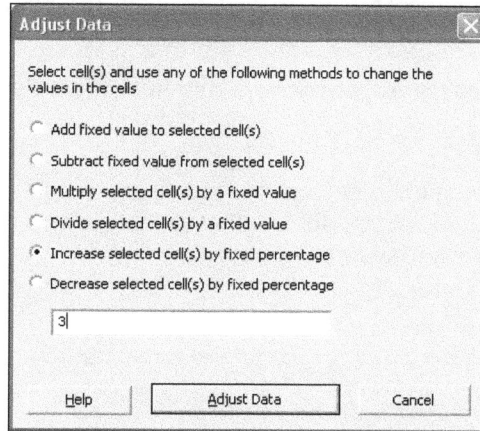

Adjust Data

Select cell(s) and use any of the following methods to change the values in the cells

- ○ Add fixed value to selected cell(s)
- ○ Subtract fixed value from selected cell(s)
- ○ Multiply selected cell(s) by a fixed value
- ○ Divide selected cell(s) by a fixed value
- ● Increase selected cell(s) by fixed percentage
- ○ Decrease selected cell(s) by fixed percentage

```
3
```

| Help | Adjust Data | Cancel |

11. Click on the **Submit Data** button on your Essbase ribbon.

12. In your Essbase ribbon, click on **Calculate**; in the **Calculation Script** menu, select **Default** under **Calculation Script**, and **Basic** under **Cube**, and then click on the **Launch** button.

13. Select another sheet in Excel, enter the selection in the following grid image to validate, and refresh your data from the `Basic` database, as shown in the following table:

	A	B	C	D	E
1		Florida	Florida	Florida	Florida
2		Adjustment Rate	Profit	Profit	Profit
3		100-10	100-10	100-10	100-10
4		Forecast	Forecast	Actual	Budget
5	Jan	0	68	68	70
6	Feb	0	63	63	80
7	Mar	0	67	67	70
8	Qtr1	0	198	198	220
9	Apr	0	73	73	90
10	May	1.03	92.7	78	90
11	Jun	1.03	113.3	99	110
12	Qtr2	0	279	250	290
13	Jul	1.03	123.6	104	120
14	Aug	1.03	123.6	104	120
15	Sep	1.03	103	86	100
16	Qtr3	0	350.2	294	340
17	Oct	1.03	92.7	64	90
18	Nov	1.03	61.8	63	60
19	Dec	1.03	82.4	73	80
20	Qtr4	0	236.9	200	230
21	Year	0	1064.1	942	1080

How it works...

In this recipe, we started by setting up two date ranges as a substitution variable so that we could determine what part of the year was `Actual` and what part was going to be the forecast. We also set up an **Adjustment Rate** measure that we used to enter the rates we wanted to use to adjust our forecast. Moreover, we added a **Forecast** scenario with the following formula:

The first `IF` statement keeps the `Adjustment Rate` from being cleared:

```
IF (NOT @ISMBR("Adjustment Rate"))
```

This nested `IF ElseIf` statement populates the `Forecast` scenario with data from both `Actual` and `Budget`. The `&CurMthTD` substitution variable, with a value of `Jan:Apr` specifies the time range that is the `Actual` data:

```
IF(@ISMBR(&CurMthTD))
```

The following line populates the `Forecast` scenario with data from the `Actual` scenario data for range `Jan` through `Apr`:

```
"Actual";
```

In the following two lines, the `Budget` scenario data is being multiplied by the `Adjustment Rate` and loaded into `Forecast` for range `May` through `Dec` as specified in substitution variable `&FcstMthTD`:

```
ELSEIF( @ISMBR(&FcstMthTD))
   "Budget" * "Adjustment Rate"->"Forecast";
```

The following three lines exclude level-zero member and use the `@SUMRANGE` function to aggregate the current `Measures`. The `@CURRMBRANGE` is used to generate a member list based on what `Year` member is currently being calculated:

```
ELSEIF(NOT @ISLEV("Year", 0))
   @SUMRANGE(@CURRMBR("Measures"), @CURRMBRRANGE(Year, LEV, 0, , 0));
```

This line removes values that are excluded from the preceding logic. This step is good practice as you want the program to remove values that are not relevant for the intended analysis:

```
ELSE
   #MISSING;
ENDIF;
ENDIF;
```

In addition, we used the `Adjust Data` menu to add three percent to our `Adjustment Rate` and submitted the data into the `Basic` database. Finally, we ran the default calculation and set up a template to validate the results.

See also

Review the recipe *Adding an Application and Database on an Essbase server* to understand how to create the `Sample Basic` database.

Using Text measures on a BSO cube

In this recipe, we will set up an `Average Daily Sales` measure with cross-dimensional operators and create a `Text` measure that will specify whether the `Average Daily Sales` ranks as high, median, or low.

Getting ready

To get started, click on the **Start** menu and navigate to **Programs | Oracle EPM System | Essbase | Essbase Administration Services | Start Administration Services Console**. In the Log in menu, enter your Administration Server, Username, Password, and click on the **Log in** button.

How to do it...

1. Drill down on the Essbase Server in EAS and the **Applications** node. Select the **Sample Basic** database, and double-click on the **Basic** outline to edit.

2. Click on the **Properties** tab and set **Type Measures enable** to **True.**

3. Click on the **Text List Manager** tab, click on the **New** button, type in **Sales_Rate** into the textbox in the **Text Lists** box, and click on the **Apply** button.

4. Click on the **Auto Generate IDs** button on the right-hand side of the **Text List Manager**. In this menu check **Auto Generate IDs**, type **1** into the **Initial value** textbox, type **1** into the **Increment** textbox, and click on **OK**. Your menu should look like the following image:

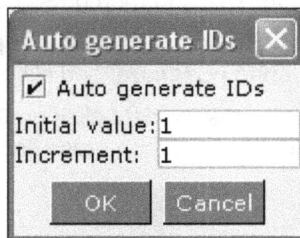

5. In **Edit Mappings – Sales_Rate**, click on the **+** sign, and enter **High**. Repeat the same step for **Median** and **Low**. Your screen will look like the following image:

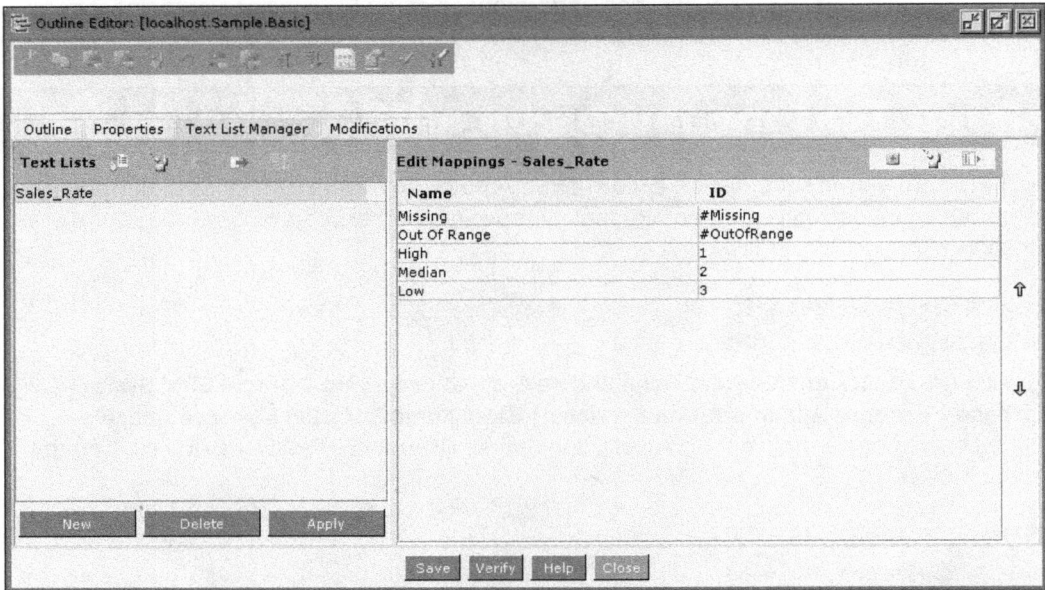

6. Click on the **Outline** tab, drill down on the **Measures** dimension, drill down on **Ratios** hierarchy, right-click on the **Profit per Ounce**, click on **Add sibling**, type in **Selling Days** in the textbox that appears, press the *Enter* key, and then press *Esc*.

7. Right-click on **Selling Days**, click on **Edit member properties**. In the **Information** tab, change the consolidation to (**~**) **ignore**, and click on **OK**.

8. Right-click on **Selling Days**, click on **Add sibling**, type in **Average Daily Sales**, press the *Enter* key, and then press *Esc*.

9. Drill down on your **Market** dimension, right-click on **Central**, click on **Add sibling**, type in **Market NA**, press the *Enter* key, and then press *Esc*.

10. Right-click on **Market NA** and click on **Edit member properties**. In the **Information** tab change the consolidation to (**~**) **ignore**, and click on **OK**.

11. Drill down in your **Product** dimension, right-click on **Diet**, click on **Add sibling**, type in **Product NA**, press the *Enter* key, and then press *Esc*.

12. Right-click on **Product NA**, click on **Edit member properties**. In the **Information** tab, change the consolidation to (**~**) **ignore**, and click on **OK**. Right-click on **Average Daily Sales** in your **Measures** dimension and click on **Edit member properties**. In the **Information** tab change the consolidation to (**~**) **ignore**, change **Two-Pass calculation** to true, and change **Data Storage** to **Dynamic Calc**.

13. Select the **Formula** tab, enter the following formula, click on the **Verify** button, and click on **OK**:

```
If ("Selling Days"->"Market NA"->"Product NA" != #MISSING  AND
  "Selling Days"->"Market NA"->"Product NA" != 0)
  "Sales" / "Selling Days"->"Market NA"->"Product NA";
EndIf;
```

14. Right-click on **Average Daily Sales**, click on **Add sibling**, type in **Sale Rating**, press the *Enter* key, and then press *Esc*.

15. Right-click on **Sales Rating**, and click on **Edit member properties**; in the **Information** tab change the **Consolidation** to (**^**) **Never**, change the **Two-Pass calculation** to **true**, change **Type** to **Text**. In the **Select Text List** combobox select **Sales_Rate**, and change **Data Storage** to **Dynamic Calc**.

16. Select the **Formula** tab, enter the following **formula**, click on the **Verify** button, click on **OK**, and then click **OK** again:

```
IF ("Average Daily Sales" < 65)
  3;
ElseIf ("Average Daily Sales" >= 65
  and "Average Daily Sales" < 75)
  2;
ElseIf ("Average Daily Sales" >= 75)
  1;
Else
  #MISSING;
EndIf;
```

17. Click on the **Save** button. In the **Restructure Database Options** menu, select **Level 0 data**, and click on the **OK** button.

18. Open an Excel session; open a connection in your in **Smart View** tab by pressing the **Open** button. In the **Smart View** panel, click on **Private Connections**, select your Essbase Server from the combobox, enter your username and password, right-click on the **Basic** database, and select **Ad hoc analysis**.

19. Set up your spreadsheet as shown in the following image without the data values, click on the **Refresh** button on your POV, and then type in the values:

	A	B
1		Market NA
2		Product NA
3		Actual
4		Selling Days
5	Jan	20
6	Feb	20
7	Mar	23
8	Apr	20
9	May	21
10	Jun	22
11	Jul	20
12	Aug	23
13	Sep	21
14	Oct	21
15	Nov	20
16	Dec	19

20. Click on the **Submit Data** button on your ribbon. Right-click on the spreadsheet, select **Essbase**, and select **Calculate**. In the **Calculation Script** menu, select **Default** under **Calculation Script**, select **Basic** under **Cube**, and click on the **Launch** button.

21. Select another spreadsheet in **Excel**, enter the selection in the following grid image to validate, and refresh your data from the basic database:

	A	B	C	D	E
1		Market NA	Florida	Florida	Florida
2		Product NA	Product	Product	Product
3		Selling Days	Average Daily Sales	Sales	Sales Rating
4		Actual	Actual	Actual	Actual
5	Jan	20	66.05	1321	Median
6	Feb	20	69.15	1383	Median
7	Mar	23	62.08695652	1428	Low
8	Qtr1	63	65.58730159	4132	Median
9	Apr	20	74.9	1498	Median
10	May	21	74.38095238	1562	Median
11	Jun	22	77.5	1705	High
12	Qtr2	63	75.63492063	4765	High
13	Jul	20	91.85	1837	High
14	Aug	23	78.86956522	1814	High
15	Sep	21	72.42857143	1521	Median
16	Qtr3	64	80.8125	5172	High
17	Oct	21	67.52380952	1418	Median
18	Nov	20	66.55	1331	Median
19	Dec	19	80.15789474	1523	High
20	Qtr4	60	71.2	4272	Median
21	Year	250	73.364	18341	Median

How it works...

In this recipe, we began by preparing the `Sample Basic` database to support `Text` measures. We also created a `Text List` for our rankings. We created a `Selling Days` measure to hold the selling days for the month. In addition, `Market NA` and `Product NA` were created as dummy members for unspecified data.

Moreover, we created the `Average Selling Days` measure with the following formula.

In this formula, we do not enter a value for `Average Selling Days` if `Selling Days` is `#MISSING` or zero. The formula will divide the `Sales` by the `Selling Day` to calculate the `Average Selling Day`.

```
If ("Selling Days"->"Market NA"->"Product NA" != #MISSING  AND
   "Selling Days"->"Market NA"->"Product NA" != 0)
   "Sales" / "Selling Days"->"Market NA"->"Product NA";
EndIf;
```

We also created the `Sale Rate Text` measure, associated it to the `Sales_Rate Text List`, and added the following formula:

```
IF ("Average Daily Sales" < 65)
   3;
ElseIf ("Average Daily Sales" >= 65 and
   "Average Daily Sales" < 75)
   2;
ElseIf ("Average Daily Sales" >= 75)
   1;
Else
   #MISSING;
EndIf;
```

This code simply sets up the values for your `Text` measure. If you recall from when we set up the `Text` list, a value of **3** was **Low**, a value of **2** was **Median**, and a value of **1** was **High**. If `Average Daily Sales` is less than 65, then the `Text` measure is Low (3). If it is 65 or greater but less than 75, then it is Median (2). If it is 75 or greater, then it is High (1).

Finally, we loaded data into `Selling Days`, submitted data to the `Basic` database, ran the Default calculation, and validated our results. In the image in step 15, you can clearly view your `Selling Days`, `Average Selling Days`, and the `Sales Rate Text` measure.

See also

Review *Adding an Application and Database on an Essbase server* to understand how to create the `Sample Basic` database.

Using Date measures on a BSO cube

In this recipe, we will set up a set of Date-stored members and load data into them. We will also determine our Shelf Life and Days to Sell value by adding the appropriate outline formulas to the two corresponding measures.

Getting ready

To get started, click on the **Start** menu and navigate to **Programs | Oracle EPM System | Essbase | Essbase Administration Services | Start Administration Services Console**. In the Log in menu, enter your Administration Server, Username, Password, and click on the **Log in** button.

How to do it...

1. Drill down on the Essbase Server in EAS and the **Applications** node, select the **Sample Basic** database, and double-click on the **Basic** outline to edit.

2. Click on the **Properties** tab, set **Type Measures enable** to **True**, and change the **Date format** value to **yyyy-mm-dd**.

3. Click on the **Outline** tab, drill down on the **Measures** dimension, drill down on the **Ratios** hierarchy, right-click on **Profit per Ounce**, click on **Add sibling**, and type in **Production Date** in the textbox that appears. Then, press the *Enter* key, and then press *Esc*.

4. Right-click on the **Production Date**, click on **Edit member properties** in the **Information** tab, and change the **consolidation** to (^) **Never**. In the **Type** property, select **Date** from the drop-down box, and click on **OK**.

5. Right-click on **Production Date**, and click on **Add sibling**, type in **Expiration Date** in the textbox that appears, press the *Enter* key, and then press *Esc*.

6. Right-click on **Expiration Date**, click on **Edit member properties**. In the **Information** tab change the **consolidation** to (^) **Never**. In the **Type** property select **Date** from the drop-down box, and click on **OK**.

7. Right-click on **Expiration Date**, click on **Add sibling**, type in **Current Date** in the textbox that appears, press the *Enter* key, and then press *Esc*.

8. Right-click on **Current Date** and click on **Edit member properties**. In the **Information** tab, change the **consolidation** to (^) **Never**. In the **Type** property, select **Date** from the drop-down box. In the **Data Storage** property click on **Dynamic Calc**, and then click on **OK**.

9. Click on the **Formula** tab, type in the following formula, click on the **Verify** button, click on **OK** when prompte, and click on **OK** to exit:

```
If("Expiration Date" <> #MISSING OR "Expiration Date" <> 0)
  @ToDateEx("yyyy-mm-dd", @FormatDate(@Today(), "yyyy-mm-dd"));
  Else
    #MISSING;
EndIf;
```

10. Right-click on **Expiration Date**, click on **Add sibling**, type in **Shelf Life** in the textbox that appears, press the *Enter* key, and then press *Esc*.

11. Right-click on **Shelf Life**, click on **Edit member properties**. In the **Information** tab change the **Consolidation** to (^) **Never**, and in the **Data Storage property** click on **Dynamic Calc**.

12. Click on the **Formula** tab, type in the following formula, click on the **Verify** button, click on **OK** when prompted, and click on **OK** to exit:

```
@DateDiff("Production Date", "Expiration Date", DP_DAY);
```

13. Right-click on **Shelf Life**, click on **Add sibling**, type in **Days to Sell** in the textbox that appears, press the *Enter* key, and then press *Esc*.

14. Right-click on **Days to Sell**, click on **Edit member properties**. In the **Information** tab change the **consolidation** to (^) **Never**. In the **Data Storage** property click on **Dynamic Calc**, and click on **OK**.

15. Click on the **Formula** tab type in the following formula. Click on the **Verify** button, click on **OK** when prompted, and click on **OK** to exit:

```
@DateDiff("Current Date", "Expiration Date", DP_DAY);
```

16. Open an Excel session. Open a connection in your **Smart View** tab by clicking on the **Open** button. In the **Smart View** panel, click on **Private Connections**. Select your Essbase Server from the **combobox**, enter your username and password, right-click on the **Basic** database, and select **Ad hoc analysis**.

17. Set up your spreadsheet as shown in the following screenshot without the data values, click on the **Refresh** button on your **POV**, type in the **'2011-01-11** for all the **Production Date** values, and **'2012-01-11** for all the **Expiration Date** values:

	A	B	C	D	E	F
1					Production Date	Expiration Date
2	Actual	100-10	Florida	Jan		
3	Actual	100-20	Florida	Jan		
4	Actual	100-30	Florida	Jan		
5	Actual	200-10	Florida	Jan		
6	Actual	200-20	Florida	Jan		
7	Actual	200-30	Florida	Jan		
8	Actual	200-40	Florida	Jan		

18. Click on the **Submit Data** button on your Essbase ribbon. Add a column to the right of **Expiration Date** called **Shelf Life**, add another column to the right of **Shelf Life** called **Days to Sell**, and **Refresh** your POV. Your screen should look like the following screenshot:

	A	B	C	D	E	F	G	H
1					Production Date	Expiration Date	Shelf Life	Days to Sell
2	Actual	100-10	Florida	Jan	1/11/2011	1/12/2012	366	270
3	Actual	100-20	Florida	Jan	1/11/2011	1/12/2012	366	270
4	Actual	100-30	Florida	Jan	1/11/2011	1/12/2012	366	270
5	Actual	200-10	Florida	Jan	1/11/2011	1/12/2012	366	270
6	Actual	200-20	Florida	Jan	1/11/2011	1/12/2012	366	270
7	Actual	200-30	Florida	Jan	1/11/2011	1/12/2012	366	270
8	Actual	200-40	Florida	Jan	1/11/2011	1/12/2012	366	270

How it works...

In this recipe, we added a **Production Date** measure that stores the day that the product was completed. We added an **Expiration Date** to make sure that we knew when the product could no longer be sold. In addition, we added the **Shelf Life** measure with the following formula:

```
@DateDiff("Production Date", "Expiration Date", DP_DAY);
```

This formula simply gives you the number of days that the product can sit on a shelf before it is sold to a customer. Moreover, we added the **Days to Sell** measure with the following formula:

```
@DateDiff(@Today(), "Expiration Date", DP_DAY);
```

This formula gives us the difference between the current day and the expiration date. Finally, we loaded data into the date measure using the yyyy-mm-dd formatted date string and validated our results in Smart View.

See also

Review the recipe *Adding an Application and Database on an Essbase server* to understand how to create the Sample Basic database.

Using different outline formula logic at parent level

In this recipe, we will set up an **Average Sale** and a **Product Sale Share** measure that shows more than just a simple aggregation at the parent level. The parent level in a BSO cube does not always have to be the aggregation of its children. In this recipe, you will learn how to get the average of the children at the parent level. Moreover, we will learn how to derive what percent of the parent a distinct **Sales | Product** combination represents.

Getting ready

To get started, click on the **Start** menu and navigate to **Programs | Oracle EPM System | Essbase | Essbase Administration Services | Start Administration Services Console**. In the Log in menu, enter your Administration Server, Username, Password, and click on the **Log in** button. Drill down on the your Essbase Server in EAS and the **Applications** node, select the **Sample Basic** database, and double-click on the **Basic** outline to edit.

How to do it...

1. Click on the **Outline** tab, drill down on the **Measures** dimension, drill down on the **Ratios** hierarchy, right-click on the **Profit per Ounce**, click on **Add sibling**, type in **Average Sale** in the textbox that appears, press the *Enter* key, and then press *Esc*.

2. Right-click on **Average Sale**, click on **Edit member properties**. In the **Information** tab, change the **consolidation** to (~) **Ignore**, and in the **Data Storage** property select **Dynamic Calc** from the drop-down box.

3. Click on the **Formula** tab; enter the following formula, click on the **Verify** button, click on **OK** on being prompted, and then click on **OK** again:

```
If(@ISLEV(Product,0))
  "Sales";
Else
  @AVGRANGE(SKIPNONE,Sales,@CHILDREN(@CURRMBR(Product)));
EndIf;
```

4. Right-click on **Average Sale**, click on **Add sibling**, type in **Product Sale Share** in the textbox that appears, press the *Enter* key, and then press *Esc*.

5. Right-click on **Product Sale Share**, click on **Edit member properties...** in the **Information** tab, change the **consolidation** to (~) **Ignore**, and in the **Data Storage** property select **Dynamic Calc** from the drop-down box.

6. Click on the **Formula** tab, enter the following formula, click on the **Verify** button, click on **OK** on the prompt, and then click on **OK** again:

```
("Sales" % @PARENTVAL( Product, "Sales")) / 100;
```

7. Click on the **Save** button on your outline to restructure, select the **Level0 Data** radio button, and click on the **OK** button.

8. Open an Excel session, open a connection in your **Smart View** tab by clicking the **Open** button. In the **Smart View** panel, click on **Private Connections**, select your Essbase Server from the combobox, enter your username and password, right-click on the **Basic** database, and select **Ad hoc analysis**.

9. Set up your spreadsheet like the following image and click on the **Refresh** button on your POV:

	A	B	C	D	E	F	G
1					Sales	Average Sale	Product Sale Share
2	Actual	100-10	East	Jan	1812	1812	0.860807601
3	Actual	100-20	East	Jan	200	200	0.095011876
4	Actual	100-30	East	Jan	93	93	0.044180523
5	Actual	100	East	Jan	2105	701.6666667	0.310471976
6	Actual	200-10	East	Jan	647	647	0.349163519
7	Actual	200-20	East	Jan	310	310	0.167296276
8	Actual	200-30	East	Jan	0	0	0
9	Actual	200-40	East	Jan	896	896	0.483540205
10	Actual	200	East	Jan	1853	463.25	0.273303835
11	Actual	300	East	Jan	1609	536.3333333	0.237315634
12	Actual	400	East	Jan	1213	404.3333333	0.178908555
13	Actual	Diet	East	Jan	620	206.6666667	0.091445428
14	Actual	Product NA	East	Jan	0	0	0
15	Actual	Product	East	Jan	6780	1233.333333	1

How it works...

In this recipe, we set up to two measures. The first measure, Average Sale, set the parent level to the average value of its children, as you can see from the image following step 9. In the Average Sales measure's formula, the If statement sets the values to Sales when Product is at level zero. If Product is not at level zero, then it takes the average of the children as the current Product member.

```
If(@ISLEV(Product,0))
  "Sales";
Else
  @AVGRANGE(SKIPNONE,Sales,@CHILDREN(@CURRMBR(Product)));
EndIf;
```

We added the Product Sale Share member next with the following formula:

```
("Sales" % @PARENTVAL( Product, "Sales")) / 100;
```

This @PARENTVAL function returns the parent value of the member being calculated. Then, the Sales value is divided by the parent value and divided by 100 to give you a decimal. This Product Sale Share measure is telling you what percent of the parent is the current member.

See also

Review the recipe *Adding an Application and Database on an Essbase server* to understand how to create the Sample Basic database.

Creating a load rule for SQL data load using substitution variables

In this recipe, we will be creating an ODBC connection to the TBC database created in the recipe *Creating TBC database and connecting to the data source* in *Chapter 2*. We will set up substitution variables for the SQL load rule and create a load rule that uses our SQL data source. This recipe was created using Window XP and may be a slightly different version of Windows or Linux. Consult your network administrator for specific instructions on setting up an ODBC.

Getting ready

To get started, click on the **Start** menu and navigate to **Programs | Oracle EPM System | Essbase | Essbase Administration Services | Start Administration Services Console**. In the Log in menu, enter your Administration Server, Username, Password, and click on the **Log in** button.

How to do it...

1. On your Essbase Windows server, click on the **Start** menu, click on **Settings**, click on **Control Panel**, select **Administrative Tools**, and double-click on **Data Source(ODBC)**. The menu in the following screenshot will appear:

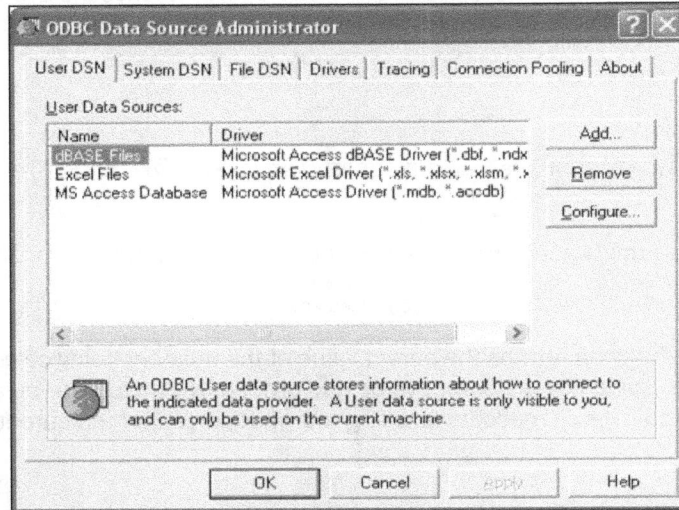

2. Click on the **System DSN** tab, click on the **Add** button, select **MERANT OEM 5.2 32-BIT SQL Server Wire Protocol** if you are using the SQL Server. Select **MERANT OEM 5.2 32-BIT Oracle Wire Protocol** if you are using Oracle, and then click on **Finish**, as shown in the following screenshot:

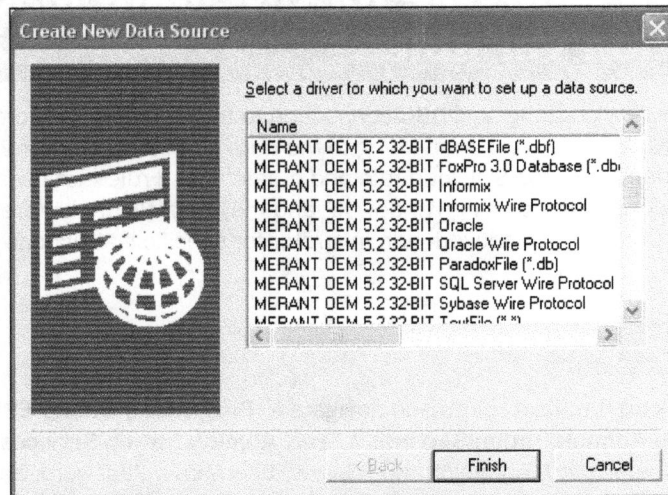

3. You will get the following menu if you are using the SQL Server. Enter **SQLTBC** for **Database Source Name**, enter your **Server Name**, and enter your **Database Name**. Click on the **Test Connect** button to test your connection, click on **OK**, and then click on **OK** again, as shown in the following screenshot:

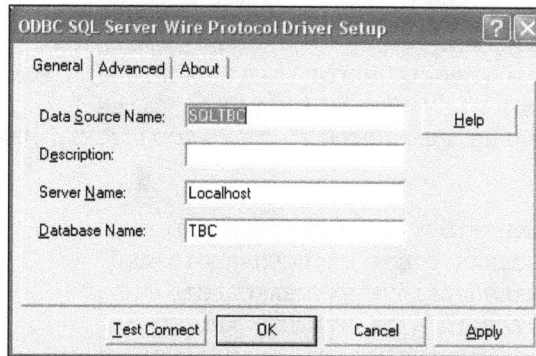

4. Right-click on your Essbase Server in EAS, select **Edit**, and click on **Variables**.

5. In the **Substitution Variables** menu, click on the cell under **Application**, select **Sample**, click on the cell under the **Database** column, and select **Basic**.

6. Click on the cell under **Variable**, type **SQLCurMth**, select the cell under **Value**, type in **"Jan"**, and click on the **Set** button. Please make sure you use double single quotes not double quotes for the value of the substitution variable. We plan to use this variable in the `Where` clause of the SQL statement and strings in SQL require the single quotes. When you refresh the variable in EAS one of the enclosed single quotes is automatically disposed of, leaving only **'Jan'**.

7. Drill down on the your Essbase Server in EAS and the **Applications** node, select the **Basic** database, right-click on the **Basic** database, select **Create**, and select **Rules File**.

8. Click on the **File** menu, click on **Open SQL** in the **Select Database** menu make sure that the **Sample** application and **Basic** database are selected, and click on **OK**, as shown in the following screenshot:

9. Select **SQLTBC** in the **SQL data sources** drop-down, and in the **Select** area or the **SQL Statement** area replace the ***** with the following script:

❑ If you are using SQL Server or T-SQL, then use the following code:

```
T2.SCENARIO                          Scenario,
   T3.SKU                            Product,
     T5.STATE                          Market,
   LEFT(DATENAME(MONTH, TRANSDATE), 3)   Year,
   AMOUNT                              Sales
FROM SALES T1, SCENARIO T2, PRODUCT T3, MEASURES T4, MARKET
T5
WHERE
T1.PRODUCTID = T3.PRODUCTID AND
   T1.SCENARIOID = T2.SCENARIOID AND
   T1.MEASURESID = T4.MEASURESID AND
   T1.STATEID = T5.STATEID AND
   LEFT(DATENAME(MONTH, TRANSDATE), 3) = &SQLCurMth AND
     T4.CHILD = 'Sales'
```

❑ If you are using Oracle PL\SQL, then use the following code:

```
T2.SCENARIO                          Scenario,
   T3.SKU                            Product,
     T5.STATE                          Market,
   TO_CHAR(TRANSDATE, 'MON')   Year,
   AMOUNT                          Sales
FROM SALES T1, SCENARIO T2, PRODUCT T3, MEASURES T4, MARKET
T5
WHERE
T1.PRODUCTID = T3.PRODUCTID AND
   T1.SCENARIOID = T2.SCENARIOID AND
   T1.MEASURESID = T4.MEASURESID AND
     T1.STATEID = T5.STATEID AND
   TO_CHAR(TRANSDATE, 'MON') = &SQLCurMth AND
     T4.CHILD = 'Sales'
```

10. Click on the **OK\Retrieve** button, type in your relational server username and password, and click on **OK**. The data should now appear in your load rule, as shown in the following screenshot:

11. Click on the **File** menu, click on the **Save** button, and type **SQLSamp** for the name of your load rule.

12. Right-click on your **Basic** database, and click on **Load Data**; in the **Data Source Type** column, select **SQL**, click on the **Find Rules File** button, select **SQLSamp.rul**, and click on **OK**.

13. In the **SQL User Name** column, type in your username. In the **SQL Password** column, enter your password, and click on **OK**. The **Data Load Results** dialog box should show **Success** for **Status**.

How it works...

In this recipe, the first thing we did was set up a DSN to connect to the relational data source on our Essbase server. We also created a substitution variable for use in the SQL load rule. Moreover, we created a load rule and placed our substitution variable into the `where` clause `&SQLCurMth` of the SQL statement to filter the data we want returned. We then used the load rule to load data directly from the TBC database into Essbase.

See also

Review the recipe *Adding an Application and Database on an Essbase server* to understand how to create the `Sample Basic` database.

Using MDX in aggregate storage applications

In this recipe, we will be adding an aggregate storage application and database using EAS and applying MDX logic for the purpose of forecast. We will begin by replacing the outline file with a completed outline and populate the database with a load rule. In addition, we will discuss the use of substitution variables in MDX as well as the additional syntax used in this recipe.

Getting ready

To get started, click on the **Start** menu and navigate to **Programs | Oracle EPM System | Essbase | Essbase Administration Services | Start Administration Services Console**. In the Log in menu, enter your Administration Server, Username, Password, and click on the **Log in** button.

How to do it...

1. In EAS, drill down on the **Essbase Servers** node, drill down on your **Essbase Server**, right-click on the **Applications**, select **Create application**, click on **Using Aggregate storage**, enter **ASOsamp** in the **Application Name** textbox, and click on the **OK** button.

2. Right-click on the **ASOsamp** application, select **Create Database**, enter **Sample** in the **Database Name** textbox, and click on the **OK** button. In this menu, you can also select **Allow Duplicate Member Name**, but you cannot set the **Database Type**. As there is no currency database type for the ASO model. You will also notice that you can only add one database to the ASO application.

3. Click on the **File** menu, select **Open**, browse to the **Sample.otl** outline file that is included with this recipe, select the outline, and click on **OK**.

4. Click on the **File** menu, select **Save As**, click on **Essbase Server**, click on the **ASOsamp** application, click on the **Sample** database, select the **Sample.otl** file, and click on the **OK** button.

5. A pop up appears asking if you want to replace the existing file. Click on **Yes**. Another prompt appears asking you, **The outline has been saved to the new location. Do you want to open it?** Click on **Yes**.

6. Right-click on the **ASOsamp** application, select **Stop,** and select **Application**.

7. Right-click on the **ASOsamp** application, select **Start**, and select **Application**.

8. Right-click on the **Sample** database and select **Load data**. In the **Data Load** menu, click on the **Find Data File** button, select the **SampleExport.txt** file that is included with this recipe, and click on the **OK** button in the menu.

9. Drill down on the **Essbase Servers** node, right-click on your **Essbase Server**, select **Edit**, click on **Variables**, and enter the **CurMthTD** and **CurYrMDX** substitution variables as follows. Refer to the recipe *Creating substitution variables* in this chapter for more details. The following table has the scope of each variable, the variable name, and the value:

Application	Database	Variable	Value
ASOsamp	Sample	CurMthTD	[Jul]
ASOsamp	Sample	CurYrMDX	[Curr Year]

10. Select the **Sample** database in the **Sample** application. Right-click on the outline and select **Edit**.

11. Drill down on the **Years** dimension, right-click member **Prev Year**, click on **Add Sibling** from the drop-down menu, enter **Forecast** as the member name, press the *Enter* key, and then press *Esc*.

12. Right-click on the **Forecast** member, click on **Edit member properties**. In the **Information** tab change the consolidation to (~) **ignore**, under **Member Solve Order** enter in **10**, and click on the **Formula** tab. Enter the following formula. Use the **Verify** button to validate the formula syntax, and click the **OK** button. The **10** in the solve order will let Essbase run all members with a lesser solve order first then execute calculation on the one marked as **10**:

```
Case When IsLevel([Time].CurrentMember, 0)
Then
  IIF(Contains([Time].CurrentMember, {[Jan]:&CurMthTD}),
  ([Time].CurrentMember, &CurYrMDX),
  (([Time], &CurYrMDX, [Measures].CurrentMember) /
    NonEmptyCount({[Jan]:&CurMthTD}, (&CurYrMDX,
    [Measures].CurrentMember)))
  )
Else
  SUM(CrossJoin({[Time].CurrentMember.Leaves}, {[Forecast]}))
End
```

13. Click on the **Save** button. The following prompt will appear. Select the **Retain all data and proceed with the restructure** radio button and click on **OK**, as shown in the following screenshot:

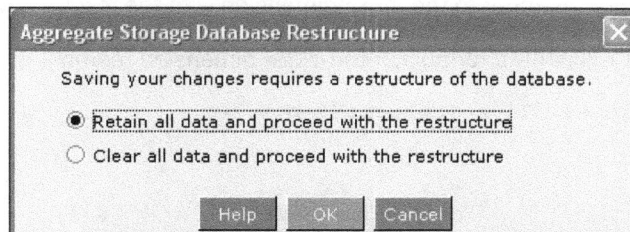

14. Open an Excel session; open a connection in your in **Smart View** tab by clicking on the **Open** button. In the **Smart View** panel, click on **Private Connections**, select your Essbase Server from the combobox, enter your username and password, right-click on the **Sample** database, and select **Ad hoc analysis**.

15. Set up your spreadsheet like the following screenshot and click on the **Refresh** button on your POV:

	A	B	C
1		Original Price	Original Price
2		Actual	Forecast
3	Jan	$ 7,498,269.25	$ 7,498,269.25
4	Feb	$ 3,543,554.00	$ 3,543,554.00
5	Mar	$ 5,625,366.50	$ 5,625,366.50
6	Qtr1	$ 16,667,189.75	$ 16,667,189.75
7	Apr	$ 3,678,482.25	$ 3,678,482.25
8	May	$ 7,394,460.00	$ 7,394,460.00
9	Jun	$ 5,400,841.00	$ 5,400,841.00
10	Qtr2	$ 16,473,783.25	$ 16,473,783.25
11	Jul	$ 4,879,566.25	$ 4,879,566.25
12	Aug	$ -	$ 5,431,505.61
13	Sep	$ -	$ 5,431,505.61
14	Qtr3	$ 4,879,566.25	$ 15,742,577.46
15	Oct	$ -	$ 5,431,505.61
16	Nov	$ -	$ 5,431,505.61
17	Dec	$ -	$ 5,431,505.61
18	Qtr4	$ -	$ 16,294,516.82
19	2nd Half	$ 4,879,566.25	$ 32,037,094.29
20	MTD	$ 38,020,539.25	$ 65,178,067.29

How it works...

In this recipe, we created an ASO application and database. We replaced the existing outline with the `Sample.otl` already populated with dimensions. In addition, we stopped and started the application as best practice as there are times that the outlines does not override the existing one immediately if you are using the file system to make changes. Moreover, we loaded the data for the `Sample` database using an export file called `SampleExtract.txt` without a load rule. In addition, we added two substitution variables to our `Sample` database and added a `Forecast` member to the `Year` dimension with the following MDX syntax.

The `Case` statement will apply a formula, if the `Time` dimension member is `Level 0`:

```
Case When IsLevel([Time].CurrentMember, 0)
Then
```

This IIF statement populates the Forecast member with data from [Jan] through &CurMthTD or [Jul] with data from substitution variable &CurrYRMDX or [Curr Year] (if the current member from the Time dimension falls between the [Jan]:[Jul] date range), as shown in the following code snippet:

```
IIF(Contains([Time].CurrentMember, {[Jan]:&CurMthTD}),
   ([Time].CurrentMember, &CurYrMDX),
```

If current members from the Time dimension do not fall between the aforementioned date range, then the member is populated with the average of the data between [Jan]:[Jul], as follows:

```
(([Time], &CurYrMDX, [Measures].CurrentMember) /
  NonEmptyCount({[Jan]:&CurMthTD}, (&CurYrMDX,
  [Measures].CurrentMember)))
)
Else
```

If the Time dimension is not at Level 0, then aggregate the Forecast dimension, as follows:

```
SUM(CrossJoin({[Time].CurrentMember.Leaves}, {[Forecast]}))
End
```

6

Creating Calculation Scripts

In this chapter, we will cover the following topics:

- ▶ Using Essbase Set and Calc All function commands to calculate cubes
- ▶ Using control flow commands, conditional, and logical operators
- ▶ Using substitution variables in calculation scripts
- ▶ Using UDAs and Calc Two Pass in calculation scripts
- ▶ Using Attributes in calculation scripts
- ▶ Clearing data and using cross-dimension operators in a calculation script
- ▶ Using allocations functions in calculation scripts
- ▶ Using Range functions in calculation scripts
- ▶ Modifying Essbase settings to improve calculation performance
- ▶ Using MDX to calculate Aggregate Storage database

Introduction

This chapter is designed to reinforce your understanding of **calculation scripts** and show some of the new functionality available in version 11.1.2.x. Calculation scripts gives Essbase developers an enormous amount of flexibility in conducting complex financial and mathematical functions. Calculation scripts allow us to run multiple passes of the Essbase outline, clear data, perform time-sensitive calculations with substitution variables, and aggregate an Essbase database, to name just a few of the functions. In addition, Essbase comes with over 300 out-of-the-box financial functions available to us via calculation scripts.

Using Essbase Set function commands and Calc All to calculate cubes

In this recipe, we are going to build a new default calculation with several commands that should allow us to view its functionality and optimize the calculation's performance. We will list the Essbase setting's descriptions and discuss how to execute the calculation the first time to make sure that it is functioning as expected. Finally, we will go over the calculation order for the Basic database when using a Calc All command. This recipe only applies to the **Block Storage Option** (**BSO**) model.

Getting ready

To get started, click on the **Start** menu and navigate to **Program | Oracle EPM System | Essbase | Essbase Administration Services | Start Administration Services Console**. In the Log in menu, enter your Administration Server, Username, Password, and click on the **Log in** button.

How to do it...

1. Drill down on the Essbase Server in EAS, expand the **Applications** node, drill down on the **Sample** application, and right-click on the **Basic** database; in the drop down menu click on **Create**, and select **Calculation Scripts**.

2. In the **Calculation Script Editor**, enter the following script:

```
SET UPDATECALC OFF;
SET CLEARUPDATESTATUS AFTER;
SET AGGMISSG ON;
SET LOCKBLOCK HIGH;
SET CACHE ALL;
SET CACHE HIGH;
SET CALCPARALLEL 3;
SET CALCTASKDIMS 2;

/*Settings during testing & development*/
SET MSG DETAIL;
SET NOTICE HIGH;

Calc All;
```

3. Click on the **Check syntax** button [ ] to verify that the syntax is correct; a prompt should pop up with the text **Syntax check was successful**. Click on **OK**.

4. Select the **File** menu, click on **Save**, enter `CalcDB` in the file name textbox, and click on **OK**.

5. Click on the **Start** menu, select **Run**, type `cmd`, and press *Enter*; in the command prompt enter command **ESSCMD**, and press *Enter*. Calculations can also be run from EAS, via MaxL, using ESSCMD, Oracle Data Integrator, using API calls, and Smart View.

6. Enter command `LOGIN`, press *Enter*. In the **Host Node** prompt enter your Essbase Server, and press *Enter*; in **User** prompt enter your username, in the **Password** prompt enter your password, and press *Enter*.

7. Enter command `SELECT Sample`, and press *Enter*; in the **Enter database name** prompt enter **Basic**, and press *Enter*.

8. Enter command `RUNCALC 2 "CalcDB";` and press *Enter* to execute calculation. You should see and review the execution of **CalcDB** in the command prompt.

9. In EAS, drill down on **Calculation Scripts** under the **Basic** database, double-click on **CalcDB**, and you should receive a prompt asking **Do you want lock calculation**, **CalcDB**. Click on **Yes**, and change the `SET MESSAGE HIGH` to `SET MESSAGE SUMMARY`.

10. In addition, change the `SET NOTICE HIGH` setting to `SET NOTICE DEFAULT`, click on the **Check syntax** button, then **OK**, and then on the **Save** button.

11. In EAS, right-click on the **Basic** database, click on **Set**, select **Default Calculation...**, click the **Use calculation script** radio button, select **CalcDB**, and click on **OK**. This step is not required but will allow you to optimize and customize the database's default calculation.

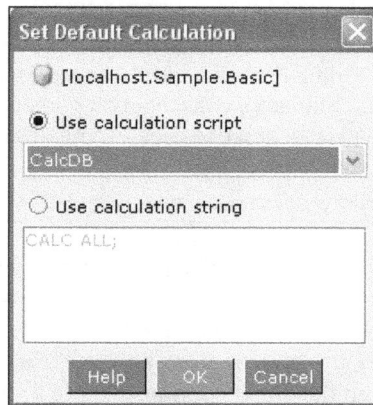

How it works...

In this recipe, we create a calculation called `CalcDB`. The following are the commands included before the Calc All and their description per Oracle documentation:

SETTINGS	DESCRIPTION
SET UPDATECALC OFF;	Turns off intelligent calc so that data is aggregate whether the block is marked as dirty or not.
SET CLEARUPDATESTATUS AFTER;	Sets blocks to clean after the calculation even when you are calculating a subset of the database.
SET AGGMISSG ON;	Sets Essbase to consolidate #MISSING values in the database.
SET LOCKBLOCK HIGH;	Specifies the maximum number of blocks that Essbase can get addressability to concurrently.
SET CACHE ALL;	Essbase uses the calculator cache even when only calculating part of a sparse dimension.
SET CACHE HIGH;	Specifies the size of the calculator cache.
SET CALCPARALLEL 3;	Enables parallel calculation and specifies the amount of threads used. This set function requires as parameter, an integer from 1-4 on 32-bit platforms or from 1-8 on 64-bit platforms.
SET CALCTASKDIMS 2;	Specifies the number of sparse dimensions included in the identification of tasks for parallel calculation. In this case, Product and Market are the sparse dimensions.
SET MSG DETAIL;	The SET MSG DETAIL command provides an information message every time Essbase calculates a data block. It is useful for testing your database's consolidation path, but this command can cause a high level of processing overhead so remember to remove the function after testing.
SET NOTICE HIGH;	Provides completion notices at intervals during the calculation.

You may have asked yourself, why not just right-click on the database and select **Execute Calculation**? The answer to that question is simple. Calculations on cubes that are not optimized, or in the beginning phases of development, can take hours to run only to give wrong results or worse, run for hours and crash when they fill up the hard drive. In order to avoid these issues, we should run the calculation from a MaxL or ESSCMD script to see the progress on the screen and detect problems early. If you see any problem as the calculation is taking place, then you can kill the calculation by right-clicking on your Server node. Click on **Edit...** and select **Session**. Select the calculation's session, select **Kill** from the drop-down, and click on the **Apply** button. We would then fix the calculation and continue.

[💡 When conducting a calculation consider using Smart View in Excel to view the results of the calculation as it progresses.]

Moreover, the `Calc ALL` command is optimized for calculating an entire cube. It should come as no surprise that `Calc All` is the default calculation when you first build an Essbase cube.

The calculation order for the Basic database using `Calc All` is as follows:

1. The dimension tagged as `Account` is calculated first, in this case the `Measures` dimension.

2. The dimension tagged as `Time` is second, in this case the `Year`.

3. Then, all other dense dimensions are processed in the order that they appear in the outline from top to bottom. The only other dense dimension is `Scenario`.

4. If no `Account` or `Time` dimension existed, then the order would have been all dense dimensions from top to bottom.

5. All sparse dimensions top to bottom. In this case, the `Market` dimension will be calculated first and then the `Product` dimension.

In each dimension, this is how calculations will take place:

1. Consolidations will be performed as per Member Properties, including formulas and rollups for the level zero members of the dimension being calculated.

2. Calculation then continues from bottom up by default to Level 1 members, and so on up the hierarchy.

Finally, we set up our `CalcDB` calculation as the `Basic` database's `Default` database.

[💡 Only use `SET CALCPARELLEL` if the ratio of Empty tasks, as specified in the application log (to the Calculation Task scheduled, in the ESSCMD or MaxL script screen) is less than 50 %. A high ratio of empty tasks means that parallelism may not improve performance. There are cases where the use of `CALCPARELLEL` slows down calculations as the calculation is meant to work in serial.]

See also

Review the recipe *Adding an Application and Database on an Essbase server* in *Chapter 5, Using EAS for Development* to understand how to create the sample basic database. The recipe *Modifying Essbase settings to improve calculation performance* can be used to understand how the settings like SET LOCKBLOCK HIGH and SET CACHE HIGH are changed. You should also review *Executing Calculation using MaxL* in *Chapter 7, Using MaxL to Automate Processes*, to learn how you automate calculations using MaxL.

Using control flow commands, conditional, and logical operators

In this recipe, we will control the calculation flow and apply conditional logic to a calculation by using FIX\ENDFIX and IF\ENDIF. We will also learn how to aggregate and calculate the database using the AGG and CALC DIM commands. Moreover, we will use the SET CREATEBLOCKONEQ command to make sure that blocks are created for our calculated measure. Finally, we will review the logical operators that you can use in the calculations and discuss the @RETURN function new to 11.1.2.x. This recipe only applies to the BSO model.

Getting ready

To get started, click on the **Start** menu and **Program | Oracle EPM System | Essbase | Essbase Administration Services| Start Administration Services Console**. In the Log in menu, enter your Administration Server, Username, Password, and click on the **Log in** button.

How to do it...

1. Drill down on the Essbase Server in EAS. Expand the **Applications** node, drill down on the **Sample** application, right-click on the **Basic** database, right-click on the **Outline**, and select **Edit** from the drop-down.

2. Drill down on the **Measures** dimension and the **Ratios** hierarchy. Right-click the member **Profit per Ounce**, click on **Add Sibling** from the drop down menu, enter Weighted Sales as the member name, press the *Enter* key, and then press *Esc*.

3. Click on the **Verify** outline button, click on **OK** at the prompt, click on the **Save** button, select the **Level 0** data radio button in the **Restructure Options** menu, and click on **OK**.

4. Drill down on the Essbase Server in EAS, expand the **Applications** node, drill down on the **Sample** application, right-click on the **Basic** database in the drop-down menu, click on **Create**, and select **Calculation Scripts**.

5. In the **Calculation Script Editor**, enter the following script:

```
SET UPDATECALC OFF;
SET AGGMISSG ON;
SET LOCKBLOCK HIGH;
SET CACHE ALL;
SET CACHE HIGH;
SET CALCPARALLEL 3;
SET CALCTASKDIMS 2;

FIX(@Relative("Product", 0), @Relative("Market", 0))
  SET CREATEBLOCKONEQ ON;
  "Weighted Sales" (
    IF (@ISLEV("Year", 0))
      IF ("Sales" <=100)
        "Sales" + ("Sales" * .03);
        ElseIf ("Sales" > 100)
          "Sales" + ("Sales" * .06);
          Else
/*@RETURN is a new function in 11.1.2.1*/
              @RETURN(@CONCATENATE(
                @CONCATENATE("Negative number for: Product [",
                @NAME(@CURRMBR("Product"))),
                "] has a negative sale.")
              , WARNING);

      EndIf;
    EndIf;
  );
  SET CREATEBLOCKONEQ OFF;
CALC DIM("Measures");
ENDFIX;
AGG("Market", "Product");
```

6. Click on the **Check syntax** button to verify that the syntax is correct. A prompt should pop up with the text **Syntax check was successful**. Click on **OK**.

7. Select the **File** menu, click on **Save**, enter `CalcAgg` in the filename textbox, and click on **OK**.

8. Open an Excel session; open a connection to your database in **Smart View** by clicking on the **Open** button in the **Smart View** ribbon. Select **Private Connections** in your **Smart View** panel, enter your username and password in the **Connect to Data Source** menu, and click on **Connect**.

9. Drill down on **Sample** application; right-click **Basic** database, and click **Ad hoc analysis**.

10. Set up your spreadsheet like the following screenshot and click on **Refresh** in your **POV** menu:

	A	B	C	D	E
1			Florida	Florida	Florida
2			Actual	Actual	Actual
3			400-10	400-20	400-30
4	Sales	Jan			
5		Feb			
6		Mar			
7		Qtr1			
8	Weighted Sales	Jan			
9		Feb			
10		Mar			
11		Qtr1			
12		Apr			

11. In your Essbase ribbon, click on **Calculate**. In the **Calculation Script** menu, select **CalcAgg** under **Calculation Script** and **Basic** under **Cube**, and click on the **Launch** button.

12. Click on the **Refresh** button on your POV to see the results.

How it works

In this recipe, we used set functions that were described in detail in the recipe *Using Essbase Set function commands and Calc All to calculate cubes* in this chapter. We used control flow in the following session of the calculation script:

```
FIX(@Relative("Product", 0), @Relative("Market", 0))
```

This `FIX` statement returns data blocks for level zero of sparse dimensions `Product` and `Market`. The `@Relative` member relational function is used to retrieve existing data blocks at the level specified at the second parameter.

> The number of blocks is determined by the sparse dimension members with data. Reducing the amounts of blocks that you need to bring into memory is a simple way of optimizing a calculation. For this reason, it is important for optimization of a calculation to `FIX` on sparse dimensions. A simple rule of thumb is to `FIX` on sparse and `IF` on dense.

Because we are fixing on an existing data block, we need a function that allows us to create new blocks when a calculation function uses any equation other than a constant for our Weighted Sales measure. The set function CREATEBLOCKONEQ is set to ON to create blocks on equations.

> When you use SET CREATEBLOCKEQ ON, make sure that the function is used inside of a FIX as this set function is processor intensive. When you are done with the equation it is important that you use SET CREATEBLOCKEQ OFF. An alternative to using the CREATEBLOCKONEQ set function is to use a DATACOPY to create blocks based on an existing data block. We can also create blocks by submitting data in Smart View or loading data via a load rule.

The Weighted Sales measure has an IF statement that uses the Boolean function @ISLEV ("Year", 0), which returns level zero members of the dense dimension **Year**. Our Weighted Sales measure uses a nested IF conditional function and logical operators to assign the formula:

```
"Weighted Sales" (
  IF (@ISLEV("Year", 0))
    IF ("Sales" <=100)
      "Sales" + ("Sales" * .03);
    ElseIf ("Sales" > 100)
      Sales" + ("Sales" * .06);
    Else
      @RETURN(@CONCATENATE(
        @CONCATENATE("Negative number for: Product [",
        @NAME(@CURRMBR("Product"))), "] has a negative sale.")
        , WARNING);

    EndIf;
  EndIf;
);
SET CREATEBLOCKONEQ OFF;
```

The following are the conditional and logical operators that you can use in your equation as per the Oracle Essbase Technical Reference:

Conditional\Logical Operators	Description
IF\ ELSEIF \ ELSE \ ENDIF	Calculates a formula based on the conditional results of the test
= =	Equal to
>=	Greater than or equal to
<=	Less than or equal to

Conditional\Logical Operators	Description
<	Less than
>	Greater than
<> or !=	Not equal to
OR	Results in TRUE if either of the condition is TRUE
AND	Results in TRUE if both of the conditions are TRUE
NOT	Return FALSE if condition is TRUE

The @RETURN function will exit the equation when a specific condition is met. This function uses an error message and one of three priority levels (INFO, ERROR, or WARNING) as parameters, as follows:

```
@RETURN ("ErrorMessage", [, INFO|ERROR|WARNING])
```

Moreover, we use the CALC DIM function to calculate all level zero members of the Measures dimension. The important thing to note here is that the other two dense dimensions, Year and Scenario, have all equations and parent-level members set to either Dynamic Calc or Label Only data storage so they are calculated on the fly when you retrieve. Therefore, you do not need to calculate them in **Basic** database's case. Finally, the AGG function is used as it is faster than the CALC function when calculating sparse dimensions. This is due partially to the fact that the AGG function ignores member calculations and only aggregates the hierarchy based on the outline structure. The following screenshot is the result of this calculation in Excel:

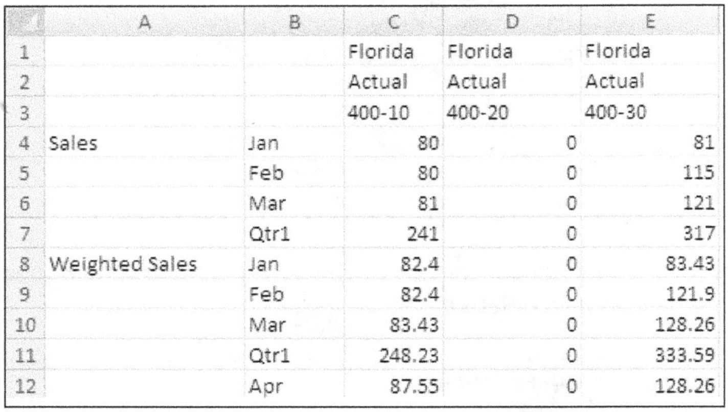

	A	B	C	D	E
1			Florida	Florida	Florida
2			Actual	Actual	Actual
3			400-10	400-20	400-30
4	Sales	Jan	80	0	81
5		Feb	80	0	115
6		Mar	81	0	121
7		Qtr1	241	0	317
8	Weighted Sales	Jan	82.4	0	83.43
9		Feb	82.4	0	121.9
10		Mar	83.43	0	128.26
11		Qtr1	248.23	0	333.59
12		Apr	87.55	0	128.26

Review the recipe *Adding an Application and Database on an Essbase server* in *Chapter 5* to understand how to create the sample basic database. Review the recipe *Using Essbase Set function commands and Calc All to calculate cubes* to understand the command function used in this recipe in this chapter.

Using substitution variables in calculations script

Substitution variables are global place holders for values that change often in our Essbase application. Substitution variables have many functions in Essbase, but in this recipe, we will use a substitution variable in a nested `FIX/ENDFIX` statement to copy data for the `Year` dimension member specified in our substitution variable. We will also use the substitution variable as the parameter in our `ACCUM` and `MOVAVG` range and financial functions. This recipe only applies to the BSO model.

Getting ready

To get started, click on the **Start** menu and navigate to **Program | Oracle EPM System | Essbase | Essbase Administration Services | Start Administration Services Console**. In the Log in menu, enter your Administration Server, Username, Password, and click on the **Log in** button.

How to do it...

1. Right-click on your Essbase Server in EAS, select **Edit...,** and click on **Variables....**

2. In the **Substitution Variables** menu, click down on the cell under **Application**, select **Sample**, click down on the cell under the **Database** column, and select **Basic**.

3. Click on the cell under **Variable**, type `CurMth`, select the cell under the **Value**, type in `Mar`, and click on the **Set** button.

4. Drill down on the Essbase Server in EAS, expand the **Applications** node, drill down on the **Sample** application and **Basic** database, right-click on the **Outline**, and select **Edit** from the drop down.

5. Drill down on the **Measures** dimension and the **Ratios** hierarchy. Right-click on the member **Profit per Ounce**. Click on **Add Sibling** from the drop-down menu, enter `YTD Sales` as the member name, press the *Enter* key, and then *Esc*.

6. Click on the **YTD Sales** member and select the ~ (tilde) or **Exclude from Consolidate** button.

7. Right-click on the **YTD Sales** member, click on **Add Sibling** from the drop-down menu, enter `MovAvg Sales` as the member name, press the *Enter* key, and then *Esc*.

8. Click on the **MovAvg Sales** member and select the ~ (tilde) or **Exclude from Consolidate** button.

9. Click on the **Verify** outline button. Click on **OK** at the prompt. Click on the **Save** button, select the **Level 0 data** radio button in the **Restructure Options** menu, and click on **OK**.

10. Right-click on the **Basic** database. In the drop down menu, click on **Create**, and select **Calculation Scripts**.

11. In the **Calculation Script Editor**, enter the following script:

```
SET UPDATECALC OFF;
SET AGGMISSG ON;
SET LOCKBLOCK HIGH;
SET CACHE ALL;
SET CACHE HIGH;
SET CALCPARALLEL 3;
SET CALCTASKDIMS 2;


FIX(@Relative("Product", 0), @Relative("Market", 0))
  FIX(&CurMth)

    "YTD Sales" = @ACCUM(Sales, Jan:&CurMth);

    "MovAvg Sales" = @MOVAVG(Sales,3,Jan:&CurMth);

      CALC DIM("Measures");
    ENDFIX;
  ENDFIX;
AGG("Market", "Product");
```

12. Click on the **Check syntax** button to verify that the syntax is correct. A prompt should pop up with the text **Syntax check was successful**. Click on **OK**.

13. Select the **File** menu, click on **Save**, enter `CalcSV` in the file name textbox, and click on **OK**.

14. Open an **Excel** session, open a connection to your **Smart View** by pressing the **Open** button in the **Smart View** ribbon, select **Private Connections** in your **Smart View** panel, enter your username and password in the **Connect to Data Source** menu, and click on **Connect**.

15. Drill down on the **Sample** application. Right-click on the **Basic** database, and click **Ad hoc analysis**.

16. Set up your spreadsheet, as shown in the following screenshot, and click on **Refresh** on your POV menu:

	A	B	C	D
1		Actual	Actual	Actual
2		Market	Market	Market
3		Product	Product	Product
4		Jan	Feb	Mar
5	Sales			
6	YTD Sales			
7	MovAvg Sales			

17. In your Essbase ribbon, click on **Calculate**; in the **Calculation Script** menu, select **CalcSV** under **Calculation Script** and **Basic** under **Cube**, and click on the **Launch** button.

18. Click on the **Refresh** button on your POV to see results.

How it works...

We begin this recipe setting up a substitution variable CurMth for the CalcSV calculation script. We then add a set of functions that were described in detail in the recipe *Using Essbase Set function commands and Calc All to calculate cubes* in this chapter. Moreover, we used the FIX statement to retrieve existing blocks and then used a nested FIX statement to only bring in blocks with the @CurMth substitution variable, which is the dense member Mar. In this scenario, the nested FIX was used in place of an IF conditional operator, as follows:

```
FIX(@Relative("Product", 0), @Relative("Market", 0))
  FIX(&CurMth)

    "YTD Sales" = @ACCUM(Sales, Jan:&CurMth);

    "MovAvg Sales" = @MOVAVG(Sales,3,Jan:&CurMth);

      CALC DIM("Measures");
    ENDFIX;
  ENDFIX;
AGG("Market", "Product");
```

Moreover, we used the @ACCUM function to get the year to date value of the Sales. The @ACCUM financial function has a member name and a range list parameter as depicted in the following code:

```
@ACCUM (mbrName [, rangeList])
```

We used the `Jan:&CurMth` to include all `Year` dimension members between `Jan` and `Mar`. Finally, we used the `@MOVAVG` function to take a moving average based on the last three months. The `@MOVAG` uses a member name or combination, an optional positive integer that specifies the amount of values to average, and a comma delimited list, cross-dimensional member, or member set function or range.

```
@MOVAVG (mbrName [, n [, XrangeList]])
```

The following screenshot has the results of the calculation. You may notice that cell **C6** has the year-to-date value for range **B5:C5** and cell **D6** has the YTD value for range **B5:D5** for **Sales**. In addition, take note that cell **D7** has the average of range **B5:D5**, which is the three month moving average for March.

	A	B	C	D
1		Actual	Actual	Actual
2		Market	Market	Market
3		Product	Product	Product
4		Jan	Feb	Mar
5	Sales	31538	32069	32213
6	YTD Sales	31538	63607	95820
7	MovAvg Sales	31538	32069	31940

See also

Review the recipe *Using control flow commands, conditional operators, and logical operators* in this chapter for details on why the `Calc Dim` and `Agg` commands are used in this recipe. Review the recipe *Adding an Application and Database on an Essbase server* in *Chapter 5* to understand how to create the sample basic database.

Using UDAs and Calc Two Pass in calculation scripts

In this recipe, we will use the `@UDA` function to list the members that we want to include in our calculation. We will also set up a formula using the `@ISUDA` Boolean function to retrieve the shares of the total `Payroll` for each `Major Markets` in the `Market` dimension. Finally, we will accomplish this same task by using an outline formula and `Calc Two Pass` instead. This recipe only applies to the BSO model.

Getting ready

To get started, click on the **Start** menu and **Program | Oracle EPM System | Essbase | Essbase Administration Services | Start Administration Services Console**. In the Log in menu, enter your Administration Server, Username, Password, and click on the **Log in** button.

How to do it...

1. Drill down on the Essbase Server in EAS, expand the **Applications** node, drill down on the **Sample** application and **Basic** database, right-click on the **Outline**, and select **Edit** from the drop down.

2. Drill down on the **Measures** dimension and the **Ratios** hierarchy. Right-click on member **Profit per Ounce**, click on **Add Sibling** from the drop-down menu, enter `Major Mkt Payroll Shares` as the member name, press the *Enter* key, and then hit *Esc*.

3. Click on the **Major Mkt Payroll Shares** member and select the ~ (tilde) or **Exclude from Consolidate** button.

4. Drill down on the **Market** dimension, right-click on the **East** member, select **Edit member properties...**, select the **UDAs** tab in the **Member Properties** menu, click on the **Major Market** UDA in the **UDAs assigned to East** listbox, click on the **Unassign** button, and then click on **OK**. Repeat this same step for the `Central` market member.

5. Click on the **Verify** outline button. Click on **OK** at the prompt, click on the **Save** button, select the **Level 0 data** radio button in the **Restructure Options** menu, and click on **OK**.

6. Right-click on the **Basic** database. In the drop down menu, click on **Create**, and select **Calculation Scripts**.

7. In the **Calculation Script Editor**, enter the following script:

```
SET UPDATECALC OFF;
SET AGGMISSG ON;
SET LOCKBLOCK HIGH;
SET CACHE ALL;
SET CACHE HIGH;
SET CALCPARALLEL 3;
SET CALCTASKDIMS 2;

FIX(@UDA("Market", "Major Market"), @Relative(Product, 0))

  CALC DIM ("Measures");
ENDFIX;

AGG("Market", "Product");

"Major Mkt Payroll Shares" (
  IF (@ISUDA(Market, "Major Market"))
    Payroll /
    @SUMRANGE(Payroll, @UDA(Market, "Major Market"));
  ELSEIF (NOT @ISLEV("Market", 0))
```

```
      @SUM(@Relative(@CURRMBR("Market"), 0));
    ELSE
      #MISSING;
    ENDIF;
  );
```

8. Click on the **Check syntax** button to verify that the syntax is correct. A prompt should pop up with the text **Syntax check was successful**. Click on **OK**.

9. Select the **File** menu, click on **Save**, enter `CalcUDA` in the file name textbox, and click on **OK**.

10. Open an Excel session. Open a connection to your **Smart View** by clicking on the **Open** button in the **Smart View** ribbon. Select **Private Connections** in your **Smart View** panel. Enter your username and password in the **Connect to Data Source** menu, and click on **Connect**.

11. Drill down on **Sample** application. Right-click on the **Basic** database, and click **Ad hoc analysis**.

12. Set up your spreadsheet like the following screenshot and click on the **Refresh** button on your **POV** menu:

	A	B	C
1		Actual	Actual
2		Product	Product
3		Payroll	Major Mkt Payroll Shares
4		Jan	Jan
5	New York		
6	Massachusetts		
7	Florida		
8	California		
9	Texas		
10	Illinois		
11	Ohio		
12	Colorado		

13. In your Essbase ribbon click on **Calculate**, in the **Calculation Script** menu select **CalcUDA** under **Calculation Script** and **Basic** under **Cube**, and click on the **Launch** button.

14. Click on the **Refresh** button on your POV to see results.

How it works...

We begin this recipe by creating a **Major Mkt Payroll Shares** member in our outline to use in the `CalcUDA` calculation script. In addition, we remove the `Major Market` UDA from the `East` and `Central` parent markets; even though these show how UDAs can be assigned to multiple levels in a hierarchy, they would have a negative impact on the results of our calculation.

> **UDA** stands for **User-Defined Attribute** and can be used in our Essbase outline to filter specific members based on the assigned attributes. Unlike an `Attribute` dimension, UDAs can be assigned to dense and sparse dimensions and cannot be used for cross tab reporting using Smart View. An advantage that UDAs have over `Attribute` dimensions is that the same UDA can be assigned to multiple levels in an Essbase hierarchy.

We then added a set of functions in our `CalcUDA` calculation that were described in detail in the recipe *Using Essbase Set function commands and Calc All to calculate cubes* in this chapter, before we executed the following lines of code:

```
FIX(@UDA("Market", "Major Market"), @Relative(Product, 0))
    CALC DIM ("Measures");
ENDFIX;
```

We used the `@UDA` function in our preceding `FIX\ENDFIX` statement to limit our data blocks to `Market` members with the `Major Market` user-defined attribute. We also used the `FIX` with the `@Relative(Product,0)` to run our calculation on the lowest level of the Product dimension. We also calculated the `Measures` dimension only as the parent values of other two dense dimensions `Scenario` and `Year` are either dynamic calc or label only, and do not have stored formulas associated with any of their leaf level members. As a result, we do not have to include the `Year` and `Scenario` in our calculation. Next, we used the `AGG` command to aggregate our sparse dimensions `Products` and `Markets` as these two dimensions do not have any stored formulas and the `AGG` command works faster on sparse dimension that only need to be rolled up as depicted in the following line of code:

```
AGG("Market", "Product");
```

Then, we use an `IF\ENDIF` with the Boolean function `@ISUDA`, which checks if a particular `Market` member has the `Major Market` user-defined attribute string:

```
"Major Mkt Payroll Shares" (
  IF (@ISUDA(Market, "Major Market"))
    Payroll /
      @SUMRANGE(Payroll, @UDA(Market, "Major Market"));
    ELSEIF (NOT @ISLEV("Market", 0))
      @SUM(@Relative(@CURRMBR("Market"), 0));
    ELSE
      #MISSING;
  ENDIF;
);
```

Moreover, we divide `Payroll` by the function `@SUMRANGE`, which sums the values of measure `Payroll` across the list of `Major Market` members returned by function `@UDA`. Finally, we use the `@SUM` function in our `ELSEIF` session to sum the leaf level values for the currently selected none level 0 members in our `Market` dimension. The result of this calculation is in the following screenshot:

	A	B	C
1		Actual	Actual
2		Product	Product
3		Payroll	Major Mkt Payroll Shares
4		Jan	Jan
5	New York	195	0.12195122
6	Massachusetts	139	0.086929331
7	Florida	198	0.123827392
8	California	302	0.188868043
9	Texas	135	0.084427767
10	Illinois	197	0.123202001
11	Ohio	211	0.131957473
12	Colorado	222	0.138836773
13	Market	4056	1

There's more...

There were several steps conducted in the `CalcUDA` script that were meant to run several passes of the Essbase outline, and in essence bring back the correct values for the `Major Mkt Payroll Shares` measure. We could have accomplished the same task by assigning the formula in the Essbase outline, setting the member's Two-Pass calculation property to true, and running the command `Calc TwoPass` in the calculation script instead. The `Calc TwoPass` command does exactly what we discussed above as it runs a second pass of the database for members in the Measure dimension that have been marked for the Two Pass calculation. You should have completed steps 1 through 4 of the recipe *Using UDAs and Calc Two Pass in calculation scripts* before running the following instructions:

1. Open the **Basic** outline to edit in **EAS**, drill down on the **Measure** dimension, right-click on the **Major Mkt Payroll Shares** member, and select **Edit member properties...**.

2. Select the **Formula** tab in the **Member Properties** menu, enter the following formula, and click on the **Verify** button.

```
IF (@ISUDA(Market, "Major Market"))
   Payroll /
   @SUMRANGE(Payroll, @UDA(Market, "Major Market"));
   ELSEIF (NOT @ISLEV("Market", 0))
      @SUM(@Relative(@CURRMBR("Market"), 0));
   ELSE
      #MISSING;
ENDIF;
```

3. Click the **Information** tab, set the **Two-Pass calculation** property to **True**, and click on **OK**.

4. Click on the **Verify** outline button, click on **OK** at the prompt, click on the **Save** button, select the **Level 0 data** radio button in the **Restructure Options** menu, and click on **OK**.

5. Right-click on the **Basic** database and in the drop-down menu, click on **Create**, and select **Calculation Scripts**.

6. In the **Calculation Script Editor**, enter the following script:

```
SET UPDATECALC OFF;
SET AGGMISSG ON;
SET LOCKBLOCK HIGH;
SET CACHE ALL;
SET CACHE HIGH;
SET CALCPARALLEL 3;
SET CALCTASKDIMS 2;

Calc All;
   Calc TwoPass;
```

7. Click on the **Check syntax** button to verify that the syntax is correct; a prompt should pop up with the text **Syntax check was successful**. Click on **OK**.

8. Select the **File** menu, click on **Save**, enter `ClcUDATP` in the file name textbox, and click on **OK**.

9. Right-click on the **Basic** database, click on **Execute Calculation**, click on **ClcUDATP**, and then on **OK**.

10. You can verify the results in Excel as in the preceding exercise. The results should be the same as before.

See also

Review *Adding an Application and Database on an Essbase server* in *Chapter 5* to understand how to create the sample basic database. Review the recipe *Using control flow commands, conditional operators, and logical operators* in this chapter for details on why the `Calc Dim` and `Agg` commands are used in this recipe.

Using Attributes in calculation scripts

In this recipe, we will use the `@Attribute`, `@WithAttr`, and `@AttributeVal` functions to limit the scope of our script and allow us to rank sales in the `Sample.Basic` database. We will use the `@Rank` function in our calculation to rank the sales of certain products for the New York market. This recipe only applies to the BSO model.

Getting ready

To get started, click on the **Start** menu and navigate to **Program | Oracle EPM System | Essbase | Essbase Administration Services | Start Administration Services Console**. In the Log in menu, enter your Administration Server, Username, Password, and click on the **Log in** button.

How to do it...

1. Drill down on the Essbase Server in EAS, expand the **Applications** node, drill down on the **Sample** application and **Basic** database, right-click on the **Outline**, and select **Edit** from the drop-down.

2. Drill down on the **Measures** dimension and the **Ratios** hierarchy. Right-click member **Profit per Ounce**, click on **Add Sibling** from the drop-down menu, enter `Rank 12 Ounce Drinks` as the member name, press the *Enter* key, and then press *Esc*.

3. Click on the **Rank 12 Ounce Drinks** member and select the ^ (karrot) or **Never consolidate member** button.

4. Click on the **Verify** outline button, click on **OK** at the prompt, click on the **Save** button, select the **All data** radio button in the **Restructure Options** menu, and click on **OK**.

5. Right-click on the **Basic** database; in the drop-down menu, click on **Create**, and select **Calculation Scripts**.

```
SET UPDATECALC OFF;
SET AGGMISSG ON;
SET LOCKBLOCK HIGH;
SET CACHE ALL;
SET CACHE HIGH;
SET CALCPARALLEL 3;
SET CALCTASKDIMS 2;

FIX (
   @WITHATTR(Ounces,"==","12"),
   @ATTRIBUTE("Can"),
   @Relative(Product, 0),
   @MEMBER("New York")
   )

   "Rank 12 Ounce Drinks" (
   IF (@ATTRIBUTEVAL("Intro Date") >=
     @TODATE("mm-dd-yyyy","03-25-1996") and
     @ISLEV("Year", 0) and
     @ISMBR("Actual")
     )
     @RANK(SKIPMISSING,"Sales"->"New York",
     @RANGE("Sales"->"New York",@LIST(@Relative(Product, 0)))));
   ELSE
     #MISSING;
   ENDIF;);
ENDFIX;
```

6. Click on the **Check syntax** button to verify that the syntax is correct. A prompt should pop up with the text **Syntax check was successful**. Click on **OK**.

7. Select the **File** menu, click on **Save**, enter `CalcAttr` in the file name textbox, and click on **OK**.

8. Open an Excel session. Open a connection to your database in **Smart View** by clicking on the **Open** button in the **Smart View** ribbon. Select **Private Connections** in your **Smart View** panel, enter your username and password in the **Connect to Data Source** menu, and click on **Connect**.

9. Drill-down on the **Sample** application, and right-click **Basic** database and click on **Ad hoc analysis**.

10. Set up your spreadsheet as shown in the following screenshot and click on **Refresh** on your **POV** menu:

	A	B	C	D	E	F	G
1		New York	Actual				
2		Jan		Feb		Mar	
3		Sales	Rank 12 Ounce Drinks	Sales	Rank 12 Ounce Drinks	Sales	Rank 12 Ounce Drinks
4	100-10						
5	200-10						
6	200-40						
7	300-10						
8	300-20						
9	400-10						
10	400-20						
11	400-30						
12	Product						

11. In your Essbase ribbon, click on **Calculate**. In the **Calculation Script** menu, select **CalcAttr** under **Calculation Script** and **Basic** under **Cube**, and click on the **Launch** button.

12. Click on the **Refresh** button on your POV to see the results.

How it works...

We began this recipe by creating a `Rank 12 Ounce Drinks` member in our outline to use in the `CalcAttr` calculation script. We then added a set of functions to our `CalcAttr` calculation that were described in detail in the recipe *Using Essbase Set function commands and Calc All to calculate cubes* in this chapter. The `FIX\ENDFIX` statement in this script has several key attribute functions that allow us to filter members of the Product base dimension based on the values of the specific attributes that have been assigned to them. The following is our `FIX` statement:

```
FIX (
  @WITHATTR(Ounces,"==","12"),
  @ATTRIBUTE("Can"),
  @Relative(Product, 0),
  @MEMBER("New York")
)
```

The @WITHATTR in these FIX states brings back Products with the Ounce numeric attribute assigned to a value equal to 12. We could have also used several other operators in this case, as depicted in the following grid and as discussed in the *Oracle Essbase Technical Reference*:

Operator	Description
IN	In
= =	Equal to
>	Greater than
<	Less than
<=	Less than or equal to
>=	Greater than or equal to
!= or <>	Not equal to

The @ATTRIBUTE function is different to the @WITHATTR as it cannot verify condition. In other words, you cannot use an operator like the preceding ones. We use the FIX statement to bring back only products that have been assigned the attribute Can. The @Relative function returns only level zero members of the Product dimension and the @MEMBER function is used to return only the New York market from the Market dimension. The next portion of the script conducts the conditional logic and formula of the script as follows:

```
DATACOPY "Sales" to "Rank 12 Ounce Drinks";

    "Rank 12 Ounce Drinks" (
    IF (@ATTRIBUTEVAL("Intro Date") >=
      @TODATE("mm-dd-yyyy","03-25-1996") and
      @ISLEV("Year", 0) and
      @ISMBR("Actual")
    )
      @RANK(SKIPMISSING,"Sales"->"New York",
      @RANGE("Sales"->"New York",@LIST(@Relative(Product, 0))));
    ELSE
      #MISSING;
    ENDIF;);
ENDFIX;
```

We used the DataCopy command to make sure that blocks are created for our Rank 12 Ounce Drinks member. Next, we used the @ATTRIBUTEVAL function in our IF\ENDIF statement to limit the @RANK calculation only to Products with an Intro Date attribute greater or equal to 03-25-1996. In addition, we limit the ranking to the lowest level of the Year dimension and the Scenario Actual. Finally, the @RANK function is used to complete the ranking of Products for the New York market.

The @RANK function takes three parameters as follows:

@RANK (SKIPNONE | SKIPMISSING | SKIPZERO | SKIPBOTH, value, expList)

The first parameter SKIPNONE | SKIPMISSING | SKIPZERO | SKIPBOTH specifies what values to include in the ranking. The second parameter value is the member or member combination for which the rank is calculated, and the third is a comma delimited list, variables, functions, or numeric expressions. The expList parameter returns a lists of value across which the rank is calculated. Our @RANK function will skip any missing value, will rank based on Sales for New York, and will return values for Sales for New York at the lowest level of the product dimension.

> The @RANK function will return the same rank for duplicate values.

The results of the function are in the following screenshot:

	A	B	C	D	E	F	G
1		New York	Actual				
2		Jan		Feb		Mar	
3		Sales	Rank 12 Ounce Drinks	Sales	Rank 12 Ounce Drinks	Sales	Rank 12 Ounce Drinks
4	100-10	678	1	645	1	675	1
5	200-10	61	#Missing	61	#Missing	63	#Missing
6	200-40	490	2	580	2	523	2
7	300-10	483	3	495	3	513	3
8	300-20	180	6	180	7	182	7
9	400-10	234	4	232	5	234	4
10	400-20	219	5	243	4	213	5
11	400-30	134	7	189	6	198	6
12	Product	2479	#Missing	2625	#Missing	2601	#Missing

See also

Review *Adding an Application and Database on an Essbase server* in *Chapter 5* to understand how to create the sample basic database.

Clearing data and using the cross- dimensional operators in a calculation script

In this recipe, we will use the `ClearData` and `ClearBlock` commands to clear intersections of our data. We will also use an `IF/ENDIF` conditional statement to set data to `#MISSING` if it meets certain criteria. Clearing data is a task that you are going to conduct frequently, specifically if your data is transactional. We are also going to be using the **cross-dimensional operator** in our calculation frequently. The cross-dimensional operators point to specific intersections of member combinations and can be recognized by the hyphen followed by the right-angle bracket sign, which is **->**. This recipe only applies to the BSO model.

Getting ready

To get started, click on the **Start** menu and navigate to **Program | Oracle EPM System | Essbase | Essbase Administration Services | Start Administration Services Console**. In the Log in menu, enter your Administration Server, username, and password, and click on the **Log in** button.

How to do it...

1. Right-click on your Essbase Server in EAS, select **Edit...**, and click on **Variables...**.

2. In the **Substitution Variables** menu, click down on the cell under **Application**, and select **Sample**. Click down on the cell under the **Database** column, and select **Basic**.

3. Click on the cell under the **Variable**, type **CurMth**, and select the cell under the **Value**. Type in **Mar**, and click on the **Set** button.

4. Drill down on the Essbase Server in EAS, expand the **Applications** node, and drill down on the **Sample** application and **Basic** database. Right-click on the **Outline**, and select **Edit** from the drop-down.

5. Drill down on the **Measures** dimension and the **Ratios** hierarchy. Right-click the member **Profit per Ounce**, click on **Add Sibling** from the drop-down menu, enter **Budget Prep** as the member name, press the *Enter* key, and then press *Esc*.

6. Click on the **Budget Prep** member and select the **~** (tilde) or **Exclude from Consolidate** button.

7. Click the **Verify** outline button and click on **OK** at the prompt. Click on the **Save** button, select the **All data** radio button in the **Restructure Options** menu, and click on **OK**.

8. Right-click on the **Basic** database; in the drop-down menu, click on **Create**, and select **Calculation Scripts**.

```
SET UPDATECALC OFF;
SET AGGMISSG ON;
SET LOCKBLOCK HIGH;
SET CACHE ALL;
SET CACHE HIGH;
SET CALCPARALLEL 3;
SET CALCTASKDIMS 2;

CLEARBLOCK UPPER;

FIX(@Relative("Product", 0), @Relative("Market", 0))
  CLEARDATA &CurMth->"Budget Prep"->"Budget";
  SET CREATEBLOCKONEQ ON;
  "Budget Prep"
    (
    IF(@ISMBR(&CurMth))
      IF("Payroll"->"Actual"  ==  #Missing)
        "Budget Prep"->"Budget" =  #Missing;
      ELSEIF ("Payroll"->"Actual"  >=  1)
        "Budget Prep"->"Budget" = "Payroll"->"Actual" +
          ("Payroll"->"Actual" * .05);
      ELSE
        "Budget Prep"->"Budget" = #Missing;
      ENDIF;
    ENDIF;
    );
  SET CREATEBLOCKONEQ OFF;
ENDFIX;
CALC ALL;
```

9. Click on the **Check syntax** button to verify that the syntax is correct, a prompt should pop up with the text **Syntax check was successful**. Click on **OK**.

10. Select the **File** menu, click on **Save**, enter ClrDB in the file name textbox, and click on **OK**.

11. Right-click on the **Basic** database, click on **Execute Calculation**, click on **ClrDB**, and click on **OK**.

12. Click on **File** in EAS, click **Editor**, click **MDX Script Editor**, enter the following script, and click the **Execute Script** button ⬛ to check the result of the calculations in the MDX script editor.

```
SELECT
Market.Levels(0).Members ON ROWS,
{(Payroll, Actual, &CurMth), ([Budget Prep], Budget, &CurMth)}
   ON COLUMNS
FROM [Sample].Basic
```

How it works

We began this recipe by creating the `CurMth` substitution variable for our `Basic` database. We also added a `Budget Prep` member to our outline to use in the `ClrDB` calculation script. We then added a set of functions to our ClrDB calculations that were described in detail in the recipe *Using Essbase Set function commands and Calc All to calculate cubes* in this chapter. Our first clear script is `CLEARBLOCK UPPER`, which removes all upper level or consolidation-level blocks. The `CLEARBLOCK` command has the parameters depicted in the following grid:

Parameter	Description
ALL	Clears and removes all blocks.
NONINPUT	Removes blocks that are derived by the running of calculations. Command excludes the block into which values were loaded.
UPPER	Clears and removes upper-level or consolidation-level blocks.
DYNAMIC	Removes block that contain values derived by Dynamic Calc Stores calculations.
EMPTY	Removes blocks that are empty.

```
FIX(@Relative("Product", 0), @Relative("Market", 0))
   CLEARDATA &CurMth->"Budget Prep"->"Budget";
```

The `FIX/ENDFIX` control flow in the preceding code is retrieving blocks from the leaf level of sparse dimensions `Product` and `Market`. The `CLEARDATA` command is used to clear data without removing the block for any data at the intersection `&CurMth` or Mar, `Budget Prep`, and `Budget`. This is an example of a more granular approach to clearing data using cross dimensional operators.

> When clearing data it is important for optimization of a calculation to `FIX` on sparse dimensions. A simple rule of thumb is to `FIX` on sparse and `IF` on dense.

You use CLEARDATA, in this case, instead of the CLEARBLOCK command, because your formula is going create these blocks again, so there really is no need to remove them.

```
SET CREATEBLOCKONEQ ON;
  "Budget Prep"
  (
    IF(@ISMBR(&CurMth))
      IF("Payroll->"Actual"  ==  #Missing)
        "Budget Prep"->"Budget" =  #Missing;
      ELSEIF ("Payroll"->"Actual"  >=  1)
        "Budget Prep"->"Budget" = "Payroll"->"Actual" +
          ("Payroll"->"Actual" * .05);
      ELSE
        "Budget Prep"->"Budget" = #Missing;
      ENDIF;
    ENDIF;
  );
  SET CREATEBLOCKONEQ OFF;
ENDFIX;
```

Next, we increase the Payroll values by five percent where Actual is greater or equal to 1. If Actual for Payroll is #Missing, zero, or negative, then the Budget Prep members are set to #Missing, which is another way of clearing data. Finally, we run our CALC All to create the consolidations removed by CLEARBLOCK UPPER, and we used MDX to verify our results using the **MDX Script Editor**. The results of the MDX are shown in the following screenshot:

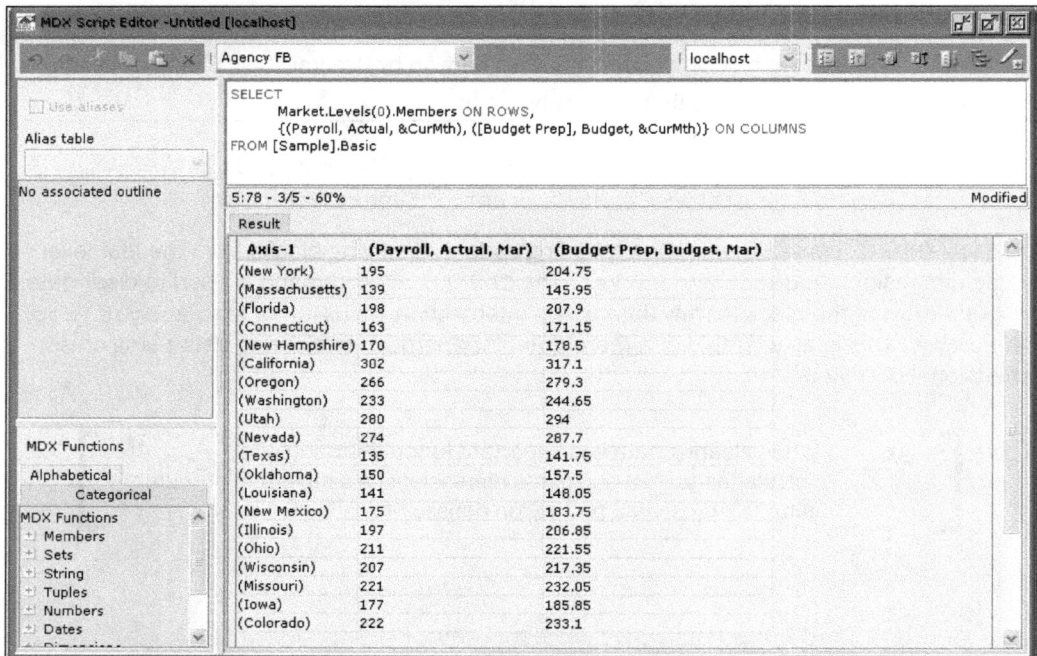

See also

Review *Adding an Application and Database on an Essbase server* in *Chapter 5* to understand how to create the basic sample database.

Using allocation functions in calculation scripts

In this recipe, we will use the @MDALLOCATE function to allocate data from upper-level members of our Product and Market dimension to the lower-levels across both dimensions. We will then go over the @MDALLOCATE functions parameters as used in our recipe. In this recipe, we will be using the Sample.Basic database as @MDALLOCATE is a BSO command.

Getting ready

To get started, click on the **Start** menu and navigate to **Program | Oracle EPM System | Essbase | Essbase Administration Services | Start Administration Services Console**. In the Log in menu, enter your Administration Server, Username, Password, and click on the **Log in** button.

How to do it...

1. Drill down on the Essbase Server in EAS, expand the **Applications** node, drill down on the **Sample** application and **Basic** database, right-click on the **Outline**, and select **Edit** from the drop-down.

2. Drill down on the **Scenario** dimension, right-click member **Actual**, click on **Add Sibling** from the drop-down menu, enter Actual 2010 as the member name, and press the *Enter* key.

3. Enter in member name Budget 2011 in the outline, press the *Enter* key, and then press *Esc*.

4. Click on the **Actual 2010** member and select the ~ (tilde) or the **Exclude from Consolidate** button. Repeat the same step for scenario **Budget 2011**.

5. Click the **Verify** outline button, click on **OK** at prompt, click on the **Save** button, select the **All data** radio button in the **Restructure Options** menu, and click on **OK**.

6. Right-click on the **Basic** database; in the drop-down menu, click on **Create**, and select **Calculation Scripts**.

```
SET UPDATECALC OFF;
SET AGGMISSG ON;
SET LOCKBLOCK HIGH;
SET CACHE ALL;
```

```
SET CACHE HIGH;
SET CALCPARALLEL 3;
SET CALCTASKDIMS 2;

   /*We use this DataCopy function to populate
 Actual 2010 for the purpose of our recipe only*/
   DATACOPY Actual to "Actual 2010";

 FIX(@ICHILDREN("Central"),@ICHILDREN("200"))
   "Budget 2011" =
   @MDALLOCATE("Budget 2011"->"Central"->"200"->
     "Sales",2, @CHILDREN("Central"),@CHILDREN("200"),
"Actual 2010"->"Sales",,share);
   ENDFIX;
CALC DIM("Measures");
AGG("Market", "Product");
```

7. Open an **Excel** session, open a connection to your database in **Smart View** by clicking on the **Open** button in the Smart View ribbon. Select **Private Connections** in your **Smart View** panel, enter your username and password in the **Connect to Data Source** menu, and click on **Connect**.

8. Drill down on the **Sample** application, right-click **Basic** database, and **Ad hoc analysis**.

9. Set up your spreadsheet as follows and click on the **Refresh** button on your **POV** menu:

	A	B
1		Budget 2011
2		Central
3		200
4		Sales
5	Jan	
6	Feb	
7	Mar	
8	Apr	
9	May	
10	Jun	
11	Jul	
12	Aug	
13	Sep	
14	Oct	
15	Nov	
16	Dec	

10. Select **B5**, enter 2500 as the value, and copy and paste the value to cell **B6** to **B16**. The cells should turn yellow.

11. Click on the **Submit Data** button on your Essbase ribbon.

12. In your Essbase ribbon, click on **Calculate**; in the **Calculation Script** menu, select **CalcMDA** under **Calculation Script** and **Basic** under **Cube**, and click on the **Launch** button.

13. Select another sheet in Excel, enter the selection in the following grid image to validate, and refresh your data from the **Basic** database:

	A	B	C	D
1			Sales	Sales
2			Year	Year
3			Actual 2010	Budget 2011
4	200-10	Illinois	7151	7337.70
5		Ohio	3810	3924.75
6		Wisconsin	2068	2122.75
7		Missouri	1315	1357.37
8		Iowa	613	631.06
9		Colorado	2276	2325.37
10		Central	17233	17698.99
11	200-20	Illinois	5875	6031.21
12		Ohio	1418	1458.50
13		Wisconsin	1074	1098.17
14		Missouri	1125	1155.42
15		Iowa	516	530.65
16		Colorado	1965	2027.06
17		Central	11973	12301.01
18	200	Illinois	13026	13368.91
19		Ohio	5228	5383.24
20		Wisconsin	3142	3220.92
21		Missouri	2440	2512.80
22		Iowa	1129	1161.70
23		Colorado	4241	4352.43
24		Central	29206	30000

How it works...

We begin this recipe by adding an Actual 2010 and a Budget 2011 scenario to be used as the basis and target of our allocation. Next, we submitted 2,500 dollars in each month for a Total Sales of 30,000 dollars. These are the sales numbers that we want to allocate into Budget 2011. We then execute our CalcMDA calculation, which first runs a DATACOPY of Actual to Actual 2010 for this recipe only to populate the prior year scenario with sample data.

The following lines of code conduct our allocation:

```
FIX(@ICHILDREN("Central"),@ICHILDREN("200"))
  "Budget 2011" =
    @MDALLOCATE("Budget 2011"->"Central"->"200"->"Sales",
    2,
    @CHILDREN("Central"),@CHILDREN("200"),
    "Actual 2010"->"Sales", ,share);
ENDFIX;
```

We begin this script with a `FIX` on children's of Central market and the `200` family of products including members `Central` and `200`. The parameters for the `@MDALLOCATE` function are specified in the following script:

```
@MDALLOCATE (amount,
Ndim,
allocationRange1 ... allocationRangeN,
basisMbr,
[roundMbr],
method [, methodParams] [, round
[, numDigits] [, roundErr]])
```

The parameters we used in our script and their descriptions are listed as follows:

Parameter	Description
amount	A value, member, or cross-dimensional member. In our case, the values that we submitted in Excel in step 11 of our recipe. "Budget 2011"->"Central"->"200"->"Sales"
Ndim	Number of dimension to allocate across. We specified two dimensions.
allocationRange1 ... allocationRangeN	The dimensions that the values are allocated to as specified by range functions, comma-delimited, or member set function. @CHILDREN("Central"),@CHILDREN("200").
basisMbr	A value, member, or cross dimensional member that specifies the values that are going to be used as the basis for the allocation. "Actual 2010"->"Sales".
roundMbr	A member or cross dimensional member that is used to add rounding errors. We left the parameter empty as it is an optional parameter.
method	An expression that is used to specify how values are to be allocated. We used the value share in our allocation.

See also

Review *Adding an Application and Database on an Essbase server* in *Chapter 5* to understand how to create the sample basic database.

Modifying Essbase settings to improve calculation performance

In this recipe, we will execute a few steps that should improve the performance of your calculation script. This recipe is meant to be used as a list of components that you should consider. This is not a one-size-fits-all list of steps as there may be many factors that you have to take into account. We will discuss some of the other points you should consider. This recipe only applies to the BSO model.

Getting ready

To get started, click on the **Start** menu and navigate to **Program | Oracle EPM System | Essbase | Essbase Administration Services | Start Administration Services Console**. In the Log in menu, enter your Administration Server, Username, Password, and click the **Log In** button.

How to do it...

1. Drill down on the Essbase Server in EAS, expand the **Applications** node, drill down on the **Sample** application, right-click on the **Basic** database, click on **Edit**, and then on **Properties**.

2. Right-click on the **Start** menu; click **Explore**, browse to `..\ ..\Oracle\ Middleware\user_projects\epmsystem1\EssbaseServer\ essbaseserver1\app\Sample\Basic`, and keep a note of the size of your `*.pag` and `*.ind` files. We can also view `*.pag` and `*.ind` size by right-clicking on the **Basic** database in EAS. Click on **Edit**, select **Properties**, and then click on the **Storage** tab.

Name ▲	Size	Type	Date Modified
trig		File Folder	5/18/2011 11:02 AM
Basic	1 KB	Data Base File	6/15/2011 8:32 AM
Basic.dbb	1 KB	DBB File	6/15/2011 8:10 AM
Basic.esm	2 KB	ESM File	6/15/2011 9:07 AM
Basic.ind	1 KB	IND File	6/15/2011 8:32 AM
Basic.otl	11 KB	OTL File	6/15/2011 8:32 AM
Basic.tct	1 KB	TCT File	6/15/2011 9:07 AM
ess00001.ind	8,024 KB	IND File	6/15/2011 9:07 AM
ess00001.pag	1,182 KB	PAG File	6/15/2011 9:07 AM

3. Open your Essbase Administrative Services, click on the **Database Properties** menu, click on the **Caches** tab, select the value **Index cache current value (KB)** setting combobox, and change the value to the size of your *.ind index file or in this case, **8024 KB**.

4. Click on the **Data cache setting (KB)** combo box and set the value **3072 KB** as that is the minimum for this setting. You would have normally set it to the combined size of your *.pag files multiplied by 0.125, which would be 148 KB as the page file was 1182 KB. We set it to 3072 kg as 148 kb falls below that minimum.

5. The **Data file cache setting (KB)** is only used when you set **Pending I/O access mode** in the **Storage** tab to **Direct I/O**. So leave it at the default value.

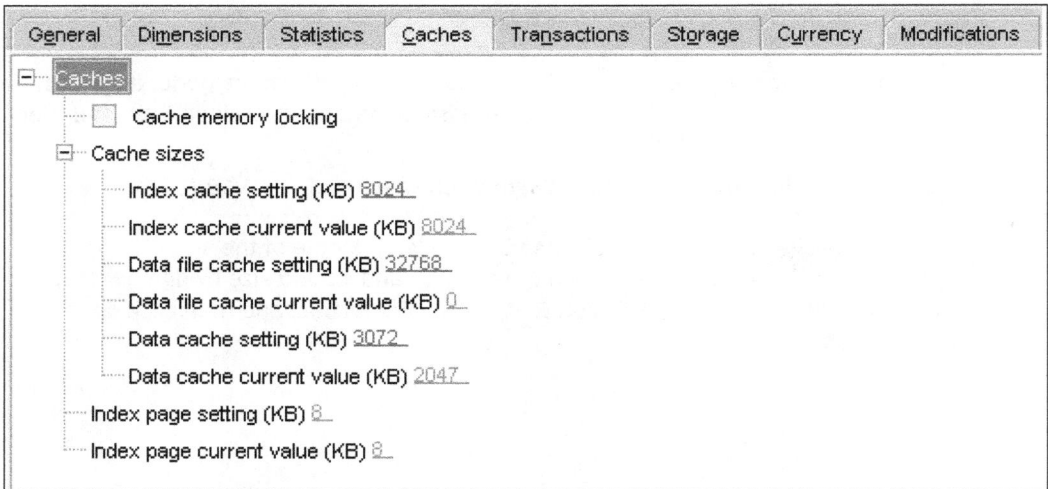

General	Dimensions	Statistics	Caches	Transactions	Storage	Currency	Modifications

```
□ Caches
      □  Cache memory locking
   □ Cache sizes
         Index cache setting (KB) 8024
         Index cache current value (KB) 8024
         Data file cache setting (KB) 32768
         Data file cache current value (KB) 0
         Data cache setting (KB) 3072
         Data cache current value (KB) 2047
   Index page setting (KB) 8
   Index page current value (KB) 8
```

6. Click on the **Dimensions** tab. Verify that that the database is an hour glass shape with the largest dense dimension, per Members Stored, at the top and the largest sparse dimension at the button. Take note of what the order should be. Note **Sample. Basic** database `Scenario` dimension is a flat dense dimension and as such is the anchor dimension. Click on the **Apply** button, and then click on **Close**.

Transactions	Storage	Currency		Modifications	
General		Dimensions		Statistics	Caches

Number of dimensions **10**

Dimension	Type	Members in Dimension	Members Stored
Year	Dense	19	12
Scenario	Dense	6	3
Product	Sparse	23	20
Population	Sparse	15	0
Pkg Type	Sparse	3	0
Ounces	Sparse	5	0
Measures	Dense	21	10
Market	Sparse	26	26
Intro Date	Sparse	8	0
Caffeinated	Sparse	3	0

7. Right-click on the **Basic Outline**, click on **Edit**, click on the **Properties** tab, and change the dense or sparse setting on the **Data Storage | Dimension storage type**'s session. You can do this only if you found discrepancies in step 6. Make sure you have a database export of the data before you continue.

```
Outline Properties
    Case-sensitive members: false
    Outline type: Block Storage
    Duplicate member names allowed false
    Typed Measures enabled true
    Date format yyyy-mm-dd
    Varying attributes enabled false
  + Alias tables
  + Attribute settings
  - Data storage
      Auto configure false
      - Dimension storage types
          Year Dense
          Measures Dense
          Market Sparse
          Product Sparse
          Scenario Dense
          Caffeinated Sparse
          Ounces Sparse
          Pkg Type Sparse
          Population Sparse
          Intro Date Sparse
```

8. Click on the **Outline** tab, right-click on the **Dimension**, and drag in the correct order. You can do this only if you found discrepancies in step 6.

9. Click on the **Verify** button, click on **Save**, and in the **Restructure Database Options** menu select **Discard all data** and click on **OK**. Note this task will cause a dense restructure, which will take a long time to complete. It is recommended to take an export of the data before you complete steps 7 through 9, **Discard all data** on the restructure, and then reload data later from the export file.

10. Right-click on the **Sample** application, click on **Stop**, and select **Application**.

11. Right-click on the **Sample** application, click on **Start**, and select **Application** for the properties to take effect.

12. Right-click on your Essbase Server node, click on **Edit**, and click on **Properties**.

13. Enter the following lines under the last line. Click on **Apply**, click on **OK** at the prompt, and click on **Close**.

```
CALCCACHEHIGH      20000
CALCCACHEDEFAULT 15000
CALCCACHELOW       10000

CALCLOCKBLOCKHIGH       10000
CALCLOCKBLOCKDEFAULT  5000
CALCLOCKBLOCKLOW        2500
```

14. Click on the **Oracle EPM System | Essbase | Essbase Server**, click on **Stop Essbase**, and click on **Start Essbase**.

How it works...

In this recipe, we adjusted our **Index Cache**, **Data File Cache**, and **Data Cache**. A description of these three settings is in the following grid:

Cache Type	Description
Index Cache	This is a buffer that controls how much of the index (.ind files) can be held in memory.
Data File Cache	This is a buffer that controls the number of compress data files (.pag files) that can be held in memory. Only used with Direct I/O.
Data Cache	This is a buffer that holds uncompressed blocks.

We also set our `Sample.Basic`'s dense and sparse settings based on the members stored. Moreover, we made sure that our outline was in an hour glass shape with the largest dense dimension on top and the largest sparse dimension on the bottom. The hour glass shape is a good guideline when you are first building your database but ultimately your dimension order should be based on the sparsity of your data by dimension. The correct dense and sparse combination for your database is not always obvious. The developer should test multiple dense and sparse configurations during testing and gauge calculation performance with each scenario. A good way of gauging the correct dense and sparse combination is by selecting the combination with the highest **Block Density** and a **Block Size** between 8 kb and 100 kb, which should provide optimal performance. These statistics can be viewed in the **Database Properties** menu and **Statistics** tab.

Finally, we change the CALCLOCKBLOCK and CALCCACHE settings to be used SET LOCKBLOCK and SET CACHE functions, respectively. We discuss the set functions in the recipe *Using Essbase Set function commands and Calc All to calculate cubes*. Developers should increase the values assigned to these settings depending on calculation performance, and to fix errors such as Dynamic Calc processor not being able to lock more than [100] ESM blocks during the calculation.

There are several things to keep in mind when defining what good calculation performance is.

The first thing is that we must maintain is a balance between calculation time and the user's experience. What I mean by user's experience is the retrieval speed in reporting applications such as Smart View, Financial Reports, or Web Analysis. If the retrieval speed of the cube is poor, calculation speed may not matter to the end user.

The second consideration is making sure that your calculation accomplishes the business's requirements. Correct results are obviously more important than fast calculation speed.

The third consideration is the frequency of execution. When a calculation is running once a night, speed of execution is not as important as if it is running, for instance, on demand.

The fourth is the scope of the calculation with regards to the user who is running it. The user may only have access to a slice of the database, and therefore, does not need be able to calculate the entire database. In this situation, improving calculation performance may mean narrowing the scope of the calculation. In summary, the developer needs to look for an acceptable balance while taking all these different points into account.

See also

Review the recipe *Adding an Application and Database on an Essbase server* in *Chapter 5* to understand how to create the sample basic database.

Using MDX to calculate Aggregate Storage database

In this recipe, we will be using MDX to run a calculation off an **Aggregate Storage Option** (**ASO**) database. Calculating an ASO database is a functionality that was not available in Essbase prior to version 11.1.2.x; as such, it is one of the more compelling reasons to upgrade from the previous versions. Although calculation in the ASO cube is a relatively new technology and does not have the breadth and depth of the BSO calculation script, it presents an exciting option to the traditional calculation options in the BSO cube. Note this recipe requires that you have the ASOsamp database added in the recipe *Using MDX in aggregate storage applications* in *Chapter 5*.

Getting ready

To get started, click on the **Start** menu and navigate to **Program | Oracle EPM System | Essbase | Essbase Administration Services | Start Administration Services Console**. In the Log in menu, enter your Administration Server, Username, Password, and click on the **Log in** button.

How to do it...

1. Drill down on the Essbase Server in EAS, expand the **Applications** node, drill down on the **ASOsamp** application and **Sample** database, right-click on the **Outline**, and select **Edit** from the drop-down.

2. Drill down on the **Years** dimension, right-click the member **Prev Year**, click on **Add Sibling** from the drop-down menu, enter **Forecast** as the member name, and press the *Enter* key

3. Click on the **Forecast** member and select the ~ (tilde) or **Exclude from Consolidate** button.

4. Click on the **Verify** outline button, click on **OK** at the prompt, click on the **Save** button, select the **Retain all data and proceed with the restructure** radio button in the **Aggregate Storage Database Restructure** menu, and click on **OK**.

5. Click on the **Start** menu, click on **Run**, enter Notepad, press *Enter*, and type the following code:

```
([Forecast], [Original Price], [Sale]) :=
([Curr Year], [Original Price], [Sale]) * 1.1;
([Forecast],[No. of Packages], [Sale]) :=
  (([Curr Year], [No. of Packages], [Sale]) +
  ([Prev Year], [No. of Packages], [Sale])) / 2;
```

6. Click on the **File** menu, click on **Save As**, browse to the following URL, enter in MDX for the filename, and click on **Save**. . \Oracle\Middleware\user_projects\ epmsystem1\EssbaseServer\essbaseserver1\app\ASOsamp\Sample

7. In the EAS, click on the **File** menu, and click on **Editors**. Then, click on **MaxL Script Editor**, and enter the following scripts in the editor:

```
execute calculation on database ASOsamp.Sample with local
  script_file
"C:\Oracle\Middleware\user_projects\epmsystem1\EssbaseServer\es
  sbaseserver1\app\ASOsamp\Sample\MDX.txt"

POV "Crossjoin(Descendants(Stores, Stores.Levels(0)),
  Crossjoin(Descendants([All Merchandise], [All
   Merchandise].Levels(0)),
  Crossjoin(Descendants(Age, Age.Levels(0)),
  Crossjoin(([Income Level].Children),
  Crossjoin ({[Sale]},
  Crossjoin(([Promotions].Children),
  Crossjoin(([Payment Type].Children),
  Crossjoin ({[Jan], [Feb], [Mar]},
  Descendants(Geography, Geography.Levels(0)))))))))))"
  SourceRegion   "Crossjoin({[Original Price], [No. of Packages]},
  Crossjoin({[Curr Year], [Prev Year]},
  Crossjoin({[Jan], [Feb], [Mar]}, {[Sale]})))";

execute aggregate process on database 'ASOsamp'.'Sample';
```

8. Click on the **Execute script** button 📋↓ to execute the MaxL script.

9. Open an Excel session; open a connection to your **Smart View** by clicking on the **Open** button in the **Smart View** ribbon. Select **Private Connections** in your **Smart View** panel, enter your username and password in the **Connect to Data Source** menu, and then click on **Connect**.

10. Drill-down on the **ASOsamp** application; right-click **Sample** database, and select **Ad hoc analysis**.

11. Set up your spreadsheet as shown in the following screenshot and click on **Refresh** on your **POV** menu:

	A	B	C	D	E
1			Sale	Sale	Sale
2			Current Year	Previous Year	Forecast
3	Original Price	Jan	$ 7,080,780.75	$ 5,309,504.75	$ 7,788,858.83
4	Original Price	Feb	$ 3,347,300.25	$ 5,379,979.25	$ 3,682,030.28
5	Original Price	Mar	$ 5,296,496.50	$ 5,401,877.50	$ 5,826,146.15
6	No. of Packages	Jan	41,932.00	31,182.00	36,557.00
7	No. of Packages	Feb	20,766.00	31,974.00	26,370.00
8	No. of Packages	Mar	31,578.00	31,152.00	31,365.00

How it works...

In this recipe, we began by adding a `Forecast` member to our `Years` dimension in the `ASOsamp.Sample` database. We then create a script to conduct the math for aggregate storage calculation, which we save in a text file. The first of the scripts calculates the **Current Year** for **Original Price** for **Sale** transaction type. It increases the number by 10 percent and places the result in the `Forecast` member of the **Original Price** measure and **Sale** transaction type. The second script takes the average of the **Current Year** and **Previous Year** for **No. Of Packages**, where transaction type equals **Sale**. The results of the following formula can be seen in the screenshot after step 11 of this recipe.

```
([Forecast], [Original Price], [Sale]) :=
([Curr Year], [Original Price], [Sale]) * 1.1;
([Forecast],[No. of Packages], [Sale]) :=
  (([Curr Year], [No. of Packages], [Sale]) +
  ([Prev Year], [No. of Packages], [Sale])) / 2;
```

We also run a MaxL script, in the MaxL Script Editor, which executes the aforementioned calculation in the `Sample` database.

Execute a calculation on database `ASOsamp.Sample` with local `script_file`, as follows:

```
C:\Oracle\Middleware\user_projects\epmsystem1\EssbaseServer\ess
  baseserver1\app\ASOsamp\Sample\MDX.txt

POV "Crossjoin(Descendants(Stores, Stores.Levels(0)),
   Crossjoin(Descendants([All Merchandise], [All
    Merchandise].Levels(0)),
   Crossjoin(Descendants(Age, Age.Levels(0)),
   Crossjoin(([Income Level].Children),
   Crossjoin ({[Sale]},
   Crossjoin(([Promotions].Children),
   Crossjoin(([Payment Type].Children),
   Crossjoin ({[Jan], [Feb], [Mar]},
```

```
Descendants(Geography, Geography.Levels(0)))))))))))"
SourceRegion    "Crossjoin({[Original Price], [No. of
  Packages]},
Crossjoin({[Curr Year], [Prev Year]},
Crossjoin({[Jan], [Feb], [Mar]}, {[Sale]})))";
```

The POV and SourceRegion are required in this MaxL\MDX script to narrow the scope of the calculation. The following table is the definition of the POV and SourceRegion:

Keyword	Description
POV	Defines the region where the calculation is performed. The calculation will execute once for every cross-product in the POV's context region. This keyword is required for the calculation.
SourceRegion	Specify the region referred to by the formula. This region should include all members on the right side of the equation at a minimum. This keyword is required.

Finally, we used a MaxL statement to aggregate the ASOsamp.Sample database. The following aggregation process line is only needed if the aggregation views do not currently exist for ASOsamp.Sample:

```
execute aggregate process on database 'ASOsamp'.'Sample';
```

7
Using MaxL to Automate Process

In this chapter, we will cover the following topics:

- ▶ Setting up folder structure and other files needed for MaxL automation
- ▶ Executing Dimension Build Rules using MaxL
- ▶ Executing Load Rules using MaxL
- ▶ Executing Calculation using MaxL
- ▶ Executing Partitions using MaxL
- ▶ Executing Report Scripts using MaxL
- ▶ Adding or changing substitution variables with MaxL
- ▶ Using ASO incremental data loads
- ▶ Using encryption in MaxL scripts
- ▶ Deploying dimension created in Essbase Studio

Introduction

In this chapter, we will first build the folder structure to maintain MaxL scripts, error files, and logs. This folder structure is the foundation of your automation and is required before completing most of the other recipes in this chapter. The first recipe will also show the reader how to maintain a username and password in one administrative batch file and pass this information as parameters to their MaxL scripts. This technique will reduce the overhead of having to change the login information required when moving processes from development to production. We will also review how to automate the running of calculations, dimension build rules, load rules, partitioning data, executing report scripts, and changing substitution variables. Moreover, we will go over how to add data to an ASO model incrementally by adding slices. Finally, we will discuss the process of encrypting a MaxL script and deploying dimensions built in Essbase Studio using MaxL.

Setting up folder structure and other files needed for MaxL automation

In this recipe, we will set up the folder structure needed to run most Essbase processes, keep track of error files, and view process log files. We will also work through some techniques that can help a developer replicate the functionality shown here for all their applications. The steps in this recipe will be done once for each application, then the folder structure and objects will be copied for the purpose of automating other applications' processes. In a sense, the techniques used here were designed for portability and ease of migration from development to production. Finally, we will execute a MaxL script that will add the `Sample2` application and `Basic` database.

Getting ready

To get started, right-click on the **Start** menu, select **Explore**, and browse to your **C** drive.

How to do it...

1. Right-click on your **C** drive in Windows Explorer, click on **New**, click **Folder**, type **AUTOMATION** in the folder name, and press *Enter*.

2. Open the **AUTOMATION** folder, click on **New**, select **Folder**, type **ADMIN** for the folder name, and press *Enter*.

3. Select the **Start** menu, select **Run**, enter **notepad**, and press *Enter*.

4. Enter the following code into Notepad. Make sure to modify the Essbase Server, admin, username, and password with your information, as follows:

```
@ECHO OFF
SET ESS_SERVER=Essbase Server
SET ESS_USER=admin user name
SET ESS_PASSWORD=admin password
```

5. Click on the **File** menu, select **Save**, browse to C:\AUTOMATON\ADMIN, enter **ini.bat** in the **File Name**, select **All Files** under **Save as Type**, and click on **Save**.

6. Browse to the C:\AUTOMATION folder, click on **New**, select **Folder**, type **Sample2** for the folder name, and press _Enter_.

7. Open the **Sample2** folder, right-click, select **New | Folder**, type **Batch** for the folder name, and press _Enter_. Repeat the same step for the **Data, Errors, Logs, Admin,** and **MaxL** folders.

8. Select the **Start** menu, click on **Run**, enter **notepad**, and press _Enter_.

9. Enter the following code into Notepad:

```
SET APP='Sample2'
SET DB='Basic'
```

10. Select the **File** menu, click on **Save**, browse to C:\AUTOMATON\Sample2\Admin, enter **App.bat** in the **File Name**, select **All Files** under **Save as Type**, and click on **Save**.

11. Select the **Start** menu, click on **Run**, enter **notepad**, and press _Enter_.

12. Enter the following code into Notepad:

```
/* This script is used to create application & database

   Variables sent from command files:
   1 Host (Server)
   2 User Name
   3 Password
   4 App name
   5 Database Name
   6 Job Name
*/

/*Login to database */
login $2 identified by $3 on $1;
/*Create log file*/
spool on to ".\\Logs\\$6.log";
echo 'Login to database';

/*Create Sample2 application*/
```

```
create application $4;
/*Go to error handle CreateAppError if application creation
  failed*/
if error 'CreateAppError';

/*Create Sample2.Basic database*/
create database $4.$5;
/*Go to error handle CreateDbError if database creation
  failed*/
if error 'CreateDbError';

spool off;
logout;
exit 0;

define label 'CreateAppError';
echo "Error detected: Creating Application Failed.";
spool off;
logout;
exit 6;

define label 'CreateDbError';
echo 'Error detected: Creating Database Failed.';
spool off;
logout;
exit 6;
```

13. Select the **File** menu, click on **Save**, browse to C:\AUTOMATON\Sample2\MaxL, enter **Database.mxl** in the **File Name**, select **All Files** under **Save as Type**, and click on **Save**.

14. Select the **Start** menu, click on **Run**, enter **notepad**, and press *Enter*.

15. Enter the following code into Notepad:

```
SET JOB_NAME=%1
echo %JOB_NAME%

cd /d %~dp0

CALL ..\Admin\ini.bat
if %errorlevel% NEQ 0 GOTO ErrorHandler2
CALL .\Admin\App.bat
if %errorlevel% NEQ 0 GOTO ErrorHandler3

echo ----------------------------------------------------------
echo Deleting old error, warning, and log files...
```

```
if exist .\errors\%JOB_NAME%*.err del /f
   .\errors\%JOB_NAME%*.err
if %errorlevel% NEQ 0 GOTO ErrorHandler4
if exist .\Logs\%JOB_NAME%*.log del /f .\Logs\%JOB_NAME%*.log
if %errorlevel% NEQ 0 GOTO ErrorHandler5
echo ----------------------------------------------------------

echo Check if MaxL script exist
IF NOT EXIST .\Maxl\%JOB_NAME%.mxl GOTO ErrorHandler7
if %errorlevel% NEQ 0 GOTO ErrorHandler7

echo Execute Maxl %JOB_NAME%
essmsh .\Maxl\%JOB_NAME%.mxl %ESS_SERVER% %ESS_USER%
   %ESS_PASSWORD% %APP% %DB% %JOB_NAME%
if %errorlevel% NEQ 0 GOTO ErrorHandler6

EXIT 0

:ErrorHandler2
echo Ini is missing or has errors
EXIT 2

:ErrorHandler3
echo App file is missing or has errors
EXIT 3

:ErrorHandler4
echo Error with deleting of error file
EXIT 4

:ErrorHandler5
echo Error with deleting of log file
EXIT 5

:ErrorHandler6
echo Error with job
EXIT 6

:ErrorHandler7
echo Cannot find Maxl script for the job
EXIT 7
```

16. Select the **File** menu, click on **Save**, browse to `C:\AUTOMATION\Sample2`, enter
    Call_MaxL.bat in the **File Name**, select **All Files** under **Save as Type**, and click
    on **Save**.

17. Select the **Start** menu, click on **Run**, enter **notepad**, and press *Enter*.

18. Enter the following code into Notepad:

    ```
    C:\AUTOMATION\Sample2\Call_MaxL.bat Database
    ```

19. Select the **File** menu, click **Save**, browse to C:\ AUTOMATION\Sample2\Batch, enter **Database.bat** in the **File Name**, select **All Files** under **Save as Type**, and click on **Save**.

20. In the file system, double-click on C:\AUTOMATION\Sample2\Batch\Database. bat. You should see a black command prompt pop up and close when it completes the tasks in the MaxL Script.

21. Double-click on C:\AUTOMATION\Sample2\Logs\Database.log to open the log. You will see the following file:

22. Click on the **Start** menu; navigate to **Program | Oracle EPM System | Essbase | Start Administration Services Console**, and log in using your server, username, and password. You should see the **Sample2** application when you drill down on your Essbase Server and the Applications node.

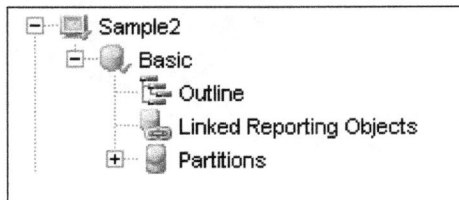

23. Right-click on the **AUTOMATION** folder, click on **Properties**, click on the **Security** tab, and click on the users you want to remove, and use the **Remove** button in order to remove users and group that should not have access to the admin password. Click on **OK**.

How it works

In this recipe, we set up the following folder structure to execute our MaxL commands:

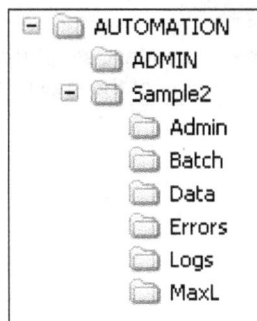

In addition, we added the following lines in an `ini.bat` file in the `C:\AUTOMATION\ADMIN` folder to set our Essbase Server, username, and password information.

```
@ECHO OFF
SET ESS_SERVER=Essbase Server
SET ESS_USER=admin user name
SET ESS_PASSWORD=admin password
```

We also created a file in `C:\AUTOMATION\Sample2\Admin` called `App.bat` to set our Essbase application and database names.

```
SET APP='Sample2'
SET DB='Basic'
```

In addition, we created a MaxL script called `Database.mxl`. This script is self-documented for clarity and is expecting a set of parameters from the `ini.bat`, `App.bat`, and the `Database.bat`.

> The down side of hard coding usernames, passwords, and host names is obvious when you move scripts from development to production, change the admin username and password, or upgrade your Essbase version; every script that has these parameters hard coded has to be modified as a result. Using the techniques, this recipe will allow you to only have to change these parameters in one location and to move scripts as is from development to production.

The following table shows us the parameters you need for the `Database.mxl` script and their descriptions:

Variable	Description
$1	Host (Essbase Server)
$2	User Name
$3	Password
$4	Application Name
$5	Database Name
$6	Job Name or name of the MaxL script that needs to be executed. This will also be the name of the log file produced.

The first five parameters are provided by the `ini.bat` and `App.bat` files. These parameters will be the same for every MaxL script. The sixth parameter is the job name, MaxL script, and name of the log file. This parameter is specified in the `Database.bat` batch file in the `C:\AUTOMATION\Sample2\Batch` directory. The `Call_MaxL.bat` script in `C:\AUTOMATION\Sample2` is the generic script that conducts the following tasks:

- Takes one parameter `JOB_NAME` or the MaxL script name
- Captures directory where the batch file resides
- Retrieves `ESS_SERVER`, `ESS_USER`, `ESS_PASSWORD`, `APP`, and `DB` parameters
- Removes any existing errors, warnings, or log files for the MaxL (`JOB_NAME`)
- Checks whether the MaxL script with the `JOB_NAME` parameter name exists
- Runs the MaxL script with the parameters specified
- Handles any errors by returning descriptive exit codes
- The lists of exit codes returned by the `Call_MaxL.bat` batch file are as follows:

Exit Codes	Descriptions
0	Successfully ran all tasks
1	Warning in running tasks
2	Ini file is missing or has errors
3	App file is missing or has errors
4	Error deleting error file
5	Error deleting log file
6	Error running MaxL Script
7	Cannot find Maxl script for the job

The important point to note about this recipe is that this folder structure will only have to be built once. We can create another application folder by copying the `Sample2` folder, pasting it under the `AUTOMATION` folder, modifying the `Copy of Sample2` folder name to your application's name, and then changing the application and database names in the `App.bat` file under the new `Admin` folder. These techniques keep you from having to re-invent the wheel.

There's more...

There are many ways of automating the building, loading, calculating, and validation of Essbase cubes. A few of the other tools you may want to consider to this end are as follows:

- **Oracle Data Integrator** (**ODI**)
- Financial Data Quality Manager
- MaxL Perl Module
- API Languages, C++, Java, Visual Basic, and so on
- Star Analytics (Star Command Center)

Executing dimension build rules using MaxL

In this recipe, we will build the dimensions for the entire `Basic` database using **Essbase Administration Services** (**EAS**). We will then use dimension build rules and MaxL dimension build commands to build the hierarchies for each dimension. You should complete the recipe *Setting up folder structure and other files needed for MaxL automation* before you continue as we are going to need the folder structure and script created in that recipe.

Getting ready

To get started, click on the **Start** menu and navigate to **Program | Oracle EPM System | Essbase | Start Administration Services Console**. In the Log in menu, enter your Administration Server, Username, Password, and click on the **Log in** button.

How to do it...

1. Expand the Essbase Server in EAS, expand the **Applications** node, drill down on the **Sample2** application, click on the **Basic** database, right-click on the **Outline**, and click on **Edit**.
2. Right-click on the **Outline: Basic** node in the **Outline Editor**, selects **Add Child**, enter **Measures**, press *Enter*, and then press *Esc*.
3. Click on the **Measures** dimension and then click the **Account Dimension Type** button.
4. Click on the **Add a sibling to selected member** button, enter **Product**, and press *Enter*.

5. Enter **Market** for the dimension name and press *Enter*.

6. Enter **Ounces** for the dimension name, press the *Enter* key, and then press *Esc*. Click on the **Ounces** dimension, click on the **Add a child to selected member** button, and enter **32**.

7. Click on the **Ounces** dimension, click on **Attribute Dimension Type**, click **Yes** when the prompt pops up, click on the **Edit properties for the selected member(s)** button, change the **Attribute Type** to **Numeric**, click on **OK**, and click on **Yes** when the prompt pops up.

8. Click on the **Ounces** dimension, click on the **Add a sibling to selected member** button. Then enter **Population**, press *Enter*, and then press *Esc*.

9. Click on the **Population** dimension, **Add a child to selected member** button, enter **Small**, press the *Enter* key, and then press *Esc*. Click on member **Small**, click on the **Add a child to selected member** button, enter **3000000**, press the *Enter* key, and then press *Esc*.

10. Click on the **Population** dimension, click on the **Add a sibling to selected member** button, enter **Caffeinated**, press the *Enter* key, and then press *Esc*. Click on **Caffeinated**, click on the **Attribute Dimension Type** button, and click on **Yes**.

11. Click on the **Edit properties for the selected member(s)** button, change the **Attribute Type** to **Boolean**, click on **OK**, and then click on **Yes**.

12. Click on the **Add a sibling to selected member** button, enter **Intro Date**, press the *Enter* key, and then press *Esc*. Click on the **Intro Date** dimension, then on the **Add a child to selected member** button, and enter **03-25-1996**.

13. Click on the **Intro Date** dimension, click on the **Attribute Dimension Type** button, click on **Yes** when the prompt pops up, click on the **Edit properties for the selected member(s)** button, change the **Attribute Type** to **Date**, click on **OK**, and click on **Yes** when the prompt pops up.

14. Click on the **Add a sibling to selected member** button, enter **Pkg Type**, press the *Enter* key, then press *Esc*.

15. Right-click on the **Market** dimension, click on **Edit member properties...**, click on the **Attributes** tab, select **Population**, click on the **Assign** button, and click on **OK**.

16. Right-click on the **Product** dimension, click on **Edit member properties...**, click on the **Attribute** tab, select **Caffeinated, Intro Date, Ounces**, and **Pkg Type**. Click on the **Assign** button, and then click on **OK**.

17. Click on **Verify** and **Save** in the **Outline Editor** window. Your outline should look like the following image:

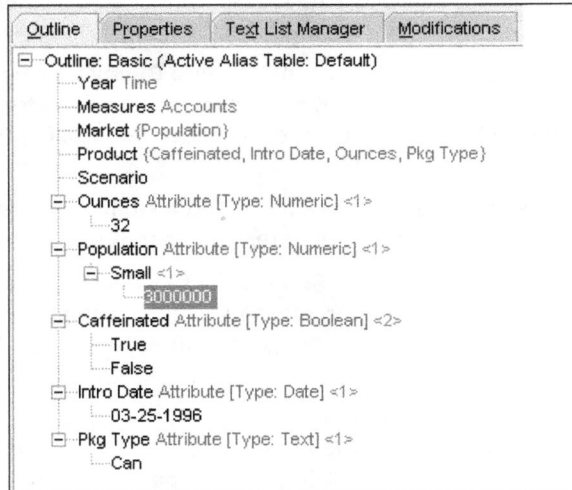

18. Copy the following file to the directory:
    `.\Oracle\Middleware\user_projects\epmsystem1\EssbaseServer\`
    `essbaseserver1\app\Sample2\Basic`

File	Description
Measures.rul	Measures parent-child dimension build rule
Product.rul	Product dimension build
Market.rul	Market dimension build rule
AttrMkt.rul	Market attribute association build rule
Measures.txt	Measures dimension meta-data
Markets.txt	Market dimension meta-data
Product.txt	Product dimension meta-data

19. Select the **Start** menu, click on **Run**, enter **notepad**, and press *Enter*.

20. Enter the follow code into Notepad:

```
/* This script is used to build Basic Outline
Variables sent from command file:
1 Host (Server)
2 User Name
3 Password
4 App name
5 Database Name
```

```
    6 Job Name
*/


/*Login to database */
login $2 identified by $3 on $1;

/*Create log file*/
spool on to ".\\Logs\\$6.log";
echo 'Login to database';


/*Build the Basic outline but suppress verification of outline
  until all dimensions have been built. Append errors to file in
  Errors directory.*/
import database  $4.$5 dimensions
from server text data_file 'Measures'
using server rules_file 'Measures' suppress verification,
from server text data_file 'Markets'
using server rules_file 'Market' suppress verification,
from server text data_file 'Product'
using server rules_file 'Product' suppress verification,
from server text data_file 'Markets'
using server rules_file 'AttrMKT' suppress verification
preserve input data on error append to "'.\\Errors\\$6.err'";
/*Go to error handle DimBuildError if dimension build failed*/
iferror 'DimBuildError';

spool off;
logout;
exit;

define label 'DimBuildError';
echo "Error in dimension build rule";
spool off;
logout;
exit 6;
```

21. Select the **File** menu, click on **Save**, browse to `C:\AUTOMATION\Sample2\MaxL`, enter **DimBuild.mxl** in **File Name**, select **All Files** under **Save as Type**, and click on **Save**.

22. Select the **Start** menu, click on **Run**, enter **notepad**, and press *Enter*.

23. Enter the following code into Notepad:

    ```
    C:\AUTOMATION\Sample2\Call_MaxL.bat DimBuild
    ```

24. Select the **File** menu, click on **Save**, browse to `C:\AUTOMATION\Sample2\Batch`, enter **DimBuild.bat** in **File Name**, select **All Files** under **Save as Type**, and click on **Save**.

25. Double-click on `C:\AUTOMATION\Sample2\Batch\DimBuild.bat`. You should see a black command prompt pop up and close when it completes the tasks in the MaxL Script.

How it works...

In this recipe, we add three stored dimension and five attribute dimensions as the backbone of our outline. We also assign dimension types and associate our attribute dimensions to their corresponding base dimensions. Moreover, we copy the dimension build rules and metadata files to our `Sample2.Basic` directory so that we do not have to specify the URL path of each file in our MaxL script.

> This outline is not complete without the Year and Scenario dimensions. The fact that you don't have a Time dimension will cause a few members to kick out during dimension build due to the Measures dimension time balance properties. Consider cross dimensional formula and property dependencies when creating your dimension build rules. For this reason, it is in some cases best to create your members first and then add properties and formulas.

Our MaxL script has comments on each of the major tasks and takes the following parameters:

Variable	Description
$1	Host (Essbase Server)
$2	User Name
$3	Password
$4	Application Name
$5	Database Name
$6	Job Name or name of the MaxL script that needs to be executed. This will also be the name of the error and log files produced.

See also

Review the following recipes in *Chapter 5, Using EAS for Development*, to understand how to create dimension build rules:

▶   *Using dimension build rules to add parent-child dimension*

▶ _Creating dimension build rules to add a base and attribute dimensions_

▶ _Using dimension build rules to add parents to attribute dimensions_

The `Scenario` and `Year` dimension can be built manually using the recipe _Using the outline editor to add dimensions_ in _Chapter 5_.

Executing load rules using MaxL

In this recipe, we will load data into our database using a load rule and MaxL script. We will also create a generic load rule batch with parameters. You should complete recipe _Setting up folder structure and other files needed for MaxL automation_ before you continue as we are going to need the folder structure and script created in that recipe. In addition, the recipe _Using the outline editor to add dimensions_ in _Chapter 5_ completes the `Sample Basic` outline started in this chapter. We will need the dimensions `Scenario` and `Year` to complete this recipe.

Getting ready

To get started, click on the **Start** menu, click on **Run**, enter **notepad**, and press _Enter_.

How to do it...

1. Select the **Start** menu, click on **Run**, enter **notepad**, and press _Enter_.

2. Enter the following code into Notepad:

```
SET JOB_NAME=%1
SET LOAD=%2
SET RULE=%3

cd /d %~dp0

echo Retrieve Host name, User Name, Password, Application, and
  Database
CALL ..\Admin\ini.bat
if %errorlevel% NEQ 0 GOTO ErrorHandler2
CALL .\Admin\App.bat
if %errorlevel% NEQ 0 GOTO ErrorHandler3

echo -------------------------------------------------------------
echo Deleting old error, warning, and log files...
if exist .\errors\%JOB_NAME%*.err del /f
  .\errors\%JOB_NAME%*.err
if %errorlevel% NEQ 0 GOTO ErrorHandler4
```

```
if exist .\Logs\%JOB_NAME%*.log del /f .\Logs\%JOB_NAME%*.log
if %errorlevel% NEQ 0 GOTO ErrorHandler5
echo ------------------------------------------------------------

echo Execute data load MaxL script with specified parameters
essmsh .\MaxL\LOAD.mxl %ESS_SERVER% %ESS_USER% %ESS_PASSWORD%
  %APP% %DB% %JOB_NAME% %LOAD% %RULE%
if %errorlevel% NEQ 0 GOTO ErrorHandler6

EXIT 0

:ErrorHandler2
echo Ini is missing or has errors
EXIT 2

:ErrorHandler3
echo App file is missing or has errors
EXIT 3

:ErrorHandler4
echo Error with deleting of error file
EXIT 4

:ErrorHandler5
echo Error with deleting of log file
EXIT 5

:ErrorHandler6
echo Error with loading of file
EXIT 6
```

3. Click on **File**, click on **Save**, make sure that **All Files** have the **Save As Type** combobox selected, enter C:\AUTOMATION\Sample2\Load.bat in the **File name** textbox, select **All Files** under **Save as Type**, and click on Save.

4. Click on **Start**, select **Run**, type **notepad**, and press *Enter*.

5. Enter the following MaxL script:

```
/* This script is used to Load Data
   Variables sent from command file:
   1 Host (Server)
   2 User Name
   3 Password
   4 App name
   5 Database Name
   6 Job Name
```

```
     7 Load File
     8 Rule File
*/

/*Login to database*/
login $2 identified by $3 on $1;

/*Create log file*/
spool on to ".\\Logs\\$6.log";
echo 'Login to database';

/*Begin Load using data file and load rules specified by
  variables $7 (Load File) and $8 (Rule File)*/
import database $4.$5 data
from  data_file  "'$7'"
using server rules_file "$8"
on error write to "'.\\Errors\\$6.err'";
/*If load fails go to LoadError handle*/
iferror 'LoadError';

spool off;
logout;
exit;

define label 'LoadError';
echo "Error in Load build rule";
spool off;
logout;
exit 6;
```

6. Click on **File**, click on **Save**, make sure that **All Files** in the **Save As Type** combobox is selected, enter C:\AUTOMATION\Sample2\MaxL\Load.mxl in the **File name** textbox, and click on **Save**.

7. Copy the LoadRuleExample.txt file to C:\AUTOMATION\Sample2\Data. This text file was created in the recipe *Creating load rules for flat file data loads*.

8. Copy the LDSamp.rul file to .\Oracle\Middleware\user_projects\ epmsystem1\EssbaseServer\essbaseserver1\app\Sample2\Basic.

9. Click on **Start**, select **Run**, type **notepad**, press *Enter,* and enter the following code. Click on **File**, click on **Save**, make sure that **All Files** in the **Save As Type** combobox is selected, in the **File Name** type C:\AUTOMATION\Sample2\Batch\LDSamp.bat, and click on **Save**.

```
cd /d C:\AUTOMATION\Sample2
Load.bat LoadBasic .\Data\LoadRuleExample.txt LDSamp
```

10. Double-click on `C:\AUTOMATION\Sample2\Batch\LDSamp.bat`. You should see a black command prompt pop up and close when it completes the tasks in the MaxL Script.

How it works...

In this recipe, we created a batch file `Load.bat`, which we will use to pass the following parameters to our MaxL script:

Variables	Description
$1	Host (Essbase Server)
$2	User Name
$3	Password
$4	Application Name
$5	Database Name
$6	Job Name or name of the MaxL script that needs to be executed. This will also be the name of the log file produced.
$7	Load file path
$8	Load rule name file located on server.

Our **Load.mxl**, has a comment before each major task and requires an additional two parameters LOAD and RULE specified in the `LDSamp.bat` batch file. The `cd /d C:\AUTOMATION\Sample2` line in the `LDSamp.bat` sets the current directory where the rest of the code will be run. The `Load.bat LoadBasic .\Data\LoadRuleExample.txt LDSamp` line passes to the `Load.bat` batch file created in step 2 the job name, load file path, and load rule name.

See also

Review *Creating load rules for flat file data loads* in *Chapter 5* to understand how to create a load rule.

Executing calculations using MaxL

In this recipe, we will create a calculation script with a MaxL script command and then execute that calculation with a MaxL script that takes a set of parameters for portability. You should complete the recipe *Setting up folder structure and other files needed for MaxL automation* before you continue as we are going to need the folder structure and scripts created in that recipe.

Getting ready

To get started, click on the **Start** menu and navigate to **Program | Oracle EPM System | Essbase | Start Administration Services Console**. In the Log in menu, enter your Administration Server, Username, Password, and click on the **Log in** button.

How to do it...

1. In EAS, click on **File**, click on **Editors**, click on **MaxL Script Editor**, type the following MaxL script, and click on the **Execute Script** button.

    ```
    create or replace calculation Sample2.Basic.CalcAll
    'SET UPDATECALC OFF;
    SET CLEARUPDATESTATUS AFTER;
    SET AGGMISSG ON;
    SET LOCKBLOCK HIGH;
    SET CACHE ALL;
    SET CACHE HIGH;
    SET CALCPARALLEL 3;
    SET CALCTASKDIMS 2;

    Calc All;';
    ```

2. Click on **Start**, select **Run**, type **notepad**, press *Enter*, enter the following MaxL script, click on **File**, and click on Save. Make sure that **All Files** in the **Save As Type** combobox is selected, type in `C:\AUTOMATION\Sample2\MaxL\Calc.mxl` in the **File name** textbox, and click on **Save**.

    ```
    /* This script is used to Calculate $4.$5

       Variables sent from command file:
       1 Host (Server)
       2 User Name
       3 Password
       4 App name
       5 Database Name
       6 Job Name
       7 Calc script

    */

    /*Login to database*/
    login $2 $3 on $1;

    /*Create log file*/
    ```

```
spool on to ".\\Logs\\$6.log";

/*Begin executing calculation where is the $4(Application),
  $5(Database), and $7 (Calculation script)*/
execute calculation $4.$5.$7;

/*If load fails go to CalcError handle*/
if error 'CalcError';

spool off;
logout;
exit;

define label 'CalcError';
echo "Error in executing calculation script";
spool off;
logout;
exit 6;
```

3. Click on **Start**, select **Run**, type **notepad**, press *Enter*, enter the following code, click on **File**, click on **Save**, make sure that **All Files** have the **Save As Type** combobox selected, type in `C:\AUTOMATION\Sample2\Calc.bat` in the **File Name** textbox, and click on **Save**.

```
SET JOB_NAME=%1
SET CALC=%2

cd /d %~dp0

echo Retrieve Host name, User Name, Password, Application, and
  Database
CALL ..\Admin\ini.bat
if %errorlevel% NEQ 0 GOTO ErrorHandler2
CALL .\Admin\App.bat
if %errorlevel% NEQ 0 GOTO ErrorHandler3

echo ----------------------------------------------------------------
---
echo Deleting log file...
if exist .\Logs\%JOB_NAME%*.log del /f .\Logs\%JOB_NAME%*.log
if %errorlevel% NEQ 0 GOTO ErrorHandler5
echo ----------------------------------------------------------------
---

echo Execute Calc script with specified parameters
```

```
essmsh .\Maxl\CALC.mxl %ESS_SERVER% %ESS_USER% %ESS_PASSWORD%
  %APP% %DB% %JOB_NAME% %CALC%
if %errorlevel% NEQ 0 GOTO ErrorHandler6

EXIT 0

:ErrorHandler2
echo Ini is missing or has errors
EXIT 2

:ErrorHandler3
echo App file is missing or has errors
EXIT 3

:ErrorHandler5
echo Error with deleting of log file
EXIT 5

:ErrorHandler6
echo Error in calculating the database
EXIT 6
```

4. Click on **Start**, select **Run**, type **notepad**, press *Enter*, enter the following script, click on **File**, click on **Save**, make sure that **All Files** in the **Save As Type** combobox is selected, in the **File Name** type C:\AUTOMATION\Sample2\Batch\CalcAll.bat, and click on **Save**.

```
cd /d C:\AUTOMATION\Sample2
Calc.bat CalcAll CalcAll
```

5. Double-click on C:\AUTOMATION\Sample2\Batch\CalcAll.bat. You should see a black command prompt pop up and close when it completes the tasks in the MaxL Script.

6. Double-click on the C:\AUTOMATION\Sample2\Logs\Calc.log to open the log and view the execution of the calculation of CalcAll.

How it works...

In this recipe, we execute a MaxL script in the MaxL Script Editor to add a calculation called `CalcAll` to the `Sample2.Basic` database. We also created a batch file `Calc.bat`, which we use to pass the following parameters to our MaxL script:

Variables	Description
$1	Host (Essbase Server)
$2	User Name
$3	Password
$4	Application Name
$5	Database Name
$6	Job Name or name of the MaxL script that needs to be executed. This will also be the name of the log file produced.
$7	Calculation Name

Our MaxL, `Calc.mxl`, has comments before each major task explaining the content of each step. `Calc.mxl` requires an additional parameter `CALC` specified in the `CalcAll.bat` batch file. The `cd /d C:\AUTOMATION\Sample2` line in `CalcAll.bat` sets the current directory where the rest of code will be run. The `Calc.bat CalcAll` line passes to the `Calc.bat` batch file, the job name, and calculation name required by our `Calc.mxl` MaxL script. We decided to name the job the same as the calculation for simplicity, but you can change the first parameter to a more descriptive job name.

Executing partitions using MaxL

In recipe, we will create a copy of the `Sample2.Basic` database, create a partition, and execute the partition to move data from `Sample2.Basic` to our new application using MaxL. You should complete the *Setting up folder structure and other files needed for MaxL automation and Executing Dimension Build Rules using MaxL* in this chapter as we will need the `AUTOMATION` folder structure and the dimensions built.

Getting ready

To get started, click on the **Start** menu and navigate to **Program | Oracle EPM System | Essbase | Start Administration Services Console**. In the Log in menu, enter your Administration Server, Username, Password, and click on the **Log in** button.

How to do it...

1. In EAS, click on **File**, click on **Editors**, click on **MaxL Script Editor**, type the following MaxL script, and click on the **Execute Script** button.

```
/*Create an application Sample4 as a copy of Sample2*/
create application Sample4 as Sample2;

/*Clear the new Sample4.Basic database*/
alter database Sample4.Basic reset;

/*
This script creates a replicate partition where Sample2.Basic
   is the Source and Sample4.Basic is the Target. Replicate
   partitions replicate the data from the Source database to the
   Target. You should change the localhost with your Essbase
   Server, Admin with your user name, and password with your
   password.
*/
create or replace replicated partition Sample2.Basic
area '@Relative("Year",0),@Relative("Profit",0),
   @Relative("Market",0), @Relative("Product",0),
   @Relative("Scenario", 0)'
to Sample4.Basic at localhost
as Admin identified by 'password'
area '@Relative("Year",0),@Relative("Profit",0),
   @Relative("Market",0), @Relative("Product",0),
   @Relative("Scenario", 0)'
update allow;
```

2. Open an Excel session, open a connection to your in **Smart View** by clicking on the **Open** button in the **Smart View** ribbon, select **Private Connections** in your **Smart View** panel, enter your username and password in the **Connect to Data Source** menu, and click on **Connect**.

3. Drill down on the **Sample2** application, right-click on the **Basic** database, and click on **Ad hoc analysis**.

4. Set up your spreadsheet as shown in the following image. Click on **Refresh**, on your **POV** menu, enter the numbers as they appear in the image, and click on the **Submit Data** button on your Essbase ribbon. This is to make sure that you have some data available to partition. The following image shows a portion of the data that will be pushed from **Sample2** to **Sample4**:

	A	B
1		Actual
2		New York
3		100-10
4		COGS
5	Jan	271
6	Feb	258
7	Mar	270
8	Apr	284
9	May	302
10	Jun	356
11	Jul	364
12	Aug	364
13	Sep	316
14	Oct	260
15	Nov	249
16	Dec	279

5. Click on **Start**, select **Run**, enter **notepad**, and press *Enter*.

6. Enter the following code, click on **File**, click on **Save**, make sure that **All Files** is selected in the **Save As Type** combobox, type in `C:\AUTOMATION\Sample2\ParititionTo.bat` in the **File name** textbox, and click on **Save**.

```
SET JOB_NAME=%1
SET SourceApp=%2
SET SourceDb=%3
SET SourceHost=%4


cd /d %~dp0

echo Retrieve Host name, User Name, Password, Application, and
   Database
CALL ..\Admin\ini.bat
if %errorlevel% NEQ 0 GOTO ErrorHandler2
CALL .\Admin\App.bat
```

```
if %errorlevel% NEQ 0 GOTO ErrorHandler3

echo ----------------------------------------------------------------
---
echo Deleting log file...
if exist .\Logs\%JOB_NAME%*.log del /f .\Logs\%JOB_NAME%*.log
if %errorlevel% NEQ 0 GOTO ErrorHandler5
echo ----------------------------------------------------------------
---

echo Call partition MaxL script with specified paramaters
essmsh .\Maxl\PartitionTo.mxl %ESS_SERVER% %ESS_USER%
   %ESS_PASSWORD% %APP% %DB% %JOB_NAME% %SourceApp% %SourceDb%
   %SourceHost%
if %errorlevel% NEQ 0 GOTO ErrorHandler6


EXIT 0
:ErrorHandler2
echo Ini is missing or has errors
EXIT 2

:ErrorHandler3
echo App file is missing or has errors
EXIT 3

:ErrorHandler4
echo Error with deleting of error file
EXIT 4

:ErrorHandler5
echo Error with deleting of log file
EXIT 5

:ErrorHandler6
echo Error in partition failed
EXIT 6
```

7. Click on **Start**, select **Run**, type **notepad,** and press *Enter*.

8. Enter the following code, click on **File**, click on **Save**, make sure that **All Files** is selected in the **Save As Type** combobox, type in C:\AUTOMATION\Sample2\MaxL\ ParititionTo.mxl in the **File Name** textbox, and click on **Save**.

```
/* This script is used to Partition data
   Variables sent from command file:
```

```
      1 Host (Server)
      2 User Name
      3 Password
      4 App name
      5 Database Name
      6 Job Name
      7 Source Application
      8 Source Database
      9 Source Host (Server)
*/

/*Login to database */
login $2 $3 on $1;

/*Create log file*/
spool on to ".\\Logs\\$6.log";

/*Replicate data from Sample2.Basic to Sample4.Basic*/
refresh replicated partition $4.$5 to $7.$8 at $9 all data;

/*If partition fails go to PartitionError handle*/
if error 'PartitionError';

spool off;
logout;
exit;

define label 'PartitionError';
echo "Error in executing Partition";
spool off;
logout;
exit 6;
```

9. Click on **Start**, select **Run**, type **notepad**, and press *Enter*.

10. Enter the following script:

```
cd /d C:\AUTOMATION\Sample2
Partitionto.bat ReplicatePartition Sample4 Basic localhost
```

11. Click on **File**, click on **Save**, make sure **All Files** is selected in the **Save As Type** combobox, in the **File Name** type C:\AUTOMATION\Sample2\Batch\ReplicatePartition.bat, and click on **Save**.

12. Double-click on `C:\AUTOMATION\Sample2\Batch\ ReplicatePartition.bat`. You should see a black command prompt pop up and close when it completes the tasks in the MaxL Script.

13. Double-click on the `C:\AUTOMATION\Sample2\Logs\ReplicatePartition.log` to open the log and view the execution of partition.

How it works...

In this recipe, we executed a MaxL script in the MaxL Script Editor to create a copy of application `Sample2`. Clear the data out of the new database `Sample4.Basic`, and create a replicate partition. The following table explains the parts of the create partition script:

Key words	Description
create or replace replicated	Creates a replicate partition to copy data from Source to Target database.
to	Specifies a partition definition between the source and target database
Area	Specifies the target database session that you want to partition from Source database
As	Identifies the username needed to connected to the Source database
area	Specifies the Sources database session that you want partitioned to the Target database
update allow;	Specifies that you want to allow the updating of the data to the Target database

We also created a batch file `PartitionTo.bat`, which we use to pass the following parameters to our MaxL script:

Variables	Description
$1	Host (Essbase Server)
$2	User Name
$3	Password
$4	Application Name
$5	Database Name
$6	Job Name or name of the MaxL script that needs to be executed. This will also be the name of the log file produced.
$7	Source Application
$8	Source Database
$9	Source Host (Essbase Server)

Our MaxL, `PartitionTo.mxl`, has comments before each major task that explain each step. The `PartitionTo.mxl` requires an additional four parameters' job name, source application, source database, and source host specified in the `ReplicatePartition`. `bat`. The `cd /d C:\AUTOMATION\Sample2` line in `ReplicatePartition.bat` sets the current directory where the rest of the code will be run. The `PartitionTo.bat` `ReplicatePartition Sample4 Basic localhost` line passes to the `PartitionTo.` `bat` batch file; the job name, the source application, the source database, and source host are required by our `PartitionTo.mxl` MaxL script. This partition specifies the lowest level of our entire set of stored dimensions so all level zero data should have been moved from `Sample2.Basic` to `Sample4.Basic`.

Executing report scripts using MaxL

In this recipe, we will create a simple report script that we will use to extract data from the `Sample2.Basic` database. You should complete the *Setting up folder structure and other files needed for MaxL automation and Executing Dimension Build Rules using MaxL* in this chapter as we will need the AUTOMATION folder structure and the dimensions built.

Getting ready

To get started, click on the **Start** menu and **Program | Oracle EPM System | Essbase | Start Administration Services Console**. In the Log in menu, enter your Administration Server, Username, Password, and click on the **Log in** button.

How to do it...

1. Drill down on the Essbase Server in EAS, expand the **Applications** node, drill down on the **Sample2** application, and right click on the **Basic** database. In the drop-down menu click **Create** and select **Report Scripts**.

2. In the **Report Script** editor, click on the **Check Syntax** button, click on **File**, click on **Save**, in the **File Name** textbox enter **Rpt**, and click on **OK**.

```
{ SUPCOMMAS }
{ SUPBRACKETS }
{ SUPHEADING }
{ ROWREPEAT }

<SETUP { TabDelimit } { decimal 2 } { NOINDENTGEN } <SYM <END
<SUPSHARE
<Sym
<Page(Year, Sales)
Year Sales
  <Column (Scenario)
```

```
Actual Budget

<Row (Product, Market)
"Lev0,Product"
"Lev0,Market"
!
```

3. Copy `Calcdat.txt` under `.\Oracle\Middleware\user_projects\` `epmsystem1\EssbaseServer\essbaseserver1\app\Sample2\Basic.`

4. In EAS, click on **File**, click on **Editors**, click on **MaxL Script Editor**, type the following MaxL script, and click on the **Execute Script** button.

```
/*Load Data without load rule*/
import database Sample2.Basic
data from server data_file "Calcdat'"
on error abort;
/*Calculate database*/
execute calculation default on 'Sample2'.'Basic';
```

5. Click on **Start**, select **Run,** type **notepad**, and press *Enter*. Enter the following code, click on **File**, click on **Save**, make sure that **All Files** have the **Save As Type** combobox selected, type in `C:\AUTOMATION\Sample2\Report.bat` in the **File name** textbox, and click on **Save**.

```
SET JOB_NAME=%1
SET REPORT_SCRIPT=%2
SET REPORT_FILE=%3

cd /d %~dp0

CALL ..\Admin\ini.bat
if %errorlevel% NEQ 0 GOTO ErrorHandler2
CALL .\Admin\App.bat
if %errorlevel% NEQ 0 GOTO ErrorHandler3

echo -------------------------------------------------------------
---
echo Deleting log files...
if exist .\Logs\%JOB_NAME%*.log del /f .\Logs\%JOB_NAME%*.log
if %errorlevel% NEQ 0 GOTO ErrorHandler5
echo -------------------------------------------------------------
---

/*Execute the report script with specified parameters*/
essmsh .\Maxl\Report_Script.mxl %ESS_SERVER% %ESS_USER%
   %ESS_PASSWORD% %APP% %DB% %JOB_NAME% %REPORT_SCRIPT%
   %REPORT_FILE%
```

```
if %errorlevel% NEQ 0 GOTO ErrorHandler6

EXIT 0
:ErrorHandler2
echo Ini is missing or has errors
EXIT 2

:ErrorHandler3
echo App file is missing or has errors
EXIT 3

:ErrorHandler4
echo Error with deleting of error file
EXIT 4

:ErrorHandler5
echo Error with deleting of log file
EXIT 5

:ErrorHandler6
echo Error with running of report script
        EXIT 6
```

6. Click on **Start**, select **Run**, type **notepad**, and press *Enter*. Enter the following code, click on **File**, click on **Save**, make sure that **All Files** have the **Save As Type** combobox selected, type in C:\AUTOMATION\Sample2\MaxL\Report_Script. mxl in the **File Name** textbox, and click on **Save**.

```
/* This script is used to Run Report Script $4.$5

   Variables sent from command file:
   1 Host (Server)
   2 User Name
   3 Password
   4 App name
   5 Database Name
   6 Job Name
   7 Report Script
   8 Report File
*/

/*Login to database */
login $2 $3 on $1;

/*Create log file*/
```

```
spool on to ".\\Logs\\$6.log";

/*Execute report script*/
export database $4.$5 using server
report_file "'$7'" to data_file "'$8'";

/*If report script fails go to ReportError handle*/
iferror 'ReportError';

spool off;
logout;
exit;

define label 'ReportError';
echo "Error in executing report script";
spool off;
logout;
    exit 6;
```

7. Click on **Start**, select **Run**, type **notepad**, and press *Enter*. Enter the following code, click on **File**, click on **Save**, make sure that **All Files** in the **Save As Type** combobox is selected. In the **File Name** type C:\AUTOMATION\Sample2\Batch\ExecuteReport.bat, and click on **Save**.

```
cd /d C:\AUTOMATION\Sample2
Report.bat RepReportScript Rpt .\Data\ReportScriptExample.txt
```

8. Double-click on C:\AUTOMATION\Sample2\Batch\ ReplicatePartition. bat. You should see a black command prompt pop up and close when it completes the tasks in the MaxL Script.

9. Double-click on the C:\AUTOMATION\Sample2\Data\ ReportScriptExample. txt to open report.

How it works...

In this recipe, we execute a MaxL script in the MaxL Script Editor to load the export file for the Sample2.Basic database and run the default calculation. We also created a batch file Report.bat, which we used to pass the following parameters to our MaxL script:

Variables	Description
$1	Host (Essbase Server)
$2	User Name
$3	Password
$4	Application Name

Variables	Description
$5	Database Name
$6	Job Name or name of the MaxL script that needs to be executed. This will also be the name of the log file produced.
$7	Report Script Name
$8	Report File Path

Our MaxL, `Report_Script.mxl`, has comments before each major task explaining the content of each step. `Report_Script.mxl` requires additional parameters `Report Script` and `Report File Path` specified in the `ReportScript.bat` batch file. The `cd /d C:\AUTOMATION\Sample2` line in `ReportScript.bat` sets the current directory where the rest of code will be run. The `Report.bat RepReportScript Rpt .\Data\ReportScriptExample.txt` line passes to the `Report.bat` batch file; the job name, the report script name, and the report file path are required by our `Report_Script.mxl` MaxL script. The results or our report script are saved in `C:\AUTOMATION\Sample2\Data\ReportScriptExample.txt`.

Adding or changing substitution variables with MaxL

In this recipe, we create a set of substitution variables, change their values, and display the results in our log files. You should complete the recipe *Setting up folder structure and other files needed for MaxL automation* before you continue as we are going to need the folder structure and the script created in that recipe.

Getting ready

To get started, click on the **Start** menu and navigate to **Program | Oracle EPM System | Essbase | Start Administration Services Console**. In the Log in menu, enter your Administration Server, Username, Password, and click on the **Log in** button.

How to do it...

1. In EAS, click on **File**, click on **Editors**, click on **MaxL Script Editor**, type the following MaxL script, and click on the **Execute Script** button.

   ```
   /*Create substition variables for Prior Month, Current Month,
     and Next Month*/
   alter database 'Sample2'.'Basic' add variable 'PriMth' 'May';
   alter database 'Sample2'.'Basic' add variable 'CurMth' 'Jun';
   alter database 'Sample2'.'Basic' add variable 'NextMth' 'Jul';
   ```

2. Click on **Start**, select **Run**, type **notepad**, and press *Enter*. Enter the following code, click on **File**, click on **Save**, make sure that **All Files** have the **Save As Type** combobox selected, and type in `C:\AUTOMATION\Sample2\MaxL\SubVar_Jul.mxl` in the **File Name** textbox. Click on **Save**.

```
/* This script is used to display substitution variables $5

    Variables sent from command file:
    1 Host (Server)
    2 User Name
    3 Password
    4 App name
    5 Database Name
    6 Job Name

*/

/*Login to database */
login $2 $3 on $1;

/*Create log file*/
spool on to ".\\Logs\\$6.log";

/*Display Substitution Variables Before*/
Display variable on database $4.$5;

/*If substitution variable change fails go to SubVarError handle*/
iferror 'SubVarError';

alter database $4.$5 set variable 'PriMth' 'Jun';
alter database $4.$5 set variable 'CurMth' 'Jul';
alter database $4.$5 set variable 'NextMth' 'Aug';

/*Display Substitution Variables After*/
Display variable on database $4.$5;

/*If substitution variable change fails go to SubVarError handle*/
iferror 'SubVarError';

spool off;
logout;
exit;

define label 'SubVarError';
echo "Error in display substitution variable";
spool off;
logout;
    exit 6;
```

3. Click on **Start**, select **Run**, type **notepad**, and press *Enter*. Enter the following code, click on **File**, click on **Save**, make sure that **All Files** in the **Save As Type** combobox is selected, in the **File Name** type **C:\AUTOMATION\Sample2\Batch\Variable_Jul.bat**, and click on **Save**.

```
cd /d C:\AUTOMATION\Sample2
C:\AUTOMATION\Sample2\Call_MaxL.bat SubVar_Jul
```

4. Double-click on **C:\AUTOMATION\Sample2\Batch\Variable_Jul.bat**. You should see a black command prompt pop up and close when it completes the tasks in the MaxL Script.

5. Double-click on the **C:\AUTOMATION\Sample2\Logs\SubVar_Jul.log** to open the log. This log shows the execution of the substitution variable changes.

How it works...

In this recipe, we execute a MaxL script in the MaxL Script Editor to add three substitution variables to our `Sample2.Basic` database. All the parameters required for this recipe were discussed in recipe *Setting up folder structure and other files needed for MaxL automation*. Our MaxL `SubVar_Jul.mxl` has comments before each major task explaining each step. There are many methods of changing substitution variable. All languages that can use Essbase API have the ability to change substitution variables.

See also

Review the tools discussed in *Setting up folder structure and other files needed for MaxL automation* to understand what your options are with regards automating the changing of substitution variables values.

Using ASO incremental data loads

In this recipe, we will set up a MaxL script to create a data load buffer, load data into that buffer, and merge the incremental slice created. The `ASOsamp.Sample` database was created in *Chapter 5* recipe *Using MDX in aggregate storage applications*. This recipe is only for the aggregate storage application.

Getting ready

To get started, click on the **Start** menu and navigate to **Program | Oracle EPM System | Essbase | Start Administration Services Console**. In the Log in menu, enter your Administration Server, Username, Password, and click on the **Log in** button.

How to do it...

1. Copy the `LDASO.rul` file and `LoadSample.txt` to `.\Oracle\Middleware\` `user_projects\epmsystem1\EssbaseServer\essbaseserver1\app\` `ASOSamp\Sample\`.

2. In EAS, click on **File**, click on **Editors**, click on **MaxL Script Editor**, type the following MaxL script, and click on the **Execute Script** button.

```
/*
Variables sent from command file:
 1 Host (Server)
 2 User Name
 3 Password
 4 App name
 5 Database Name
*/


/* A temporary buffer in memory is initilized for loading
   data.*/
alter database $4.$5 initialize load_buffer with buffer_id 1;


/*Load data from server*/
import database $4.$5 data
from  server data_file  "LoadSample"
using server rules_file "LDASO"
to load_buffer with buffer_id 1
on error write to "C:\\LoadASO.err";


/*Remove the content of the slice and override data with data
   in load buffer.*/
import database $4.$5 data
from load_buffer with buffer_id 1
override incremental data;


/*Merges all incremental data slices*/
/*alter database $4.$5
merge incremental data;*/
```

3. You will receive the prompt for each variable $4 and $5. Enter **ASOsamp** in the textbox for $4 and click on **OK**. Enter **Sample** in the textbox for $5 and click on **OK**.

How it works...

In this recipe, we placed a load rule and load file on the server to be able show an incremental load of data into the `ASOsamp.Sample` aggregate storage database. We create a load buffer to hold the data temporarily in memory and then imported the data overriding incremental slices. We also provide the following piece of code commented so you can merge all slices into one:

```
alter database $4.$5
merge incremental data;
```

You would want to schedule your incremental slice code throughout the day at your preferred intervals and then schedule the merge incremental data once a day to merge all your slices. This gives you a close to real time data update for your ASO database.

There's more...

If your data is transactional there may be a need to clear out the data from the entire region before you load more data. We can accomplish this task with a physical clear or logical clear. A physical clear removes the input cells physically from the ASO database. The logical clear creates an incremental data slice and in essence places into that incremental data slice a delta set of values that causes the slice you wanted to clear to add up zero. The following example is a physical clear of a region in the `ASOsamp.Sample` database:

1. In EAS, click on **File,** click on **Editors,** click on **MaxL Script Editor,** type the following MaxL script, and click on the **Execute Script** button.

```
alter database AsoSamp.Sample clear data in region '
CROSSJOIN({[Sale]},
   CROSSJOIN({[Curr Year], [Prev Year]}, {([No Promotion],
[31 to 35 Years], [70,000-99,999],
[Camcorders], [004118], [33135])})))' physical;
```

Using encryption in MaxL scripts

In this recipe, we will retrieve a public key and private key using MaxL commands. Then we will encrypt a MaxL script and modify the command line to successfully run the MaxL command.

Getting ready

To get started, click on **Start,** select **Run,** type **cmd,** and press *Enter.*

How to do it...

1. Type in `essmsh -gk` into the **command** screen and press *Enter*. The following text will appear. Keep a note of the **Public Key** and **Private Key** as they appear on this screen.

```
C:\WINDOWS\system32\cmd.exe                                     _ □ ×

Microsoft Windows XP [Version 5.1.2600]
(C) Copyright 1985-2001 Microsoft Corp.

C:\Documents and Settings\          >essmsh -gk

Essbase MaxL Shell - Release 11.1.1
Copyright (c) 2000, 2009, Oracle and/or its affiliates.
All rights reserved.


Public Key for Encryption: 17917,2349698789
Private Key for Decryption: 910754293,2349698789

 MaxL Shell completed

C:\Documents and Settings\          >
```

2. In EAS, click on **File**, click on **Editors**, click on **MaxL Script Editor**, type the following MaxL script, click on **File**, then on **Save script as**, browse to the C drive, type **SubVarD** in the **File Name**, and click on **OK**.

```
/*Login to database */
login Admin password on localhost;

/*Create log*/
    spool on to 'C:\Display.txt'

/*Display Substitution Variables Before*/
Display variable on database Sample.Basic;

logout;
spool off;
exit;
```

3. Return to your command line and type in `essmsh -E scriptname.mxl PUBLIC-KEY` or based on the pubic key return on step 1 `essmsh -E C:\SubVarD.mxl 17917,2349698789`. A **Maxl Shell completed** prompt will be returned.

4. Right-click on **Start**, click on **Explore**, and browse to your C drive. You should now see two scripts `SubVarD.mxls` and `SubVarD.mxl`.

5. Double-click on `SubVarD.mxls` to open it. Notice that the username and password were removed and a key was entered in their places.

```
/*Login to database */
login $key 354459928009656998414230787930 $key
   505353172014067508419536646014964978902 on localhost;

  /*Create log*/
  spool on to 'C:\Display.txt'

/*Display Substitution Variables Before*/
Display variable on database Sample.Basic;

logout;
spool off;
exit;
```

6. Click on **Start**, select **Run**, type **notepad**, and press *Enter*. Enter the following code, click on **File**, click on **Save**, make sure that **All Files** have the **Save As Type** combobox selected, and type in `C:\Display.bat` in the **File Name** textbox, and click on **Save**.

```
REM essmsh -D C:\SubVarD.mxls PRIVATE-KEY
essmsh -D C:\SubVarD.mxls 910754293,2349698789
```

7. Double-click on `C:\Display.log` to view script execution.

How it works...

In this recipe, we used the `essmsh -gk` to retrieve our Public and Private keys. We then created a Maxl script to encrypt. We return to our command line and enter the following script: `essmsh -E scriptname.mxl PUBLIC-KEY`. We, of course, replaced the `PUBLIC-KEY` in this script with the public key return by our `essmsh -gk` public key results. This command created a copy of the `SubVarD.mxl` called `SubVarD.mxls` and replaced the username and passwords with keys. We also created a batch file that called our `SubVarD.mxls` and entered our private key as returns with the `essmsh -gk` command.

```
REM essmsh -D C:\SubVarD.mxls PRIVATE-KEY
essmsh -D C:\SubVarD.mxls 910754293,2349698789
```

Finally, we were able to view the results of the MaxL script by opening the `Display.log` file.

Deploy dimension created in Essbase Studio

In this recipe, we will deploy the `Time` dimension from an Essbase model created in *Chapters* 2 and 3 with MaxL scripts. The ability to deploy one dimension at a time is new in version 11.1.2.1. Prior to this version, you only had the option of deploying the entire cube. This functionality gives us a lot more flexibility as in real world situations it is normally not practical or necessary to deploy the entire cube every time you have to make changes to a single hierarchy.

Getting ready

To get started, click on the **Start** menu and navigate to **Programs | Oracle EPM System | Essbase | Start Administration Services Console**. In the Log in menu, enter your Administration Server, Username, Password, and click on the **Log In** button.

How to do it...

1. Click on the **File** menu, click on **Editors**, click on **MaxL Script Editor**, enter the following outline, and click on the **Execute script** button.

   ```
   /*Create TBC2 application*/
   create application 'TBC2';


   /*Create TBC2.TBC database*/
   create database 'TBC2'.'TBC';
   ```

2. Click on **Start**, select **Run**, type **notepad**, and press *Enter*. Enter the following MaxL script, click on **File**, click on **Save**, make sure that **All Files** in the **Save As Type** combobox is selected, and type in `C:\TBCModelDeployTime.mxl` in the **File Name** textbox. Click on **Save**. Make sure you replace the Host Essbase Server with your Essbase Server Name.

   ```
   /* This script is used to build
     Variables sent from command file:
     1 User Name
     2 Password
   */

   /*Login to Essbase Server*/
   login $1 $2 on 'Host Essbase Server';
   /*Create log*/
   spool on to "C:\DeployTBC.log";

   /*Create the Time dimension from the TBCModel.*/
   deploy outline from model 'TBCModel'
   ```

```
in cube schema '\CUBE_SCHEMAS\TBC' with option incremental_load
    modify
using update for 'TIME'-<'Year'-<'Quarter'-<'Month'-<'Week'-
    <'Day'
preserve all data
login $1 identified by $2 on host 'Host Essbase Server'
to application 'TBC2' database 'TBC' using connection
    'Localhost'
keep 200 errors on error ignore dataload write to default;

logout;
spool off;
exit;
```

3. Click on **Start**, select **Run**, type **notepad**, and press *Enter*. Enter the following MaxL script, click on **File**, click on **Save**, make sure that **All Files** in the **Save As Type** combobox is selected, and type in C:\TBCModelDeployTime.bat in the **File Name** textbox. Click on **Save**. Make sure you replace the username and password with your information.

```
ESSMSH TBCModelDeployTime.mxl UserName Password
```

4. Double-click on **C:\TBCModelDeployTime.bat**. You should see a black command prompt pop up and close when it completes the tasks in the MaxL Script.

5. Click on the **Applications** node in EAS, right-click **Refresh Application List** to view the new **TBC2** application, drill down on the **TBC2** application and **TBC** database, right-click on the **Outline**, and click on **View**. You should see the Time dimension in your hierarchy.

How it works...

In this recipe, we created the TBC2.TBC database and a TBCModelDeployTime.mxl script with the following parameters. This script functionality is used in conjunction with Essbase Studio to deploy the dimension specified to the Essbase outline. Deploying the entire outline is still available in 11.1.2.1.

Variables	Description
$1	Username
$2	Password

8
Data Integration

In this chapter, we will cover the following topics:

- Using report script to extract data to a text file
- Using the DATAEXPORT function to extract data into a text file
- Using the DATAEXPORT function to extract data into a relational source
- Exporting data using column format
- Using MaxL to extract the outline in XML format
- Using @XREF functions to move data between BSO cubes
- Partitioning data from BSO to ASO cubes
- Using MDX for extracting data using API

Introduction

In this chapter, we will review several different methods of moving data from one Essbase cube to another or from Essbase to a relational environment. The **report script** is the most versatile of tools as it has a full set of commands for reporting. The downside of report script is that it does not use the calculator cache to extract data and as a result it is not as fast as the DATAEXPORT function for example. The DATAEXPORT calculation function gives developers the ability to extract large amounts of data quickly into both flat file and relational targets. The disadvantage of DATAEXPORT is that it does not have the reporting depth of report script. A less flexible, yet powerful data export function is the **export** in column format method in **Essbase Administration Services** (**EAS**). The functionality will extract the entire content of your database in a tabular format delimited by spaces. This export method gives you the ability to export and then load large amounts of data via a load rule into another Essbase database.

This method comes in handy when you want to archive an entire database or use the **reject selected record** functionality of a load rule to load portions of one database into another. Another way of sharing data is using the @XREF or @XWRITE function in calculations or outline formula developers to move or use data from another Essbase database. The @XREF or @XWRITE function is an extremely efficient method of sharing small to mid-size data between databases. On the other hand, a more efficient way of moving or sharing data between Essbase systems is the **partition**. Partitions come in three flavors: Transparent, Replicated, and Linked. We will build a **replicated partition** between a block storage and aggregate storage cube and discuss the other two partitions. In addition, we will discuss a new functionality available in 11.1.2.1 that allows developers to extract the outline or a dimension in XML format. Finally, the ability to extract data via API using MDX is a very flexible method with all the options included with the MDX language.

Using report script to extract data to a text file

In this recipe, we will create a report using the **Report Script Editor** to extract data from Essbase. Our report script will be used to extract data in a tabular format that will be ready to be loaded into a relational environment. We will use the data from the `Sample.Basic` database created in recipe *Adding an Application and Database on an Essbase server* in *Chapter 5*, *Using EAS for Development*.

Getting ready

To get started, click on the **Start** menu and navigate to **Programs | Oracle EPM System | Essbase | Essbase Administration Services | Start Administration Services Console**. In the Log in menu, enter your Administration Server, Username, Password, and click on the **Log in** button.

How to do it...

1. Right-click on your Essbase Server in EAS, select **Edit...**, and click on **Variables...**.

2. In the **Substitution Variables** menu, click down on the cell under **Application**, select **Sample**, click down on the cell under the **Database** column, and select **Basic**.

3. Click on cell under **Variable**, type **CurMth**, select the cell under the **Value**, type in **Apr**, and click on the **Set** button.

4. Drill down on the **Essbase Server | Applications | Sample | Basic**, right-click on **Report Scripts**, and click on **Create report script**.

5. Click on the **Associate Outline** button 🗐 and select the **Sample Basic** database from the dropdown. Then click on **OK**.

6. On the left side of the **Report Script Editor**, select the **Categorical** tab, drill down on the **Commands and functions | Format** hierarchy, and select the following suppression formats:

```
{ SUPCOMMAS  }
{ SUPBRACKETS }
{ SUPHEADING }
{ ROWREPEAT }
{ SUPEMPTYROWS }
{ SUPMISSINGROWS}
{ SUPZEROROWS }
{ TABDELIMIT  }
```

7. Click on **DECIMAL** and type **variable** before the } and after DECIMAL. The following is the exact line of code:

```
{DECIMAL variable }
```

8. In the **Categorical** tab, drill down on **Commands and functions | Format** tab, select NOINDENTGEN, drill down on **Command and functions | Layout**, select **<SYM**, press the *Space Bar*, and double-click on **<SUPSHARE.**

9. In the **Categorical** tab, drill down on **Command and functions | Layout**, click on **<PAGE**, drill down on **Sample.Basic** on upper left-hand side, right-click on the **Year** dimension, and select **Insert Member Name**. Your code should look as follows:

```
<PAGE ("Year")
```

10. In the line below <PAGE ("Year"), type &CurMth to specify that you want to use the substitution variable for the Year dimension.

11. Press the *Enter* key. In the **Categorical** tab, drill down on **Command and functions | Layout**, click on **<COLUMN**, click on **Sample.Basic** on upper left-hand side, click on the **Scenario** dimension, and select **Insert Member Name**. Your code should look like the following line:

```
<COLUMN ( "Scenario")
```

12. Click on the line under <COLUMN ("Scenario"), and **Sample.Basic** on the upper left-hand side, drill down on the **Scenario** dimension, and double-click on **Actual** and **Budget**.

13. Press the *Enter* key. In the **Categorical** tab, drill down on **Command and functions | Layout**, and click on **<ROW**.

14. Click on **Sample.Basic** on the upper left-hand side, click on the **Product** dimension, and select **Insert Member Name**. Repeat the steps for dimension **Market** and **Measures**. Remember to type in a comma in between dimensions. Your code should look like the following line:

```
<ROW ( "Product", "Market", "Measures")
```

15. In the line below `<ROW ( "Product", "Market", "Measures")` type `"Lev0,Product"`, press the *Enter* key, and type `"Lev0,Market"` to retrieve the lowest level of both the **Product** and **Market** dimensions.

16. Press the *Enter* key. In the **Categorical** tab, drill down on **Command and functions | Layout**, double-click **<LINK**, double-click on **<DESCENDANTS**, and edit the code as in the following code line. Make sure you add the exclamation point at the end of the code. The bang (!) character always ends each report script.

```
<LINK (<DESCENDANTS("Profit", "Lev0,Measures"))
!
```

17. Click on the **Check Syntax** button, click on **OK** at the **Syntax Check was successful** prompt, click on the **Execute Script** button, when prompted to save report script, click on **Yes**, enter **IntRept** in the **File Name** textbox, and click on **OK**. Your report should look like the following image:

```
Script

//ESS_LOCALE English_UnitedStates.Latin1@Binary
{ SUPCOMMAS }
{ SUPBRACKETS }
{ SUPHEADING }
{ ROWREPEAT }
{ SUPEMPTYROWS }
{ SUPMISSINGROWS}
{ SUPZEROROWS }
{ TABDELIMIT }
{ DECIMAL variable }
{ NOINDENTGEN }

<SYM
<SUPSHARE
|
<PAGE ( "Year")
&CurMth

<COLUMN ( "Scenario")
"Actual""Budget"

<ROW ( "Product", "Market", "Measures")
"Lev0,Product"
"Lev0,Market"

<LINK (<DESCENDANTS("Profit", "Lev0,Measures"))
!
```

18. An **Execute Report Script** menu will show; click on the **Output File** checkbox to save the results to a text file, click on **Find**, enter **C:\IntRept.txt**, change the **File as Type** to **Text file (*.txt)**, click on **OK**, and then click on **OK** again. The result of the report script will show in the console and export to the text file in tabular format.

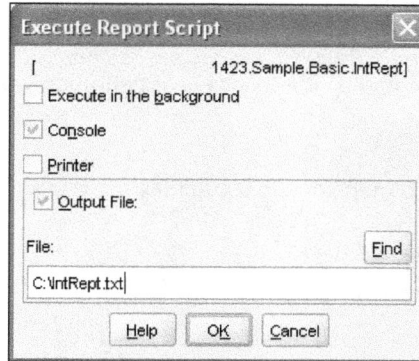

How it works...

In this recipe, we created a CurMth substitution variable to use in our report scripts. Then, we used the Report Script Editor to set up each session of our report script. We began by selecting our format settings. The following grid shows the format settings and their description:

Format Setting	Description
SUPCOMMAS	Suppresses the display of commas in numbers with more than four figures or greater than 999
SUPBRACKETS	Suppresses parentheses around negative numbers
SUPHEADING	Suppresses the column headings
ROWREPEAT	Displays all row members on each row regardless of whether it is the same as the previous row
SUPEMPTYROWS	Suppresses rows with only zero or #MISSING values
SUPMISSINGROWS	Suppresses rows with only #MISSING values
SUPZEROROWS	Suppresses rows with only zero values
TABDELIMIT	Specifies that tabs should be placed instead of commas in between columns
NOINDENTGEN	Specifies that all member names should be left aligned in the row name columns
DECIMAL VARIABLE	This setting specifies the number of decimals to show. The VARIABLE parameter allows the decimal to float.
<SUPSHARE	Suppresses shared members when using generation or level names to extract data

The layout function <SYM specifies that this will be a symmetric report regardless of data selection. Also, several other layout functions are used. The following is the syntax and description of each followed by the function and member selections:

Define the dimensions to list on the current page, as follows:

```
<PAGE ( "Year")
```

Select the Year member specified by the following substitution variable:

```
&CurMth
```

The following line defines the dimensions to list across the page:

```
<COLUMN ( "Scenario")
```

The following line defines Scenario dimension list:

```
"Actual""Budget"
```

The following line defines the dimensions to list down the page:

```
<ROW ( "Product", "Market", "Measures")
```

The following line returns the leaf level of the Product dimension:

```
"Lev0,Product"
```

The following line returns the leaf level of the Market dimension:

```
"Lev0,Market"
```

The <LINK function allows developers to combine extraction commands. In this case, we take the leaf level of Measure where these members are descendants of the Profit parent member, as follows:

```
<LINK (<DESCENDANTS("Profit", "Lev0,Measures"))
!
// Finish the report script with the bang character
```

The results of this tabular report are shown in the following image:

```
100-10   New York        Sales       712      670
100-10   New York        COGS        284      270
100-10   New York        Marketing            99       80
100-10   New York        Payroll 53           40
100-10   Massachusetts   Sales       519      490
100-10   Massachusetts   COGS        68       60
100-10   Massachusetts   Marketing            22       10
100-10   Massachusetts   Payroll 31           20
100-10   Massachusetts   Misc        1        #Missing
100-10   Florida Sales   222         210
100-10   Florida COGS    88          80
100-10   Florida Marketing           29       20
100-10   Florida Payroll 31          20
100-10   Florida Misc    1           #Missing
100-10   Connecticut     Sales       292      270
100-10   Connecticut     COGS        116      110
100-10   Connecticut     Marketing            38       30
100-10   Connecticut     Payroll 31           20
100-10   New Hampshire   Sales       125      110
```

See also

Review recipe *Creating substitution variable* in *Chapter 5* for more information on *Creating substitution variables*. Review *Executing Report Scripts using MaxL* in *Chapter 7, Using MaxL to Automate Process*, to automate the running of your report script.

Using the DATAEXPORT function to extract data into a text file

In this recipe, we will export data in a format that can easily be loaded into the relational environment. The DATAEXPORT function does not have the breadth and depth of report scripts as its purpose is to retrieve data for integration and not reporting. On the other hand, it can use the calculator cache to retrieve data in a tabular format, which makes it much faster than the equivalent report scripts. The DATAEXPORT function does not allow you to specify the order of each row or column, but you can specify what dense dimension you would like see in the columns. Another difference between a report script and the DATAEXPORT function is that these types of calculations can only be run on a **block storage cube**. This functionality is not supported in the **aggregate storage model**.

Getting ready

To get started, click on the **Start** menu and navigate to **Programs | Oracle EPM System | Essbase | Essbase Administration Services | Start Administration Services Console**. In the Log in menu, enter your Administration Server, Username, Password, and click on the **Log in** button.

How to do it...

1. Right-click on your Essbase Server in EAS, select **Edit...**, and click on **Variables...**.

2. In the **Substitution Variables** menu, click down on the cell under **Application**, select **Sample**, click down on the cell under the **Database** column, and select **Basic**.

3. Click on cell under **Variable**, type **CurMth**, select the cell under the **Value**, type in **Apr**, and click on the **Set** button.

4. Right-click on the **Start** menu, click on **Explore**, right-click on **My Computer**, select **Properties**, select the **Advanced** tab, and click on the **Environment variable** button. You should see the following menu:

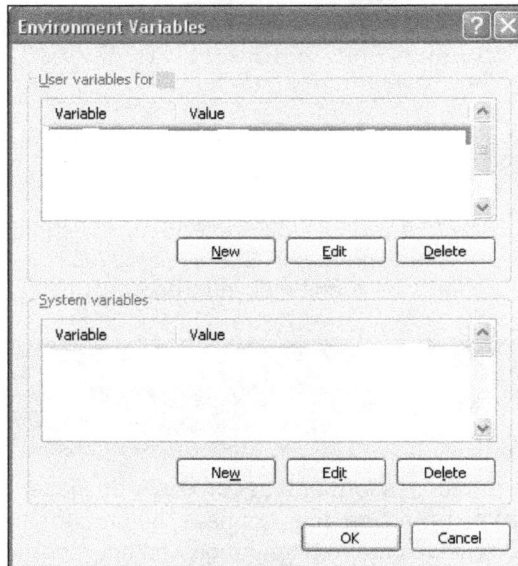

5. Click on the **New** button under the **System variables**, type **DataExportPath** in the **Variable name**, type the following `C:\Oracle\Middleware\user_projects\epmsystem1\EssbaseServer\essbaseserver1\app\Sample\Basic` in the **Variable value** textbox, click on **OK** in the **Edit System Variable** menu, click on **OK** in the **Environmental Variables** menu, and click on **OK** in the **System Properties** menu.

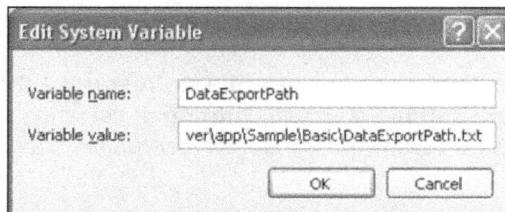

6. Drill down on the Essbase Server in EAS, expand the **Applications** node, drill down on the **Sample** application, right-click on the **Basic** database, in the drop-down menu click **Create**, and select **Calculation Scripts**.

7. In **Calculation Script Editor**, enter the following script:

```
SET LOCKBLOCK HIGH;
SET CACHE HIGH;
SET CALCPARALLEL 3;

SET DATAEXPORTOPTIONS
{
  DataExportLevel "LEVEL0";
  DataExportColFormat ON;
  DataExportOverwriteFile ON;
  DataExportDimHeader OFF;
  DataExportRelationalFile ON;
  DataExportColHeader "Scenario";
};

FIX (@Relative("Product", 0), @Relative("Market", 0))
  FIX(&CurMth, "Actual",
    "Budget", @Relative("Profit", 0))
    DATAEXPORT "File" "," $DataExportPath "0";
  ENDFIX;
ENDFIX;
```

8. Click on the **Check syntax** button to verify that the syntax is correct; a prompt should pop up with the text **Syntax check was successful**. Click on **OK**.

9. Click on the **File** menu, click on **Save**, enter **CalcExp** in the **File name** textbox, and click on **OK**.

10. Right-click on **CalcExp**, click on **Execute...**, and click on **OK** at the prompt.

How it works...

In this recipe, we created a CurMth substitution variable to use in our calculation script. We also set an environmental variable to hold the path where the DATAEXPORT function is going to drop its record set or export. The following is a description of the settings in our DATAEXPORTOPTIONS:

Option	Description
DataExportLevel	This option limits the amount of data that is to be extracted. The options are ALL / LEVEL0 / INPUT. We selected LEVEL0 to return the leaf level of data.

Option	Description
DataExportColFormat	This option specifies if data is extracted in columnar or non columnar format. The options are ON/OFF. We have set ours to ON for a columnar format.
DataExportOverwriteFile	Specifies whether a file with the same name is overwritten or if the export is aborted. The options are ON/OFF. We have set ours to ON to overwrite the existing file.
DataExportDimHeader	Specifies whether to include the dimensions as headers. The options are ON/OFF. We have set to OFF to suppress dimension headers.
DataExportRelationalFile	This option enables you to format the text export file as an input file for a relational database. The options are ON/OFF. We set our option to ON.
DataExportColHeader	Specifies the name of the dense dimension that is to be used as the column header. This option takes one dense dimension name as the parameter. We specified the Scenario dimension.

We FIX on the leaf level of the Product and Market sparse dimension. A nested FIX\ENDFIX statement includes only &CurMth Year member, the Actual, and Budget Scenario, and the lowest level of the Profit hierarchy for our Measures dimension.

Our DATAEXPORT function has the following four parameters:

Parameter	Description
"File" "Binfile" "DSN"	A keyword that determines the output type. We used "File" as we wanted to export to text file.
"delimiter"	A character that is used as a column separator. For example, ",".
"fileName"	The path of the export file. We specified the path using the $DataExportPath environmental variable.
"missingChar"	A string that is used in place of missing data. In our recipe, we used the "0" string to place a zero for each empty field.

The results of our DATAEXPORT script are shown in the following image. Notice that double quotes are used to encapsulate each outline member, commas are used as the delimiters, and the Scenario dimension is across the page as columns in the order that its members appear in the outline.

```
"100-10","New York","Sales","Apr",712,670
"100-10","New York","COGS","Apr",284,270
"100-10","New York","Marketing","Apr",99,80
"100-10","New York","Payroll","Apr",53,40
"100-10","New York","Misc","Apr",0,
"200-10","New York","Sales","Apr",66,60
"200-10","New York","COGS","Apr",125,120
"200-10","New York","Marketing","Apr",113,100
"200-10","New York","Payroll","Apr",33,30
"200-10","New York","Misc","Apr",0,
"200-40","New York","Sales","Apr",564,550
"200-40","New York","COGS","Apr",239,220
"200-40","New York","Marketing","Apr",66,60
"200-40","New York","Payroll","Apr",24,20
"200-40","New York","Misc","Apr",0,
"300-10","New York","Sales","Apr",638,490
"300-10","New York","COGS","Apr",260,190
```

See also

Review the _Executing Calculation using MaxL_ recipe in _Chapter 7_ to learn how to automate this calculation. You can also review _Using Essbase Set function commands and Calc All to calculate cubes_ in _Chapter 6_ to learn more about some of the command function used in this recipe. Moreover, you can build the Sample.Basic database used in this recipe by reviewing recipe _Adding an Application and Database on an Essbase server_ in _Chapter 5_.

Using the DATAEXPORT function to extract data into a relational source

In this recipe, we will use the DATAEXPORT function to extract data from Essbase directly into a relational table. In order to accomplish this task, you need a DSN and a table in the relational environment that is set up with the same column structure as your export. You will also need to set up your DATAEXPORT with the parameters needed for this task. This functionality is only available in the **Block Storage** (**BSO**) cube.

Getting ready

To get started, click on the **Start** menu and navigate to **Programs | Oracle EPM System | Essbase | Essbase Administration Services | Start Administration Services Console**. In the Log in menu, enter your Administration Server, Username, Password, and click on the **Log in** button. You need the TBC database that was created in _Chapter 1_ and _2_ to add a new table.

How to do it...

1. On your Essbase Windows Server, click on the **Start** menu, click on **Settings**, click on **Control Panel**, select **Administrative Tools**, and double-click on **Data Source (ODBC)**. The menu in the following image will appear.

2. Click on the **System DSN** tab, click on the **Add** button, select the **MERANT OEM 5.2 32-BIT SQL Server Wire Protocol** if you are using **SQL Server** or **MERANT OEM 5.2 32-BIT Oracle Wire Protocol** if you are using **Oracle**, then click on **Finish**.

3. You will get the following menu if you are using SQL Server; enter **SQLTBC** for the **Database Source Name**, enter your **Server Name**, enter your **Database Name**, and click on the **Test Connect** button to test your connection, click on **OK**, and then click on **OK** again.

4. If you are using **SQL Server**, then click on the **Start** menu, click on **Microsoft SQL Server 200x**, and **SQL Server Management Studio**, enter your username, password, select your server, and click on **Connect**.

5. Click on the **New Query** button, type the following SQL statement, and click on **Execute** to add the table that you are going to used to load your data.

```
USE TBC
GO
CREATE TABLE [Basic](
  PRODUCT   varchar(85) NULL,
  MARKET    varchar(85) NULL,
  MEASURES  varchar(85) NULL,
  SCENARIO  varchar(85) NULL,
  JAN       varchar(85) NULL,
  FEB       varchar(85) NULL,
  MAR       varchar(85) NULL,
  APR       varchar(85) NULL,
  MAY       varchar(85) NULL,
  JUN       varchar(85) NULL,
  JUL       varchar(85) NULL,
  AUG       varchar(85) NULL,
  SEP       varchar(85) NULL,
  OCT       varchar(85) NULL,
  NOV       varchar(85) NULL,
  [DEC]     varchar(85) NULL
);
```

6. Drill down on the Essbase Server in EAS, expand the **Applications** node, drill down on the **Sample** application, right-click on the **Basic** database, in the drop-down menu click on **Create**, and select **Calculation Scripts**.

7. In **Calculation Script Editor**, enter the following script. Make sure you replace sa and password with your username and password.

```
SET LOCKBLOCK HIGH;
SET CACHE HIGH;
SET CALCPARALLEL 3;

SET DATAEXPORTOPTIONS
  {
  DataExportLevel "LEVEL0";
  DataExportRelationalFile ON;
  DataExportColHeader Year;
  };

FIX (@Relative("Product", 0), @Relative("Market", 0))
  FIX(Jan:Dec, "Actual", "Budget", @Relative("Profit", 0))

    DATAEXPORT "DSN" "SQLTBC" "Basic" "sa" "password";
  ENDFIX ;
ENDFIX;
```

8. Click on the **Check syntax** button to verify that the syntax is correct; a prompt should pop up with the text **Syntax check was successful**. Click on **OK**.

9. Click on the **File** menu, click on **Save**, enter **ExpSQL** in the **File name** textbox, and click on **OK**.

10. Right-click on **ExpSQL**, click on **Execute...**, and click on **OK** at the prompt.

11. Return to **SQL Server Management Studio**, click on the **New Query** button, type **Select * From Basic**, and click on **Execute**. Your data should have been loaded into the **BASIC** table as shown in the following image:

	PRODUCT	MARKET	MEASURES	SCENARIO	JAN	FEB	MAR	APR	MAY	JUN	JUL	AUG	SEP	OCT	NOV	DEC
1	100-10	New York	Sales	Actual	678	645	675	712	756	890	912	910	790	650	623	699
2	100-10	New York	COGS	Actual	271	258	270	284	302	356	364	364	316	260	249	279
3	100-10	New York	Marketing	Actual	94	90	94	99	105	124	127	127	110	91	87	97
4	100-10	New York	Payroll	Actual	51	51	51	53	53	53	51	51	51	51	51	51
5	100-10	New York	Misc	Actual	0	1	1	0	1	0	0	0	1	1	0	1
6	100-10	New York	Sales	Budget	640	610	640	670	710	840	860	860	750	540	560	620
7	100-10	New York	COGS	Budget	260	240	250	270	280	340	340	340	300	210	220	250
8	100-10	New York	Marketing	Budget	80	80	80	80	90	110	110	110	90	70	70	80
9	100-10	New York	Payroll	Budget	40	40	40	40	40	40	40	40	40	30	40	40
10	200-10	New York	Sales	Actual	61	61	63	66	69	72	77	78	68	69	61	66
11	200-10	New York	COGS	Actual	105	121	125	125	121	144	162	173	121	125	121	135

How it works...

In this recipe, we created a DSN to allow our `DATAEXPORT` calculation to export data into a relation table. We set a table called **Basic** with the same format that our script uses. The following is a description of the settings in our `DATAEXPORTOPTIONS`.

Option	Description
DataExportLevel	This option limits the amount of data that is to be extracted. The options are ALL | LEVEL0 | INPUT. We selected LEVEL0 to return the leaf level of data.
DataExportRelationalFile	This option enables you to format the text export file as an input file for a relational database. The options are ON|OFF. We set our options to ON.
DataExportColHeader	Specifies the name of the dense dimension that is to be used as the column header. This option takes one dense dimension name as the parameter. We specified the Year dimension.

We `FIX` on the leaf level of the `Product` and `Market` sparse dimensions. A nested `FIX\ ENDFIX` statement includes range `Jan:Dec` from the `Year` dimension, the `Actual` and `Budget` Scenario, and the lowest level of the `Profit` hierarchy for our `Measures` dimensions.

Our `DATAEXPORT` function has the following five parameters:

Parameter	Description
"File" "Binfile" "DSN"	A keyword that determines the output type. We used "DSN" as we wanted to export to a relational environment.
"dsnName"	This parameter is the DSN used to communicate with the relational environment.
"tableName"	The relational table name where the exported data will be imported. This table needs to be created before executing this script and columns cannot contain spaces.
"userName"	Your SQL Server or Oracle relational database username.
"password"	Your SQL Server or Oracle relational database password.

See also

Review the *Executing Calculation using MaxL* recipe in *Chapter 7* to learn how to automate this calculation. You can also review *Using Essbase Set function commands and Calc All to calculate cubes* in *Chapter 6* to learn more about some of the command functions used in this recipe. Moreover, you can build the `Sample.Basic` database used in this recipe by reviewing recipe *Adding an Application and Database on an Essbase server* in *Chapter 5*.

Exporting data using column format

In this recipe, we will use a column format export to extract all the data from `Sample.Basic` at the lowest level. We will also create a separate database for the purpose of loading this columnar export via a load rule. The column format is the least flexible method of exporting data from a database as data is exported in the format of the Essbase outline. Moreover, we cannot specify a slice of the database for export with column format export. On the other, it is one of the fastest ways of extracting all data from an Essbase database.

Getting ready

To get started, click on the **Start** menu and navigate to **Programs | Oracle EPM System | Essbase | Essbase Administration Services | Start Administration Services Console**. In the Log in menu, enter your Administration Server, Username, Password, and click on the **Log in** button.

How to do it...

1. Drill down on the Essbase Server in EAS, expand the **Applications** node, drill down on the **Sample** application, right-click on the **Basic** database, and in the drop-down menu click on **Export...**.

2. In the **Export Database** menu, type **Sample\Basic\Basic.txt** in the **Export to File** textbox. The default directory is `.\Oracle\Middleware\user_projects\ epmsystem1\EssbaseServer\essbaseserver1\app`.

3. Select the **Level 0 data blocks** radio button to export only level-zero data.

4. Click on the **Export in Column format** checkbox and click on **OK**.

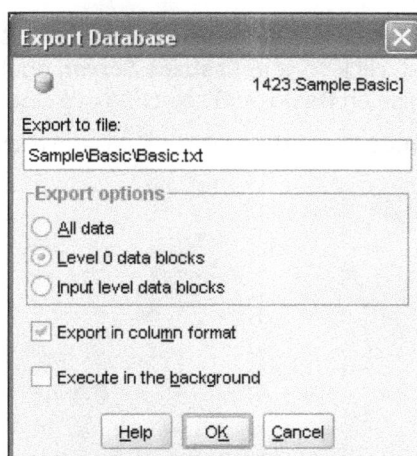

5. In EAS, click on **File**, click on **Editors**, click on **MaxL Script Editor**, type the following MaxL script, and click on the **Execute Script** button.

```
/*Create an application Sample6 as a copy of Sample*/
create application Sample6 as Sample;

/*Clear the new Sample6.Basic database*/
alter database Sample6.Basic reset;
```

6. Open the `Basic.txt` text file under `.\Oracle\Middleware\user_projects\ epmsystem1\EssbaseServer\essbaseserver1\app\Sample\Basic` with your favorite text editor and type in the following line with a space at the end of "Scenario", and Save.

`"Product" "Market" "Year" "Scenario"`

```
"Product" "Market" "Year" "Scenario" "Sales" "COGS" "Marketing" "Payroll" "Misc" "Opening Inventory"
"100-10" "New York" "Jan" "Actual" 678 271 94 51 0 2101 644 2067 718.68 678 678 0.1946564885496183 1
"100-10" "New York" "Feb" "Actual" 645 258 90 51 1 2067 619 2041 683.7000000000001 1323 645 0.194656
"100-10" "New York" "Mar" "Actual" 675 270 94 51 1 2041 742 2108 715.5 1998 666 0.1946564885496183 1
"100-10" "New York" "Apr" "Actual" 712 284 99 53 0 2108 854 2250 754.72 #Mi #Mi 0.1970260223048327 1
"100-10" "New York" "May" "Actual" 756 302 105 53 1 2250 982 2476 801.36 #Mi #Mi 0.1970260223048327
"100-10" "New York" "Jun" "Actual" 890 356 124 53 0 2476 1068 2654 943.4 #Mi #Mi 0.1970260223048327
"100-10" "New York" "Jul" "Actual" 912 364 127 51 0 2654 875 2617 966.72 #Mi #Mi 0.1946564885496183
"100-10" "New York" "Aug" "Actual" 910 364 127 51 0 2617 873 2580 964.6 #Mi #Mi 0.1946564885496183 1
"100-10" "New York" "Sep" "Actual" 790 316 110 51 1 2580 758 2548 837.4 #Mi #Mi 0.1946564885496183 1
"100-10" "New York" "Oct" "Actual" 650 260 91 51 1 2548 682 2580 689 #Mi #Mi 0.1946564885496183 2
"100-10" "New York" "Nov" "Actual" 623 249 87 51 0 2580 685 2642 660.38 #Mi #Mi 0.1946564885496183 2
"100-10" "New York" "Dec" "Actual" 699 279 97 51 1 2642 671 2614 740.9400000000001 #Mi #Mi 0.1946564
"100-10" "New York" "Jan" "Budget" 640 260 80 40 #Mi 2030 600 1990 678.4 640 640 0.1904761904761905
"100-10" "New York" "Feb" "Budget" 610 240 80 40 #Mi 1990 600 1980 646.6 1250 610 0.1904761904761905
"100-10" "New York" "Mar" "Budget" 640 250 80 40 #Mi 1980 700 2040 678.4 1890 630 0.1904761904761905
"100-10" "New York" "Apr" "Budget" 670 270 80 40 #Mi 2040 800 2170 710.2000000000001 #Mi #Mi 0.18181
"100-10" "New York" "May" "Budget" 710 280 90 40 #Mi 2170 900 2360 752.6 #Mi #Mi 0.1818181818181818
"100-10" "New York" "Jun" "Budget" 840 340 110 40 #Mi 2360 1000 2520 890.4 #Mi #Mi 0.181818181818181
"100-10" "New York" "Jul" "Budget" 860 340 110 40 #Mi 2520 800 2460 911.6 #Mi #Mi 0.1904761904761905
```

7. Right-click on the **Applications** node and select **Refresh Application Lists**, drill down on **Sample6** application, right-click on the **Basic** database, select **Create**, and click on **Rules file**.

8. Click on **File**, click on **Open** data file, select the **Essbase Server** tab, click on the **Look in** drop-down list, click on your **Essbase Server**, double-click on the **Sample** application, double-click on **Basic**, and select `Basic.txt`.

9. Click on the **Data Source Properties** button [icon], and click on the **All Spaces** radio button.

10. Click on the **Header** tab, click on **Records containing data load field names**, and enter **1** in the textbox, as shown in the following screenshot:

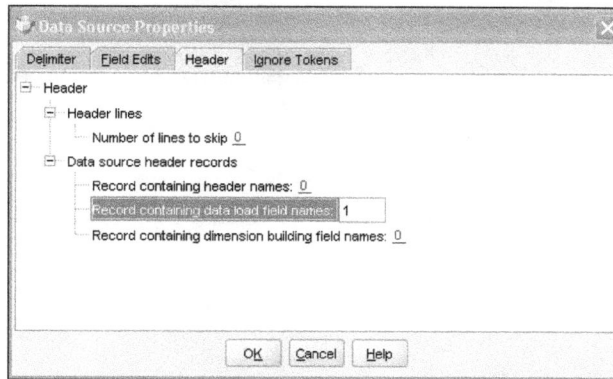

11. Select the **Sales** measure column and click on the **Field properties** button.

12. Click **Replace**, type **#Mi**, type **#Missing** in the **With** textbox, check **Match whole word**, check **Replace All Occurrences**, click on the **Next** button, repeat the same steps for each of the other Measures, and click on **OK** in the **Field Properties** menu, as shown in the following screenshot:

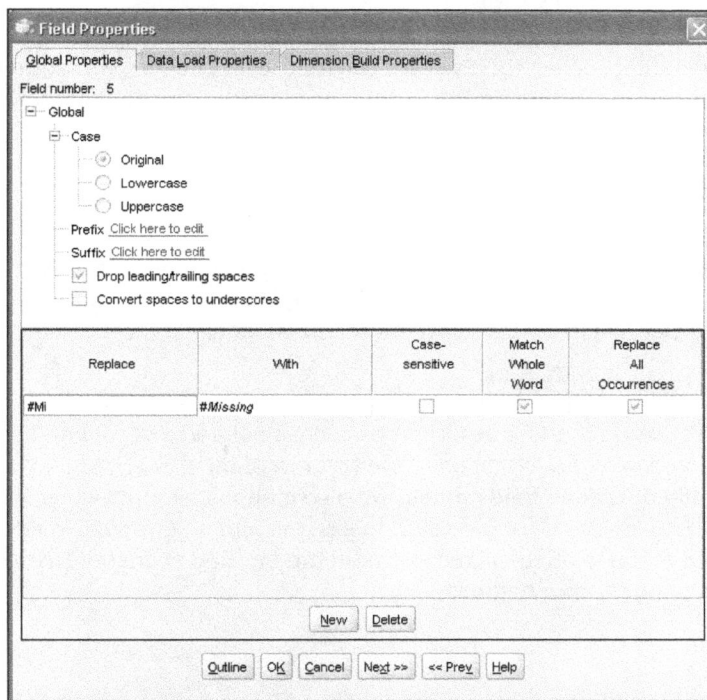

13. Click on column **Scenario**, click on the **Reject Record** button, select **String** under the **Type** column, type **Budget** in the **String/Number** column, select **Equal** in the **Condition** column, and click on **OK**.

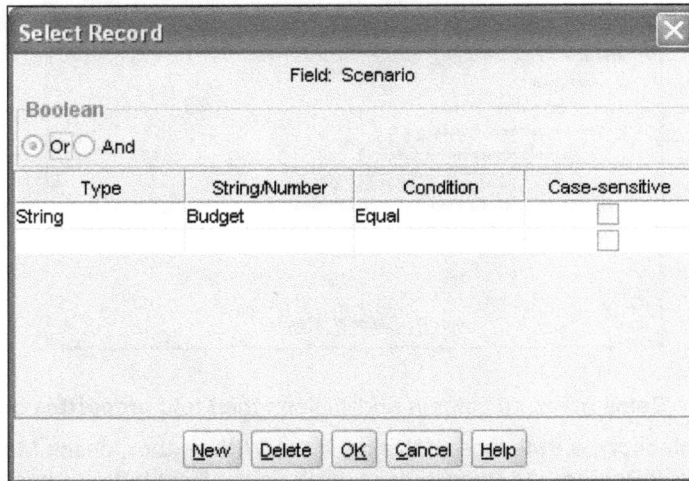

14. Click on the **Validate** button, click on **OK**, click on **File**, click on **Save**, type **LDCF** in the **File name** textbox, and click on **OK**.

15. Right-click on the **Sample6.Basic** database, click on **Load Data...**, click on the **Find Data File** button, select the **Essbase Server** tab, in **Look in** drop-down list select **Basic.txt** under the **Sample.Basic** database, click on the **Find Load Rule** button, select **LDCF**, and click on **OK**.

How it works...

In this recipe, we extracted data at the lowest level using a column format export. We then created a copy of the `Sample.Basic` database using MaxL. We added the following line to the `Basic.txt` export file in order to have all column headers in the text file:

```
"Product" "Market" "Year" "Scenario
```

The reason for this step is that the export process does not add row column headers. Moreover, we created a load rule that used the first row of the `Basic.txt` export as the **Records containing data load field names**. We also mapped all #Mi values in the measures column to #Missing as #Mi will cause data to kick out into an error file. In addition, we used the **Reject Record** menu to reject all records from the `Budget` scenario. Finally, we loaded data into our `Sample6.Basic` database.

The building of the `Sample.Basic` database used in this is discussed in the recipe *Adding an Application and Database on an Essbase server* in *Chapter 5*.

Using MaxL to extract the outline in XML format

In this recipe, we will use an Export Outline MaxL script to extract the metadata from the `Sample.Basic` database in XML format. In *Chapter 1*, *Understanding and Modifying Data Sources*, we discussed how to extract metadata using third-party tools such as the **Essbase Outline Extractor** and **Star Integration Server Manager**. The **Export Outline MaxL** is new to Oracle Essbase 11.1.2.x and allows us to share metadata information with any application or relational database that supports XML.

Getting ready

To get started, click on the **Start** menu and navigate to **Programs | Oracle EPM System | Essbase | Essbase Administration Services | Start Administration Services Console**. In the Log in menu, enter your Administration Server, Username, Password, and click on the **Log in** button.

How to do it...

1. In EAS, click on **File**, click on **Editors**, click on **MaxL Script Editor**, type the following MaxL script, and click on the **Execute Script** button:

    ```
    /*Export dimensions Measures and Year to xml file Basic*/
    Export outline Sample.Basic list dimensions {"Measures",
      "Year"} to xml_file "c:/Basic.xml";
    ```

2. Click on the **Start** menu, click on **Explore**, browse to the `C:\Basic.xml` file, and double-click to open. The file should look like as in the following image:

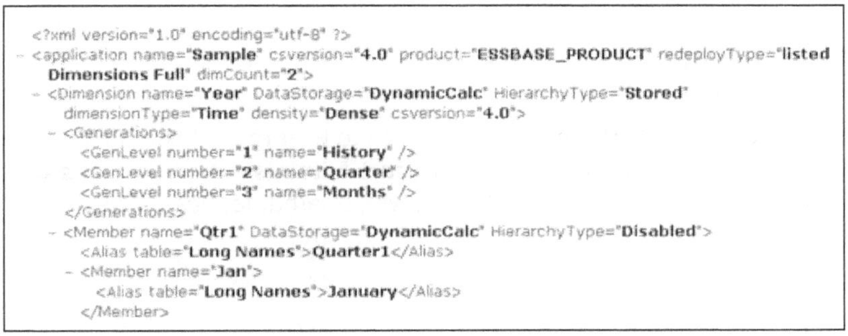

    ```
    <?xml version="1.0" encoding="utf-8" ?>
    <application name="Sample" csversion="4.0" product="ESSBASE_PRODUCT" redeployType="listed
      Dimensions Full" dimCount="2">
      <Dimension name="Year" DataStorage="DynamicCalc" HierarchyType="Stored"
        dimensionType="Time" density="Dense" csversion="4.0">
        <Generations>
          <GenLevel number="1" name="History" />
          <GenLevel number="2" name="Quarter" />
          <GenLevel number="3" name="Months" />
        </Generations>
        <Member name="Qtr1" DataStorage="DynamicCalc" HierarchyType="Disabled">
          <Alias table="Long Names">Quarter1</Alias>
          <Member name="Jan">
            <Alias table="Long Names">January</Alias>
          </Member>
    ```

How it works...

In this recipe, we used a MaxL script to export the `Measures` and `Year` dimensions' metadata from our `Sample.Basic` database. The following line and grid are the syntax for the export outline MaxL script as used in this recipe and a description of the keywords:

```
Export outline DBS-NAME list dimensions DIM-NAME to
   xml_file FILE-NAME;
```

Keyword	Description
DBS-NAME	A database name, in our case Sample.Basic.
DIM-NAME	A list of the dimensions surrounded by curly brackets and separated by commas. In our recipe the value is {"Measures", "Year"} .
FILE-NAME	The full path of the XML file or `C:/Basic.mxl`.

> There may be occasions when you want to find out what changed in outline to explain a variance from one month to the next. All you need is an XML Export for the previous month, an export for the current month, and a text editor that has file comparison functionality such as TextPad, for example. You can use the **Compare Files...** function in TextPad to compare the two XML files and find the differences quickly.

Using @XREF functions to move data between BSO cubes

In this recipe, we will use the `XREF` function in a calculation script to pull data from a source to the target Block Storage database. The value of this `XREF` function is obvious when you consider that you can assign calculation execution access to your power users and empower them to pull data from another database on demand. This function also gives you the option of sharing between databases instead of replicating load processes. Moreover, the `XREF` function does not require that outlines be identical so you can pull data from outlines with completely different dimension structures and hierarchies.

Getting ready

To get started, click on the **Start** menu and navigate to **Programs | Oracle EPM System | Essbase | Essbase Administration Services | Start Administration Services Console**. In the Log in menu, enter your Administration Server, Username, Password, and click on the **Log in** button.

How to do it...

1. In EAS, drill down on **Applications | Sample | Basic**, right-click the **Basic Outline**, and click on **Edit**.

2. Right-click on the **Ratios** member, click on **Add Sibling**, type **Exchange Rates**, press _Enter_, then _Esc_, click on **Exchange Rates**, and click on the **Excluded from consolidation** button.

3. Right-click on the **Exchange Rate** member, click on **Add Sibling**, type **EUR**, press _Enter_, then _Esc_, click on **EUR**, and click on the **Never Consolidate Member** button.

4. Drill down in your **Market** dimension, right-click on **Central**, click on **Add sibling**, type in **Market NA**, press the your _Enter_ key, then _Esc_, click on **Market NA**, and click on the **Excluded from Consolidation** button.

5. Drill down in your **Product** dimension, right-click on **Diet**, click on **Add sibling**, type in **Product NA**, press the _Enter_ key, and then _Esc_, click on **Product NA**, and click on the **Excluded from consolidation** button.

6. Click on the **Verify** button, click on **OK**, click on the **Save** button, in the **Restructure Database Options** menu select **All data**, and click on the **OK** button.

7. In EAS, click on **File**, click on **Editors**, click on **MaxL Script Editor**, type the following MaxL script, and click on the **Execute Script** button.

```
/*Create an application Sample7 as a copy of Sample*/
create application Sample7 as Sample;

/*Clear the new Sample7.Basic database*/
alter database Sample7.Basic reset;
```

8. Drill down on **Applications | Sample7 | Basic**, right-click the **Basic** database, click on **Edit**, and click on **Location aliases**.

9. Type **SampleDB** on the cell below the **Alias** column and, select your Essbase server from the **Essbase Node** drop down, select **Sample** under the **Application** column, select **Basic** under the **Database** column, type in you username under the **User Name** column, and type you password under the **Password** column.

10. Click on the **Test** button, click on the **Set** button, and click on **Close**. Your location aliases menu should look like the following image:

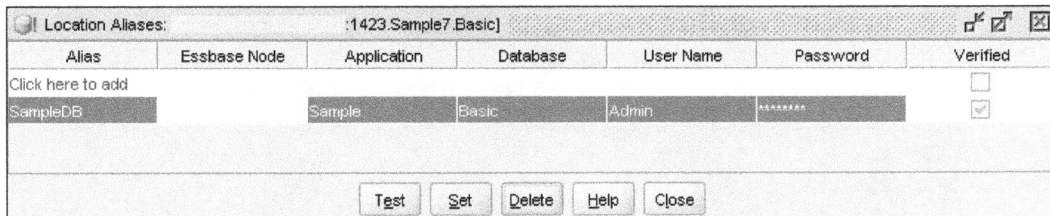

19. Open an Excel session, open a connection in your in **Smart View** tab by clicking on the **Open** button, in the **Smart View Panel**, click on **Private Connections**, select your Essbase Server from the combobox, enter your username and password, right-click on the **Sample.Basic** database, and select **Ad hoc analysis**.

20. Set up your spread sheet like the following image without the data values, click on the **Refresh** button on your POV, and then type in the values in yellow in column **B**, as shown in the following image. Click on the **Submit Data** button on your ribbon.

	A	B *	C
1		Market NA	Market
2		Actual	Actual
3		EUR	Sales
4		Product NA	Product
5	Jan	1.427048	31538
6	Feb	1.36834	32069
7	Mar	1.357478	32213
8	Apr	1.342732	32917
9	May	1.2538	33674
10	Jun	1.221068	35088
11	Jul	1.279995	36134
12	Aug	1.289995	36008
13	Sep	1.309282	33073
14	Oct	1.38971	32828
15	Nov	1.363755	31971
16	Dec	1.322704	33342

21. In EAS, drill down on the **Sample7** application, right-click on the **Basic** database, in the drop-down menu click on **Create**, and select **Calculation Scripts**.

22. In **Calculation Script Editor**, enter the following script:

```
SET UPDATECALC OFF;
SET AGGMISSG ON;
SET LOCKBLOCK HIGH;
SET CACHE ALL;
SET CACHE HIGH;

FIX(@Relative("Product", 0))
  FIX(Jan:Dec, "Actual", "Sales")
    "Market NA" =
      @XREF(SampleDB, "Actual", "Sales", "Market");
      "Market NA" = "Market NA"
 / @XREF(SampleDB, "Actual", "EUR", "Market NA", "Product NA");
  ENDFIX;
ENDFIX
Calc All;
```

23. Click on the **Check syntax** button to verify that the syntax is correct; a prompt should pop up with the text **Syntax check was successful**. Click on **OK**.

24. Click the **Execute script button**, on the **Do you want to save the file** prompt click on **Yes**, enter **CalcXREF** in the **File name** textbox, click on **OK**, and in the **Execute Calculation Script** prompt click on **OK**.

25. Return to your Excel session, select **Sheet2**, open a connection in your in **Smart View** tab by pressing the **Open** button, in the **Smart View Panel**, click on **Private Connections**, right-click on the **Sample7.Basic** database, select **Connect** from the combobox, enter your username and password, right-click on **Sample7.Basic**, and select **Ad hoc analysis**.

26. Set up your spread sheet like the following image without the data values, and click on the **Refresh** button on your POV.

	A	B
1		Market NA
2		Actual
3		Sales
4		Product
5	Jan	22100.16762
6	Feb	23436.42662
7	Mar	23730.03467
8	Apr	24514.94416
9	May	26857.55304
10	Jun	28735.5004
11	Jul	28229.79777
12	Aug	27913.28649
13	Sep	25260.4099
14	Oct	23622.19456
15	Nov	23443.36043
16	Dec	25207.45382

How it works...

In this recipe, we added a EUR measure to store the exchange rates for Euro currency and two dummy members for the Market and Product dimensions. We copied Sample.Basic and called it Sample7.Basic using MaxL, so that we could show how data can be pulled from the source to target database. We also set up of a **location alias**. A location alias is used with the @XREF function to provide a shorthand method of managing information such as host name, application name, database name, username, and password of the source database. We submitted the rates for the Euro into the Sample.Basic database to illustrate how to conduct math using data stored outside of the target of database.

We began our calculation by copying data from `Sample.Basic` to `Sample7.Basic` for the `Actual` scenario, `Sales` measure, and `Market` parent value into dummy member `Market NA`. We used our `FIX/ENDFIX` statement to specify the point of view on our data target. The `@XREF` function takes a location alias `SampleDB` and a comma-delimited list of members that qualifies the Essbase query:

```
FIX(@Relative("Product", 0))
  FIX(Jan:Dec, "Actual", "Sales")
    "Market NA" = @XREF(SampleDB, "Actual", "Sales", "Market");
```

We then divided the value we copied over with our first `@XREF` function into the target database `Sample7.Basic` with the exchange rate value for member `EUR` available in the source database `Sample.Basic`.

```
  "Market NA" = "Market NA"
 / @XREF(SampleDB, "Actual", "EUR", "Market NA", "Product NA");
  ENDFIX;
ENDFIX
Calc All;
```

Partitioning data from BSO to ASO cubes

In this recipe, we will use the **Aggregate Storage Outline Conversion Wizard** to convert the `Sample.Basic` block storage to an aggregate storage database. We will then clear the new aggregate storage database using replicate partition to load data from the source cube `Sample.Basic` to our new ASO database.

Getting ready

To get started, click on the **Start** menu and navigate to **Programs | Oracle EPM System | Essbase | Essbase Administration Services | Start Administration Services Console**. In the Log in menu, enter your Administration Server, Username, Password, and click on the **Log in** button.

How to do it...

1. In **EAS**, click on the **File** menu, click on **Wizards | Aggregate Storage Outline Conversion**, click on the **Essbase Server** tab, click on the **Look in** drop-down box, click on the **Sample** application, double-click on **Basic**, and select `Basic.otl`. Your screen should look like the following image:

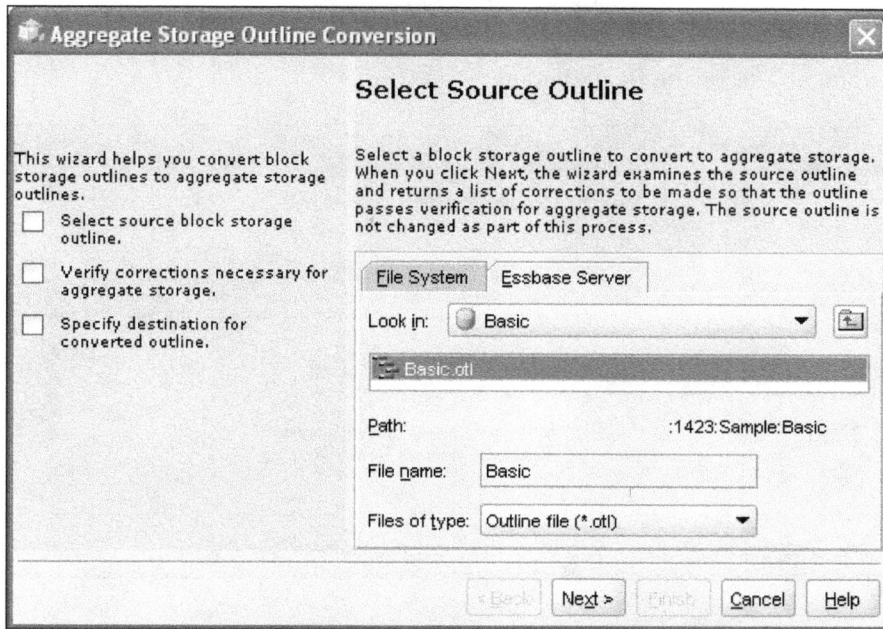

2. Click on the **Next >** button and you will get a list of errors that you can choose to fix interactively or automatically. Make sure that the **Automatic outline correction** radio button is selected and click on the **Next >** button.

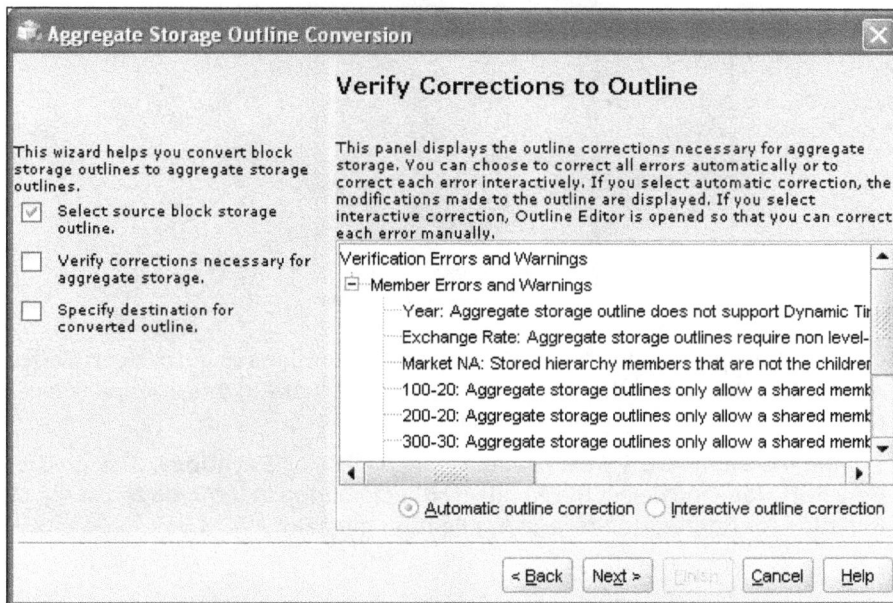

3. The **Verify Corrections to Outline** screen will let you know what corrections are needed or identify the members that need to be deleted for conversion to aggregate storage. Click on the **Next>** button.

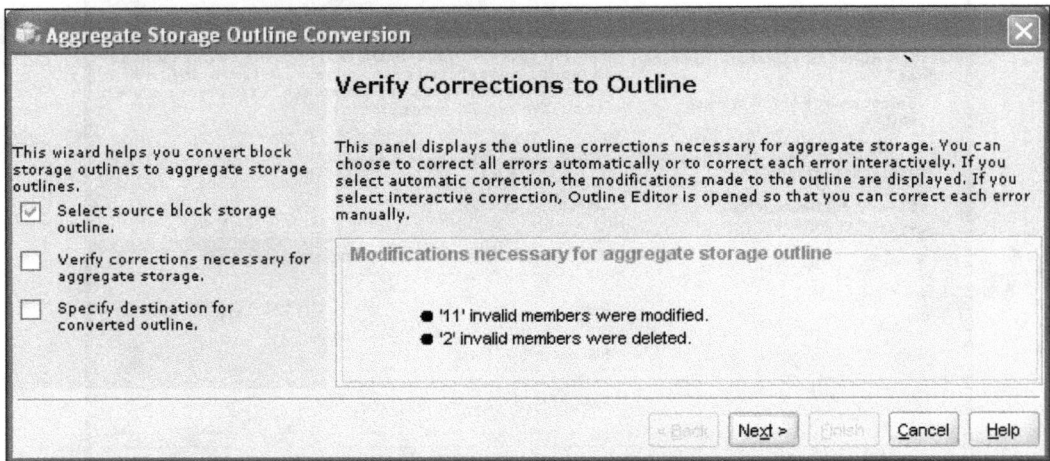

4. In the **Select Destination for Aggregate Storage Outline** screen, click on **Create Aggregate Storage Application**. In the **Create Aggregate...** menu, type **SampASO** in the application textbox, type **Basic** in the **Database** textbox, and click on **OK**.

5. Click on the **Finish** button, right-click on the **Applications** node, click on **Refresh application list**, select the **SampASO | Basic** database, right-click and select **Clear**, click on **All data**, click on **Yes**, and click on **OK**.

6. Expand the **SampASO | Basic** database, right-click on **Partitions**, click on **Create New Partition**, and select the **Replicated** radio button in the **Type** tab of the **Create Partition for Aggregate Storage Application** menu.

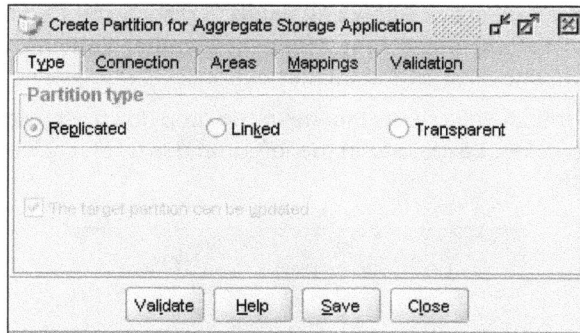

7. Click on the **Connection** tab. On the left-hand side select **Sample** for the **Data Source Application**, and select **Basic** for the **Data Source** database.

8. On the right-hand side of the **Connection** tab, select **SampASO** for the **Data Target Application**, and select **Basic** for the **Data Target** database.

9. Select an administrative username from the dropdowns on both **Data Source** and **Data Target**, and enter the password for both. A best practice is to make sure that the administrative username that you use has a password that does not have an expiration date. In other words, if the administrative username's password becomes invalid, because your companies policy forces the changing of passwords every three months, then your partition will not longer work as a result.

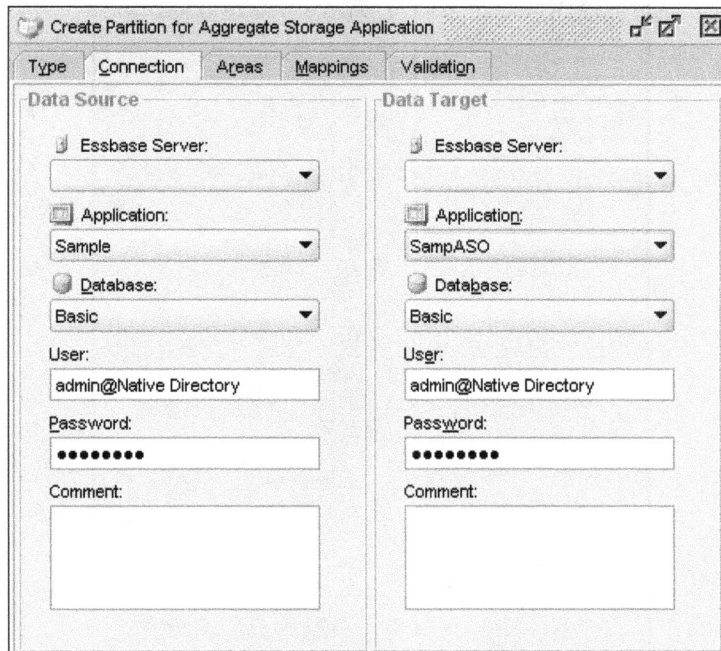

10. Select the **Areas** tab, check **Show cell count** to display the **Cell** number count, double-click on **Source**, in the **Area Mapping Member Selection** menu click on the **Year** dimension, and click on the **Subset** button.

11. In the **Subset** menu, select **Level name** in the drop-down list, click on **IS** in the center drop-down list, select **Lev0, Year** in the left drop-down list, click on the **Add** button, and then on **OK**.

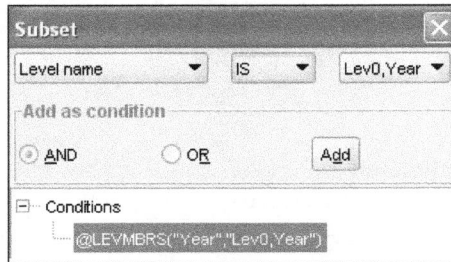

12. Repeat the step 11 for dimensions Measures, Scenario, Market, and Product.

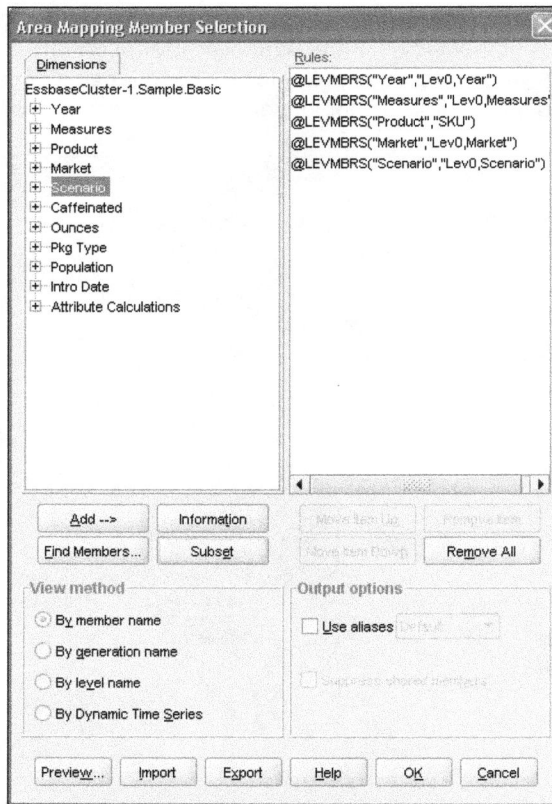

13. Click on the **OK** button in the **Area Mapping Member Selection** menu, click on the **Use text editor** radio button, in the **Area definition** menu, click inside the text area, keeping the *Shift* key pressed, drag the mouse to select all the data inside the textbox, press *Ctrl+C* to copy text, and click on **OK**, as shown in the following screenshot:

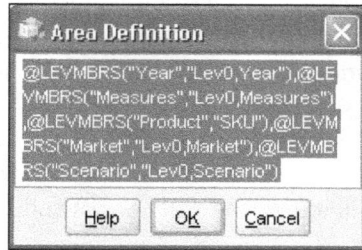

14. Double-click under the **Target** column in the text and press *Ctrl+V* to paste text. Then click on **OK**. Your area in the **Source** and **Target** should have the following text and your cell count should be the same, as shown in the following screenshot:

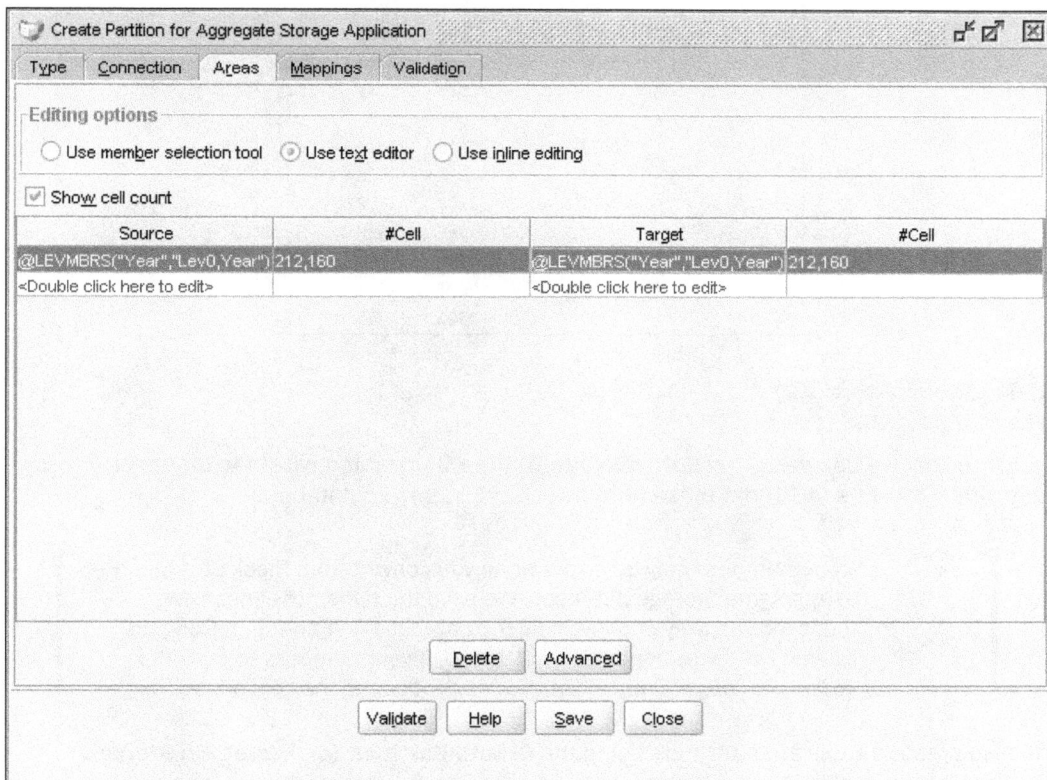

15. Click on the **Validate** button. On the **Validation was successful prompt** click on **OK**. Click on the **Save** button, click on **OK**, and click on **Close**.

16. Drill down on **SampASO | Basic | Partitions | Source Databases**, right-click on **[localhost.Sample.Basic] [Replicate]**, click on **Replicate data from source**, click on the **Update all Cells** radio button, click on **OK**, and then on **OK** at the prompt.

17. Open an **Excel** session, open a connection to your database in **Smart View** by clicking on the **Open** button in the Smart View ribbon, select **Private Connections** in your **Smart View** panel, enter your username and password in the **Connect to Data Source** menu, and click **Connect.**

18. Drill down on the **SampASO** application; right-click on the **Basic** database and **Ad hoc analysis**. Set up your spreadsheet as follows and click on **Refresh** on your **POV**:

	A	B	C	D	E
1		Actual	Actual		Actual	Actual
2		100	200		300	400
3		East	East		East	East
4		Sales	Sales		Sales	Sales
5	Jan	2105		1853	1609	1213
6	Feb	2061		1966	1621	1272
7	Mar	2126		1907	1638	1250
8	Apr	2258		1935	1753	1267
9	May	2347		1896	1779	1319
10	Jun	2625		2071	1795	1404
11	Jul	2735		1992	1926	1395
12	Aug	2673		1984	1677	1469
13	Sep	2362		1887	1539	1337
14	Oct	2094		2124	1544	1339
15	Nov	2066		2076	1605	1231
16	Dec	2288		1981	1755	1249

How it works...

In this recipe, we use the **Aggregate Storage Outline Conversion** wizard to create an **Aggregate Storage (ASO)** database from the `Sample.Basic` database.

> Note that there may be errors when you convert from Block Storage to Aggregate Storage database. We have the option of either fixing these interactively or converting the database first and then fixing the issues. These discrepancies will throw off your numbers so consider keeping a note of them while you are conducting the conversion.

We also create a replicated partition using the **Create Partition for Aggregate Storage Application** menu. The **Type** tab gives you three options for your partition types.

These partitions and their definitions are listed in the following table:

Partition Type	Partition Description
Replicated	This type of partition allows you to move slices of the Source's data to the Target database.
Transparent	This type of partition allows you to use data from the Source database as if it were stored at the Target database. However, the data is stored in another application, database, or Essbase Server.
Linked	This partition will send a user from a cell in one database to another database.

The **Connection** tab in our menu allows us to enter login information for both the source database and target database. The **Areas** tab allows us define the slice or slices that we want to partition. We check the **Show cell** count to make sure that we have the same cell count on our source database and target database for each slice. If this is not the case, then the **Replicated** partition will not validate as Essbase will not have a clean mapping of data from the Source to the Target database.

We were able to copy the same area definition to the **Target** from the **Source** as our databases had the same structure, but you may have a situation where the databases have different dimensionality. In this case, you should pick the member that you want partitioned and not exclude any dimension from the partition area. This sometimes means creating dummy members on the side of the partition with more dimensions. You would then have to use the **Mappings** tab to either map dimensions to **Void**, if they do not exist at the target or map a member from the source database to the aforementioned dummy members if the target database has more dimensions than the source.

Finally, we validate and partition our data. If your partition did not validate, then the **Validation** tab would have a list of errors for you to view and fix.

Using MDX for extracting data using API

In this recipe, we will extract data using the APIs in Excel and an MDX script. We will be using the Visual Basic editor to load the `smartviewvba.bas` file, enter the code needed to connect to Essbase, and extract data specified in our MDX script. In addition, we will conduct a similar task manually using the Execute MDX option in Smart View.

Getting ready

To get started, click on the **Start** menu and navigate to **Programs | Microsoft Office | Excel**.

How to do it...

1. In Excel, click on **Sheet1** and press *Alt+F11*. You will launch **Microsoft Visual Basic editor**, which should look like the following screenshot:

2. Right-click on **Microsoft Excel Objects** under **VBAProject** (**Book1**), click on **Import File...**, in the **Import File** menu, browse to **C:\Oracle\SmartView\Bin**, click on **SmartviewVBA.bas**, and click on the **Open** button. You should see the file imported under the **Modules** folder.

3. Double-click on the **SmartviewVBA** module and type the following database constant variables below the **Function Smartview VBA Declaration** session. Make modifications to the values on the right side of the equal sign for your environment's information.

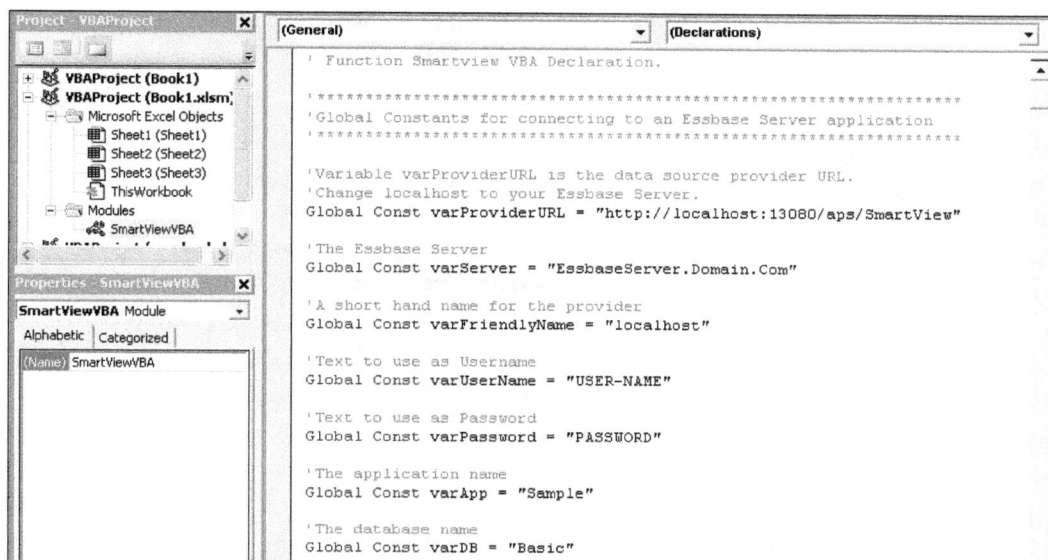

```
' Function Smartview VBA Declaration.

'*************************************************************
'Global Constants for connecting to an Essbase Server application
'*************************************************************

'Variable varProviderURL is the data source provider URL.
'Change localhost to your Essbase Server.
Global Const varProviderURL = "http://localhost:13080/aps/SmartView"

'The Essbase Server
Global Const varServer = "EssbaseServer.Domain.Com"

'A short hand name for the provider
Global Const varFriendlyName = "localhost"

'Text to use as Username
Global Const varUserName = "USER-NAME"

'Text to use as Password
Global Const varPassword = "PASSWORD"

'The application name
Global Const varApp = "Sample"

'The database name
Global Const varDB = "Basic"
```

4. Scroll down to the button of the code in the **SmartviewVBA** module and type in the following code to create a public sub for the MDX code, create the variable required for the Essbase functions, and set up your error handler.

```
Public Sub MDX()

    Dim vtBoolHideData As Variant
    Dim vtBoolDataless As Variant
    Dim vtBoolNeedStatus As Variant
    Dim vtMbrIDType As Variant
    Dim vtAliasTable As Variant
    Dim HypF As Boolean
    Dim lintRow As Integer
    Dim lstrError As String
    Dim sts As Long
    Dim vtQuery As Variant
    Dim result_Native As MDX_AXES_NATIVE
    Dim result_VBCompatible As MDX_AXES

    On Error GoTo ErrorHandler

    Exit Sub
ErrorHandler:
      MsgBox ("MDX run failed with error #: " & CStr(Err.Number)
        & ". " & lstrError)
    End Sub
```

5. Below the `On Error GoTo ErrorHandle`, type the following code to check your Essbase connection and connect to your Essbase Server:

```
HypF = HypIsConnectedToAPS() 'Check if connected

If HypF = False Then
  HypF = HypConnectToAPS() 'Connect to provider services
End If

HypF = HypConnectionExists(varFriendlyName)
'If friendly name exist then disconnect
If HypF = True Then
  HypF = HypInvalidateSSO()
  HypF = HypDisconnect(Empty, True)
  HypF = HypRemoveConnection(varFriendlyName)
End If
'Create connection
varCreateConnection = HypCreateConnection(Empty, _
  varUserName, varPassword, _
  HYP_ESSBASE, varProviderURL, _
  varServer, varApp, varDB, _
varFriendlyName, _            HYP_ANALYTIC_SERVICES)
    'Connect to Essbase Server
    varConnect = HypConnect(Empty, varUserName, varPassword, _
      varFriendlyName)
```

6. Type following code under step 5's code to concatenate your MDX script and press *Enter*:

```
vtQuery = "Select  {[Actual]} ON COLUMNS,   "
vtQuery = vtQuery + " Product.Levels(0).Members on rows "
vtQuery = vtQuerty + " From Sample.Basic"
```

7. Type the following code to check if you are connected to Essbase, set the variables you require for `HypExecuteMDXEx` function, and conduct error trapping for your `HypExecuteMDX` function. Press *Enter*.

```
'Check if connected to Essbase
If varConnect = 0 Then
  'Specify parameters for HypExecuteMDXEx
    vtBoolHideData = True
    vtBoolDataless = True
    vtBoolNeedStatus = True
    vtMbrIDType = ""
    vtAliasTable = "none"

  'Extract MDX record set into result_Native
```

```
    sts = HypExecuteMDXEx(Empty, vtQuery, vtBoolHideData, _
      vtBoolDataless, vtBoolNeedStatus, vtMbrIDType, _
      vtAliasTable, result_Native)
    'Error trapping for HypExecuteMDXEx
    If sts <> 0 Then
      lstrError = "HypExecuteMDXEx failed with error #" + sts
      Err.Raise vbObjectError + 513, "SmartViewVBA::MDX()", _
      "HypExecuteMDXEx failed with error #" + sts
    End If
```

8. Type the following code to retrieve your MDX query, create an array to hold the record set, loop through the array, and set cell values on `Sheet1`. Press *Enter*.

```
'Takes a result_Native parameter and returns array
  result_VBCompatible
    Call GetVBCompatibleMDXStructure(result_Native, _
      result_VBCompatible)



    'Select Sheet1
    With Sheet1
      .Select
      .Activate
      .Cells.Select
      .Cells.ClearContents
      .Range("A1").Select
    End With
    'Loop through result_VBCompatible retrieving product
      'member name
      For lintRow = 0 To result_VBCompatible. _
        AxisInfo(1).ClusterInfo(0). _
        DimensionInfo(0).NumMembers - 1

        ActiveCell.Value = result_VBCompatible. _
        AxisInfo(1).ClusterInfo(0) _
        .DimensionInfo(0). _
        MemberInfo(lintRow).MemberName
        ActiveCell.Offset(1, 0).Select
      Next lintRow
```

9. Type the following code to retrieve the MDX query, extract the results into **Sheet2**, disconnect from the current session, and handle error trapping:

```
'Select sheet2
With Sheet2
   .Select
   .Activate
   .Cells.Select
   .Cells.ClearContents
   .Range("A1").Select
End With

'Retrieve MDX script result set into sheet2
   sts = HypExecuteQuery(ActiveSheet.Name, vtQuery)

'Conduct error trapping for HypExcuteQuery
   If sts <> 0 Then
      lstrError = "HypExecuteQuery failed with error #" + sts
   Err.Raise vbObjectError + 514, _
   "SmartViewVBA::MDX()", _
      "HypExecuteQuery failed with error #" + sts
End If

'Disconnect
   sts = HypDisconnect(Empty, True)

If sts <> 0 Then
   lstrError = "HypExecuteQuery failed with error #" + sts
   Err.Raise vbObjectError + 515, _
   "SmartViewVBA::MDX()", _
   "HypExecuteQuery failed with error #" + sts
End If
Else
   lstrError = "Failed to connect to Essbase error #" + sts
   Err.Raise vbObjectError + 516, "SmartViewVBA::MDX()", _
      "Failed to connect to Essbase error #" + sts
End If
```

10. Click in your **MDX()** procedure; press *F8* to step through the code or *F5* to execute the code.

How it works...

In this recipe, we begin by importing the Smart View module `SmartviewVBA.bas`. This module has many declarations and functions that will be useful for this and other applications. We then add some global constants' variable declarations to make it easier for us to build on this code in the future. Our MDX procedure, starts with the declaration of variables and the checking of provider service connection. The following grid describes each variable:

Variable	Description
vtBoolHideData	A flag used to hide or unhide data in the results
vtBoolDataless	A flag used to retrieve or avoid data in the results
vtBoolNeedStatus	A flag used to retrieve or avoid status info in the results
vtMbrIDType	This variable works with vtAliasTable to specify the use of "alias"
vtAliasTable	The alias table to be used
HypF	A Boolean flag that is used to specify whether we are connected to provider services
lintRow	An integer that increments the row number in the For Next loop
lstrError	A string to keep specific error descriptions for the message box
sts	Holds the status of our HypExecuteQuery query; if successful should be zero
vtQuery	The MDX query
result_Native	The result set of our MDX function and input parameter for GetVBCompatibleMDXStructure
result_VBCompatible	An array returned by the GetVBCompatibleMDXStructure function

The `HypIsConnectedToAPS` function checks if the connection exists. If it does, then it is disconnected and reconnected to make sure that you are using the correct provider server. Then, we connect to Essbase, set our MDX script, and pass the script to the `HypExecuteMDXEx` function. The `HypExecuteMDXEx` function returns a `result_Native` record set that we use as an input to our `GetVBCompatibleMDXStructure`. The `GetVBCompatibleMDXStructure` returns a `result_VBCompatible` record set, which we use to loop through our data and drop results in `Sheet1`.

The results of this part of the code are shown in the following image:

	A
1	100-10
2	100-20
3	100-30
4	200-10
5	200-20
6	200-30
7	200-40
8	300-10
9	300-20
10	300-30
11	400-10
12	400-20
13	400-30
14	100-20
15	200-20
16	300-30

We then used our MDX script to extract the entire record set into `Sheet2` using `HypExecuteQuery`. The results of this function are in the following image:

	A	B
1		Actual
2	Cola	22777
3	Diet Cola	5708
4	Caffeine Free Cola	1983
5	Old Fashioned	7201
6	Diet Root Beer	12025
7	Sasparilla	4636
8	Birch Beer	4092
9	Dark Cream	12195
10	Vanilla Cream	2511
11	Diet Cream	11093
12	Grape	11844
13	Orange	9851
14	Strawberry	-394
15	Diet Cola	5708
16	Diet Root Beer	12025
17	Diet Cream	11093

We used several functions in this recipe that require many parameters. You can review the parameters in more detail by clicking on **Help** in your **Smart View** ribbon.

There's more...

We can also extract data via MDX using Smart View's Execute MDX functionality. This functionality is a manual task and does not require the use of API.

1. Right-click on **Sample | Basic** and in the menu select **Execute MDX**.

2. Type in the following MDX script in the **Execute Free Form MDX Query** menu and click on the **Execute** button. The MDX Query is as follows and should look like the following image:

```
Select {[Actual]} ON COLUMNS, Product.Levels(0).Members ON ROWS
    FROM Sample.Basic
```

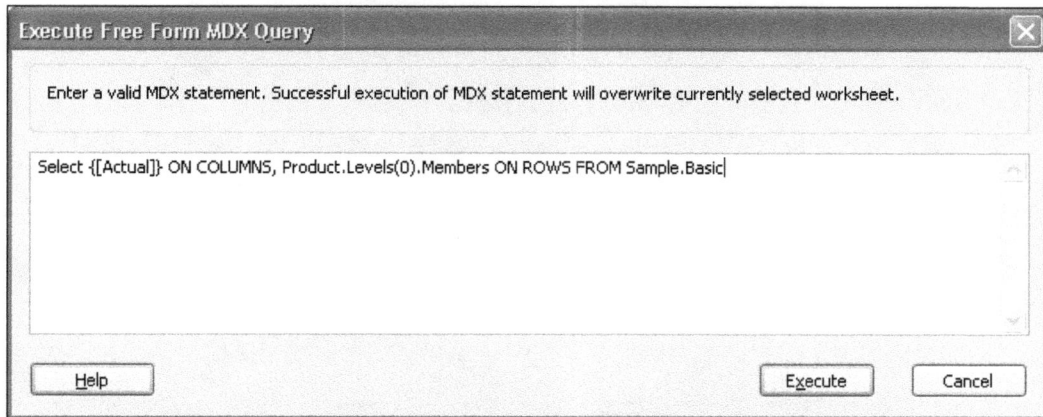

Execute Free Form MDX Query   ☒

Enter a valid MDX statement. Successful execution of MDX statement will overwrite currently selected worksheet.

Select {[Actual]} ON COLUMNS, Product.Levels(0).Members ON ROWS FROM Sample.Basic

| Help | | Execute | Cancel |

9
Provisioning Security Using MaxL Editor or Shared Services

In this chapter, we will cover the following topics:

- ▶ Using MaxL Editor to add and externalize a user
- ▶ Using Shared Services to add and provision a user
- ▶ Using MaxL Editor to set up a filter for MetaRead and Write access
- ▶ Using Shared Services to provision filters to a group
- ▶ Using Shared Services to provision calculation scripts to a group
- ▶ Using MaxL to export security files

Introduction

Security in Essbase is flexible enough to support very complicated applications with complex access requirements and restrictions. This flexibility will help a developer design an outline without having to create a very large distributed model for the same subject area. When we are developing an Essbase database, careful planning and leveraging of your security will prevent enormous amounts of maintenance going forward and keep the user experience as intuitive as possible by hiding the complexities in an Essbase outline. This task is accomplished by implementing effective group, role, and filter-level security. This chapter will not cover the whole of user and role security. For the complete User and Role Security Guide, visit http://docs.oracle.com/cd/E17236_01/epm.1112/hss_admin.pdf.

Using MaxL editor to add and externalize a user

In this recipe, we will look up the user we want to add to make sure the user does not already exist. If the user does not exist, then we will create a native group and add an external user using `Single Sign-On` in the `Shared Service` mode. Maintaining user access this way removes the Essbase Administrator from the business of keeping track of user passwords in the `Native Security` mode. The options for external directories are reviewed in the *How it works* session of this recipe. From the user standpoint, it will be easier as they keep track of one username and password, as opposed to remembering an Essbase username and password and a network username and password.

Getting ready

To get started, click on the **Start** menu and navigate to **Programs | Oracle EPM System | Essbase | Essbase Administration Services | Start Administration Services Console**. In the Log in menu, enter your Administration Server, Username, Password, and click on the **Log in** button.

How to do it...

1. In EAS, click on the **File** menu, expand the **Editors**, and select **MaxL Script Editor**.

2. In the **MaxL Script Editor**, enter **Display user all;** and click on the **Execute Script** button to display a list of your users. This MaxL script will give you a list of user information, as shown in the following screenshot:

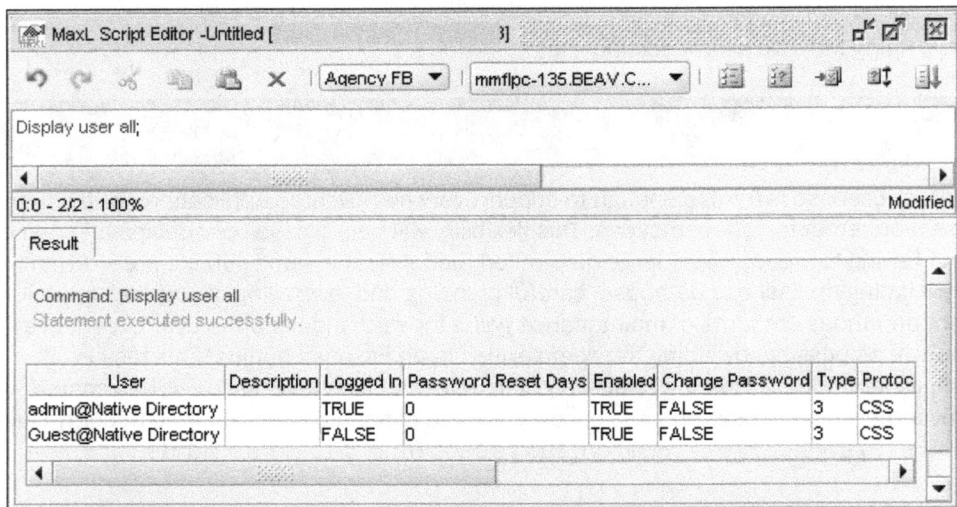

MaxL Script Editor -Untitled [   ]

Agency FB ▼   mmflpc-135.BEAV.C... ▼

Display user all;

0:0 - 2/2 - 100%   Modified

Result

Command: Display user all
Statement executed successfully.

User	Description	Logged In	Password Reset Days	Enabled	Change Password	Type	Protoc
admin@Native Directory		TRUE	0	TRUE	FALSE	3	CSS
Guest@Native Directory		FALSE	0	TRUE	FALSE	3	CSS

3. You could have also entered `display user 'Ruizj1';` and clicked on the **Execute Script** button to check if this user existed before you attempted to add it to your environment.

4. Remove the previously added code from your **MaxL Script Editor** and enter the following code to add a group, grant the group access, add the user, and grant the user access to the group. Change `Ruizj1` to the account that you want to provision.

```
/*Create Sample_Read group*/
create or replace group 'Sample_Read';

/*Assign group Sample_Read read access to the Sample.Basic
  database*/
grant read on database 'Sample'.'Basic' to 'Sample_Read';

/*Add external user Ruizj1*/
create or replace user 'Ruizj1' type external;

/*Add user Ruizj1 to group Sample_Read*/
alter user 'Ruizj1' add to group 'Sample_Read';
```

5. Verify that the external user has read access to `Sample.Basic` by having the user attempt to log in to the system.

How it works

In this recipe, we checked that the user did not have access before attempting to provision. We saw that this task could be accomplished by using either the `display user all` or `display user 'USER-NAME'` command. The `all` parameter returns all the users and the `USER-NAME` will return that user's information. Both of these MaxL scripts will return a list of the user's current settings, as shown as follows, if the user exists.

Column Output	Description
user	A string with the user's name.
description	A string with a description of the user. Optional.
logged in	A Boolean field that returns TRUE if the user has logged in or FALSE if the user has not logged in.
password_reset_days	The number of days before the password expires.
enabled	A Boolean field that returns TRUE if the account is active or FALSE if it is not.
change_password	A Boolean field that returns TRUE if the user needs to reset his/her password on the next login or else it returns FALSE.

Column Output	Description
type	Returns 0 when the user is set up using native Essbase security, 1 if no longer in use, or 3 if the user is using external authentication with Shared Services.
protocol	When using external authentication, it returns CSS, else returns blank.
conn param	This field is normally blank, but when using Native security, it may show the following string: `native://DN=cn=911,ou=People,dc=css,dc=hyperion,dc=com?USER`
application_access_type	Field returns 0 if there is no access, 1 when there is access to Essbase, 2 when there is access to Planning, and 3 when there is access to both Essbase and Planning.

We also set up the group Sample_Read and granted read access to the Sample.Basic database to that group. We could have also granted the group system, application, and database-level access using a variation of the grant commands. The following are some of the other privileges and roles you could have granted as well.

Privilege\Role	Description
create_application	Grants create application access to a user or a group
create_database	Grants create database access to a user or a group
no_access	Revokes any access the user or group has to the system, application, or database
administrator	Grants administrative rights to the system to the user or group
designer	Grants the database designer role to a user or group
read	Grants a user or group read access to a database
write	Grants a user or group write access to a database
filter	Grants a user or group filter-level access to a database
execute	Grants a user or group the ability to execute a calculation on a database

For a list of the Essbase Server or Application roles in Shared Services, review the *Using Shared Services to add and provision a user* section in this chapter. Finally, we created the user Ruizj1 using external authentication and granted that user read access to Sample. Basic by adding that user to the group Sample_Read.

Security can be an ominous time-consuming task if group or role-level security is not used properly. For this reason, we set up a group and assign read access to the `Sample.Basic` group as opposed to granting access directly to the user. Make sure that you discuss with the business what security policy fits their application best. Security will sometimes impact how you design your hierarchies, as there may be parts of your hierarchy that may need to be excluded from users, based on their areas of responsibilities. In the case of very sensitive information, it may impact the number of databases, as the risk of information getting into the wrong hands may be too high for the client.

On a side note, you should make sure that **Single Sign On** (**SSO**) authentication is enabled when you install Essbase in Shared Service mode. The user directories that can be used are **Oracle Internet Directory** (**OID**), **Microsoft Active Directory** (**MSAD**), Sun Java System Directory Server, and an LDAP-based user directory. Enabling Single Sign On authentication ensures that the password security policy used by the network administrator can be used by the Essbase environment, which removes duplication of efforts.

There's more...

In the future, if you want to grant another user the same group or role-level access as `Ruizj1`, a request that may often be asked, you could use the following command:

```
create or replace user 'Smithj1' as 'Ruizj1';
```

This command adds `Smithj1` to the group that we created and grants him the same provisioning as the user `Ruizj1`. Essbase administrators are often asked to give a user the same access as another, as opposed to specifying all the access privileges again. This script will reduce errors and keeps you from having to research another user's access.

Using Shared Services to add and provision a user

In this recipe, we will add a group, provision that group, and add a user to that group using Oracle Shared Services. We will also grant the group Server Access role, read access to `Sample.Basic`, and discuss some of the other roles that you can assign.

Getting ready

To get started, click on the **Start** menu and navigate to **Programs | Oracle EPM System | Foundation Services**, select the **Shared Services URL**, enter your username and password, and click on the **Log in** button.

How to do it...

1. On the left-hand side, under **Provisioning**, expand **User Directory | Native Directory**, right-click on **Groups**, and click on **New**.

2. Enter **Sample_Write** in the **Name** textbox, click on **Save**, and at the **Group Sample_Write created** prompt, click on **OK**.

3. Right-click on the **Users** under **Native Directory** and click on **New**. If you are using an external directory, then you could have simply added the user to your group using the **Create Group** menu in step 2. We need to set up a native user to complete this recipe.

4. In the **General** step, enter **Ruizj1** for the **User Name**, enter **password** for the **Password**, and enter **password** in the **Confirmed Password** textbox. The **First Name**, **Last Name**, **Description**, and **Email Address** are optional. Click on the **Next** button.

5. In the **Member Of** tab, select the **Group Name** textbox on the left-hand side, enter **Sample_Write**, click on **Go**, click on the checkbox next to **Sample_Write** in the checkbox list box, and click on the right arrow button.

6. Click on **Save** and click on **OK** at the prompt. Your screen should now look like the following screenshot:

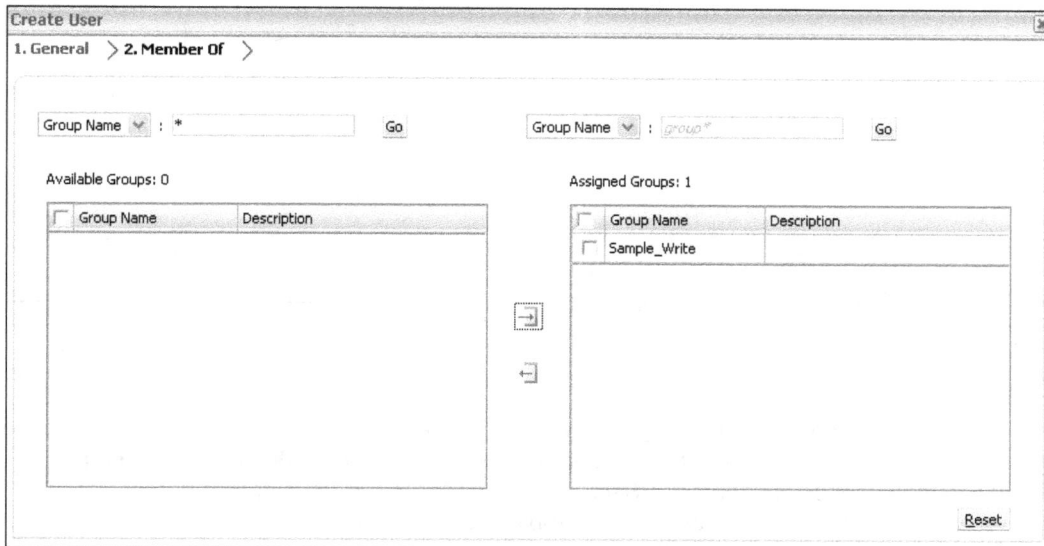

7. Double-click on **Groups**, enter **Sample_Write** under **Group Filter**, and click on **Search**.

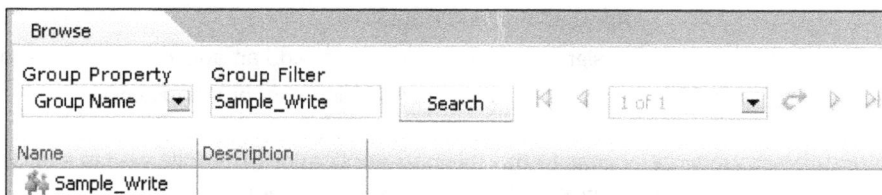

8. Right-click on **Sample_Write**, click on **Provision**, expand **EssbaseCluster-1**, drill down on **EssbaseCluster-1**, click on **Server Access**, and click on the right arrow to add to the **Selected Roles** list.

9. Drill down on the **Sample** application, left-click on **Write**, click on the right arrow to add to the **Selected Roles** list, click on **Save**, and then click on **OK**. Your screen should now look like the following screenshot:

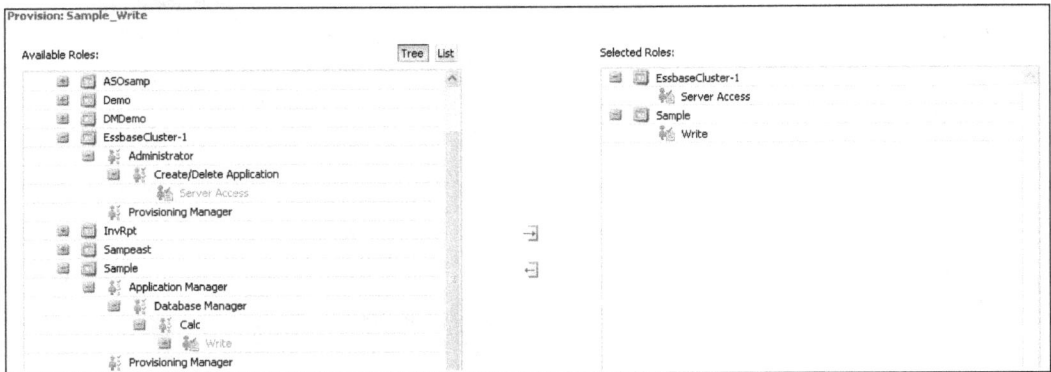

How it works...

In this recipe, we created the native group **Sample_Write**, added a native user for the purpose of the recipe, assigned the user to the group, and gave the **Sample_Write** group **Server Access** to the Essbase environment. Server Access is the minimum Essbase Server role that allows a user to have the ability to see applications and the database in Essbase. The following is a list of other Essbase Server Roles:

Server Role	Description
Administrator	Assigns full administrative rights to Essbase Server, Applications, and Database
Create/Delete Application	Assigns the ability to delete or add an application or database
Provisioning Manager	Assigns the ability to provision user or group access

We also grant the group write access to the Sample application. The following is a list of application role types that you can use for Essbase users or groups:

Application Role	Description
Application Manager	Assigns the ability to delete, create, or modify a database or application settings
Database Manager	Assigns the management of locks, sessions, database artifacts, and the database for an application
Calc	Assigns the ability to run calculations, read data values, and write to the database within a specified scope
Write	Assigns the ability to update and read data for a specific scope

Application Role	Description
Read	Assigns the ability to see the data
Filter	Assigns the ability to read the data and metadata as filtered
Start/Stop Application	Assigns the ability to Start or Stop an application
Provisioning Manager	Assigns the responsibility of provisioning users and groups

Using MaxL Editor to set up a filter for MetaRead and Write access

In this recipe, we will use a substitution variable in a security filter. This filter will be set up to use **MetaRead** and **Write** access to the Sample.Basic database. A filter is a security object that will allow users read or write access based on the specified scope. Filters can be used to revoke or allow access to hierarchies or members in your dimension. This is a powerful tool for a developer, as it makes it possible to build one outline and customize what the users can see, based on their security.

Getting ready

To get started, click on the **Start** menu and navigate to **Programs | Oracle EPM System | Essbase | Essbase Administration Services | Start Administration Services Console**. In the Log in menu, enter your Administration Server, Username, Password, and click on the **Log in** button.

How to do it...

1. Right-click on your Essbase Server in EAS, select **Create**, and click on **Variables....**
2. In the **New Variables** menu, click on the cell under **Application**, select **(all apps)**, click on the cell under the **Database** column, and select **(all dbs)**.
3. Click on the cell under **Name**, type **CurMth**, select the cell under **Value**, type in **Apr**, and click on the **OK** button.
4. In the **File** menu, expand the **Editors** and select **MaxL Script Editor**.
5. In **MaxL Script Editor**, enter the following script to add a group **Sample_Metadata**, add the user **testuser**, and assign **testuser** to the group **Sample_Metadata**.

```
create or replace group 'Sample_MetaRead';
create or replace user 'testuser' identified by 'password1'
member of group 'Sample_MetaRead';
```

6. Press *Enter* and type **create or replace filter 'Sample.Basic'**, and you will get a filter name textbox; enter **Sample_MetaRead** and press *Enter*. The following **Filter Editor** will pop up on the screen:

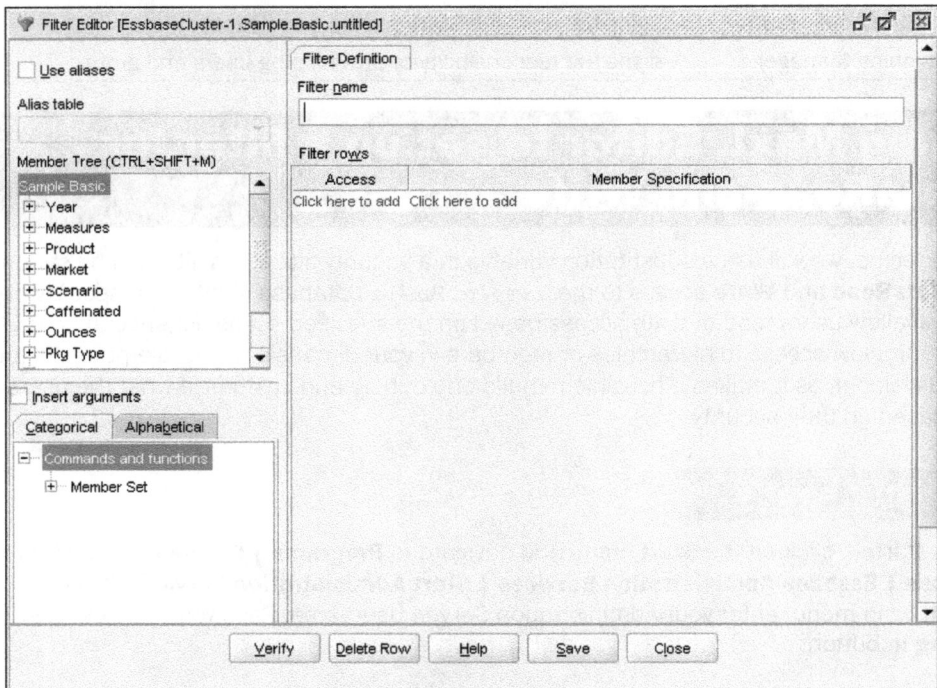

7. Click on the cell with the **Click here to add** text under the **Access** column, select **None**, click under **Member Specification**, and type **Jan:&CurMth**. This task will remove any access before you assign filter access.

8. Click on the cell with the **Click here to add** text under the **Access** column, select **MetaRead**, click under **Member Specification**, select from **@MEMBER()** the **Member Set**, drill down under the **Categorical** tab, click between the open brackets, drill down on **Scenario**, right-click on the **Budget** dimension, and click on **insert member name**.

9. Enter a comma behind @MEMBER("Budget"), select from @IDESCENDANTS() the member set, drill down under the **Categorical** tab, click in-between the open brackets, drill down on the **Market** dimension, right-click on **East**, and click on **insert member name**. This task will allow the group to view the **Budget** scenario and the **East** members of the **Market** dimension.

10. Enter a comma behind the @IDESCENDANTS("East") member set and type Jan:&CurMth.

11. Click on the cell with the **Click here to add** text under the **Access** column, select **None**, click under **Member Specification**, and type @MEMBER ("Budget"), @IDESCENDANTS("East"). This task will grant access to write to the scenario Budget and all levels of the Market dimension.

12. Enter a comma behind the @IDESCENDANTS("East") member set and type Jan:&CurMth.

13. Click on the **Verify** button. You should see **Succeeded Verify Filter** in the **Message** window below. Click on the **OK** button. Your screen should look like the following screenshot:

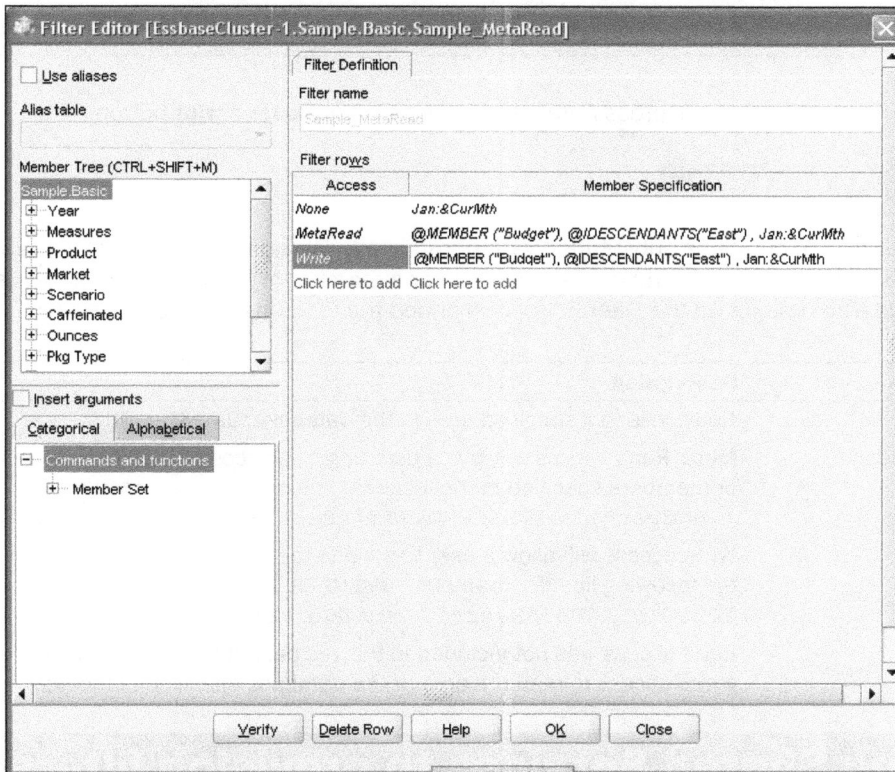

14. You should see the code in blue with white lettering. Double-click on the blue session. The entire script should show as follows:

15. Enter a semi-colon, press *Enter*, and click on the **Execute script** button.

How it works...

In this recipe, we created a substitution variable, CurMth. We added a group called Sample_MetaRead, created a user, and made the new user a member of Sample_MetaRead using MaxL. We also brought up the Filter Editor and added the following types of access:

Access	Description
none	No access to a specified area in the database. 'Jan:&CurMth'.
meta_read	Meta_Read access will give a user or group access to see the hierarchies or members specified in the following line, for example, '@MEMBER ("Budget"), @IDESCENDANTS("East"), Jan:&CurMth'.
write	Write access will allow a user to write to the area specified in the following line, for example, '@MEMBER ("Budget"), @IDESCENDANTS("East"), Jan:&CurMth'.
read	Read access was not included in this recipe, but it will give a user or a group access to read the area of the database specified in the filter.

Using Shared Services to provision filters to a group

In this recipe, we will set up a filter using MaxL and provision the filter to a group using Shared Services. Filters allow us to provision security to an Essbase database in the most granular manner possible. Using filters, you should be able to revoke access, assign read or write access, or allow metadata read access to components of the hierarchies.

Getting ready

To get started, click on the **Start** menu and navigate to **Programs | Oracle EPM System | Essbase | Essbase Administration Services | Start Administration Services Console**. In the Log in menu, enter your Administration Server, Username, Password, and click on the **Log in** button.

How to do it...

1. In EAS, click on the **File** menu, click on **Editors**, click on **MaxL Script Editors**, enter the following code, and click on **Execute script** to create a filter.

```
/*Create substitution variable*/
alter database 'Sample'.'Basic' add variable 'CurMth' 'Dec';
/*Create filter*/
    create filter 'Sample'.'Basic'.'Sample_MetaRead'
no_access on 'Jan:&CurMth',
meta_read on
'@MEMBER ("Budget"), @IDESCENDANTS("East"), Jan:&CurMth',
write on
'@MEMBER ("Budget"), @IDESCENDANTS("East") , Jan:&CurMth';
```

2. Click on the **Start** menu, expand **Programs | Oracle EPM System | Foundation Services**, and select **Shared Services URL**.

3. Under the **Application Manager** menu on the left-hand side, expand **User Directory | Native Directory**, right-click on **Groups**, and click on **New**.

4. Enter **Sample_MetaRead** in the **Name** textbox, click on **Save**, and at the **Group Sample_MetaRead created** prompt, click on **OK**.

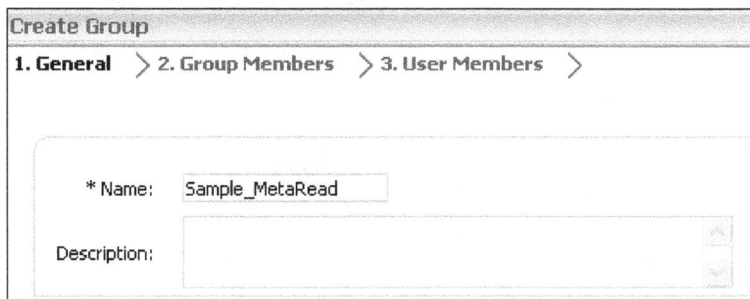

5. Double-click on **Groups**, enter **Sample_MetaRead** in the **Group Filter** textbox, and click on **Search**.

6. Right-click on **Sample_MetaRead**, click on **Provision**, expand **EssbaseCluster-1**, drill down on **EssbaseCluster-1**, click on **Server Access**, and click on the right arrow to add to the **Selected Roles** list. You could have also set up another group with **Server Access** and assigned **Sample_MetaRead** to that group. Nested groups in Shared Services will reduce the steps required.

7. Drill down on the **Sample** application, click on **Filter**, click on the right arrow to add to the **Selected Roles** list, click on **Save**, and click on **OK**. Your screen should look like the following menu:

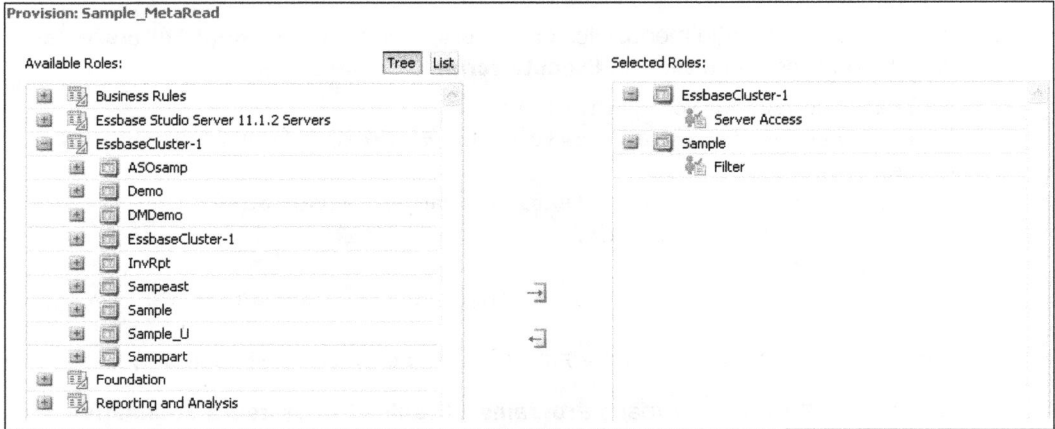

Provision: Sample_MetaRead

Available Roles: Tree List

- Business Rules
- Essbase Studio Server 11.1.2 Servers
- EssbaseCluster-1
  - ASOsamp
  - Demo
  - DMDemo
  - EssbaseCluster-1
  - InvRpt
  - Sampeast
  - Sample
  - Sample_U
  - Samppart
- Foundation
- Reporting and Analysis

Selected Roles:

- EssbaseCluster-1
  - Server Access
- Sample
  - Filter

8. Right-click on **Users** and click on **New**.

9. In the **General** step, enter **TestUser2** in the **User Name** textbox, enter **password** in the **Password** textbox, enter **password** again in the **Confirm Password** textbox, and click on the **Save** button. The **First Name**, **Last Name**, **Description**, and **Email Address** field are optional. Click on the **Next** button.

Create User

1. General > 2. Member Of >

- * User Name: TestUser2
- * Password: ••••••
- * Confirm Password: ••••••
- First Name:
- Last Name:
- Description:
- Email Address:

10. In the **Member Of** tab, select the **Group Name** textbox on the left-hand side, enter **Sample_MetaRead**, click on **Go**, click on the checkbox next to **Sample_MetaRead** in the checkbox list box, and click on the right arrow button. Your screen should look like the following image:

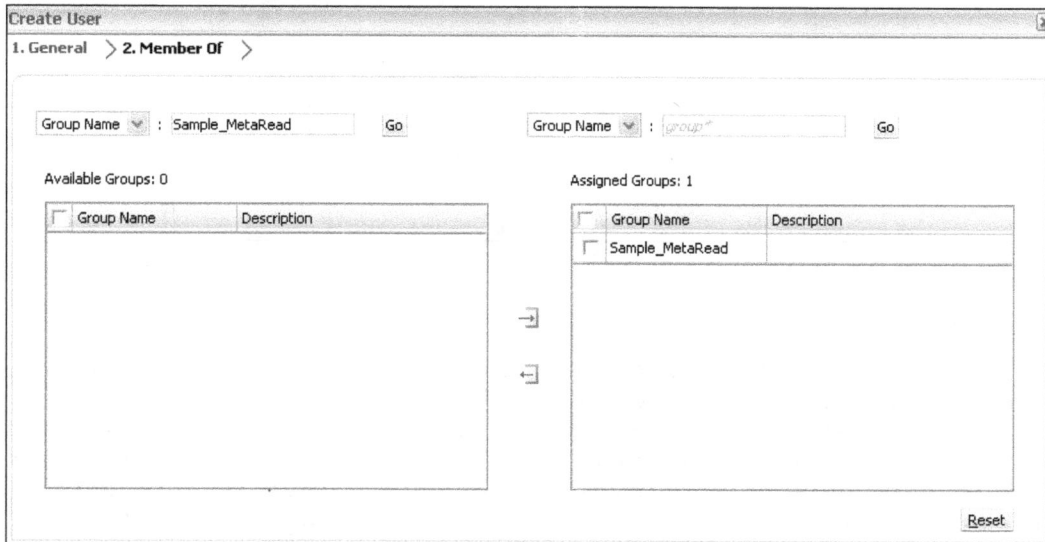

11. Click on **Save** and click on **OK** at the prompt.

12. Expand the **Application Group** node, drill down on your Essbase instance **EssbaseCluster-1**, right-click on the **Sample** application, and select **Assign Access Control** from the menu.

13. Select **Group Name** from the drop-down list on the left-hand side, enter **Sample_MetaRead** in the textbox to return the group we created or the wildcard character ***** (Asterisk) to return all groups, and click on the **Search** button.

14. Select **Sample_MetaRead** from the left **Available** list, click on the right arrow to add to the right **Selected** list, click on the **Next** button, select **Sample_MetaRead** from the filter drop-down list, and click on the check mark button ☑ next to the `Calc` list.

15. Make sure **Basic** is selected in the database drop-down list, select **Sample_ MetaRead@Native Directory**, and click on the **Save** button. Your screen should look like the following image. You will see a **Filter and calculation access has been changed successfully** dialog box.

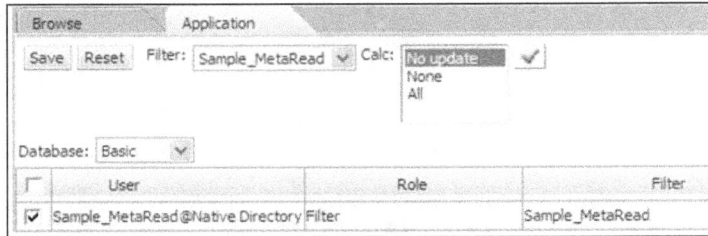

Browse	Application					
Save	Reset	Filter:	Sample_MetaRead ▾	Calc:	No update / None / All	✓

Database: Basic ▾

	User	Role	Filter
☐			
☑	Sample_MetaRead @Native Directory	Filter	Sample_MetaRead

How it works...

In this recipe, we created a substitution variable and a filter with MetaRead and Write access in our MaxL Script Editor. Our `Sample_MetaRead` filter will give the user or group that it is assigned to Write and MetaRead access to the `East` market, the range `Jan:Dec` in the `Year` dimension, and the `Budget` member in our `Scenario` dimension. We also created the `Sample_MetaRead` group and provisioned `Server Access` and `Filter` using Shared Services. Moreover, we created a user named `TestUser2` and assigned the user to the group. Finally, we assigned our group, `Sample_MetaRead`, access to the `Sample Basic` database via our `Filter`. Testing your filter access to `Sample Basic` can be done in Smart View using the `TestUser2` user created in this recipe. Your spreadsheet should look something like the following image, once you begin to navigate. Notice the `#NoAccess` label in the `Year` dimension for levels that are not part of the `Jan:Dec` range. This is data you do not have access to. Furthermore, note the fact that you cannot see any other `Market` except for `East` and any other `Scenario` except for `Budget`.

	A	B
1		Budget
2		Product
3		Sales
4		East
5	Jan	6180
6	Feb	6350
7	Mar	6360
8	Qtr1	#NoAccess
9	Apr	6610
10	May	6730
11	Jun	7250
12	Qtr2	#NoAccess
13	Jul	7360
14	Aug	7190
15	Sep	6550
16	Qtr3	#NoAccess
17	Oct	5840
18	Nov	6160
19	Dec	6370
20	Qtr4	#NoAccess
21	Year	#NoAccess

Using Shared Services to provision calculation scripts to a group

In this recipe, we will create a calculation, create a group, create a native user, assign a user to the group, and then provision the filter to the group.

Getting ready

To get started, click on the **Start** menu and navigate to **Programs | Oracle EPM System | Essbase | Essbase Administration Services | Start Administration Services Console**. In the Log in menu, enter your Administration Server, Username, Password, and click on the **Log in** button.

How to do it...

1. Drill down on the Essbase Server in EAS, expand the **Applications** node, drill down on the **Sample** application, and right-click on the **Basic** database. In the drop-down menu, click on **Create** and select **Calculation Scripts**.

2. In the **Calculation Script Editor**, enter the following script and click on the **Check syntax** button to verify that the syntax is correct; a prompt should pop up with the text **Syntax check was successful**. Click on **OK**.

```
SET UPDATECALC OFF;
SET CLEARUPDATESTATUS AFTER;
SET AGGMISSG ON;
SET LOCKBLOCK HIGH;
SET CACHE ALL;
SET CACHE HIGH;
SET CALCPARALLEL 3;
SET CALCTASKDIMS 2;

Calc All;
```

3. Click on the **File** menu, click on **Save**, enter **CalcDB** in the **File name** textbox, and click on **OK**.

4. Click on the **Start** menu, expand **Programs | Oracle EPM System | Foundation Services**, and select **Shared Services URL**.

5. Under the **Application Manager** menu on the left-hand side, expand **User Directory | Native Directory**, right-click on **Groups**, and click on **New**.

6. Enter **Sample_CalcDB** in the **Name** textbox, click on **Save**, and at the **Group Sample_ CalcDB created** prompt, click on **OK**.

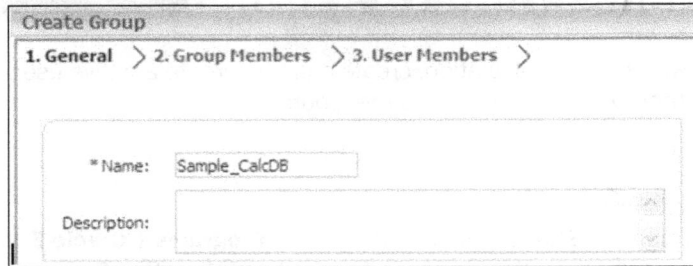

7. Double-click on **Groups**, enter **Sample_CalcDB** in the **Group Filter** textbox, and click on **Search**.

8. Right-click on **Sample_CalcDB**, click on **Provision**, expand **EssbaseCluster-1**, drill down on **EssbaseCluster-1**, click on **Server Access**, and click on the right arrow to add to the **Selected Roles** list. You could have also set up another group with **Server Access** and assigned **Sample_CalcDB** to that group. Nested groups in Shared Services will reduce the steps required to provision users and groups.

9. Drill down on the **Sample** application, click on **Filter**, click on the right arrow to add to the **Selected Roles** list, click on **Save**, and click on **OK**. Your screen should look like the following screenshot:

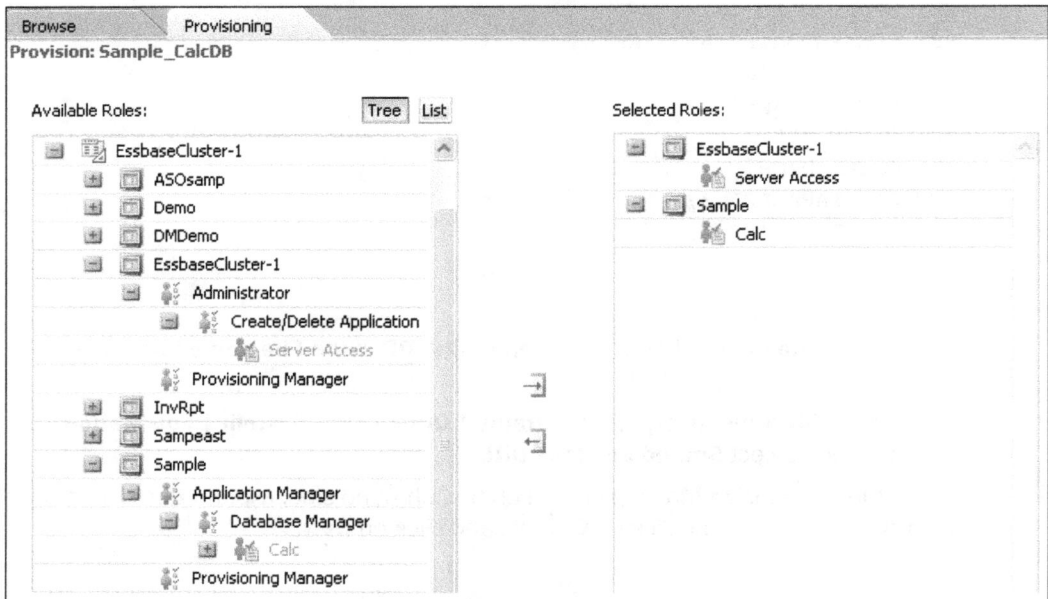

10. Right-click on **Users** and click on **New**.

11. In the **General** tab, enter **TestUser3** in the **User Name** textbox, enter **password** in the **Password** textbox, enter **password** again in the **Confirm Password** textbox, and click on the **Save** button. The **First Name**, **Last Name**, **Description**, and **Email Address** fields are optional. Click on the **Next** button.

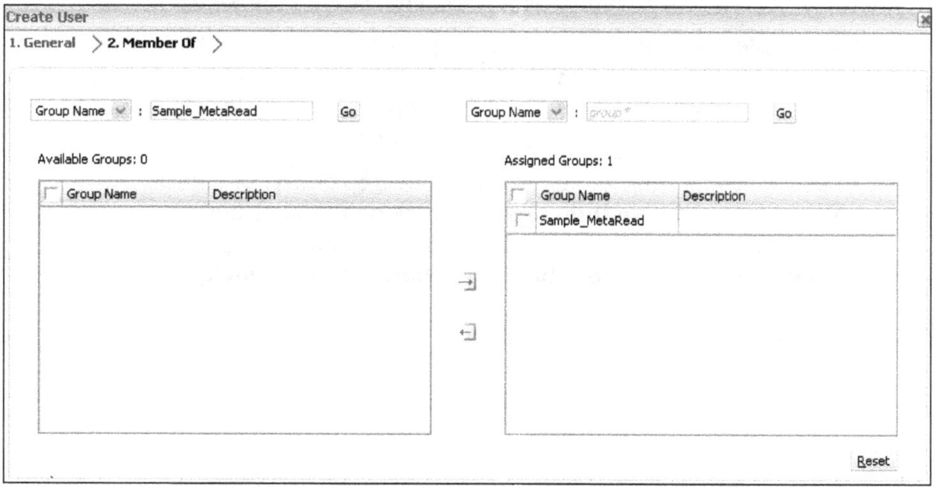

12. In the **Member Of** tab, select the **Group Name** textbox on the left-hand side, enter **Sample_CalcDB**, click on **Go**, click on the checkbox next to **Sample_CalcDB** in the checkbox list box, and click on the right arrow button. Your screen should look like the following image:

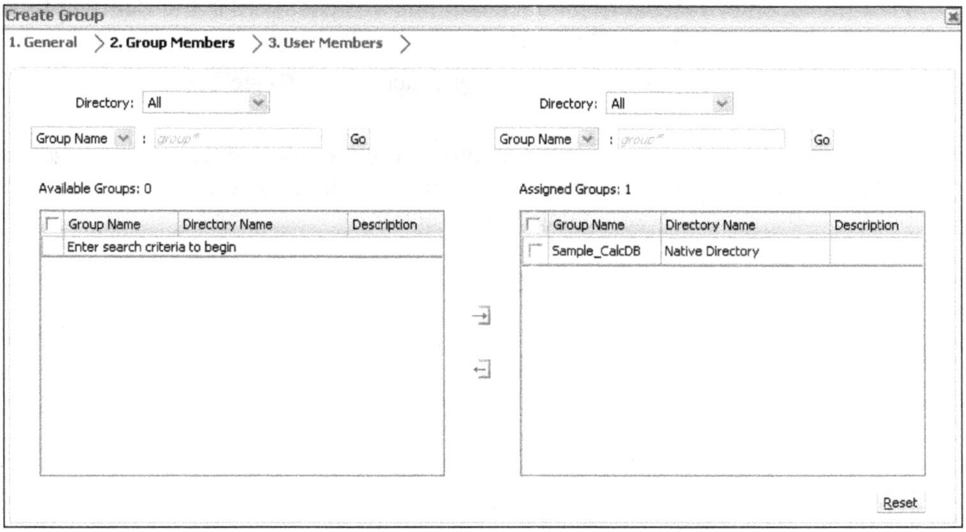

13. Click on **Save** and click on **OK** at the prompt.

14. Expand the **Application Group** node, drill down on your Essbase instance **EssbaseCluster-1**, right-click on the **Sample** application, and select **Assign Access Control** from the menu.

15. Select **Group Name** from the drop-down list on the left-hand side, enter the wildcard character * (Asterisk) to return all groups, and click on the **Search** button.

16. Select **Sample_CalcDB@Native Directory** from the left **Available** list, click on the right arrow to add to the right **Selected** list, click on the **Next** button, select **None** in the **Filter** drop-down list, and in the **Calc** drop-down list, select **CalcDB** and click on the check mark button ☑ next to the Calc drop-down list.

17. Make sure **Basic** is selected in the database drop-down list, select **Sample_CalcDB@Native Directory**, and click on the **Save** button.
    Your screen should look like the following image. You will see a **Filter and calculation access has been changed successfully** dialog box.

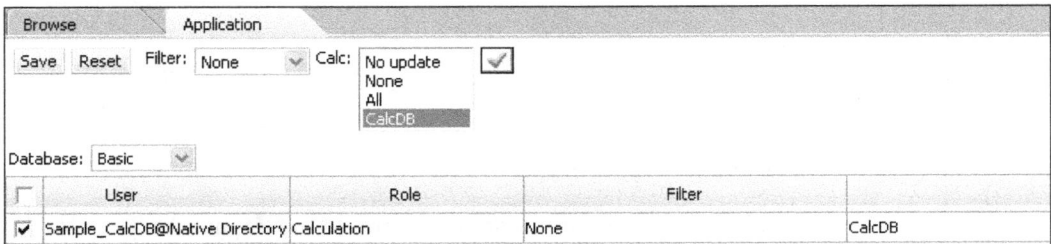

Browse	Application			
Save Reset Filter: None ▾ Calc: No update ☑ None All CalcDB				
Database: Basic ▾				
☐ User		Role	Filter	
☑ Sample_CalcDB@Native Directory	Calculation		None	CalcDB

18. Open an **Excel** session, open a connection to your in **Smart View** by pressing the **Open** button in the **Smart View** ribbon, select **Private Connections** in your **Smart View** panel, enter **TestUser3** for the username and password in the **Connect to Data Source** menu, and click on **Connect**.

19. Drill down on the **Sample** application; right-click on the **Basic** database and **Ad hoc analysis**.

20. In your Essbase ribbon, click on **Calculate**. In the **Calculation Script** menu, select **CalcDB** under **Calculation Script** and **Basic** under **Cube**, and click on the **Launch** button. You should only see **CalcDB** as an option.

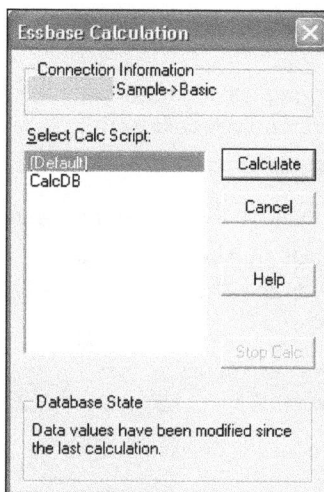

How it works...

In this recipe, we created a calculation script using EAS. We also created the Sample_ CalcDB group and provisioned Server Access and Calc access using Shared Services. Moreover, we created a user named TestUser3 and assigned the user to the group. Finally, we assigned our group Sample_CalcDB access to execute CalcDB on the sample database.

Using MaxL to export security file

In this recipe, we will execute a MaxL script to export the content of the security file to a text file. This functionality is useful when you want to see all the application, database, and server-level access for your Essbase Server in a text format. This security information may, at some point, be asked of an Essbase Administrator, in order to make sure that sensitive data is secured. Developers can use this functionality to review application, database, and filter access and compare against user requirements.

Getting ready

To get started, click on the **Start** menu and navigate to **Programs | Oracle EPM System | Essbase | Essbase Administration Services | Start Administration Services Console**. In the Log in menu, enter your Administration Server, Username, Password, and click on the **Log in** button.

How to do it...

1. In EAS, click on the **File** menu, click on **Editors**, click on **MaxL Script Editors**, enter the following code, and click on **Execute script** to create a filter.

```
Export security_file to data_file 'C:\security_file.txt';
```

2. Click on the **Start** menu, click on **Run**, enter **notepad**, and press *Enter*.

3. Click on the **File** menu, click on **Open...**, browse to C:\security_filter.txt, click on the file, and click on the **Open** button. The file should look like the following image:

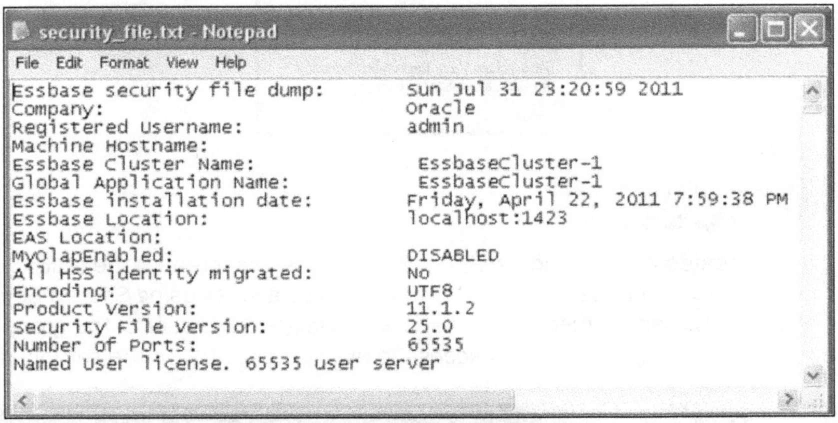

```
security_file.txt - Notepad

File  Edit  Format  View  Help

Essbase security file dump:      Sun Jul 31 23:20:59 2011
Company:                         Oracle
Registered Username:             admin
Machine Hostname:
Essbase Cluster Name:            EssbaseCluster-1
Global Application Name:         EssbaseCluster-1
Essbase installation date:       Friday, April 22, 2011 7:59:38 PM
Essbase Location:                localhost:1423
EAS Location:
MyOlapEnabled:                   DISABLED
All HSS identity migrated:       No
Encoding:                        UTF8
Product Version:                 11.1.2
Security File Version:           25.0
Number of Ports:                 65535
Named User license. 65535 user server
```

How it works...

In this recipe, we ran a following MaxL script to write the security file to a text file in the C drive. We were able to view the following content in the security file:

- ▶ Users and groups
- ▶ Applications
- ▶ Databases
- ▶ Filters
- ▶ Locked objects
- ▶ Substitution variables

10
Developing Dynamic Reports

In this chapter, we will cover the following topics:

- ► Creating a connection and using substitution variables in financial reports
- ► Using column templates and formatting reports
- ► Retrieving data using UDAs and attributes
- ► Retrieving data using children and descendant members set functions
- ► Using user prompts and the POV to select members
- ► Using conditional formatting and suppression in financial reports
- ► Adding related content to financial reports
- ► Creating a web analysis report

Introduction

This chapter will focus on the dynamic functions and aspects of the Essbase reporting tools. As with security, the value that a developer provides is a good plan to leverage the tools function with the goal of conducting flexible and sustainable reports. Sometime this means having to modify your Essbase outline to accommodate reporting needs. Reports that are designed well should not have to be touched every month. In addition, there may come a time when leveraging this functionality is the only way to continue to provide for the business needs without frequent disruptions or a perpetual heavy load of maintenance. This chapter will not cover all the functions available in both web analysis and financial reports as there are too many to discuss in full here. For more web analysis functionality you should visit `http://docs.oracle.com/cd/E17236_01/epm.1112/wa_user.pdf`. For more financial reports functionality you should visit `http://docs.oracle.com/cd/E17236_01/epm.1112/fr_user.pdf`.

Creating a connection and using substitution variables in financial reports

In this recipe, we will create three substitution variables, create a database connection to the sample basic database, and use our substitution variables in our report. Using substitution variables will allow us to change a report or set of reports quickly without having to manually modify multiple reports when we need to change default member selections. In addition, substitution variables can be easily automated, which allows us to schedule these changes.

Getting ready

To get started, click on the **Start** menu and navigate to **Programs | Oracle EPM System | Essbase | Essbase Administration Services | Start Administration Services Console**. In the Log in menu, enter your Administration Server, Username, Password, and click on the **Log in** button.

How to do it...

1. Right-click on your Essbase Server in EAS, select **Create**, and click on **Variables...**.

2. In the **New Variable** menu, click on the **Application** combobox, select **Sample**, click down on the **Database** combobox, and select **Basic**.

3. Enter **NextMth** in the **Name** textbox, in the **Value** textbox enter **Mar**, and click on **OK**.

4. Repeat steps 1 through 3 for the variables, as shown in the following table:

Application	Database	Variable	Value
Sample	Basic	PrevMth	Jan
Sample	Basic	CurMth	Feb
Sample	Basic	CurQtr	Qtr1

5. Click on the **Start** menu, select **Oracle | Financial Studio Report | Financial Studio Report**, enter your **User ID**, enter your **password**, modify the **Server URL**, and click on **OK**. Your **Server URL** should be `http://EssbaseServer:Port` if you are not using SSL.

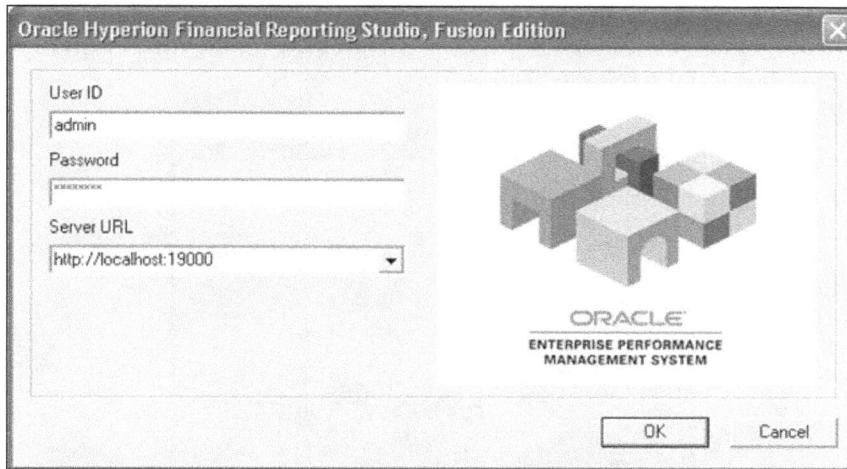

6. Click on the **Repository** menu [icon], expand the **Users** folder, right-click on **{Profiles}**, click on **New Folder**, and type **TestUser**.

7. Double-click on the **TestUser** folder, click on the **File** menu, select **New**, and click on **Report**.

8. Select the **Grid** menu [icon], click, and drag your mouse on the report designer area below to draw the grid. The **Select a Database Connection** menu will pop up requesting your connection information.

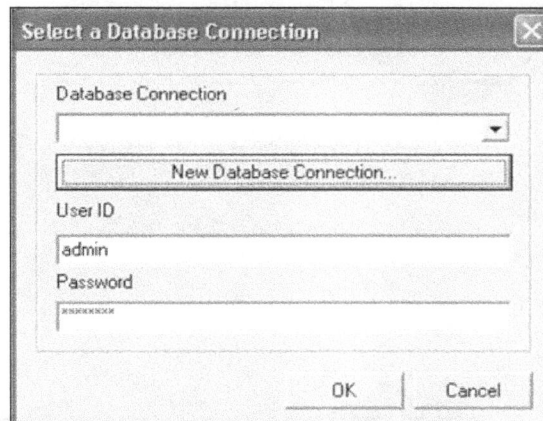

9. Click on the **New Database Connection** button to open the **Database Connection Properties** menu. Enter **Sample** for **Database Connection Name**. Make sure that the **Essbase Server**, **User ID**, and **Password** are correct.

10. Click on the button next to the **Application** textbox and select **Sample Basic** from the **Select Application\Database** menu. Your **Database Connection Properties** menu should look like the following image:

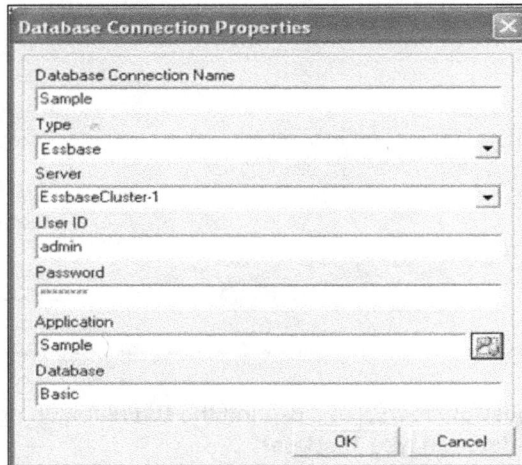

11. In the **Dimension Layout menu**, click and drag the **Measures** dimension from the **Point of View** to the **Rows**.

12. Click on the **Year** dimension and drag it to **Columns** from **Point of View**. Click on **OK**.

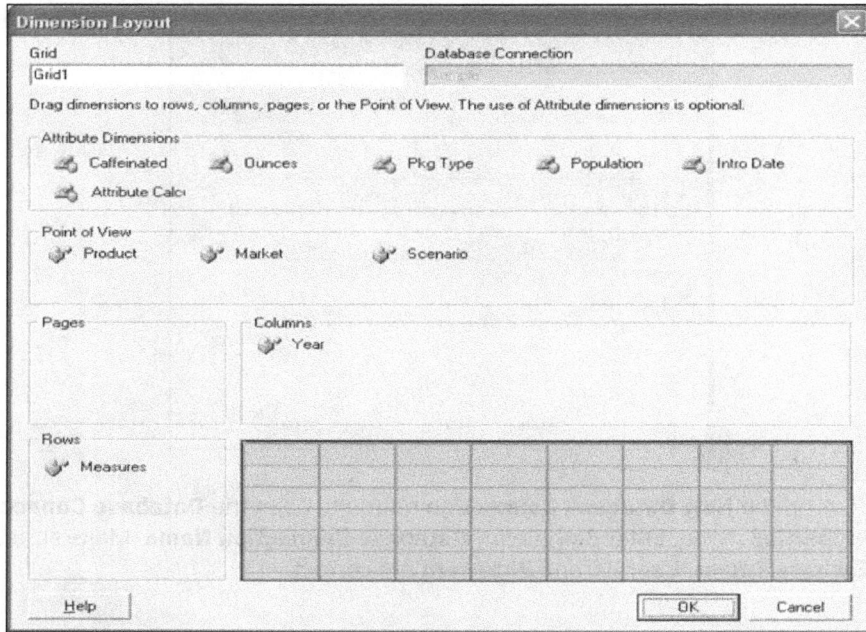

13. Double-click on the **Year** dimension under **Column A** to display the **Select Member** menu, drill down on **Substitution Variable** in the **Members** tab, press *Shift* and select the entire set of substitution variables, and click on the **Add** button to select all the variables.

14. Click on the **Year** member in the **Selected** listbox and click on the **Remove** button to unselect the member.

15. Select **PrevMth** and use the arrow buttons above the **Selected** listbox to bring the substitution variable to the top of the list. Repeat the steps for the rest of the variables so that they look like the following screenshot, and click on **OK**:

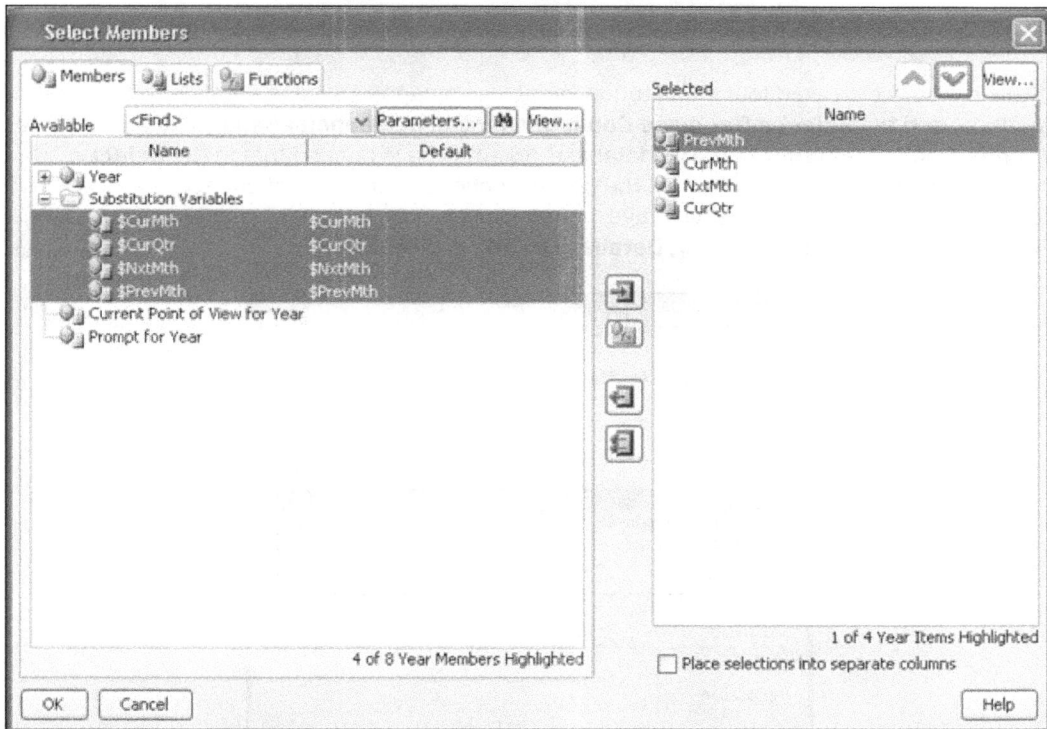

16. Double-click on the **Measures** dimension, drill down on **Measures** in the **Select Member** menu, press *Shift* and select the **Profit** and **Inventory** parent members, and click the **Add** button to select the members.

17. Click the **Measures** member in the **Selected** drop-down list, click on the **Remove** button to unselect the member, and click on **OK**.

18. Click the **Print Preview** button 🖳 to view your report. Click on **Close**, select the **Save** menu, browse to the **TestUser** folder, and **Save as** SampleSV. Your simple report should look like the following image. Notice that the substitution variable's values show as columns:

	Jan	Feb	Mar	Qtr1
Profit	8,024	8,346	8,333	24,703
Inventory	117,405	116,434	115,558	117,405

How it works...

In this recipe, we created four substitution variables using the Essbase Administrative Service. We then used the **Select a Database Connection** menu in **Financial Report Studio** to create a connection to the Sample Basic database. You may have noticed that in the **Select a Database Connection** menu we had the option of choosing the type of connection we wanted. As you can see from the following image, in financial reports you can connected to **Essbase**, **Financial Management**, **Planning Details**, **SAPBW**, and **MSOLAP**:

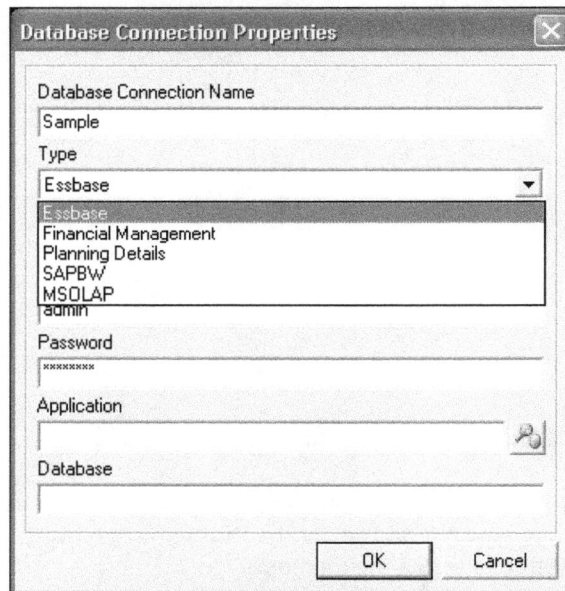

We also were immediately able to set up the layout of our report by dragging and dropping dimensions from the Point of View to the Rows and Columns using the **Dimension Layout** menu. Moreover, we selected the substitution variables we created in steps 1 through 3 as columns and also selected two parent members from the `Measures` dimension for the rows of our report. Finally, we used the **Print Preview** button to view our simple report. We can see from this recipe how simple it is to set up financial reports to dynamically pull default members using substitution variables.

See also

Review the recipe *Adding an Application and Database on an Essbase server* in *Chapter 5, Using EAS for Development*, to understand how to create the sample basic database. Review the recipe *Creating substitution variables* in *Chapter 5* to see what other options are available with substitution variables. The *Using the column templates and formatting reports* recipe in this chapter will show you how to apply formatting to the report.

Using the column templates and formatting reports

In this recipe, we will create a column template with formatting. We will save the column template, create a second report, and add our column template to this report to illustrate how you can use this functionality to reuse sections of reports with similar columns, rows, or both.

Getting ready

Click on the **Start** menu, select **Oracle | Financial Studio Report | Financial Studio Report**, enter your **User ID**, enter your **password**, modify the **Server URL**, and click on **OK**. Your **Server URL** should be `http://EssbaseServer:Port` if you are not using SSL. The default port number is 19000.

How to do it...

1. Click on the **Repository** menu , expand the **Users** folder, right-click on **{Profiles}**, click on **New Folder**, and type **TestUser**.

2. Double-click on the **TestUser** folder, click on the **File** menu, select **New**, and click on **Report**.

3. Select the **Grid** menu ▦, click, and drag your mouse on the report designer area below to draw the grid. The **Select a Database Connection** menu will pop up asking your connection information. Select the **Sample** application from the **Database Connection** combobox, make sure the **User ID** and **Password** are populated, and click on **OK**. If you do not have the database connection **Sample**, then review recipe *Creating a connection and using Substitution Variables in Financial Reports* in this chapter.

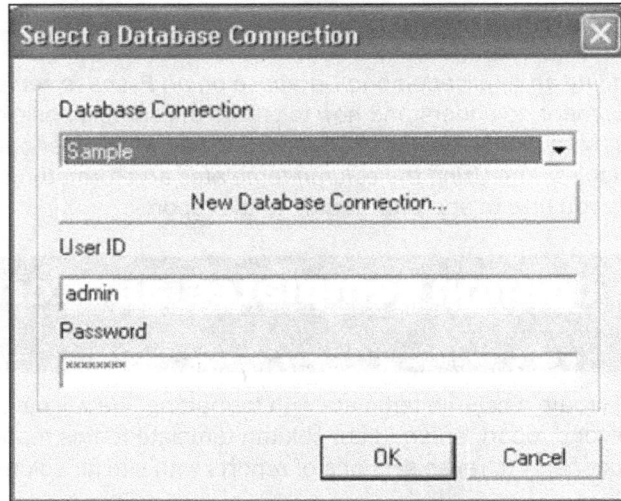

4. In the **Dimension Layout** menu, click and drag the **Measures** dimension from the **Point of View** to the **Rows**.

5. Click on the **Scenario** dimension and drag it to the **Columns** from the **Point of View**. Repeat the same step for the **Year** dimension and click on **OK**.

6. Double-click on the **Year** dimension in **Column A**. In the **Select Member** menu click on the **Lists** tab, select **Quarter** from the **Available** listbox, click on the **Add** button to add the member to the **Selected** listbox, select **Quarter**, click on the up arrow to move **Quarter** above **Year**, and select the **Place selections into separate columns** checkbox. Click on **OK**.

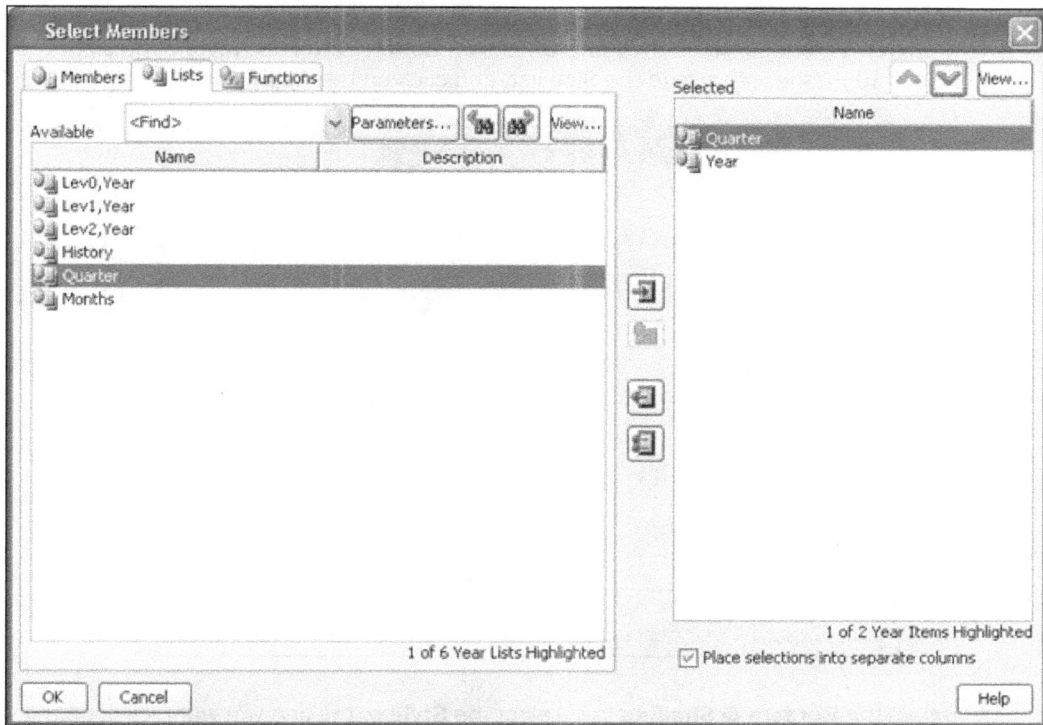

7. Select the **Scenario** cell in **Column A**. In the status bar, remove **Scenario**, type **Actual**, click on the verify checkbox ☑, and click on the report to select. Repeat the same step for the **Scenario** dimension in **Column B**.

8. Press *Shift* and select the **Scenario** cells in **Column A** and **Column B**. Right-click on the **Scenario** cells, and select **Merge**.

9. Right-click on the **Scenario** cell, click on **Format**, and in the **Format Cell** menu, select the **Alignment** tab. In the **Horizontal** combobox select **Center**, click on the **Apply** button, and click on **OK**.

10. Select all column headers in **Column A** and **B**, right-click and select **Format** in the drop-down menu, click on the **Font** tab, select **Bold** for the **Font Style** in the list, select **10** for the font size in the **Size** list, and click on the **Apply** button.

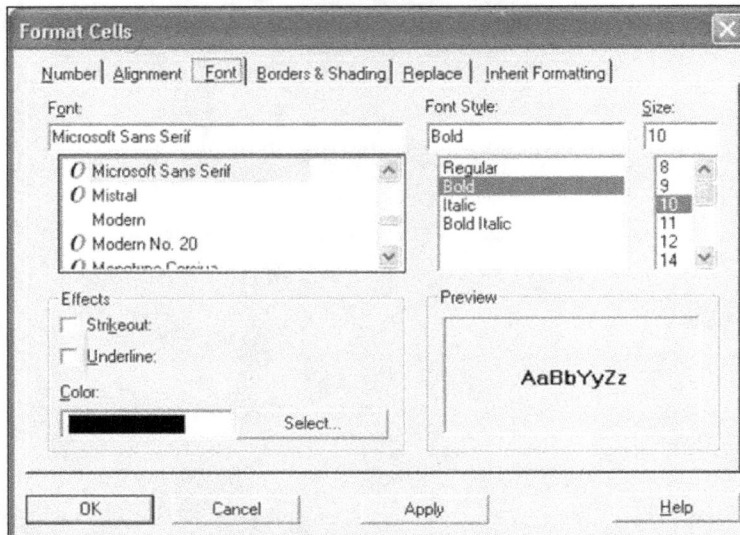

11. Select the **Borders & Shading** tab, select the **Style** of the line you want, click on the **Square** box, click on the **Select...** box in the **Shading** section, select the color yellow, click **OK** in the **Color** menu, and click on the **Apply** button. The following image shows the selections that should form a solid grid around your column headers. Click on **OK**.

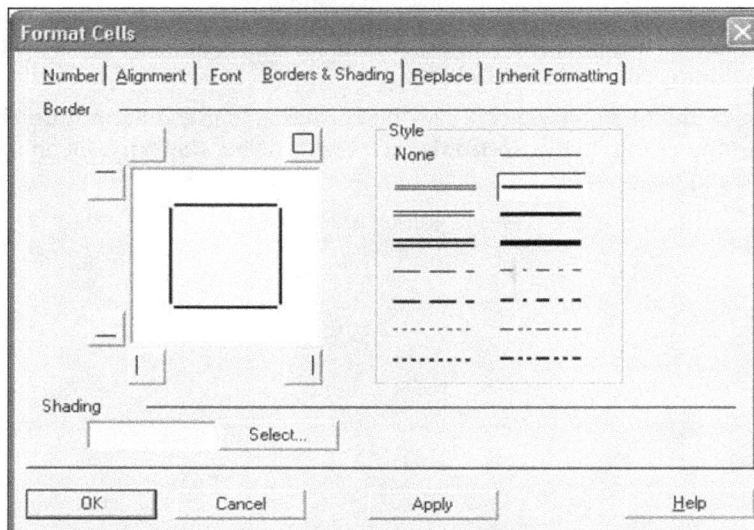

12. Click and drag your mouse to select both your data cells. These are the cells with the pound (#) signs; right-click and select **Format** from the drop-down menu.

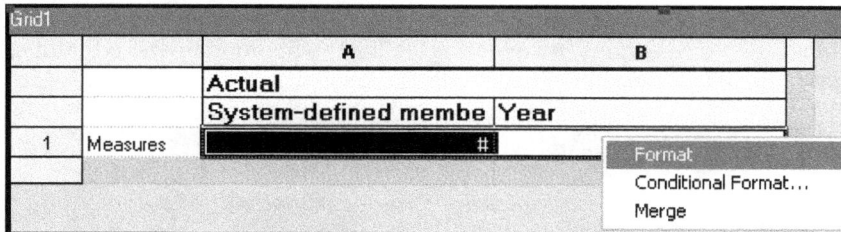

13. Click on the **Number** tab, change the **Decimal Places** to **2**, and click on the **Display in Red** checkbox for the **Negative** numbers, click on **Apply**, and click on **OK**. Your **Format** menu should look like the following image:

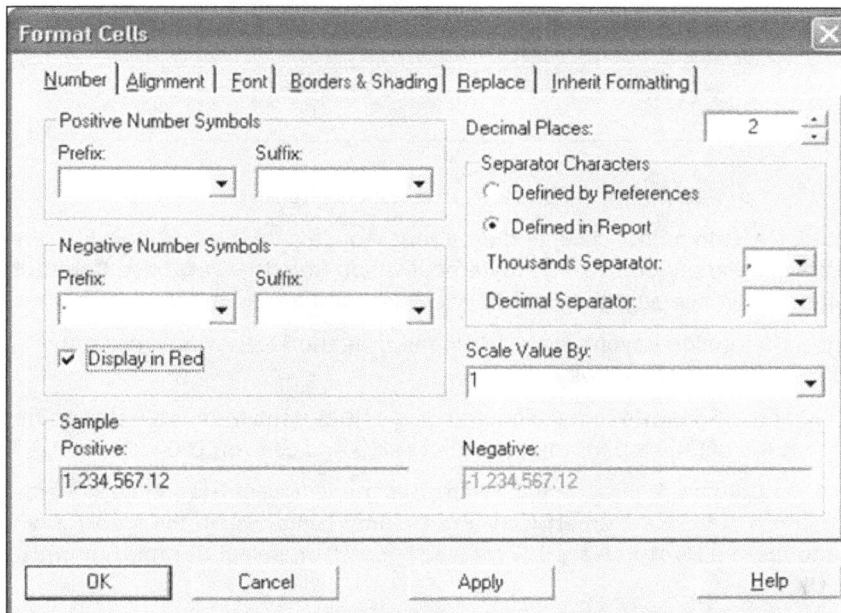

14. Right-click on the gray column next to **Column B**, click on **New Column**, and select **Data**. The reason for this step is that templates require one column or row to not be part of the template.

15. Press *Shift* and select **Column A** and **B**, right-click and select **Save as Row and Column Template**, drill down on **Root | Users | {Profiles} | TestUser** in the **Look in** dropdown, type in **SampleTemplate** in **Name**, make sure that the **Linked to Source Object** checkbox is selected, and click on **Save**. The following menu should appear. Change all the selections to **Save** by selecting the appropriate radio buttons, as shown in the following screenshot. Click on **OK**.

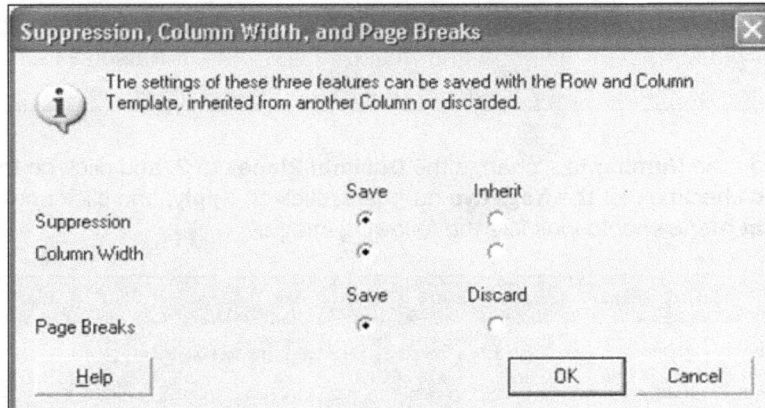

16. Click on the **File** menu, select **New**, and click on **Report**.
17. Select the **Grid** menu, click, and drag your mouse on the report designer area below to draw the grid. Select the **Sample** application from the **Database Connection** combobox, make sure the **User ID** and **Password** are populated, and click on **OK**.
18. In the **Dimension Layout** menu, click and drag the **Measures** dimension from the **Point of View** to the **Rows**.
19. Click on the **Scenario** dimension and drag to **Columns** from the **Point of View**. Repeat the same step for the **Year** dimension and click on **OK**.
20. Click on **Column A**, click on the **Properties** menu, select **Hide Always**, right-click on **Column A**, and select **Insert Row and Column Template**. In the **Insert Saved Object** menu browse **Root | Users | {Profiles} | TestUser**, select **SampleTemplate**, and click on **OK**.
21. Click on the **Print Preview** button to view your report. Click on **Close**, select the **Save** menu, browse to the **TestUser** folder created in step 1, and save as `SampleTemplate`. The column template should show as follows:

	Actual				
	Qtr1	Qtr2	Qtr3	Qtr4	Year
Measures	24,703.00	27,107.00	27,912.00	25,800.00	105,522.00

How it works...

In this recipe, we create a report and used the `Format` menu to make the report more presentable. Next, we save `Column A` and `B` of our report into a new column template called `SampleTemplate`. Before we complete the saving or our template, we will see the following menu:

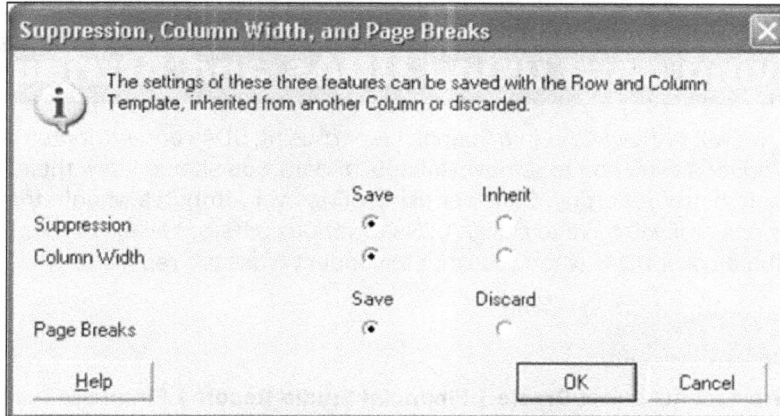

This menu allows us to select whether we want **Suppression**, **Column Width**, and **Page Breaks** saved with our template or whether we want to inherit these properties from other columns in our report. We want to keep our properties from the column template, so we choose all the **Save** radio buttons.

The **Linked to Source Object** checkbox was selected by default when you attempted to save the template. This checkbox links the template used in your report to the saved template. When you make changes the saved template those changes also take place in all the reports using that template. This functionality in essence reduces repetitive and tedious tasks and prevents disconnection between similar reports.

Finally, we add our column template to another report and view that report using **Print Preview**.

See also

Review the recipe *Adding an Application and Database on an Essbase server* in *Chapter 5* to understand how to create the `Sample Basic` database. The *Creating a connection and using substitution variables in financial reports* recipe will show you how to create a connection to the `Sample Basic` database, and the *Using the column templates and formatting reports* recipe in this chapter will show you how to apply formatting to the report.

Retrieving data using UDAs and Attributes

In this recipe, we will retrieve data in a financial report using UDAs and Attributes. Although both of these options allow you to retrieve subsets of data, you should know their strengths in order to create better reporting. Consider using UDAs over Attributes when retrieving from dense dimensions or if you have to assign UDAs to various different levels in your hierarchy. Consider Attributes over UDAs when you want to conduct cross-tab reporting.

Getting ready

Click on the **Start** menu, select **Oracle | Financial Studio Report | Financial Studio Report**, enter your **User ID**, enter your **password**, modify the **Server URL**, and click on **OK**. Your **Server URL** should be `http://EssbaseServer:Port` if you are not using SSL.

How to do it...

1. Click on the **File** menu, select **New**, and click on **Report**.
2. Select the **Grid** menu, click, and drag your mouse on the report designer area below to draw the grid. The **Select a Database Connection** menu will pop up asking your connection information. Select the **Sample** application from the **Database Connection** combobox, make sure the **User ID** and **Password** are populated, and click on **OK**. If you do not have the database connection **Sample**, then review the recipe *Creating a connection and using Substitution Variables in Financial Reports* in this chapter.

3. In the **Dimension Layout** menu, click and drag the **Market** dimension from the **Point of View** to the **Rows**.

4. Click on the **Pkg Type** attribute dimension and drag it to **Columns** from the **Attribute Dimension** section. Repeat the same step for the **Product** dimension and click on **OK**. The **Dimension Layout** window should look like the following image:

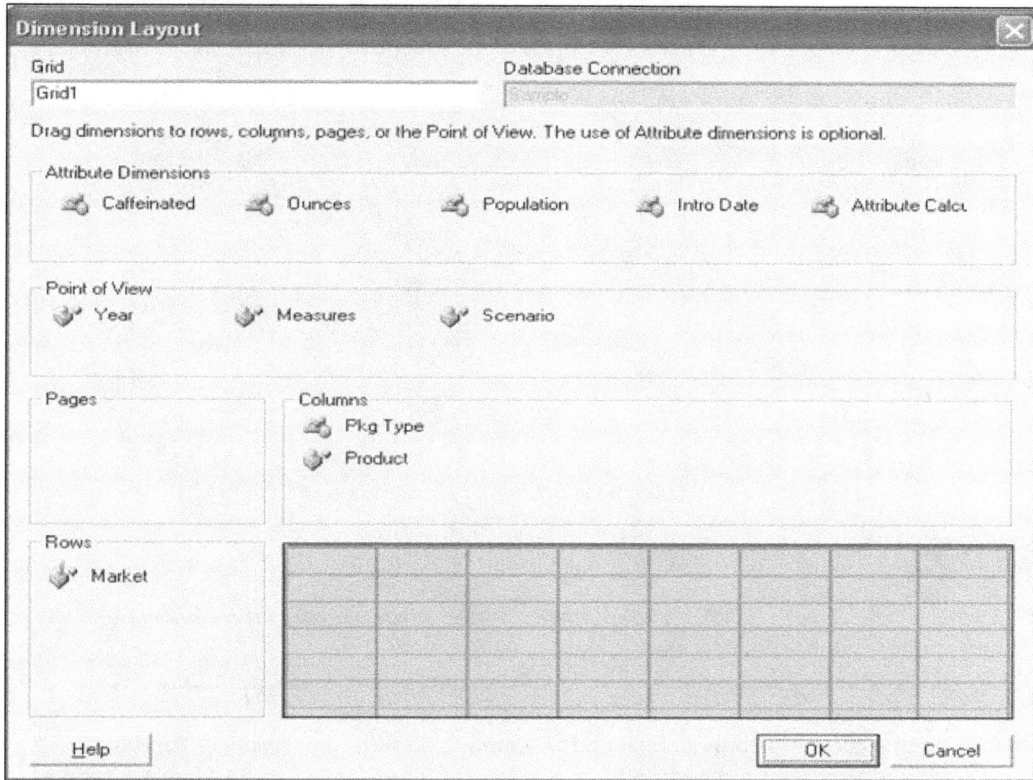

5. Double-click the **Pkg Type** attribute dimension, click on the **Remove All** button to remove **Pkg Type** from the selected listbox, expand **Pkg Type**, press *Shift* and select the **Bottle** and **Can** attributes, click on the **Add** button to select, and click on **OK**, as shown in the following screenshot:

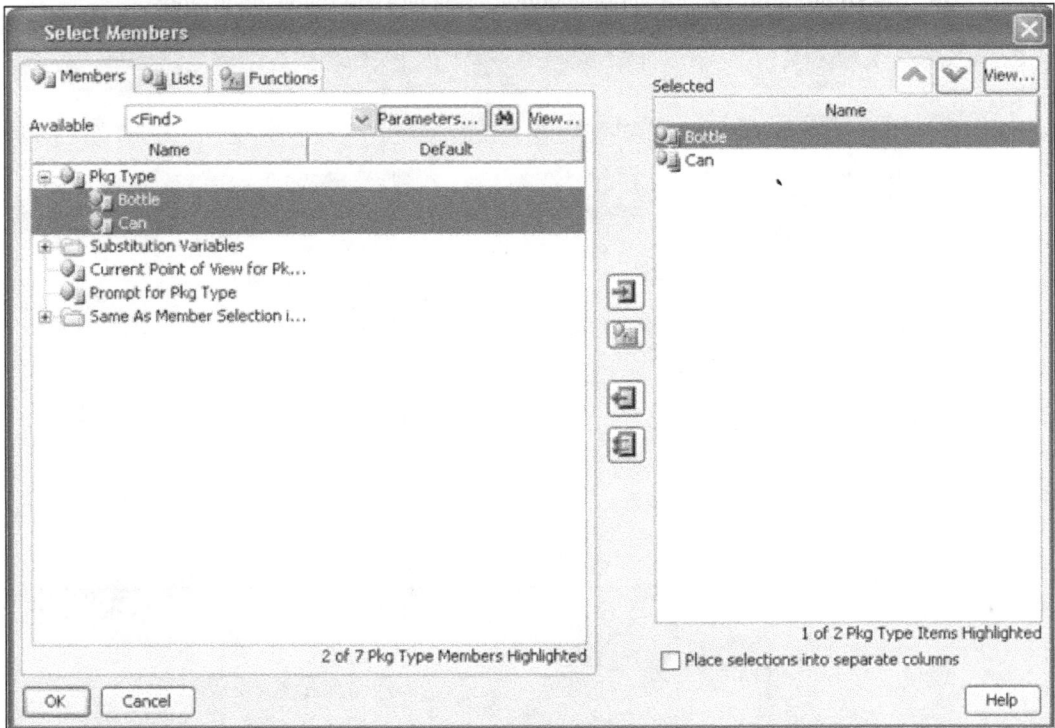

6. Double-click on **Product**, click on the **Remove All** button to unselect **Product**, expand **Product** on the left side of the **Available** listbox, press *Shift*, select children of **Product** from **100** to **400**, and click on the **Add** button to select. Select the **Place selections into separate columns** checkbox, and click on **OK**.

7. Double-click on the **Market** dimension, click on the **Functions** tab, select **Property** from the available listbox, click on the **Add** button, in the **Edit Property Function** dialog box, select **UDA** for **Property Type**, select **Major Market** for **Property Value**, click on **OK** twice. Your **Edit Property** menu should look like the following screenshot:

Edit Property Function

Parameters

Name	Description	Value
Property Type	Specify a property type, for example, "c...	UDA
Property Value	Specify a property value, for example, "...	Major Market
Property Operator	Specify the operator, for example, "!="	<None>

OK   Cancel   Help

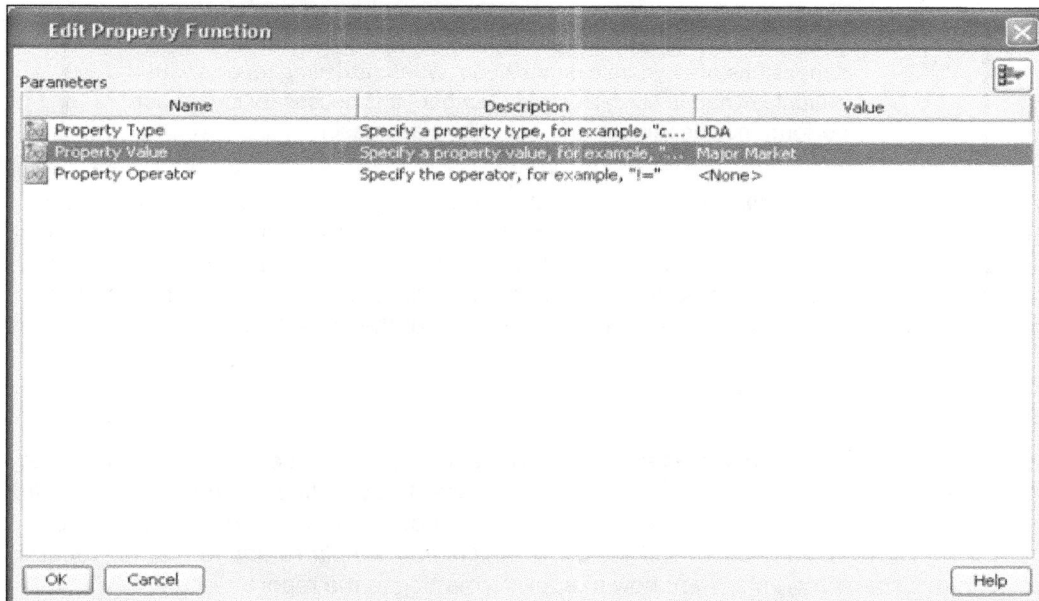

8. Click on the **Print Preview** button to view your report. The report should look like the following image:

	Bottle 100	Can 100	Bottle 200	Can 200	Bottle 300	Can 300	Bottle 400	Can 400
East	413	12,243	2,534	#MISSING	2,315	312	6,344	#MISSING
New York	#MISSING	3,498	492	#MISSING	544	#MISSING	3,668	#MISSING
Massachusett	#MISSING	5,105	972	#MISSING	149	#MISSING	486	#MISSING
Florida	#MISSING	2,056	948	#MISSING	779	312	934	#MISSING
California	-912	1,911	4,881	#MISSING	2,859	1,328	2,897	#MISSING
Texas	#MISSING	2,864	2,897	#MISSING	336	328	#MISSING	#MISSING
Central	2,080	7,410	9,578	#MISSING	4,212	5,879	9,103	#MISSING
Illinois	#MISSING	3,197	4,516	#MISSING	1,969	1,388	1,507	#MISSING
Ohio	333	280	1,230	#MISSING	286	200	2,055	#MISSING
Colorado	1,390	1,966	1,508	#MISSING	273	1,088	1,002	#MISSING

How it works...

In this recipe, we set up a report with the Pkg Type Attribute dimension going across the top as columns. We also selected a set of Product groups in the columns of our report to return a cross tab for each of the selected Product group and Pkg Type combinations.

> The values in this report are calculated on the fly as Attribute dimensions are dynamic dimensions. When retrieving reports with multiple dynamically calculated members it is necessary to monitor performance as reports may slow down as a result.

We also select the **Major Market** in our Market dimension by using the UDAs assigned to this dimension. The important thing to note about the Market dimension's retrieval by UDA is that some of the members returned are regions, such as East and Central, and some of the members returned are states, such as New York, Florida, and California. The UDA Major Market allows us to retrieve members at different levels of the same hierarchy.

See also

Review the recipe *Adding an Application and Database on an Essbase server* in *Chapter 5* to understand how to create the Sample Basic database. The *Creating a connection and using Substitution Variables in Financial Reports* recipe will show you how to create a connection to the Sample Basic database, and the *Using the column templates and formatting reports* recipe in this chapter will show you how to apply formatting to the report.

Retrieving data using children and descendants member set functions

In this recipe, we will create a report that returns members based on the specified member set functions. The strength of using member set functions in reporting is obvious when you consider the ability to make a change in one location, then have all reports change from changes made in the Essbase outline. This is valuable in terms of time savings and also has qualitative value as it would be easy to forget to make a change to a report that is not used often.

Getting ready

Click on the **Start** menu, select **Oracle | Financial Studio Report | Financial Studio Report**, enter your **User ID**, enter your **password**, modify the **Server URL**, and click on **OK**. Your **Server URL** should be http://EssbaseServer:Port if you are not using SSL.

How to do it...

1. Click on the **File** menu, select **New**, and click on **Report**.

2. Select the **Grid** menu, click, and drag your mouse on the report designer area below to draw the grid. The **Select a Database Connection** menu will pop up asking your connection information. Select the **Sample** application from the **Database Connection** combobox, make sure the **User ID** and **Password** are populated, and click on **OK**. If you do not have the database connection **Sample**, then review the recipe *Creating a connection and using Substitution Variables in Financial Reports* in this chapter.

3. In the **Dimension Layout** menu, click and drag the **Market** dimension from the **Point of View** to the **Pages**.

4. Click on the **Measures** dimension and drag from the **Point of View** to the **Rows**.

5. Click on the **Year** dimension, drag it to the **Columns,** and click on **OK**.

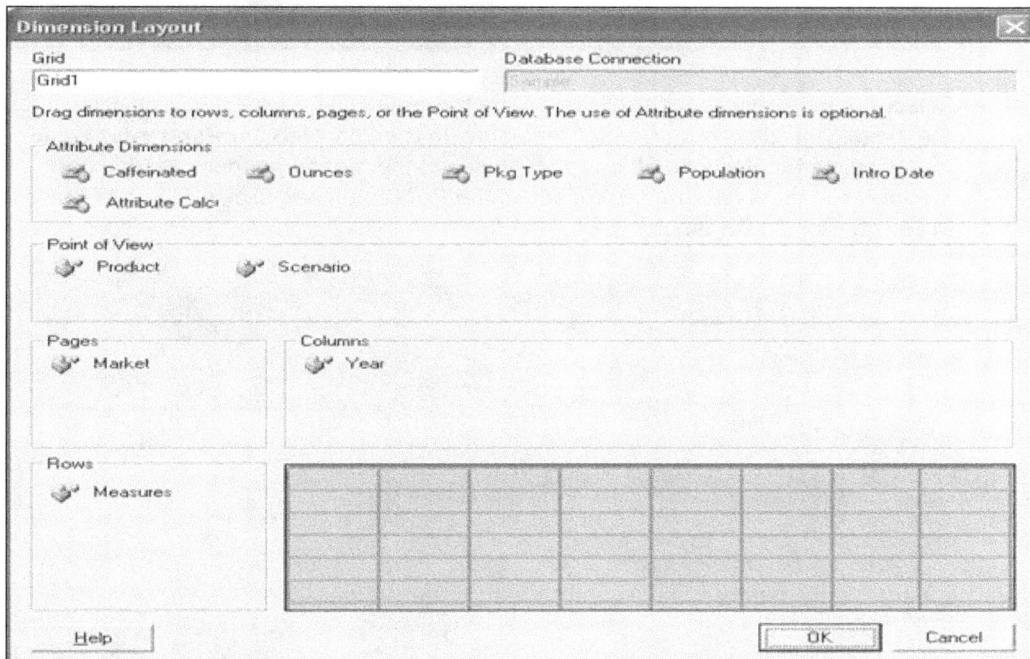

6. Double-click on the **Measures** dimension, click on the **Remove All** button to remove **Measures** from the selected list, click on the **Functions** tab, select **Descendants** from the **Available** listbox, and click on the **Add** button to select. The **Edit Descendants Function** menu should pop up, as shown in the following screenshot:

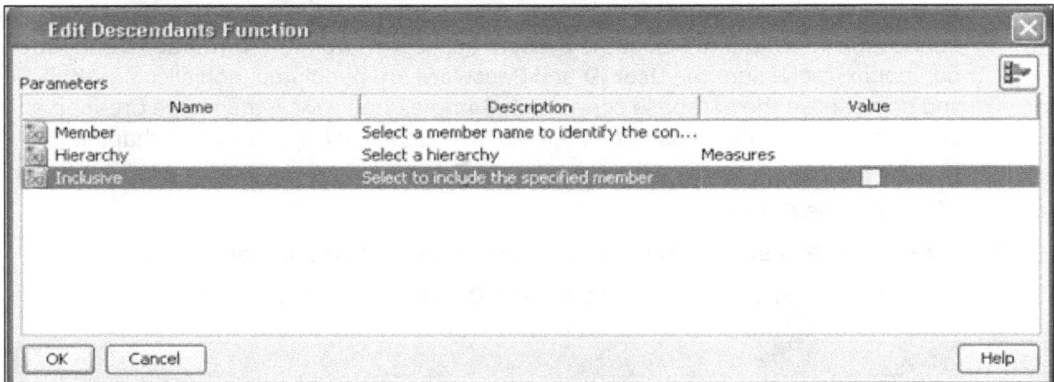

7. Select the **Inclusive** checkbox, click on the **Member** cell under **Value**, and click on the magnifying glass button to set the **Value**. In the **Edit Member Parameter Value** menu, select the **Remove All** button to unselect the **Measures** member, drill down on **Measures** in the **Available** listbox, select the **Profit** member, click on the **Add** button to select, click on **OK** thrice.

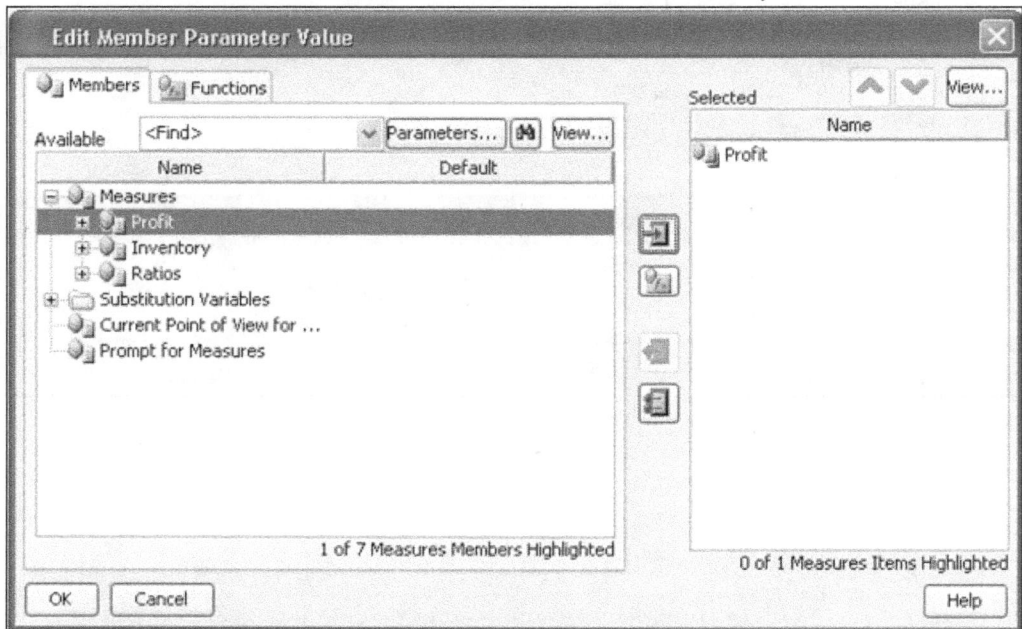

8. Double-click on the **Pages** text to the left of the **Market** combobox, select the **Functions** tab, click on **Children** in the **Available** listbox, and click on the **Add** button to select.

9. In the **Edit Children Functions** dialog box, select the **Inclusive** checkbox, click on the **Member** cell under **Value**, click on the magnifying glass button to set the **Value**, in the **Edit Member Parameter Value** menu, select the **Remove All** button to unselect the **Market** member, drill down on **Market** in the **Available** listbox, select the **East** member, click on the **Add** button to select the market, click on **OK**, click on **OK**, and click on **OK**.

10. Double-click on the **Year** dimension, select the **Functions** tab, click on **Children** in the **Available** listbox, and click on the **Add** button to select.

11. In the **Edit Children Functions** dialog box, select the **Inclusive** checkbox, click on the **Member** cell under **Value**, and click on the magnifying glass button to set the **Value**. In the **Edit Member Parameter Value** menu, select the **Remove All** button to unselect the **Year** member, drill down on **Year** in the **Available** listbox, select the **Qtr1** member, click on the **Add** button to select the member, click on **OK**, click on **OK**, and click on **OK**.

12. Click on the **Print Preview** button to view your report. The report should look like the following image:

New York

	Jan	Feb	Mar	Qtr1
Sales	2,479	2,625	2,601	7,705
COGS	1,294	1,331	1,356	3,981
Margin	1,185	1,294	1,245	3,724
Marketing	474	494	504	1,472
Payroll	195	195	195	585
Misc	4	4	3	11
Total Expenses	673	693	702	2,068
Profit	512	601	543	1,656

How it works...

In this recipe, we created a report with a `Page`, `Column`, and `Row` axis to illustrate the value of member set functions. We modified the retrieve of the Measures to bring back `Descendants` of the member `Profit` using the **Edit Descendants Function** menu. We also modified the retrieve of the `Markets` dimension in the `Pages` axis to bring back `Children` of the `East` market. What this task did was place the Market on the top of each page and create a page break for each state in the `East` market. Finally, we used the **Edit Children Function** menu on the `Year` dimension to bring back the children of `Qtr1`.

See also

Review the recipe *Adding an Application and Database on an Essbase server* in *Chapter 5* to understand how to create the `Sample Basic` database. The *Using the column templates and formatting reports* recipe in this chapter will show you how to apply formatting to the report.

Using User Prompts and the POV to select members

In this recipe, we will set up a report that uses **User Prompts** and the **Point of View** (**POV**) to allow users to make selections at runtime. Using these functions, we can empower the users by allowing them to make selections and filter the data they would like to see in the report.

Getting ready

Click on the **Start** menu, select **Oracle | Financial Studio Report | Financial Studio Report**, enter your **User ID**, enter your **password**, modify the **Server URL**, and click on **OK**. Your server URL should be `http://EssbaseServer:Port` if you are not using SSL.

How to do it...

1. Click on the **Repository** menu, expand the **Users** folder, right-click on **{Profiles}**, click on **New Folder**, and type **TestUser**.

2. Click on the **File** menu, select **New**, and click on **Report**.

3. Select the **Grid** menu, click, and drag your mouse on the report designer area below to draw the grid. The **Select a Database Connection** menu will pop up asking your connection information. Select the **Sample** application from the **Database Connection** combobox, make sure the **User ID** and **Password** are populated, and click on **OK**. If you do not have the database connection **Sample**, then review the recipe *Creating a connection and using Substitution Variables in Financial Reports* in this chapter.

4. In the **Dimension Layout** menu, click and drag the **Measures** dimension from the **Point of View** to the **Rows**.

5. Click on the **Year** dimension and drag it to the **Columns** from the **Point of View**. Click on **OK**.

6. Double-click on the **Year** dimension, click on the **Remove All** button to unselect **Year**, select **Prompt for Year**, click on the **Add** button twice to add two prompts, and click on **OK**.

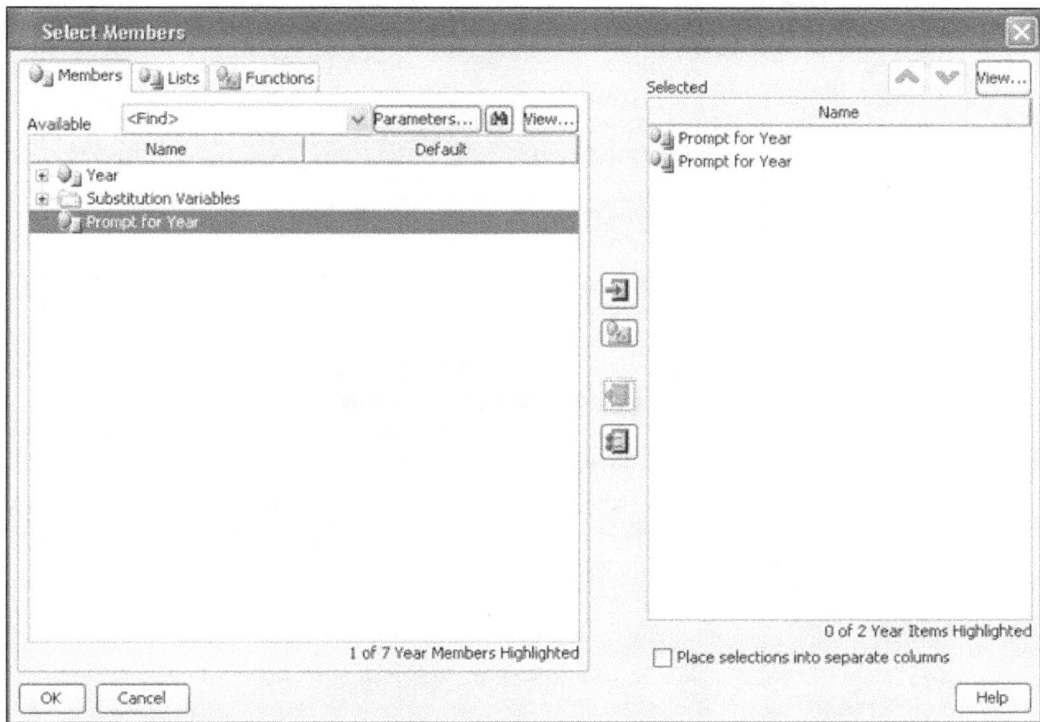

7. The **Define** prompt menu should pop up. Select the prompt you want to modify, click on the **Title** and change to **Enter Current Month**. Click on the **Choice List** magnifying glass button.

8. Click on the **Remove All** button to unselect the **Year** member, select the **Functions** tab, click on **Descendants** in the **Available** listbox, and click on the **Add** button to select.

9. In the **Edit Descendants Functions** dialog box, select the **Inclusive** checkbox, click on the **Member** cell under **Value**, and click the magnifying glass button to set the **Value**. In the **Edit Member Parameter Value** menu, select the **Remove All** button to unselect the **Year** member, select the **Year** member, click on the **Add** button to select, click on **OK**, and click on **OK**.

10. Select **Alias** in the **Member Label** in the **Prompt Selection Dialog** combobox.

11. Repeat the last four steps for the second prompt but change the **Title** of the prompt to **Enter Previous Month**. Click on **OK**. Your menu should look like the following screenshot:

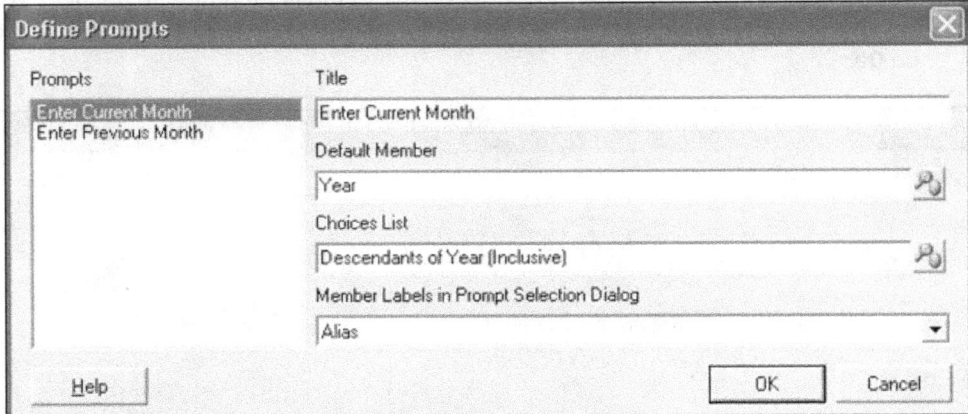

12. Double-click on the **Measures** dimension, click on the **Lists** tab, click on the **Remove All** button to remove the **Measures** member, select **Lev1, Measures**, click on the **Add** button to select, and click on **OK**. Select the **Save** menu, browse to the **TestUser** folder created in step 1, and save as **SamplePrompt**.

13. Select **Web Preview**, and the following prompts should show. Click on both **Edit Member Names** checkboxes, type **Aug** in the **Current Month** textbox, type **Jun** in the **Previous Month** textbox, as shown in the following screenshot, and click on the **OK** button.

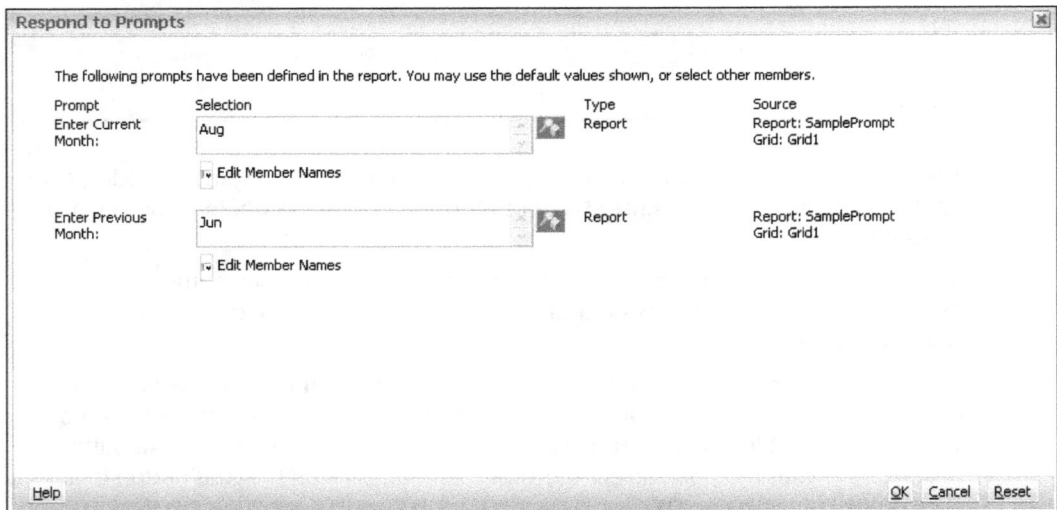

14. Click on the **Market POV** and the following menu will pop up. Expand the **Market** hierarchy, select the **East** radio button, and click on **OK**, as follows:

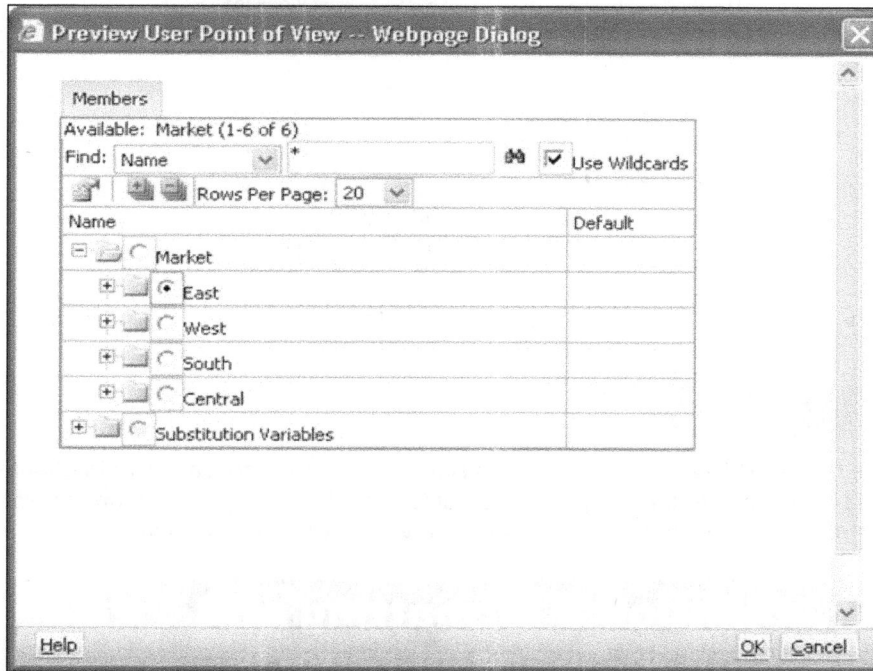

How it works...

In this recipe, we created a report with two prompts. We executed the report and at runtime were able change both prompts. We also changed our Market POV to the East market.

The User Prompt and the POV have some differences with regards to scope. We can set up a User Prompt for the Pages, Rows, and Columns axis of a Grid in the report. The POV, on the other hand, is used for the entire report or the Grid. User Prompts essentially provide a more granular control of what is displayed in the report.

The generated report looks like the following image:

Product: Product	Market: East	Scenario: Scenario

	Aug	Jun
Margin	4,331	4,577
Total Expenses	2,236	2,169
Inventory	30,641	29,768
Ratios	56	58

Export In Query Ready Mode

See also

Review the recipe *Adding an Application and Database on an Essbase server* in *Chapter 5* to understand how to create the `Sample Basic` database. The *Using the column templates and formatting reports* recipe in this chapter will show you how to apply formatting to the report.

Using conditional formatting and suppression in financial reports

In this recipe, we will be using conditional formatting to emphasize areas of our reports. We will also be using conditional suppression to hide portions of the reports that are not relevant to our analysis or add no value. These two tools allow us to provide reports that will change based on specified conditions.

Getting ready

Click on the **Start** menu, select **Oracle | Financial Studio Report | Financial Studio Report**, enter your **User ID**, enter your **password**, modify the **Server URL**, and click on **OK**. Your server URL should be `http://EssbaseServer:Port` if you are not using SSL.

How to do it...

1. Click on the **Repository** menu, expand the **Users** folder, right-click on **{Profiles}**, click on **New Folder**, and type **TestUser**.

2. Click on the **File** menu, select **New**, and click on **Report**.

3. Select the **Grid** menu, click, and drag your mouse on the report designer area below to draw the grid. The **Select a Database Connection** menu will pop up asking your connection information. Select the **Sample** application from the **Database Connection** combobox, make sure the **User ID** and **Password** are populated, and click on **OK**. If you do not have the database connection **Sample**, then review the recipe *Creating a connection and using Substitution Variables in Financial Reports* in this chapter.

4. In the **Dimension Layout** menu, click and drag the **Measures** dimension from the **Point of View** to the **Rows**.

5. Click on the **Scenario** dimension and drag it to the **Columns** from the **Point of View**. Click on **OK**.

6. Double-click on **Scenario**, click on the **Remove All** button to unselect scenarios, expand **Scenario** in the **Available** listbox, press *Shift*, and select **Actual**, **Budget**, and **Variance %**. Click on the **Add** button to select, click on the **Place selections into separate columns** checkbox, and click on **OK**.

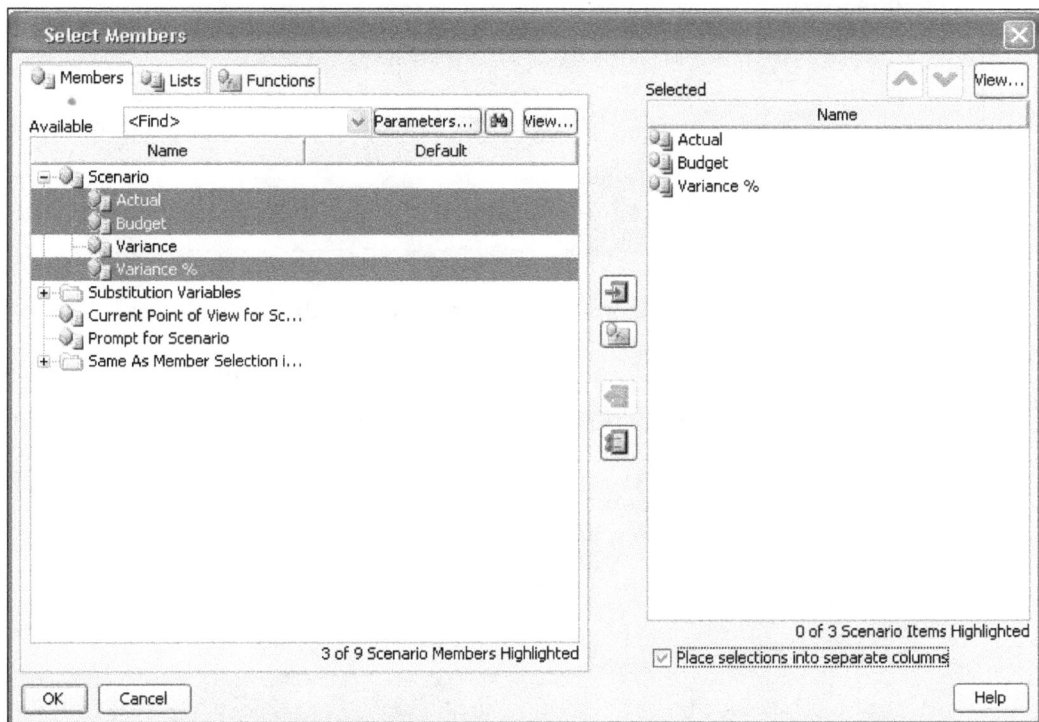

7. Double-click on the **Measures** dimension, click on the **Remove All** button to remove **Measures** from the selected list, click on the **Functions** tab, select **Descendants** from the **Available** listbox, and click on the **Add** button.

8. In the **Edit Descendants Function** menu, select the **Inclusive** checkbox, click on the **Member** cell under **Value**, and click on the magnifying glass button to set the **Value**. In the **Edit Member Parameter Value** menu, select the **Remove All** button to unselect the **Measures** member, drill-down on **Measures** in the **Available** listbox, select the **Profit** member, click on the **Add** button to select, and click on **OK**.

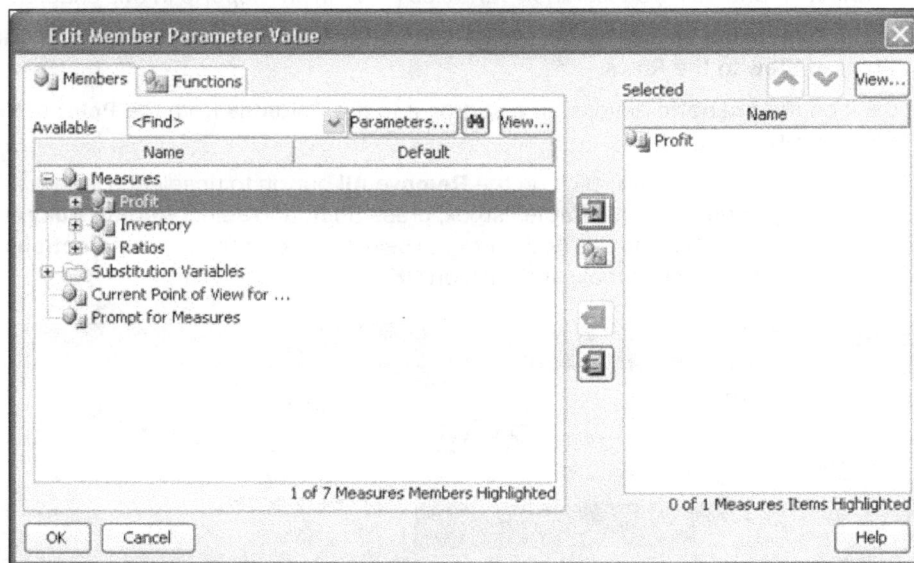

9. Click on **OK** on **Edit Descendants Function**, and click on **OK** on the **Select Members** menu.

10. Click on the **Print Preview** button to view your report before conditional formatting and suppression is applied. Click on **Close**. Your report should look as follows:

	Actual	Budget	Variance %
Sales	87,398	78,950	11
COGS	37,927	32,250	-18
Margin	49,471	46,700	6
Marketing	14,721	11,210	-31
Payroll	10,389	7,100	-46
Misc	200	#MISSING	#MISSING
Total Expens	25,310	18,310	-38
Profit	24,161	28,390	-15

11. Click on cell **C1**, select the **Format** menu, and select **Condition Format...**.

12. In the **Condition 1: If** combobox, select **Column Value**. In the combo box that is second from left, select column **C**. Select the greater than sign (**>**) in the combobox that is third from left, leave **Value** selected, and enter **30** for the value in the last text box.

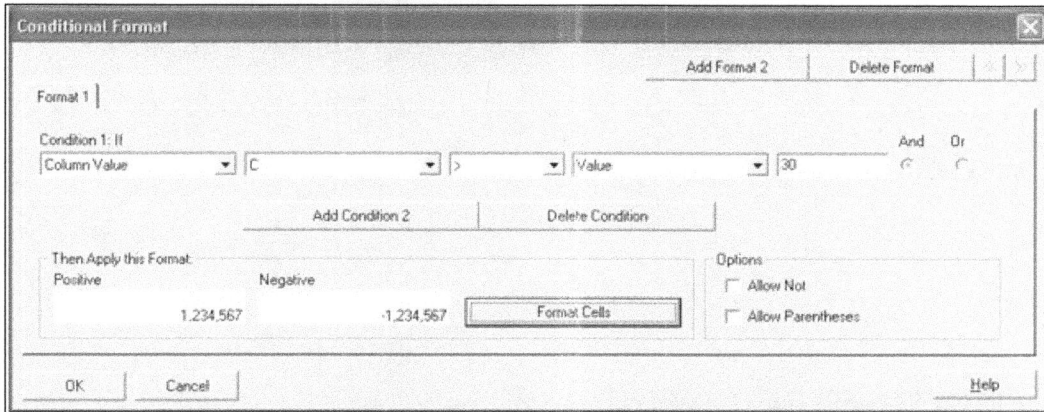

13. Click the **Format Cells** command button, select the **Borders & Shade** tab, click on the **Select** button, select **Red** from the **Color** pallet, click on **OK**, and click on **OK**. The following is the image of the Color pallet:

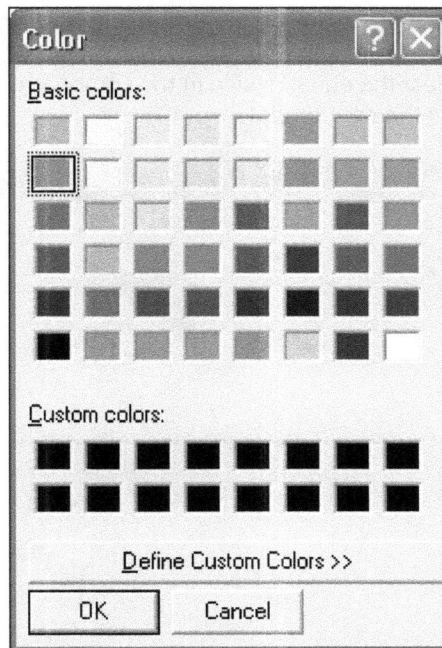

14. In the **Conditional Format** menu, select the **Or** radio button, and click on the **Add Condition 2** button. In the **Condition 2: If** combobox select **Column Value**. Then in the second to the right combobox select column **C**. Select the less than sign in the combobox that is third from left, leave **Value** selected, and enter **-30** for the value in the last textbox. Click on **OK**.

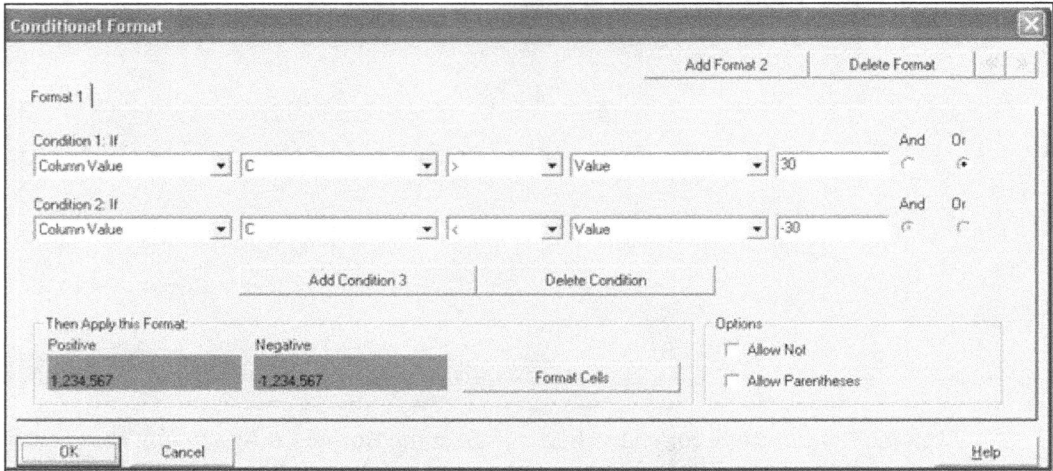

15. Click on **Row 1** in **Grid1** to select the row. In the **Row 1** properties menu, select the **Advance Options** checkbox, click on the **Setup...** button, and in the **Suppress Row If:** combobox select **Data Values in Column**. In the combobox that is second from left select column **C**, select the equal to sign in the combobox, which is third from the left, and select **Zero** from the right drop-down.

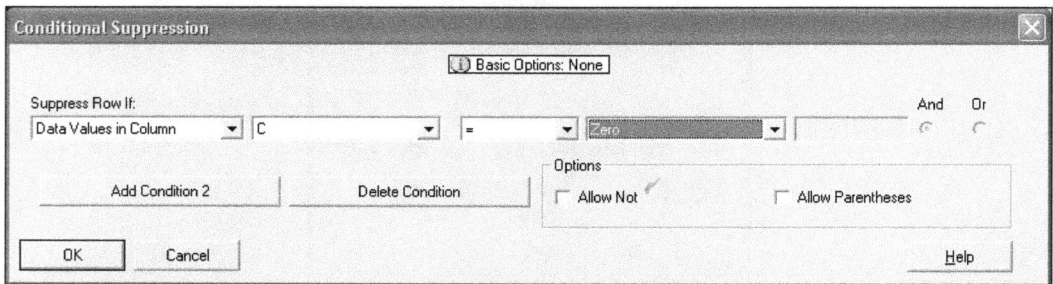

16. Click on **Add Condition 2**, select the **Or** operator radio button, in the **Suppress Row If** combobox select **Data Values in Column**, in the second to the right combobox select column **C**, select the equal to sign in the combobox, which is third from the left, select **No Data** from the right drop down, and click on **OK**.

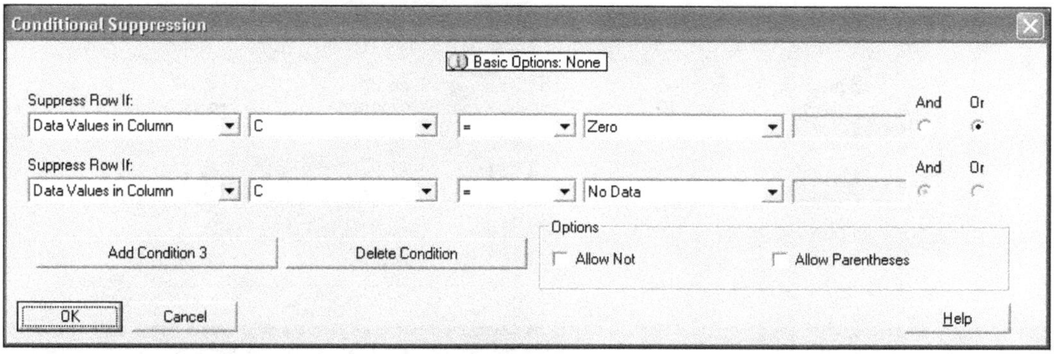

17. Click on the **Print Preview** button to view the report. Your report should look like the following screenshot:

	Actual	Budget	Variance %
Sales	87,398	78,950	11
COGS	37,927	32,250	-18
Margin	49,471	46,700	6
Marketing	14,721	11,210	-31
Payroll	10,389	7,100	-46
Total Expenses	25,310	18,310	-38
Profit	24,161	28,390	-15

How it works...

In this recipe, we created a report with scenarios `Actual`, `Budget`, and `Variances %` across the top as columns and `Measures` going down as rows. We ran the report and found that it was returning `#missing` values for `Variance %` and there was formatting in any cell. The following is the report before conditional formatting:

	Actual	Budget	Variance %
Sales	87,398	78,950	11
COGS	37,927	32,250	-18
Margin	49,471	46,700	6
Marketing	14,721	11,210	-31
Payroll	10,389	7,100	-46
Misc	200	#MISSING	#MISSING
Total Expens	25,310	18,310	-38
Profit	24,161	28,390	-15

We then added conditional formatting to the Variance % so that values greater 30 and less than -30 were highlighted in red. In addition, we added conditional suppression to remove Variance % with either zero or no data. The results of our conditional formatting and suppression are shown below. Notice that Misc is no longer in the report as it had Variance % with #MISSING or no data. Also, all Variance % values less than -30 are now red.

	Actual	Budget	Variance %
Sales	87,398	78,950	11
COGS	37,927	32,250	-18
Margin	49,471	46,700	6
Marketing	14,721	11,210	-31
Payroll	10,389	7,100	-46
Total Expenses	25,310	18,310	-38
Profit	24,161	28,390	-15

Adding related content to financial reports

In this recipe, we will use **Related Content** to navigate from a report with a summary of our data to a report with more detail. Related Content is a functionality used to add documents or other reports to a cell in your report, which gives users more information on that number. Although this recipe discusses related content from one Financial Report to another, this functionality is not limited to Financial Reports and Web Analysis. We can use related content to navigate to any document including OBIEE reports.

Getting ready

Click on the **Start** menu, select **Oracle | Financial Studio Report | Financial Studio Report**, enter your **User ID**, enter your **password**, modify the **Server URL**, and click on **OK**. Your server URL should be http://EssbaseServer:Port if you are not using SSL.

How to do it...

1. Click on the **Repository** menu, expand the **Users** folder, right-click on **{Profiles}**, click on **New Folder**, and type **TestUser**.

2. Click on the **File** menu, select **New**, and click on **Report**.

3. Select the **Grid** menu, click and drag your mouse on the report designer area below to draw the grid. The **Select a Database Connection** menu will pop up asking your connection information. Select the **Sample** application from the **Database Connection** combobox, make sure the **User ID** and **Password** are populated, and click on **OK**. If you do not have the database connection **Sample**, then review the recipe *Creating a connection and using Substitution Variables in Financial Reports* in this chapter.

4. In the **Dimension Layout** menu, click and drag the **Measures** dimension from the **Point of View** to the **Rows**.

5. Click on the **Scenario** dimension and drag it to the **Columns** from the **Point of View**. Click on **OK**.

6. Double-click on the **Measures** dimension, click on the **Remove All** button to remove **Measures** from the selected list, click on the **Functions** tab, select **Descendants** from the **Available** listbox, and click on the **Add** button to select.

7. In the **Edit Descendants Function** menu, select the **Inclusive** checkbox, click on the **Member** cell under **Value**, and click on the magnifying glass button to set the Value. In the **Edit Member Parameter Value** menu, select **Measures** on the left-hand side, click on the **Add** button to add Measures to the **Selected** list, click on **OK**, click on **OK**, and click on **OK**.

8. Select the **Save** menu, browse to the **TestUser** folder, and save as **SampleRC**.

9. Click on the **File** menu, select **New**, and click on **Report**.

10. Select the **Grid** menu, click, and drag your mouse on the report designer area below to draw the grid. The **Select a Database Connection** menu will pop up asking your connection information. Select the **Sample** application from the **Database Connection** combobox, make sure the **User ID** and **Password** are populated, and click on **OK**.

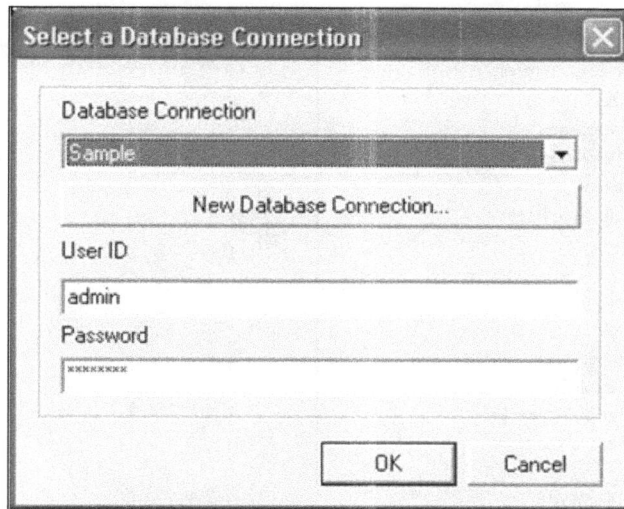

11. In the **Dimension Layout** menu, click and drag the **Measures** dimension from the **Point of View** to the **Rows**.

12. Click on the **Scenario** dimension and drag it to the **Columns** from **Point of View**. Click on **OK**.

13. Select cell **A1**, click on the **Cell Properties** menu, select the **Add Related Content** checkbox, and click on **Setup...**. The following is an image of the **Cell Properties** menu with the selections:

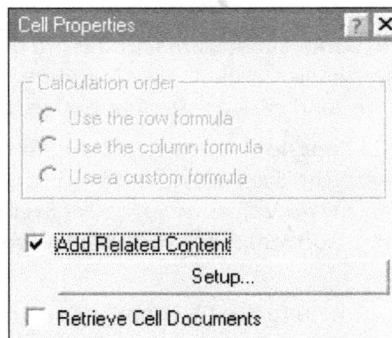

14. Expand the **Oracle Hyperion Reporting and Analysis** on the `http://localhost:19000` folder, drill down on **Users | {Profiles} | TestUser**, select **SampleRC**, click on the **Add** button, and click on **OK**.

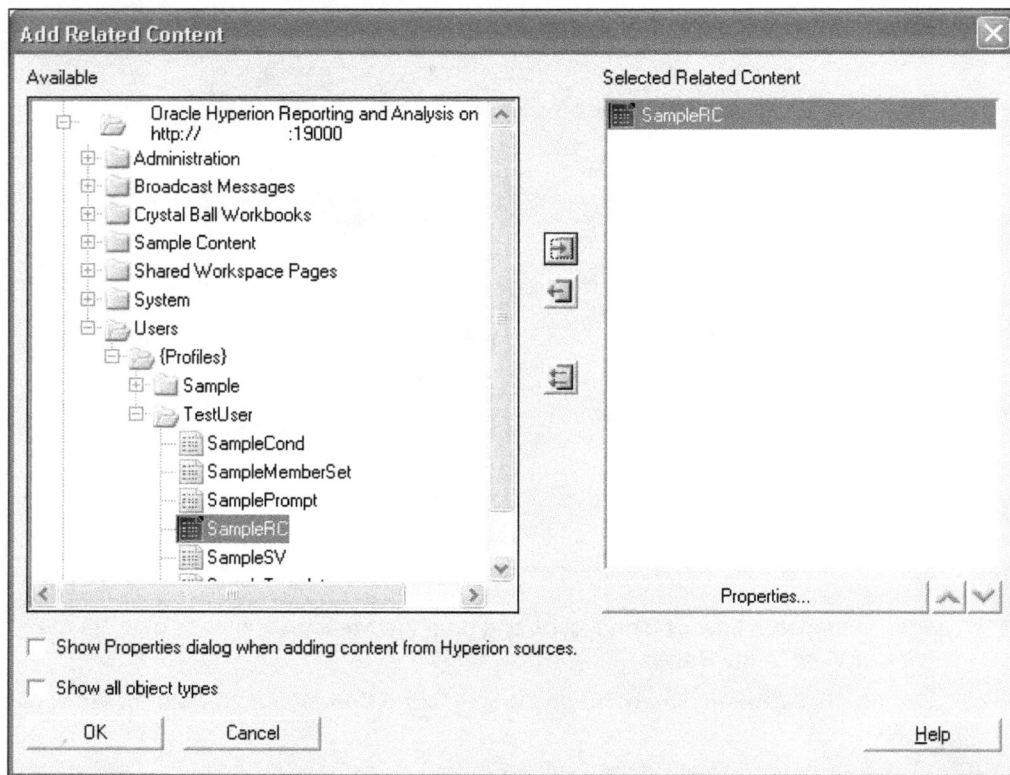

15. Select the **Save** menu, browse to the **TestUser** folder, and save as
SampleRCSummary.

16. Click on the **Web Preview** button to view your report. The simple report should display
as shown in the following screenshot. Notice the line under the data cell:

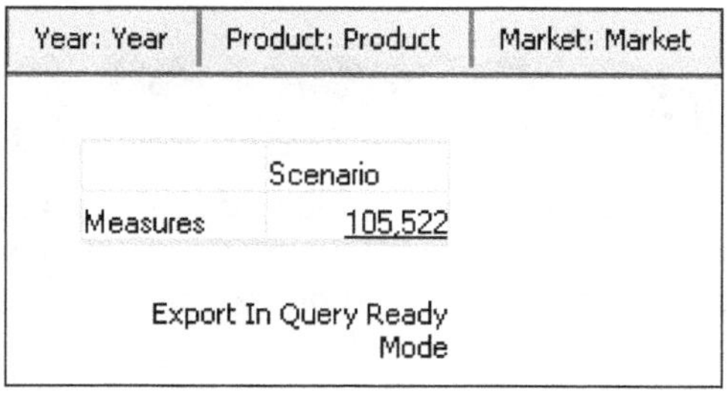

Year: Year	Product: Product	Market: Market
	Scenario	
Measures	105,522	
	Export In Query Ready Mode	

17. Click on the data cell to display the report **SampleRC**. The report should display
as follows:

/Users/{Profiles}/TestUser/SampleRC		
Year: Year	Product: Product	Market: Market
	Scenario	
Sales	400,855	
COGS	179,336	
Margin	221,519	
Marketing	66,237	
Payroll	48,747	
Misc	1,013	
Total Expenses	115,997	
Profit	105,522	
Opening Inventory	117,405	
Additions	429,774	
Ending Inventory	146,324	
Inventory	117,405	
Margin %	55	
Profit %	26	
Profit per Ounce	#MISSING	
Ratios	55	

How it works...

In this recipe, we navigate from a report with summary data to a report with more detail using related content. This functionality gives us the ability to share content among our reports and open any URL or document.

Creating a web analysis report

In this recipe, we will create a **Database Connection**, use the **Document Wizard** to set up the layout of our report, and modify the selections on our report with the Data Layout menu. **Web analysis reports** are about the most dynamic reports we can build as they allow drilling into and drilling out at runtime by the end users.

Getting ready

Click on the **Start** menu and select **Programs | Oracle EPM System | Reporting and Analysis | Web Analysis URL**.

How to do it...

1. You may have the following dialog pop up. Click on **Run**, enter your **User ID**, enter your **password** in the **Hyperion Web Analysis Studio screen**, and click on **Login**.

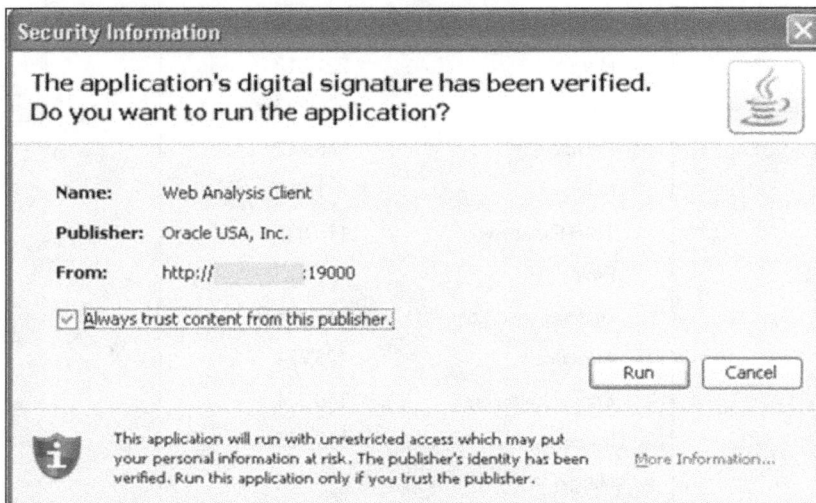

Security Information

The application's digital signature has been verified.
Do you want to run the application?

Name:	Web Analysis Client
Publisher:	Oracle USA, Inc.
From:	http:// :19000

☑ Always trust content from this publisher.

[Run] [Cancel]

This application will run with unrestricted access which may put your personal information at risk. The publisher's identity has been verified. Run this application only if you trust the publisher.   More Information...

2. Click on **Files | New | Database Connection | Analytics Services**.

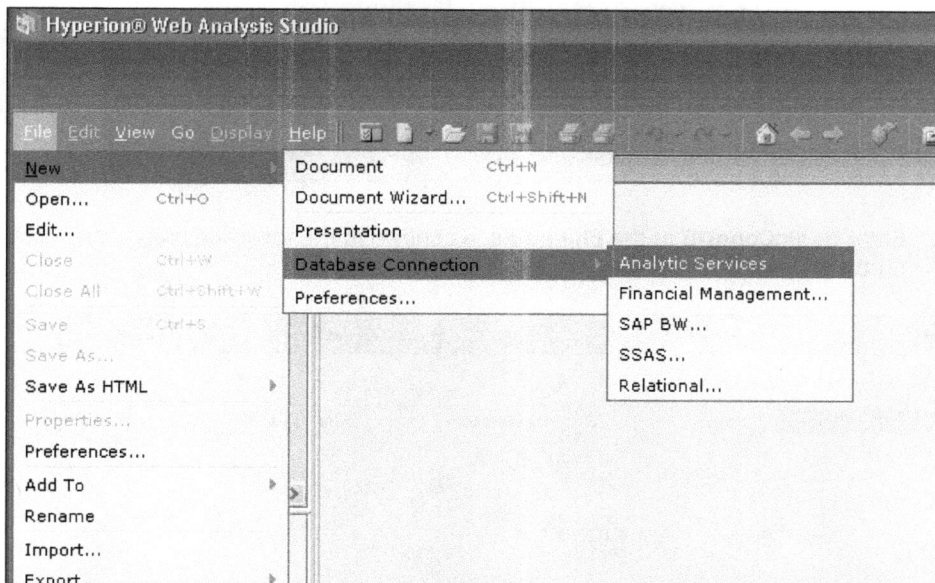

3. Enter your server name, administrative username, and password.

4. Select the **Save User ID and Password** checkbox, as shown in the following screenshot, and click on **Next**.

Developing Dynamic Reports

5. Double-click on **Sample | Basic** from the listbox on the right and click on **Finish**.

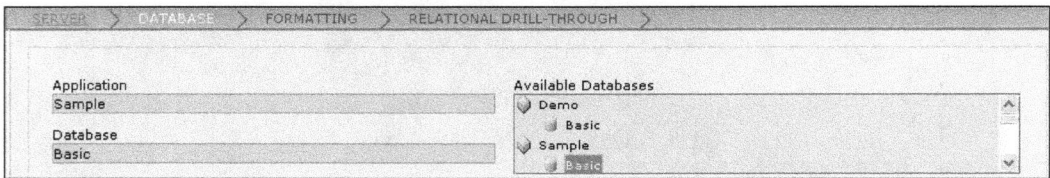

6. Enter **BasicConnDB** in the **File name**, as shown in the following image, and click on **OK**.

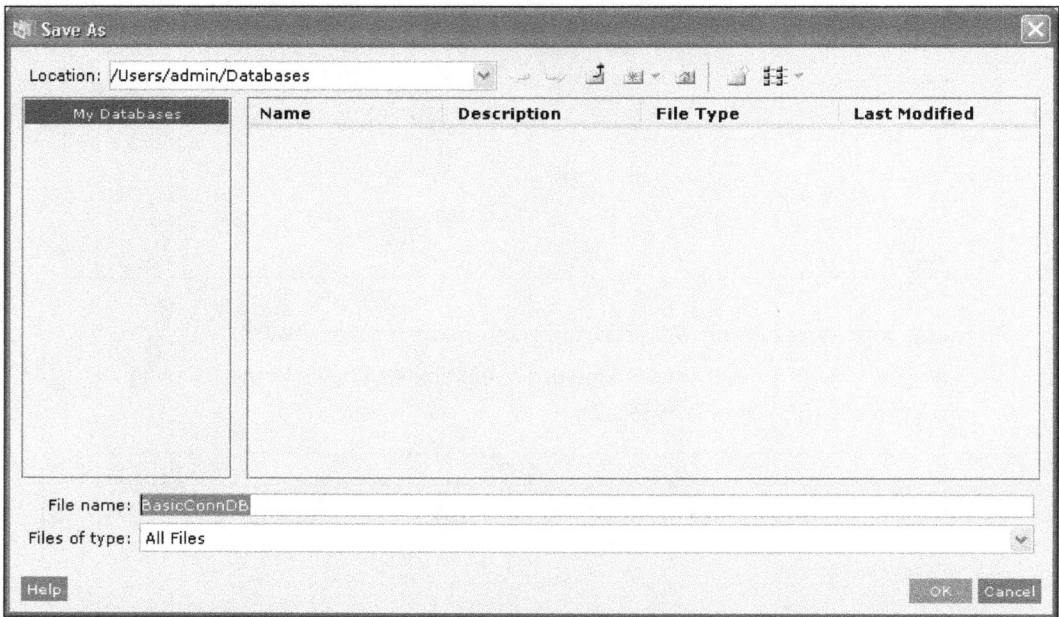

7. Click on **File | New | Document Wizard...**, click on **Browse**, select **BasicConnDB**, and click on **OK**.

8. Click on the **Use Point Of View** checkbox and click on **Next**.

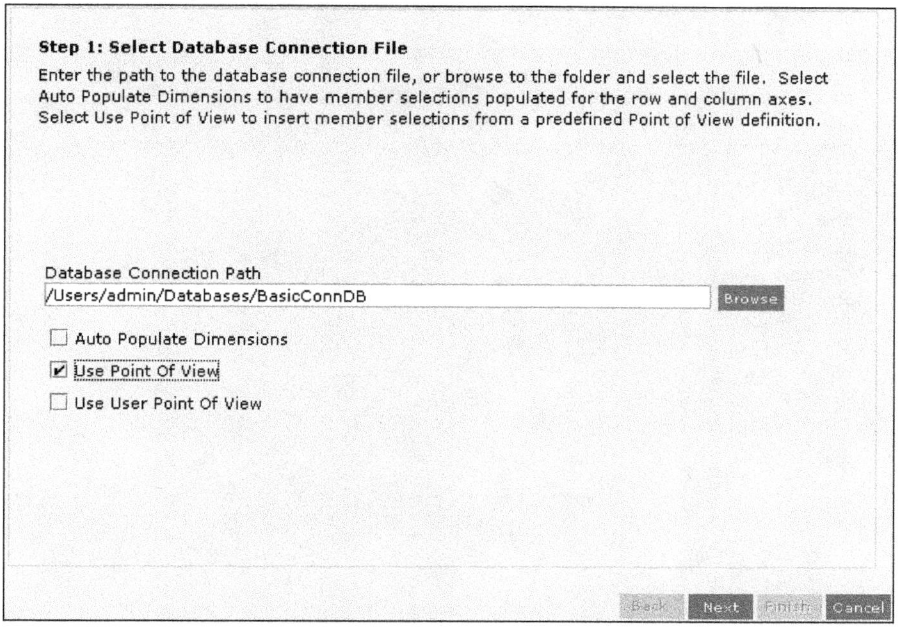

Step 1: Select Database Connection File

Enter the path to the database connection file, or browse to the folder and select the file. Select Auto Populate Dimensions to have member selections populated for the row and column axes. Select Use Point of View to insert member selections from a predefined Point of View definition.

Database Connection Path
/Users/admin/Databases/BasicConnDB   Browse

☐ Auto Populate Dimensions
☑ Use Point Of View
☐ Use User Point Of View

Back Next Finish Cancel

---

9. Select the **Measures** dimension, click on the **Add** button, and click on **Next**.

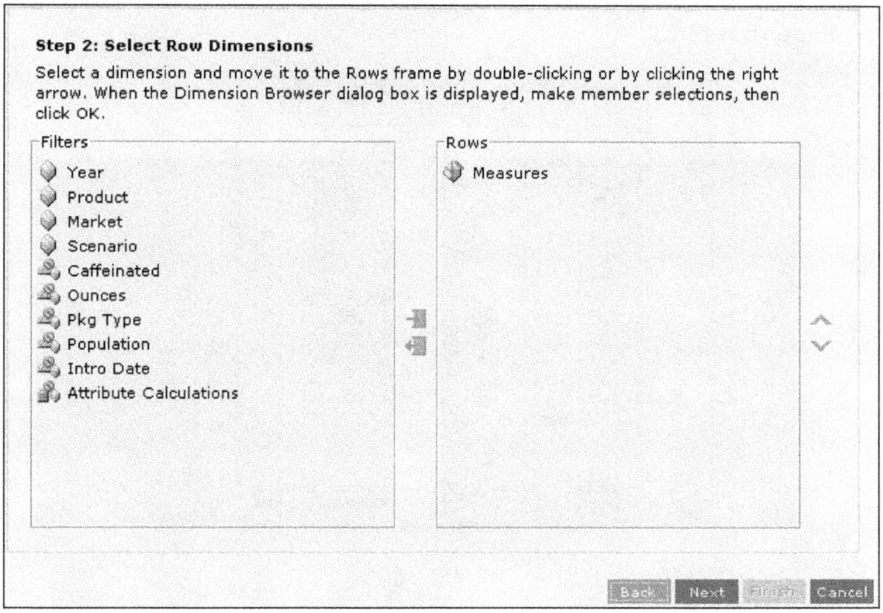

Step 2: Select Row Dimensions

Select a dimension and move it to the Rows frame by double-clicking or by clicking the right arrow. When the Dimension Browser dialog box is displayed, make member selections, then click OK.

Filters   Rows

🌐 Year   🌐 Measures
🌐 Product
🌐 Market
🌐 Scenario
🔹 Caffeinated
🔹 Ounces
🔹 Pkg Type
🔹 Population
🔹 Intro Date
🔹 Attribute Calculations

Back Next Finish Cancel

---

10. Select **Year**, click on the **Add** button, and click on **Next**.

11. Select **Scenario**, click on the **Add** button, and click on **Finish**.

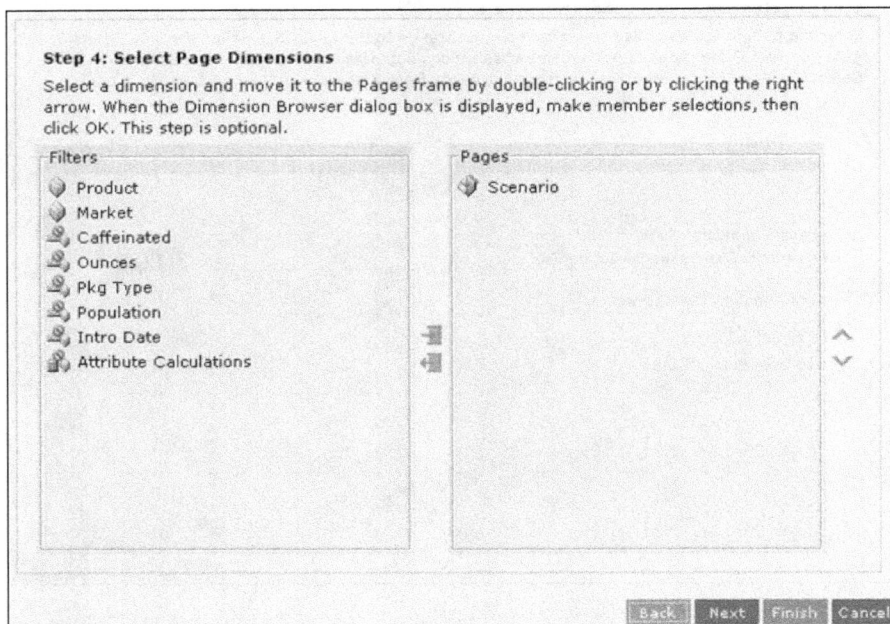

Step 4: Select Page Dimensions

Select a dimension and move it to the Pages frame by double-clicking or by clicking the right arrow. When the Dimension Browser dialog box is displayed, make member selections, then click OK. This step is optional.

Filters

- Product
- Market
- Caffeinated
- Ounces
- Pkg Type
- Population
- Intro Date
- Attribute Calculations

Pages

- Scenario

Back   Next   Finish   Cancel

12. Click on the **Switch to Document Designer** button, double-click on the **Grid**, and click on **ReportDataSrc1**.

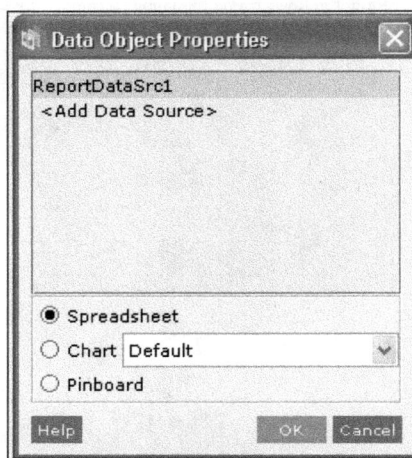

Data Object Properties

ReportDataSrc1
<Add Data Source>

- ● Spreadsheet
- ○ Chart Default
- ○ Pinboard

Help   OK   Cancel

13. In the **Data Layout** menu, double-click on **Year** and select **Quarter** on the left-hand side. Remove **Year** for the selection, and click on **OK**. Repeat the same step. Select **Actual** for **Scenario** on the Page, and **Profit** for **Rows**.

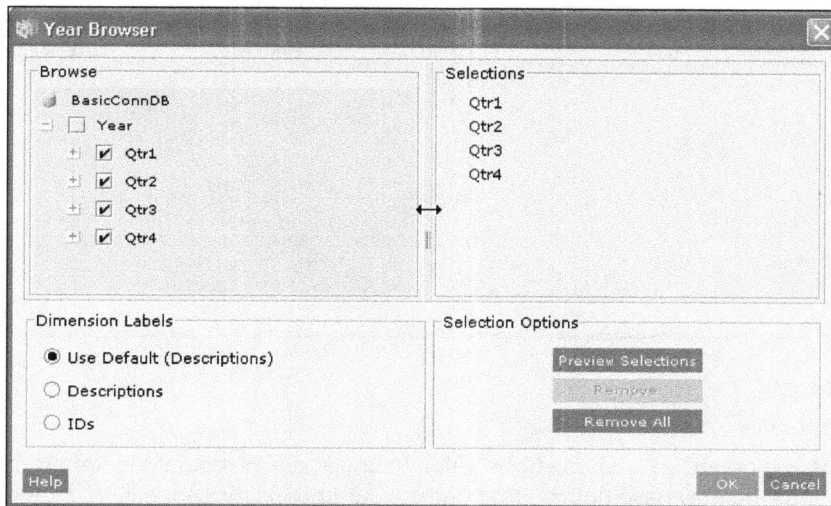

14. Click on **OK** twice and click on the ▣ **Switch to Analyze View** button. Double-click on the **Profit** measure to view all the children, and double-click on **Qtr1**.

15. Click on **File | Save**, enter **WebReport1**, and click on **Save**.

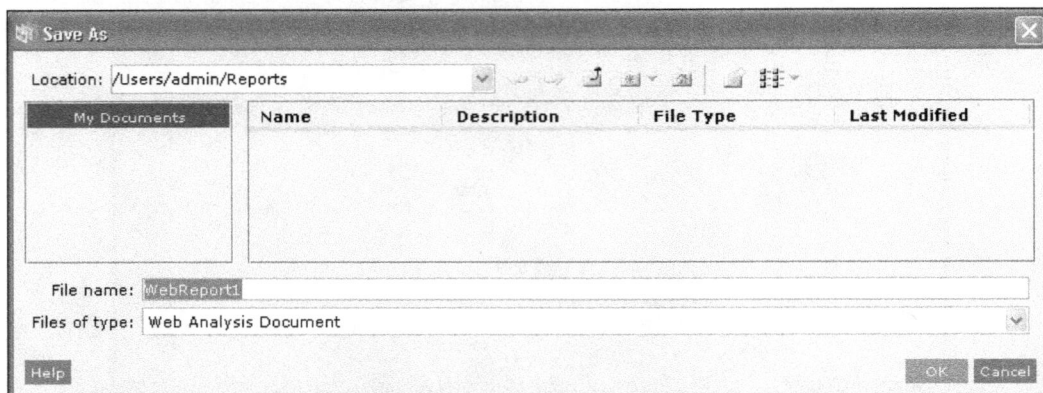

How it works...

In this recipe, we create a Database Connection to use in our Web Analysis Report called `BasicConnDB`. You may have noticed that one of your options for connection is relational. This database connection gives Web Analysis some flexibility. The other Database Connection options are as follows:

- Analytics Services
- SAP BW
- SSAS

We are able to use the Database Wizard to set up our dimension on the row, column, and page. We do not set up filters, but instead choose to use the POV, which means that our `Product` and `Market` dimensions will be set to the POV. We are also able to use our **Data Layout** menu to select the members we want in row, column, and page. Although not shown in these recipes, consider using Web Analysis Reports to create executive dash boards and score card type applications for example. Web Analysis Reports are among the most presentable and flexible reports.

> Although Web Analysis Reports are popular in the field, developers should begin looking at **OBIEE Answers** for their dashboard applications as this may be a solution that is more in line with Oracle's long-term dashboard reporting tool set.

Index

Symbols

A

J

joins setup, in minischema
about 57
steps 57-59
working 59, 60

K

key words
Area 259
As 259
create or replace replicated 259
to 259
Update allow 259

L

Launch button 174
linked, partition types 303
lintRow variable 309
load rule, for SQL data load
creating, substitution variables used 181-185
working 185
load rules
executing, MaxL used 247-250
location alias 295
logged in 315
logical operators
using 196
working 198-201
Log in button 63
Login button 38
lstrError variable 309

M

Margin % Sales 20
MaxL
dimension build rules, executing 242-246
using, for calculation execution 250-254
using, for load rules execution 247-250
using, for outline extraction in XML format 291
using, for partitions execution 254-260
using, for report script execution 260
working 292

MaxL automation
folder structure, setting up 234-239
folder structure, working 239-241
MaxL editor
using, for MetaRead setup 321-324
using, for user addition 314-317
using, for user externalization 314-317
using, for Write access setup 321-324
working 315
MaxL script
using, for security file export 333, 334
MDX
using, for ASO calculation 228, 229
using, for data extraction 303-308
using, in aggregate storage applications 186-189
working 309-311
MDX Script Editor 218
Measures dimension
building, from fact table 123
properties 125, 126
setting up, parent-child reference used 8-12
working 125
MEASURES table
additional tables, adding 20
columns 12
Member button 293
MetaRead
setting up, MaxL Editor used 321-324
method parameter 222
Microsoft Active Directory. *See* **MSAD**
minischema
building 53- 56
joins, setting up 57
tables, adding to 60
working 57
Minischemas tab 57
Minischema Wizard 57
Move Field button 160
MSAD 317
Multidimensional Expressions (MDX) 18

N

Ndim parameter 222
New Connection button 40
NONINPUT parameter 217

O

OLAP metaoutline , EIS
creating 111
creating, steps 112-117
working 117
OLAP Model, in EIS
creating 104, 105
working 111
Oracle Data Integrator (ODI) 242
Oracle Essbase Road Map 45
Oracle Essbase Studio User's Guide 119
Oracle Internet Directory (OID) 317
outline editor
using, for dimensions addition 143-145
working 146
outline formula logic
using, at parent level 179, 180
working 181
outline formulas
If/Else logic, using 167-170
substitution variables , using 167-170

P

parent-child dimension
adding, dimension build rules used 147-150
working 150
parent-child reference table
about 74
hierarchies, creating 74-76
working 77
partition
about 274
executing, MaxL used 254-260
password_reset_days 315
Period dimension 138
PeriodsToDate function 137
Point of View. *See* **POV**
POV
using 356-359
working 359, 360
Preview button 82
Print Preview button 340, 341
privilege
administrator 316
create_application 316

create_database 316
designer 316
execute 316
filter 316
no access 316
read 316
write 316
Profit % Sales 20
protocol 316

R

Rebuild button 104
Refresh button 198
reject selected record functionality 274
relational tables
hierarchies, determining 29-32
working 33-36
replicated partition 274
replicated, partition types 303
report
formatting 347, 348
report script
about 273
executing, MaxL used 260
Report Script Editor
about 274
using, for data extraction to text file 274-278
working 277-279
Repository menu 337
result_Native variable 309
result_VBCompatible variable 309
roles. *See* **privilege**
rules
creating, for flat file data loads 161-164

S

SALESMAN attribute 103
Sample Basic database 156
security file
exporting, MaxL script used 333, 334
Select Table tab 120
Server Access 320
server.datafile.dir property 66
server.properties file 66
SET MSG DETAIL command 194

[PACKT] enterprise
PUBLISHING
professional expertise distilled

Thank you for buying
Oracle Essbase 11 Development Cookbook

About Packt Publishing

Packt, pronounced 'packed', published its first book "*Mastering phpMyAdmin for Effective MySQL Management*" in April 2004 and subsequently continued to specialize in publishing highly focused books on specific technologies and solutions.

Our books and publications share the experiences of your fellow IT professionals in adapting and customizing today's systems, applications, and frameworks. Our solution-based books give you the knowledge and power to customize the software and technologies you're using to get the job done. Packt books are more specific and less general than the IT books you have seen in the past. Our unique business model allows us to bring you more focused information, giving you more of what you need to know, and less of what you don't.

Packt is a modern, yet unique publishing company, which focuses on producing quality, cutting-edge books for communities of developers, administrators, and newbies alike. For more information, please visit our website: www.PacktPub.com.

About Packt Enterprise

In 2010, Packt launched two new brands, Packt Enterprise and Packt Open Source, in order to continue its focus on specialization. This book is part of the Packt Enterprise brand, home to books published on enterprise software – software created by major vendors, including (but not limited to) IBM, Microsoft and Oracle, often for use in other corporations. Its titles will offer information relevant to a range of users of this software, including administrators, developers, architects, and end users.

Writing for Packt

We welcome all inquiries from people who are interested in authoring. Book proposals should be sent to author@packtpub.com. If your book idea is still at an early stage and you would like to discuss it first before writing a formal book proposal, contact us; one of our commissioning editors will get in touch with you.

We're not just looking for published authors; if you have strong technical skills but no writing experience, our experienced editors can help you develop a writing career, or simply get some additional reward for your expertise.

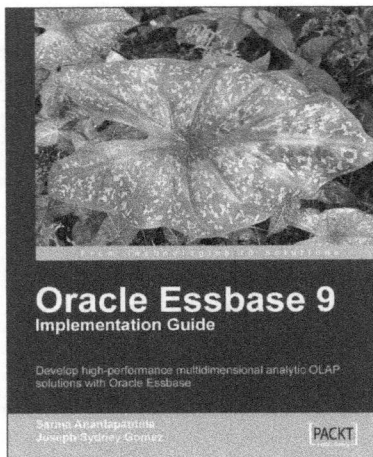

Oracle Essbase 9 Implementation Guide

ISBN: 978-1-847196-86-6   Paperback: 444 pages

Develop high-performance multidimensional analytic OLAP solutions with Oracle Essbase

1. Build multidimensional Essbase database cubes and develop analytical Essbase applications

2. Step-by-step instructions with expert tips from installation to implementation

3. Can be used to learn any version of Essbase starting from 4.x to 11.x

4. For beginners as well as experienced professionals; no Essbase experience required

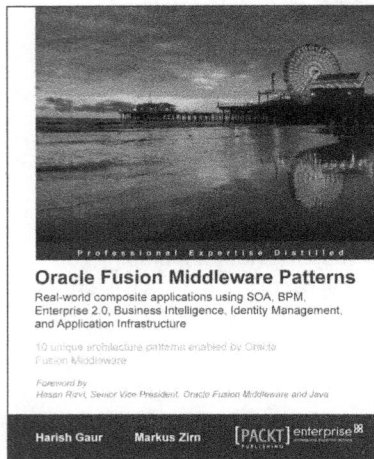

Oracle Fusion Middleware Patterns

ISBN: 978-1-847198-32-7   Paperback: 224 pages

10 unique architecture patterns enabled by Oracle Fusion Middleware

1. First-hand technical solutions utilizing the complete and integrated Oracle Fusion Middleware Suite in hardcopy and ebook formats

2. From-the-trenches experience of leading IT Professionals

3. Learn about application integration and how to combine the integrated tools of the Oracle Fusion Middleware Suite - and do away with thousands of lines of code

Please check **www.PacktPub.com** for information on our titles

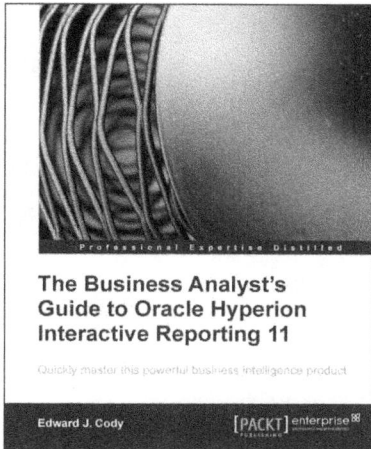

The Business Analyst's Guide to Oracle Hyperion Interactive Reporting 11

ISBN: 978-1-84968-036-3   Paperback: 232 pages

Quickly master this powerful business intelligence product

1. Get to grips with the most important, frequently used, and advanced features of Oracle Hyperion Interactive Reporting 11

2. A step-by-step Oracle Hyperion training guide packed with screenshots and clear explanations

3. Explore the features of Hyperion dashboards, reports, pivots, and charts

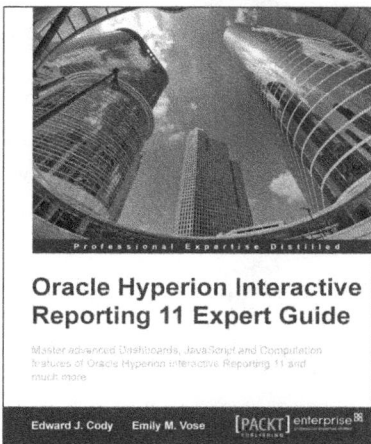

Oracle Hyperion Interactive Reporting 11 Expert Guide

ISBN: 978-1-84968-314-2   Paperback: 276 pages

Master advanced Dashboards, JavaScript and Computation features to Oracle Hyperion Interactive Reporting 11 and much more

1. Walk through a comprehensive example of a simple, intermediate, and advanced dashboard with a focus on Interactive Reporting best practices

2. Explore the data analysis functionally with an in-depth explanation of built-in and JavaScript functions.

3. Build custom interfaces to create batch programs and exports for automated reporting.

4. Demonstrate expertise by learning to build a central code repository.

Please check **www.PacktPub.com** for information on our titles